D1476913

the
gastronomica
reader

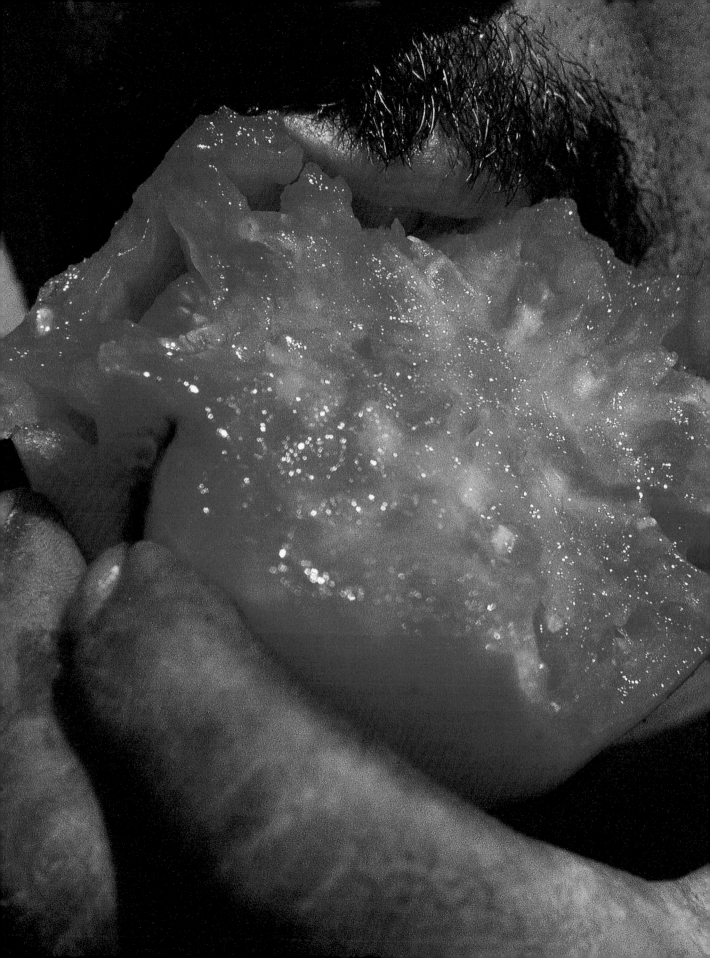

the gastronomica reader

edited by darra goldstein

University of California Press   *Berkeley Los Angeles London*

The publisher gratefully acknowledges the generous support
of the Ahmanson Foundation Humanities Endowment Fund
of the University of California Press Foundation.

University of California Press, one of the most distinguished
university presses in the United States, enriches lives around the
world by advancing scholarship in the humanities, social sciences,
and natural sciences. Its activities are supported by the UC Press
Foundation and by philanthropic contributions from individuals
and institutions. For more information, visit www.ucpress.edu.

University of California Press
Berkeley and Los Angeles, California

University of California Ltd.
London, England

Library of Congress Cataloging-in-Publication Data

The Gastronomica reader / edited by Darra Goldstein.
    p.   cm.
  Includes bibliographical references.
  ISBN 978-0-520-25939-3 (cloth : alk. paper)
  1. Gastronomy.   2. Food.   3. Food—Social aspects.
I. Goldstein, Darra.   II. Gastronomica.
  TX341.G37   2010
  641.013—dc22
                                        2009012445

Designed and composed by Frances Baca
Text: Electra 10.25/14
Display: Akzidenz Grotesk Extended
Printed and bound by CS Graphics, Pte. Ltd.
Printed in Singapore

18   17   16   15   14   13   12   11   10
10   9   8   7   6   5   4   3   2   1

The paper used in this publication meets the minimum
requirements of ANSI/NISO Z 39.48-1992 R 1997)
(Permanence of Paper).

contents

Editor's Introduction **1**

appetites

Women Who Eat Dirt | *Susan Allport* **10**
Badlands: Portrait of a Competitive Eater | *John O'Connor* **23**
"Don't Eat That": The Erotics of Abstinence in American Christianity | *R. Marie Griffith* **34**
A Shallot | *Richard Wilbur* **51**

the family table

Delicacy | *Paul Russell* **54**
The Unbearable Lightness of Wartime Cuisine | *A. Marin* **60**
One Year and a Day: A Recipe for Gumbo and Mourning | *James Nolan* **75**
The Prize Inside | *Toni Mirosevich* **87**
Messages in a Bottle | *Barbara Kirshenblatt-Gimblett* **89**
dinner, 1933 | *Charles Bukowski* **100**

social constructs

Otto Horcher, Caterer to the Third Reich | *Giles MacDonogh* **104**
The Cooking Ape: An Interview with Richard Wrangham | *Elisabeth Townsend* **116**
How Caviar Turned Out to Be *Halal* | *H. E. Chehabi* **129**
"La grande bouffe": Cooking Shows as Pornography | *Andrew Chan* **139**
Recipe for S&M Marmalade | *Judith Pacht* **149**

the art of food

Man Ray's *Electricité* | *Stefanie Spray Jandl* **152**
Food + Clothing = | *Robert Kushner* **158**
Vik Muniz's *Ten Ten's Weed Necklace* | *Vanessa Silberman* **170**
Zhan Wang: Urban Landscape | *John Stomberg* **174**
The First Still Life | *Lawrence Raab* **178**

personal journeys

Waiting for a Cappuccino: A Brief Layover along the Spice Trail | *Carolyn Thériault* **182**
Include Me Out | *Fred Chappell* **187**
Evacuation Day, or A Foodie Is Bummed Out | *Merry White* **190**
Ripe Peach | *Louise Glück* **194**

how others eat

My McDonald's | *Constantin Boym* **198**
Great Apes as Food | *Dale Peterson* **202**
The Bengali *Bonti* | *Chitrita Banerji* **212**
The Best "Chink" Food: Dog Eating and the Dilemma of Diversity | *Frank H. Wu* **218**

close to the earth

Organic in Mexico: A Conversation with Diana Kennedy | *L. Peat O'Neil* **234**
Mr. Clarence Jones, Carolina Rice Farmer | *Jennie Ashlock* **247**
"GM or Death": Food and Choice in Zambia | *Christopher M. Annear* **255**
Wine, Place, and Identity in a Changing Climate | *Robert Pincus* **267**
Episode with a Potato | *Eric Ormsby* **277**

technologies

A Plea for Culinary Modernism: Why We Should Love New, Fast, Processed Food | *Rachel Laudan* **280**
The Patented Peanut Butter and Jelly Sandwich: Food as Intellectual Property | *Anna M. Shih* **293**
The Clockwork Roasting Jack, or How Technology Entered the Kitchen | *Jeanne Schinto* **302**
Grinding Away the Rust: The Legacy of Iceland's Herring Oil and Meal Factories | *Chris Bogan* **314**

pleasures of the past

A la recherche de la tomate perdue: The First French Tomato Recipe? | *Barbara Santich* **326**
The Egg Cream Racket | *Andrew Coe* **332**
Frightening the Game | *Charles Perry* **345**
Alkermes: "A Liqueur of Prodigious Strength" | *Amy Butler Greenfield* **347**
Food for Thought | *Eamon Grennan* **356**

Acknowledgments **358**
Contributors **359**
Illustration Credits **365**

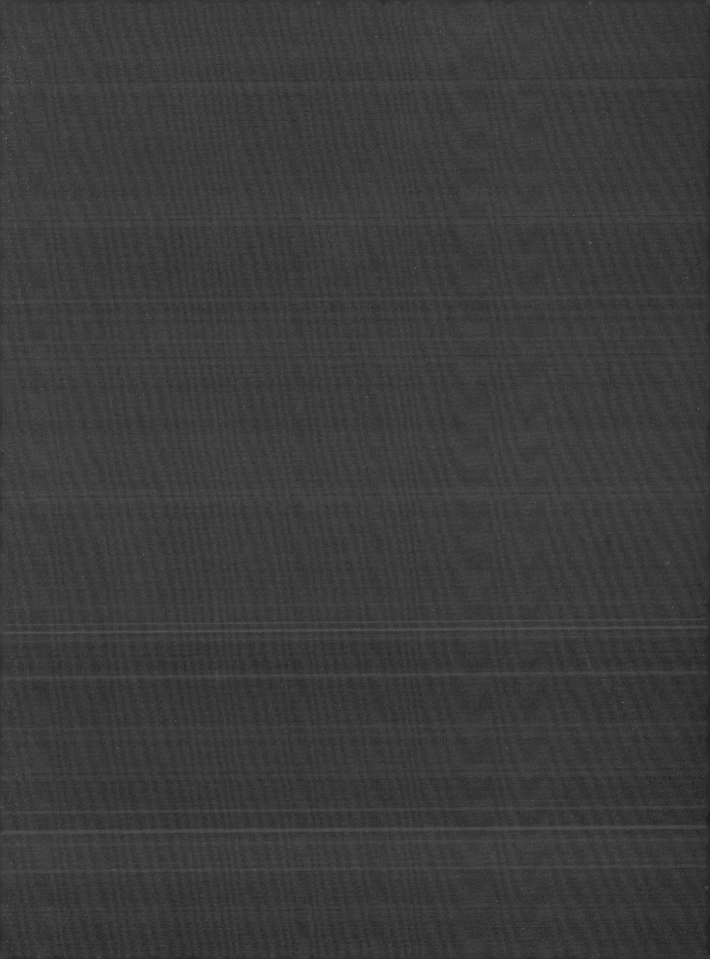

to provoke
and to please

RIOTS BROKE OUT when Luis Buñuel's surrealist film *L'Âge d'Or* was first screened in Paris in 1930. Right-wing vigilantes threw ink at the screen and set off smoke bombs. Even the pope got involved, threatening to excommunicate the film's financial sponsor, the vicomte de Noailles. For almost fifty years, the film was suppressed due to its erotic imagery and mockery of the bourgeoisie.

Times change, fortunately. Seventy-one years later, in February 2001, the charter issue of *Gastronomica: The Journal of Food and Culture* appeared with a still from *L'Âge d'Or* on its cover. No riots broke out, but people from all over the country wrote to protest the image of Lya Lys sucking her lover's hand. They found it repulsive, or at least too erotically charged for a food magazine. I was surprised, but I have to confess I was also pleased that by hinting at both the darker and more sensual sides of orality I had provoked a reaction.

Fast-forward another six years, to August 2007. *Gastronomica* stares boldly out of the pages of the Pottery Barn catalog, featured at a kitchen desk under the headline "Work Smart." Finally, some commercial attention! But my initial thrill turned quickly to worry: if *Gastronomica* was being displayed alongside such popular cookbooks as *Martha Stewart's Hors d'Oeuvres Handbook* and Paul Bertolli and Alice Waters's *Chez Panisse Cooking*, had it lost its provocative edge?

I decided it was time to run an article I had been holding about the artist Chrissy Conant, who harvests eggs—human eggs, that is—from her own body. She packages them like the finest caviar and puts them on display. Conant's work is a social commentary both on caviar as a luxury food and on the practice of young women selling their eggs as a commodity. Such art is admittedly repulsive, but shock and aversion help make Conant's point. So we called our own bluff. Unlike the popular magazines that lure readers with images of beautiful food eaten by beautiful people, *Gastronomica* aims to be edgy, hoping to make its readers think about what lies *behind* the meal, which often includes guts and gore and the exploitation of others, both human and animal. For better and for worse, most of the food we eat these days is manipulated, so it is important to consider the larger implications of what we eat and how we eat it, whether they are political, social, or just plain grotesque. Although the journal celebrates food as a source of comfort and pleasure, conviviality and beauty, we want to push against the conventions that define our eating habits and the ways in which we think about them.

With these goals in mind, for the past ten years *Gastronomica* has been publishing articles and essays, poetry and fiction, as well as provocative works of art that examine food in relation to society and culture. The quirky, the challenging, the whimsical, and the unexpected all find a place at *Gastronomica*'s table. Over the years, readers have learned about parrot eating in the Renaissance, the diet of sumo wrestlers in Japan, the ethics of eating apes, the cultural ramifications of the Atkins diet, the resistance to genetically modified foods in Zambia, the meaning of *terroir*, the effect of global warming on wine, and the phenomenon of competitive eaters who chow down for dollars (see John O'Connor's illuminating essay on 420-pound Eric "Badlands" Booker in this volume). We rarely publish recipes, but when we do, they usually have a twist. Aglaia Kremezi's recipe for Easter Leg of Lamb Stuffed with Greens, Fennel, and Feta is delicious. But instead of illustrating the instructions with a photograph of the glorious finished dish, we showed a deadeyed butcher carrying two skinned kids over his shoulder. Spoilsport, perhaps, but we like to remind ourselves of the cost of our pleasure.

The pages of *Gastronomica* offer reproductions as lush as those in any art journal, yet they rarely aestheticize their subjects in expected ways. Instead of gussying up food for visual consumption, *Gastronomica* presents stark images that are brazen in their simplicity or disturbing in their elaboration. Lest I begin to sound defensive, let me make my point as a suggestion: if readers are willing to engage with the images, they will discover that what initially seemed repulsive more often than not opens up as a thing of beauty.

The journal's covers have elicited particularly strong responses. Some two and a half years after Buñuel's stirring image, Emily Eveleth's *Nigh* (Winter 2003) provoked considerable discomfort. In this painting, a lone doughnut lies against a flat, empty background, its textured airiness and sugary glaze heightened by the work's spareness. Suffused with shimmering light, it tempts us to pleasure—who doesn't like to bite into a jelly doughnut? Yet this is no larger-than-life pop art confection in candy colors. It captures instead isolation, an existential longing. For some, the image apparently carried sexual connotations as well.

One reader wrote to say that he would never be able to look at a doughnut innocently again. But really, dear readers, it was just a doughnut, beautifully rendered.

Tomatoes proved even more controversial than the doughnut. An early issue of *Gastronomica* featured Catherine Chalmers's vivid *Food Chain*, a series of hyperreal C-prints of a perfect tomato being devoured by a horned tomato worm, which is itself ultimately devoured by a praying mantis (which is, in turn, devoured by a tarantula beyond the journal's pages). Perhaps because tomatoes are such a predictable, and therefore comforting, part of the American diet, the drama of their consumption, depicted up close and in brilliant color, upset people. But that's life! The Fall 2002 cover triggered an even more outraged response. Gail Skoff's close-up portrait of a swarthy migrant worker in southern France captured him at a moment of great pleasure, as he brought a lush tomato to his darkly mustachioed mouth. Here was the perfect conjunction of ripeness and desire, an image to recall the earthy essence of summer during the dark days of November. Skoff's photograph reconnects us with the soil and with those who labor for our food. It celebrates the organic and reminds us of the sensory pleasure of biting into an utterly ripe tomato fresh from the vine—a tomato that has been neither gassed to ripen nor packaged in cellophane; one that is not hard to the touch but lush and juicy. I fell for the photograph the minute I saw it! But others reacted differently. The cover so upset the owner of a Los Angeles cookbook store that she called me at home to tell me that she would no longer carry *Gastronomica*. And one newspaper columnist wrote: "The Fall, 2002, issue sports an extreme close-up of a mustachioed man's mouth consuming a tomato, which is held by an extremely dirty hand. Ahem." Ahem? His hand is dirty because he has been working in the soil.

I am not objecting to the sensibilities of some of *Gastronomica*'s readers so much as describing what we are up against when we represent food. It is generally expected that food and its depictions should be a source of easy pleasure. Popular magazines necessarily work hard to please their readers. After all, who wants to pay good money for something that turns our stomach? Food, being visceral, always has the power to induce squeamishness. Of course, we should enjoy our comfort foods, and we should indulge in sweets—I certainly do. But it's also necessary to know the weight they carry, and I don't mean just the potential pounds. When discomfort opens dialogue and elicits deeper reflection, it's not such a bad thing. Vanessa Silberman's analysis of Vik Muniz's portrait *Ten Ten's Weed Necklace* makes us think beyond sweetness to consider the conditions of child labor in St. Kitts's sugarcane fields; Paul Russell's bittersweet memoir, "Delicacy," explores the often-painful dynamics of the family table. As the articles in *Gastronomica* explore the social dimensions of food, they also make us consider, as cultural anthropologists have long admonished us to do, what is good to think and not just good to eat.

As you'll discover in this volume, *Gastronomica* aims not only to provoke, but also to please, by celebrating food in its many permutations, not to mention the pleasures of eating, of taste, and of sharing meals. North Carolina writer Fred Chappell introduces us to the glories of real southern ice tea by, perversely, disavowing it ("Include Me Out"), while Barbara Santich, in "*A la recherche de la tomate perdue*," evokes the lushness of tomatoes boiled into a conserve with cinnamon and cloves (tomatoes again! though no one objected to them this time). Food can be fun, and so we publish cartoons and ruminations on such topics as the fanciful architecture of American drive-ins, deep-fried candy bars, and a Viennese orchestra composed entirely of instruments fashioned from vegetables. *Gastronomica* has displayed naked women, both thin and fat, cavorting with pasta; several pages of "critter cuisine" showing armadillos, tadpoles, worms, and snakes in beautifully composed still lifes; and a "porcineograph" of the United States, with frolicking pigs presenting the favorite pork dishes of the constituent states.

We like to indulge readers at least as often as we pull them up short. Other food magazines may set out to be useful by offering new recipes and techniques, and by reviewing appliances and restaurants, but *Gastronomica* is unabashedly nonutilitarian in its delights: occasional humor, ironic essays, and lagniappes. In fact, the word *lagniappe* comes close to defining our philosophy. It means something extra, a little bonus beyond the necessary. *The Gastronomica Reader* may not feature Chrissy Conant's eggs or other of our most outré articles, but it reflects the basic *Gastronomica* belief that only the unexpected can make a familiar subject new.

Gastronomica and the Study of Food

In addition to serving up food for thought, *Gastronomica* harbors another purpose: to breach the divide between academic inquiry and popular writing about food. For many years this separation was a source of great frustration for me. I would publish articles in the popular press that were fun to write but offered little space to enter into my subject deeply. They seemed too breezy. By contrast, the articles I labored long over and published in scholarly journals were read by only a handful of specialists. I wanted there to be a place for published work that straddled the narrowly academic and the inescapably light. So during a sabbatical year in 2000, I began dreaming of a journal that would offer a venue for new thoughts and new findings, a place where food enthusiasts both inside and outside of academia could share work and engage in meaningful dialogue, where those of us researching food could be liberated from the isolation of our own narrow fields and build on one another's findings. I dreamed of the kind of publication that I myself would like to read: a lively periodical that would distinguish itself from the glossy food magazines with their unfailingly upbeat lifestyle stories and staged photographs. Not a corrective, exactly, but an additional opportunity, a journal where writers could examine the darker sides of food—the eating disorders, the marketing that fosters obesity, the abuse of food to wield power. The list of ambitions spread out from there. A journal truly interdisciplinary in its approach would, I hoped, help bring credibility to the emerging field of food studies.

The birth of *Gastronomica* occurred at a fortuitous time, just as food studies was finally beginning to be taken seriously in the United States (critical research into food has been conducted in Europe for decades). Even though food is one of the best, and most immediate, ways of understanding culture, on American shores it has long been considered unworthy of serious intellectual inquiry. Since everyone eats, food has been taken for granted or seen as a mundane commonality, something that pertains to lowly bodily functions, not to the realm of the cerebral. Until fairly recently, food scholars were disdained, and food itself dismissed as women's work that belongs more properly in the domestic sphere. The first generation of feminist scholars worked hard to get women out of the kitchen, so they were understandably wary of studying food, which threatened to pull them back in. By the time *Gastronomica* launched, however, there was a growing realization among American academics that the study of food could, in important ways, add to our understanding not only of women's lives but also of society as a whole.

I titled my first editor's letter "Food Studies Come of Age," writing that

> Metaphors for the symbiotic relationship between mind and body have become so familiar that by now they're clichés. We speak of intellectual hunger and food for thought, but we forget that these concepts were once the subject of serious inquiry—from Erasmus, who advised readers to digest material rather than merely memorize it, to Montaigne, who described education and digestion as parallel functions. *Gastronomica: The Journal of Food and Culture* aims to renew this connection between sensual and intellectual nourishment by bringing together many diverse voices in the broadest possible discourse on the uses, abuses, and meanings of food. It's time that we set a central table for this sort of conversation, if not quite in the boisterous manner of the great Renaissance banquets, then at least in the wide, egalitarian spirit of Virginia Woolf's *To the Lighthouse*, where all dinner-party guests get a few featured pages in the limelight of narrative point of view.

Gastronomica helped to set that food-studies table, and I like to think that the journal is still broadly inclusive in all that it embraces. Our pages are open to chefs and food professionals, novelists, poets, and all sorts of other articulate food amateurs. Where the inaugural issue featured articles on the global food supply, biotechnology, futuristic food, and visionary kitchen architecture, the Summer 2008 issue explores jail food, eating on the run, philosophy's historic contempt for food, and the nature of celebrity chefs and those who dine in their restaurants. Then as now the articles are intended to encourage readers to think seriously, widely, and deeply about what appears on their plates. Food for thought— what an apt cliché!

There is no question that the study of food has entered into the mainstream. Not only has the number of food books published yearly increased exponentially, but social movements surrounding food sustainability and artisanal traditions have gained broad political traction. The venerable *Oxford English Dictionary* even named *locavore* the 2007 word of the year. Culinary traditions are being considered under UNESCO's Convention for the Safeguarding of the Intangible Cultural Heritage. And as a subdiscipline of cultural studies, food studies is making inroads into academia. Eyebrows are no longer raised when graduate students decide to write dissertations on food using the methodologies of anthropology, history, nutrition, sociology, economics, literature, biology, and other fields. Fueled in part by the commercial market—the celebrity chefs and off-the-chart cookbook sales—the study of food has become chic. It sometimes seems as though everyone is writing about the subject.

The problem now is not whether food is worthy of study, but how to contextualize it, to figure out where it belongs.

Unsurprisingly, turf wars have broken out. Some academics, newly arrived on the food bandwagon, express disdain for independent scholars, insisting that popular voices will discredit the still-evolving field. Yet it was these writers who, free of disciplinary constraints, pioneered our knowledge of food over the past half century. Elizabeth David, Reay Tannahill, M. F. K. Fisher, Alan Davidson—all approached food in a wide-ranging and often idiosyncratic way. We owe them a tremendous debt. On the other hand, popular writers can be too jaunty in their handling of information, since meticulous research is by definition time-consuming. By placing itself in the breach, *Gastronomica* has reached in two directions, demanding greater substantiation from nonscholars and insisting on more vivid writing and a smaller remove from the kitchen from scholars. An admittedly eclectic publication, the journal seeks to present new work that looks at food and culture in a way that is simultaneously accessible and substantive, and to convey an aesthetic experience of food, not just an intellectual one.

In 2003, the Dutch government awarded the prestigious Erasmus Prize for contributions to European culture to culinary historian Alan Davidson, who took his place among such previous recipients as Claude Lévi-Strauss, Václav Havel, Isaiah Berlin, and Martin Buber. Davidson's acceptance speech made a case for the independent scholars whose quirkiness and enthusiasms, unconstrained by the demands of the academy, often lead to genuine discovery. As the study of food continues to evolve, *Gastronomica* offers a model of lively prose that conveys solid information. In the journal's pages, glamour serves science, and analysis tempers eagerness. *Gastronomica* offers a place at the table for everyone who brings passion and rigor to the study of food.

The Gastronomica Reader

With articles on all manner of topics, as well as memoirs, photo essays, interviews with chefs, and more, *Gastronomica* is, as the Columbia University sociologist Priscilla Parkhurst Ferguson has written, "a kind of banquet"—or at least a buffet. On this, the journal's tenth anniversary, we want to reflect back on our writers' exquisite offerings, which represent some of the best articles and essays about food that have appeared anywhere. This volume could easily have been several times as long. Indeed, it was painful to let go the marvelous photo essays we have published, such as Aya Brackett's study of street food in Japan, or Carlos Poveda's domestic landscapes fashioned from industrial refuse. It was equally hard to give up the scholarly articles. I happen to be an avid reader of footnotes, but I've discovered over the years that many others are not (one overwhelmed reviewer actually counted the footnotes in the inaugural issue, all 160 of them!). So, for the most part, this reader does not contain the longer articles that make up the "Investigations" rubric in each issue, the irresistible exceptions being R. Marie Griffith's incisive look at Christian diet movements and Andrew Chan's witty analysis of cooking shows as pornography. Despite all my words about provocation, you'll find this sampling to be not only exciting but also highly palatable fare.

The great nineteenth-century French chef Carême recognized food as an art form. He once famously said that the fine arts are five in number: painting, sculpture, poetry, music, and architecture, whose main branch is confectionary. *Gastronomica* follows in that spirit. It is a journal that celebrates the art of food, its beauties and its provocations. In an early review in the *National Journal*, media critic William Powers wrote about *Gastronomica:* "This is a magazine that cares not just about food as pleasure but food as idea, one that wants to be serious about eating without losing the fun of it.…This is, both literally and figuratively, a transcendent magazine." Transcendent? Yes and no.

A friend of mine, an art historian, was recently reviewing a painting by one of her favorite artists, Caravaggio. She clicked on her laptop, and from across the centuries there appeared his *Supper at Emmaus*, in all its resplendency. I marveled at the supernatural intensity of the divine light, but what my friend remarked on was off to the right, where the extended arms of the apostle Luke appear disembodied against the sensual, velvety depth of the black ground. Does this darkness suggest evil? I suppose so, if the light is divine, but my friend's point was less metaphysical than practical. Only in maximum contrast is there maximum pleasure. The light is more awe inspiring for the way it radiates against the dark.

Gastronomica is, of course, no Caravaggio. It's a quarterly, by definition a transitory publication. But whatever small transcendence the journal may have achieved is thanks to the contrasts that it provides: light and dark, pleasurable and provocative, tasteful and, sometimes, tasteless. Only by confronting the black—the darker side of food—can we challenge the palate and reveal the ultimate beauty of food, casting it into even deeper relief. I hope you enjoy the taste. ☺

appetites

Women Who Eat Dirt | *Susan Allport* **10**

Badlands: Portrait of a Competitive Eater | *John O'Connor* **23**

"Don't Eat That": The Erotics of Abstinence in American Christianity | *R. Marie Griffith* **34**

A Shallot | *Richard Wilbur* **51**

susan allport |

Women Who Eat Dirt

NOT TOO LONG AGO, I received a package from a village in Nepal, high in the foothills of the Himalayas. It was from the brother of the shipping clerk in my husband's office, and it contained, as clearly written on the outside, two kinds of mud: red and white. These are the muds that the inhabitants of that faraway village use to plaster their houses, red for the bottom and white for the top. They are also the muds that the women of that village are known to snack on, especially during pregnancy. Victor Ghale, my husband's shipping clerk, knew I was interested in people who include dirt or clay in their diet, and so he asked his brother to send samples of these muds to me in New York.

The package arrived, fortunately, before fears of anthrax had made us all suspicious of envelopes containing powdery substances. So I had no reservations about opening it and deciding to give these two chunks of hardened clay a try. The first was the white one, which was gritty and gummy-tasting as it dissolved, very slowly, in my mouth. It was hard to swallow and seemed to give me an almost instantaneous allergic reaction, since I itched all over for about an hour. The red mud, which I waited a day to try, was also gritty and gummy-tasting. But in some ways, it was like a good wine. While it dissolved, I sensed on the back of my palate the smell of fresh earth just after a rain.

As I savored the smell, I remembered the words that Victor had used when he told me about this gastronomic habit from Nepal. "The clays smell so good when it rains," he had said almost enviously.

"How handy to be able to snack on your own house," I had joked. "Every woman has her own twenty-four-hour convenience store."

"Nobody gives it much thought," he said with a shrug. "It's just something women do."

BUT THE FIRST THING that everyone should know about these women who eat dirt—and about this widespread habit of snacking on special clays or muds that has been reported among women in almost every part of the world—is that it's not just women who eat dirt. Dirt or clay eating is more usual among women, especially pregnant women, in many parts of the world, in Nepal, Africa, India, Central America, and the American South. But in other parts of the world, and at other times in history, entire populations have been known to consume dirt. In Northern California and in Sardinia, where acorns used to be the

Right: A trader from Western Nigeria sorting bags of eko clay at the market in Uzalla, Nigeria. This woman buys clay in volume, then sells it to individual marketers over great distances. She came to the market in a ten-ton truck.
COURTESY OF DONALD VERMEER

dietary staple, the traditional bread was made by mixing acorn flour with clay and water, then baking the mixture in a slow oven.[1] In Germany in the last century, some of the poorer workers and their families used very fine clays to "butter" their bread. In China, as in other parts of the world, clay was eaten by much of the population during times of severe want. Some clays, such as smectite, have a tendency to swell when they take up water, and these clays are present in famine food samples from China.[2]

The list goes on and on and should make those with a peculiarly "female" explanation of dirt eating ("geophagy," as it is known in scientific circles) question their assumptions. Geophagy has often been attributed to mood swings, hormonal rushes, magical and superstitious beliefs, and/or beliefs in the fertility of the earth—causes more closely associated with the distaff population. But any cogent explanation of this behavior, any explanation that pretends to make real and lasting sense, must also account for these examples of universal consumption.

The second thing that everyone should know is that it's not just humans—men, women, and children—who eat dirt. Dirt eating is also widespread among animals. It's been reported in many species of birds; many species of herbivores (antelopes, elk, bison, elephants, and the like); and many species of omnivores (porcupines, bears, rats, gorillas, and chimpanzees). No strict carnivores have ever been reported eating dirt (for reasons I will come to), but carnivores do hang around the dirt sites used by other animals because of the hunting opportunities they present.

Many of us are familiar with dirt eating in the animal kingdom, at least with such descriptive place names as Licking Hollow, Elk Lick, and Three Bed Lick,[3] which portray the activity of animals at specific dirt sites. So many of us don't find anything surprising about this behavior in other animals. But dirt eating in animals can shed a lot of light on dirt eating in humans. And it can help us to question our assumptions about diet and the nature of what should and should not be eaten.

Like humans, other animals are very selective about the dirt they eat. No adult animal, it seems, eats just any dirt—a kind of indiscriminate, exploratory behavior seen only in very young animals, including children. A troop of gorillas or a herd of elephants concentrates on just a few sites that they return to again and again. East African elephants routinely excavate the caves of certain hillsides where they are able to access iodine-rich salt deposits. According to some scientists, elephants are particularly prone to iodine deficiency, and even their familiar, elephantine habits of wallowing in mud and throwing dirt on their hides are attempts to absorb iodine through the rich blood supply in their skin.[4]

Mountain gorillas in Rwanda are not the regular dirt eaters that elephants are, but they do visit sites five or six times a year where all the members of a group occupy themselves in digging and eating soil for about thirty minutes at a time. This soil, located high up on the side of a volcano, is rich in both salt and iron, and observers suspect that the gorillas may be after those two important nutrients. Mountain vegetation, after all, is usually very low in sodium, and gorillas, like all mammals living at high altitudes, need extra iron for the extra red-blood-cell production that is required at those altitudes.[5] The easiest way for them to get this extra iron may be these volcanic soils.

And here's another insight into human geophagy that animals help us to see. Just as strict carnivores do not eat dirt or clay, human populations that include a lot of animal products in their diet also do not eat dirt or clay. Clay eating is rare, even nonexistent, among the Maasai of Kenya, cattle-herders whose diet consists largely of milk and blood. But it is extremely common among the neighboring Kikuya, agriculturalists whose diet is based largely upon plants.[6]

Animal products are important for both what they have and what they don't have. They have most of the minerals that humans and other animals need to survive, including sodium, iron, phosphorus, zinc, selenium, and calcium (but only if the bones are chewed, since meat itself is low in calcium). And they don't have the many toxins that plant foods have: the tannins in acorns, the glycoalkaloids in potatoes, the phytates in soybeans. Because so many of the plants we eat in the United States have been bred to lessen their toxic load, we have the luxury of knowing very little about these chemicals, which were designed to protect plants from being attacked by funguses, as well as animals. But they can cause severe and sometimes fatal damage. Some limit the nutrients available for growth, while others act as poisons, releasing cyanides, carcinogens, and other dangerous substances, bursting red blood cells and damaging neurons, kidneys, and the endocrine system.

Plant eaters are not entirely at the mercy of plants, though, and many find ways around these toxins. Some plant eaters process plants to remove the most toxic parts, and some have become specialists in handling certain toxins, like the koala, which eats only eucalyptus. Others consume clay along with toxic plants so that the clay particles can absorb most of the toxins. Clays are ideal antitoxins for several reasons. Their very fine particles give them a large surface area and make it likely that those particles will come into contact with the toxins in foods. And their crystalline structure is layered with positively charged ions, primarily of silicon and aluminum. Since many organic toxins are also positively charged particles, they essentially trade places with the ions in the clays, then pass harmlessly through the digestive system.[7]

Animals seem to be aware of the benefits of adding clay to a plant-based diet, and in some animals, detoxification of plant foods seems to be the primary reason for eating dirt. In a study of the daily, dirt-eating behavior of tropical, plant-eating birds in New Guinea, Jared Diamond found that the soil chosen by these birds (cockatoos, parrots, and pigeons) is particularly good at binding the positively charged molecules of strychnine, quinine, and tannic acid that lace their diet of seeds and unripe fruits. The soil is not rich in any minerals that the birds might need, but it binds one-tenth of its own weight in toxins and has 50 percent more binding capacity than the surrounding soils that the birds do not eat.[8]

Dirt eating in animals also allows us to see how irrational we can be about dirt eating in humans and how differently we regard the behavior of our own species. While few scientists question the underlying functionality of this behavior in other animals, in humans, such arguments have usually been dismissed. Dirt eating is seen as a sensible, instinctive way that animals can compensate for deficiencies in their diet and/or remove toxins from their foods. In humans, it is a perverse activity that few educated persons would ever admit to.

Which brings me to the third thing that we need to know in order to understand the human practice of geophagy. In fact, most of us *are* geophagists in that we seek salt from

the earth or the oceans to add to our diet. We usually don't think of salt as dirt, but salt is a deposit found in rocks, and clay and dirt are nothing more than weathered rocks. Animals that are carnivores don't need to add salt to their diet because the muscles and the guts of their prey have sodium enough to meet their needs. But most herbivores and omnivores—and that includes humans—cannot rely on diet alone for adequate amounts of this nutrient, essential to nerve transmission, muscle contraction, and the maintenance of fluid balance. Because salt is scarce in many parts of the planet, and hence in the plants that grow in those places, many animals must seek out salt licks or salt mines. The problem is particularly acute for inland vegetarians, such as the mountain gorillas of Rwanda, or much of the population of India. Because of this inverse correlation between meat consumption and salt requirements, a poor man, in general, needs more salt than a rich one. And a poor country needs more salt per head than a rich one, a fact of nature that led Gandhi to protest the British policy of salt taxation and take his followers on a "salt march" to the sea.[9]

We so take for granted this almost universal form of geophagy—the saltshaker—that we don't even see it as geophagy. And, therefore, we don't understand that geophagy is neither an uncommon, nor an abnormal behavior, but a reflection of the fact that being an omnivore is a tricky business in many parts of the world. Humans need forty or fifty different nutrients to stay healthy, and sometimes we have to go outside the bounds of what is

Above: Edible clays at a market in Accra, Ghana. The disks and pegs are from Togo; the spindle-shaped pieces from Ghana; the large, crudely shaped pieces from the Accra area; and the one plate of eko (bottom left) from Nigeria. Other plates hold medicinal herbs and plant materials. COURTESY OF DONALD VERMEER

considered food to find them. Or we have to add things to our diet, like clay, in order to turn toxic foods into nutritious ones. Since women, especially pregnant women, have a harder time meeting their nutritional needs, and since pregnant women must also protect the child that is growing inside them from the toxins in food, women tend to eat more dirt.

Calcium and iron present two of the biggest nutritional problems that women face over the course of their lives. A woman's need for calcium increases dramatically during pregnancy, from 800 to 1200 mg per day, a challenge everywhere on earth, but especially in places where calcium levels in the soil are naturally low and/or in cultures where milk and milk products are not a part of the diet. A woman's ability to absorb calcium from the foods she eats increases during pregnancy, but to get the same amount of calcium as in one glass of milk, she would have to eat two and one-half cups of beans or two cups of cooked collards. Tofu is almost as good a source of calcium as dairy products, so Asian women have no harder time meeting their calcium needs than women in dairy cultures, but women all over the world can easily consume too little calcium during pregnancy and lactation, shortfalls that they will pay for later with bone fractures and other signs of osteoporosis.

Some of the clays eaten by pregnant women in Africa provide large amounts of calcium, up to 80 percent of a pregnant woman's RDA, assuming a consumption pattern of 100 grams per day (the equivalent of a stick of butter). Others, however, provide only trace amounts of calcium. But, as Andrea Wiley and Solomon Katz point out in a theoretical paper on the role that calcium might play in geophagy, clay consumption can help a woman's calcium balance in ways other than by actually providing her with calcium. Clays can slow down the motility of the gastrointestinal system and thereby increase the time during which calcium can be absorbed from foodstuffs. And by binding with secondary compounds in plant foods, clays can also release minerals, including calcium, with which these compounds often form complexes.[10] The traditional method of preparing corn tortillas in much of Mexico and Central America, by boiling the corn with limestone, markedly improves the calcium, as well as the protein, content of the tortillas and is probably the reason for the low incidence of osteoporosis in those same areas.

Iron presents an even longer-term problem for women, from the onset of puberty until menopause, from around fifteen to fifty-one. Women have higher iron requirements than men, but they consume fewer calories. So even Western diets—diets that include many more iron-rich types of meat than those in less-developed countries—can leave women with shortages of iron. Iron deficiency, not surprisingly, is the most common nutrient deficiency in the world.

In the United States, women make up for shortages of iron with supplements and fortified foods (or by consuming more food than they need—a subject for another article). Elsewhere, they might visit clay pits or termite mounds. The clays of termite mounds are rich in both calcium and iron and supply a woman who eats at least 20 grams a day with more than 100 percent of her RDA for iron.[11] It has never been proved that women eat these clays in order to obtain extra calcium and iron, but it is telling that, in certain parts of Africa at least, most of the pregnant population makes it a habit of visiting termite mounds. And telling, too, that women must compete for these same clays with many other animals, including giraffes, chimpanzees, and cattle. The cattle, in their rush for these mineral-rich clays, have been known to knock women and children down.[12]

Another problem that becomes more difficult for women during pregnancy—and one that also inclines them toward dirt eating—is the problem of plant toxins. Many substances that are mildly toxic to adults are extremely toxic to developing embryos. Some researchers have speculated that the nausea and food aversions that plague women during the first trimester help women to avoid the ingestion of these harmful substances,[13] but for women who have no choice but to eat foods that are loaded with toxins, a daily dose of clay could help to minimize their effects. Small amounts of clay might also directly relieve the symptoms of pregnancy by changing the acidity of the stomach and/or by absorbing excessive amounts of saliva. Whatever the actual reasons why pregnant women eat dirt, dirt eating is an integral part of the behavior of pregnant women in many parts of the world. "That's how you know when you are pregnant," as one African informant says.[14]

With all the examples I've given of dirt eating in humans and other animals, with all the possible benefits that dirt eating can provide, especially to pregnant women, I'm not arguing that all dirt eating in our species serves a clear nutritional purpose. Nor that all dirt eating is benign.[15] Humans can abuse clay just like anything else they put into their mouths, and eating too much clay can cause intestinal blockages that may have to be surgically removed and sometimes result in death. Clay eating also causes tooth abrasion (some dentists are able to pick out the geophagists in their patient population by the amount of wear on their teeth) and is suspected of causing, not curing, nutrient deficiencies, especially iron deficiency anemia, a suspicion that has been around since ancient times.

The relationship between clay eating and anemia is a complex one that has never been clearly resolved. Physicians have long observed that many of their patients who eat dirt are anemic, but is clay eating a cause of anemia or a consequence? Part of the confusion, investigators are beginning to realize, stems from the fact that different clays have very different effects on a person's nutritional status. Certain clays are rich in easily absorbable minerals, but others actually rob the body of nutrients and minerals. When clays are ingested with food, the cations in the clays trade places with the cations in the food. So there can be a net gain or loss of mineral nutrition depending on the clay and the food. A clay may pick up an iron particle and leave behind an aluminum particle, a net loss for the consumer. Or it may pick up a toxic particle and leave behind an iron particle, a substantial gain. Human and animal populations presumably learn what clays to eat through trial and error and over many generations, but if that knowledge is interrupted through voluntary or forced dislocation, new clays that may be substituted by these populations can do more harm than good.

The experience of slaves in the New World may be an example of this. When slaves were forcibly removed from Africa, they brought their well-established clay-eating traditions with them, and plantation owners were soon commenting on their "mania for eating dirt." Owners came to blame this practice for much of the illness they saw in the Black population and for a new and often fatal syndrome they called Cachexia Africana, or *mal d'estomac*, a syndrome characterized by sluggishness, anemia, and mental insensibility, as well as dirt eating.

"The only appreciable signs of mental activity exhibited during the course of this disease," wrote F.W. Cragin, a physician who described the syndrome of Cachexia Africana in 1835, "are the crafty and cunning plans which the patient most subtily [*sic*] matures, and as stealthily executes, to procure his desired repast…of charcoal, chalk, dried mortar, mud, clay, sand, shells, rotten wood, shreds of cloth or paper, hair, or occasionally some other unnatural substance."[16] Slave owners attributed these unnatural appetites to willfulness on the part of their slaves and viewed geophagy as a slow method of suicide. And they tried, largely unsuccessfully, to break their slaves of the habit (and to protect their economic investment) by chaining perpetrators or by forcing them to wear cone-shaped mouth locks, tin masks that covered the entire face.

In recent years, several researchers have revisited this once-common syndrome, second only to yellow fever as a cause of death among slaves in parts of the South. Some have suggested that a deficiency of B vitamins, along with hookworm infestation and intestinal parasites, brought on the symptoms of earth eating, as well as those of weakness, anemia, edema, and heart failure; others, that the clays eaten by the slaves acted to bind dietary potassium and iron and cause all the symptoms of the disease. But dirt eating is still very common in the South, and physicians see very few patients with symptoms similar to those described by pre–Civil War physicians.[17] So though it is conceivable that the specific clays the slaves ate in the New World initiated a new and often fatal medical syndrome, it is more likely that slaves ate more and more clay when their circumstances and diet left them malnourished, overworked, and unable to fight infections.

Questions about the cause and the nature of this syndrome still remain, though, and they underscore the lack of solid information that accompanies almost every instance of human geophagy. In the South, as in most places where dirt eating has been observed, the usual reaction has been to repress, not study, the habit. From the earliest writings on the subject of geophagy, a term used by Aristotle in the fourth century B.C., medical practitioners have regarded the practice with a skepticism bordering on contempt. Many recognized the usefulness of clay in treating cases of poisoning. But as to the daily consumption of dirt, one physician who lived in A.D. 1000 wrote of the necessity of controlling it, "in boys by use of the whip, in older patients by restraints, prison and medical exhibits, while incorrigible ones are abandoned to the grave."[18] Clay eating, until recently, has been synonymous with pica, a perversion of appetite that causes one to ingest strange and unsuitable substances.

Perhaps part of this negative attitude toward geophagy has been due to the misconception that dirt eaters eat surface dirt, a truly inappropriate food, since surface dirt is loaded with bacteria, parasites, and other potentially harmful substances. In truth, most edible clays are taken from the band of clay-enriched soil ten to thirty inches below the surface, and the fact that they are usually dried or baked further reduces the possibility of contamination. Perhaps part of the attitude comes from a population that has always had enough meat and dairy in their diet to make geophagy less vital and necessary. Whatever the cause, the effect has been to cover up an aspect of human gastronomy that has been extremely important to the survival of the human omnivore. And extremely ancient. Edible clays have been found at archeological sites once occupied by early man, and the fact that chimpanzees regularly ingest clays suggests that this practice predates our evolution as a species.

Attitudes toward geophagy have been changing, though, largely as the result of the work of two scientists, Donald Vermeer and Timothy Johns, who both "stumbled across" the practice of dirt eating in the course of other research. Vermeer, a geographer with Louisiana State University and George Washington University before he retired in 1996, was the first researcher to recognize the great similarity between edible clays sold all over West Africa and the commercial pharmaceutical Kaopectate. Johns is a plant biologist at McGill University in Canada, best known for his work on the role that plant toxins have played in shaping human diet and medicine.

In 1960, when Vermeer was preparing for his first trip to Africa, he came across occasional references to the practice of geophagy in the scientific and medical literature and assumed that dirt eating must play a persistent but fairly insignificant role in the dietary habits of the people of West Africa. When he actually got to Nigeria, though, he found evidence for the habit everywhere: in pestles full of clay pieces outside almost every home; in the pouches of edible clays that women wore around their waists; in the marketplaces where clay was sold and sometimes consumed in public. He once watched a woman eat about 150 grams of clay in five minutes. But the usual amount, he learned, is a small handful of clay (30 to 50 grams) consumed over the course of a day.

Vermeer began to wonder if geophagy might in fact be almost universal in West Africa, at least among pregnant women, and he decided to investigate the mining, processing, and marketing of geophagical clays. He found that four hundred to five hundred tons of eko, a clay from the village of Uzalla in Nigeria, were being produced each year and sold in markets as far away as Liberia, Ghana, and Togo. Irregular blocks of these clays were sun-dried, then smoked and hardened for two to three days over a smoldering fire. In the process, they were transformed from their original gray shale color into the rich chocolate color and sheen of eko, the final product.

Vermeer also reported on how West Africans use this clay medicinally and was the first, as I've said, to demonstrate the striking similarity between eko and Kaopectate, widely used in the United States to counteract gastric upsets and diarrhea. Kaopectate is made of pectin and kaolin, a type of clay that forms a protective coating on the mucous membranes of the digestive tract and is capable of adsorbing bacterial and plant toxins. Eko and Kaopectate have X-ray diffraction patterns that reveal an almost identical quantity and size of kaolin particles; not surprisingly, eleven of the nineteen preparations that village medicine men make out of eko are intended for stomach and intestinal problems, including diarrhea. The other eight are for problems associated with pregnancy.

"The extent to which the many different ethnic groups in West Africa are aware of the antidiarrheal properties of eko is uncertain," Vermeer concludes a paper in the journal *Science*. "The fact that so many medicinal preparations in the village of Uzalla use eko, however, supports the notion that the therapeutic qualities of the clay are recognized by those who supply it to the West African market system and possibly by those who purchase it."[19]

Why was he the first Westerner to document the uses and composition of eko? I once asked Vermeer, a tall, unassuming, and very genial geographer. We were having lunch one day when he was in New York to attend the annual meetings of the Association of American Geographers, and I was struck by the fact that so many tons of this clay are produced and sold every year, yet only Africans had been aware of its existence.

"I don't know," Vermeer answered in the soft, raspy voice he has acquired from his ongoing treatments for throat cancer. "People must have had blinders on. They must have automatically condemned this practice."

"And why didn't you?" I pursued.

Then Vermeer told me about a childhood spent largely outdoors, in the hills outside of Oakland, California, where he grew up, and in the deserts of New Mexico, where he visited his missionary uncle and played and rode bareback with Navaho children. He has been looking at rocks and soils all his life, he said, so he couldn't *not* see them in the markets of Africa. In order to better understand the practice of geophagy, Vermeer also began sampling clays in Africa, and the good ones, he says, dissolve like a piece of chocolate in the mouth. He has tried hundreds of different clays, and most taste like chalk. He has yet to detect the pleasant "sour" taste that many women say they enjoy about eating clay.

Eko is not the only clay consumed in West Africa, and as Vermeer continued to investigate the practice of geophagy, he found numerous examples that did not paint as neat a picture as eko and Kaopectate. There were coastal groups in Ghana that regularly consumed sand, a totally inert substance, a habit for which he has yet to come up with any kind of plausible explanation other than that it was a habit that formerly interior-living people took with them to the coast. There were groups for which clay clearly seemed to serve a nutritive purpose, such as the Tiv of Nigeria, where women eat a clay that is very high in calcium. But they live right next door, so to speak, to groups where the same explanation doesn't hold. The Igbo people live near the Tiv, and theirs is also a nondairy culture. Igbo women have the same need for calcium as Tiv women, yet the clay they routinely consume has very little of this mineral.

The mystery of why people eat clay continued to expand with Vermeer's work in the American South, where the habit was once so widespread that clay removal caused considerable damage to roads, and some states posted signs requesting that local inhabitants not dig into the banks.[20] Since most of the southerners who eat clay are Blacks, the usual explanation for the clay-eating habit in America is that slaves brought it to this country from Africa. But clay eating has never been an exclusively Black habit—in Africa or in the South. In Africa, Europeans used to carry their stashes of edible clays in little silver cases; David Livingstone once observed that both slaves and rich men were affected.[21] In the South, the appellations "sand lickers," "sand lappers," and "sand hillers" refer to the practice among poor Whites. During the course of his research, Vermeer has also come across numerous examples of Whites eating clay, such as the nurse in Holmes County, Mississippi, with a Master of Science degree in public health. She pulled Vermeer aside one day to say, "I just wanted you to know that I am also a practitioner."

Clay eating in the South is more prevalent, though, in the Black population, and in the 1970s, 50 percent of Black women admitted to eating clay, about four times the frequency among White women. The percentage of Blacks admitting to clay eating has dropped since then, as clay eaters have become increasingly aware of the stigma attached to their practice and have either broken their habit or switched to eating corn starch or laundry starch (a switch, by the way, that spares women from the humiliation of being known as dirt eaters, but adds only calories to their diets), but the practice is still widespread.

As in Africa, the clays commonly eaten in the South are dug from clay deposits below the surface. And, as in Africa, clays are usually dried before they are eaten, either in the oven or on top of the stove. Clay consumption averages 1 to 2 ounces (30 to 50 grams) daily, and clay eating among Blacks often occurs under social conditions, like watching TV, while the habits of White women, on the other hand, are much more private and covert.[22]

As Vermeer began to look into the reasons why southern women consume dirt, however, he could find no consistent mineral content in clays that could explain the habit. Nor could he find any consistent medical or nutritional problems, such as anemia, diarrhea, toxins in foods, parasite infection, etc., associated with eating clay. He concluded that clay eating in the South does not stem from either a physiological or nutritional need but is, rather, "a common custom arising from traditional values and attitudes."[23]

"Millions around the world practice geophagy, and I hope I've encouraged the medical establishment to approach geophagy with a more open mind," says Vermeer. Yet all that he can say with certainty about the practice is that it is "neither good nor bad." It has the chance for being beneficial in some settings; in other settings, it seems to serve a purely psychological or cultural purpose, transferred from one generation to the next, like smoking or dipping snuff. And he warned me, as I began my research, that I will get as many answers about why people eat dirt as people I ask.[24]

Timothy Johns, on the other hand, is much more convinced of the underlying nutritional and medical reasons for most dirt eating, a conviction that stems in part from his knowledge of the ubiquitousness of plant toxins.

Like Vermeer, Johns saw his first edible clays in a market, but a market in the mountains of Peru, where the clays were being sold alongside potatoes. Johns was in South America to study the domestication of the potato, so he was, of course, curious. He knew that wild potatoes growing at high altitudes are full of toxic, bitter-tasting chemicals called glycoalkaloids, which can cause stomach pains, vomiting, and even death if consumed in sufficient quantity. But he had always assumed that Indians living in the Andes ate a domesticated and less toxic version of that wild and bitter food. So it was an eye-opening experience for him to learn that the clays were being sold alongside the potatoes because the Indians ate the clays with their potatoes in order to take the bitterness out. They boil the potatoes, then dip them into a slurry of clay and water before each bite.[25]

"This sounds pretty awful," Johns said when we were discussing this novel gastronomic technique over the phone, "but the clays are very fine, and their texture isn't at all gritty. The taste is in fact quite pleasant, reminiscent of unsalted butter or margarine." Eating their potatoes in this way, the Indians consume several grams of clay at a meal, and that is enough, Johns has found through extensive absorption studies, to take up most of the toxic glycoalkaloids in the potatoes. The clays that the Andean Indians choose to consume with their potatoes are particularly fine, and they have cation exchange qualities that make them magnets for positively charged substances, particularly glycoalkaloids.

Johns's experience in the Andes gave him a new perspective on geophagy and the role that geophagy probably played in human dietary history. "It's all very well to say that humans have reduced the toxic load of their plants through domestication, but what did they eat before domestication?" he asks. His findings suggest that clay eating gave humans the flexibility to eat a broader range of plants, and this flexibility was important not just in the Andes, but all over the world. The use of clays in Africa had not before been linked to the detoxification of plants. Vermeer, for instance, had not considered the role of detoxification, because he had never seen clays being eaten in combination with specific foods. But when Johns tested edible clays from Africa, as well as from California and Sardinia, he found that they all share this ability to absorb plant toxins.[26]

According to Johns, then, clay eating has allowed us to adapt to an ever-changing array of foods. It is an important part of the behavioral repertoire of experimental omnivores like us and is "a kind of buffer, or protective device, for quelling gastrointestinal stress induced by barely tolerable wild plants or pangs of hunger." It could also make a significant nutritional contribution to the diet, in terms of calcium, iron, or zinc, but this role of clays is harder to pin down because the mineral content of edible clays varies greatly from one clay to the next. Until researchers invest the time and the money to examine geophagy very thoroughly—an unlikely occurrence in this day of cheap mineral substitutes and many more pressing medical problems—we may never know all the reasons why people eat dirt. Perhaps it is enough to know that there are many good reasons and that women, with the extra demands of pregnancy and lactation, have the most reasons of all. "Earth," says Johns, "may not be to everyone's taste, but it is one of the oldest tastes known to humankind."[27]

A FEW DAYS AFTER my conversation with Johns, I received a second sample of dirt in the mail, this time from the Down Home Georgia White Dirt Company in Griffin, Georgia. A company spokesman assured me that this dirt, kaolin from a private mine, is sold strictly as a novelty item (the label says "Not Suggested For Human Consumption"). But the person who first told me about it, the owner of Mrs. Bea's Kitchen in Atlanta, said that all her customers for the dirt were women looking for edible clays. She stocks it behind the cash register, along with the candy and cigarettes, and charges $1.29 for a one-pound bag.[28]

I broke open the bag that was sent to me and bit off a small piece of one of the white chunks. It was fine, not gritty at all, but very gummy and chalk-like. I can't imagine craving this stuff, and craving it more than food, a feeling that many dirt eaters have reported. But, hey, I'm an omnivore (and a woman too), and so I will keep my dietary options open. ◉

NOTES

1. Timothy Johns and Martin Duquette, "Detoxification and Mineral Supplementation as Functions of Geophagy," *American Journal of Clinical Nutrition* 53 (1991): 448–456.

2. S. Aufreiter, R. G. V. Hancock, W. C. Mahaney, A. Stambolic-Robb, and K. Sanmugadas, "Geochemistry and Minerology of Soils Eaten by Humans," *International Journal of Food Sciences and Nutrition* 48 (1997): 293–305.

3. Jared Diamond and Dugald Stermer, "Eat Dirt," *Discover* 19, no. 2 (1998): 70–76.

4. "Elementary Elephant Control," *The Economist*, 2 September 2000, 74.

5. William C. Mahaney, David P. Watts, and R. G. V. Hancock,"Geophagy by Mountain Gorillas (*Gorilla gorilla beringei*) in the Virunga Mountains, Rwanda," *Primates* 31 (1990): 113–120.

6. Derek Denton, *The Hunger for Salt* (New York: Springer Verlag, 1982), 421.

7. Timothy Johns, "Well-Grounded Diet," *The Sciences* (September/October 1991): 38–43.

8. Diamond and Stermer, "Eat Dirt," 74.

9. Denton, *The Hunger for Salt*, 84.

10. Andrea S. Wiley and Solomon H. Katz, "Geophagy in Pregnancy: A Test of a Hypothesis," *Current Anthropology* 39, no. 4 (1998): 532–545.

11. John M. Hunter, "Macroterme Geophagy and Pregnancy Clays in Southern Africa," *Journal of Cultural Geography* 14 (1993): 69–92.

12. Ibid., 80.

13. Margie Profet, "The Evolution of Pregnancy Sickness as Protection to the Embryo against Pleistocene Teratogens," *Evolutionary Theory* 8 (1988): 177–190.

14. Hunter, "Macroterme Geophagy," 75.

15. Eating clay is anything but benign in a place like Anniston, Alabama, where the Monsanto Company "routinely discharged toxic waste into a West Anniston creek and dumped millions of pounds of PCBs into oozing open-pit landfills," as reported in an article in the *Washington Post* (1 January 2002, p.A01). Anniston residents who ate their local clay have been among those complaining of health problems and high PCB levels.

16. F. W. Cragin, "Observations on Cachexia Africana or Dirt-Eating," *American Journal of the Medical Sciences* 17 (1835): 356–364.

17. Charles E. Mengel, William A. Carter, and Edward S. Horton, "Geophagia with Iron Deficiency and Hypokalemia," *Archives of Internal Medicine* 114 (1964): 470–474; Harry W. Severence, Jr., Thomas Holt, Nicholas A. Patrone, and Lynne Chapman, "Profound Muscle Weakness and Hypokalemia Due to Clay Ingestion," *Southern Medical Journal* 81, no. 2 (1988): 272–274.

18. James A. Halsted, "Geophagia in Man: Its Nature and Nutritional Effects," *American Journal of Clinical Nutrition* 21, no. 12 (1968): 1384–1393.

19. Donald E. Vermeer and Ray E. Ferrell, Jr., "Nigerian Geophagical Clay: A Traditional Antidiarrheal Pharmaceutical," *Science* 227 (1985): 634–636.

20. Donald E. Vermeer, "Geophagy in the American South," *Bulletin of the Shreveport Medical Society* 37 (1986): 38; Donald E. Vermeer and Dennis A. Frate, "Geophagy in a Mississippi County," *Annals of the Association of American Geographers* 65, no. 3 (1975): 412–424.

21. Halsted, "Geophagia in Man," 1388–1389.

22. Vermeer, "Geophagy in the American South," 38.

23. Vermeer and Frate, "Geophagy in a Mississippi County," 424.

24. I was reminded of this warning when I was visiting friends in North Carolina and got into a conversation with their babysitter, a woman who had eaten clay and laundry starch all through her childhood. After discussing the circumstances of her youth—she was one of thirteen children raised by a family of women in rural Virginia—we came to the somewhat humorous realization that in her case, at least, part of the appeal of clay and laundry starch was that they were the only snack foods in the house. Everything else had to be boiled, fried, and, in the case of chicken, killed and plucked before it could be eaten. All of her siblings and cousins also ate clay, but she gave up the habit when she got married and began seeing a doctor. "Every other day, I had to have a piece of that dirt," this woman still remembers. "It was the prettiest dirt you ever saw."

25. Johns, "Well-Grounded Diet," 40.

26. Johns and Duquette, "Detoxification," 451.

27. Johns, "Well-Grounded Diet," 43.

28. Down Home Georgia White Dirt and Mrs. Bea's Kitchen appear to no longer be in business.

Spring 2002, volume 2, number 2

john o'connor |

Badlands

Portrait of a Competitive Eater

BADLANDS WAS HUNGRY. And by hungry I don't mean peckish, or pleasantly empty, or that he had that faint grumble you get an hour or so before dinner. No, this was a different breed of hunger altogether. It was a murderous, desert island hunger, the kind you feel deep in your eyeballs, when all of your rational faculties have atrophied and your brain feels like it's dribbling out of your nostrils and the only thing you desire in this world is FOOD, any kind of food, RIGHT NOW.

Let it be said that Badlands is not accustomed to this kind of hunger. Normal hunger, sure. He's usually hungry. In fact, a satiated Badlands is a rare creature indeed. But tonight was different. Tonight it was as if a small mammal, say, a badger (those most capable burrowers of the weasel family), had crawled down his gullet, hollowed out his stomach, and lay there growling and scratching away at his insides.

You see, Badlands does not usually fast before contests, as he believes this can lead to "shrinkage" of his stomach, thereby reducing his intake of food. He'll eat a normal breakfast the day of an event, sometimes lunch, too, and maybe even a snack shortly before the start whistle. All of which sets Badlands at ideological odds with the vast majority of competitive eaters, called "gurgitators," who generally hold that an empty stomach equals increased stuffing capacity. Physiologically speaking, both theories are half-baked. But for some reason a few acolytes of the fasting school have had recent success on the circuit, so tonight Badlands was experimenting, and it was clear from the look on his face that the experiment was killing him.

To make matters worse, George Shea, the brains and impeccable hair of the International Federation of Competitive Eating (IFOCE), which had organized the contest, had asked gurgitators to arrive well ahead of time as insurance against start whistle snafus, which are routine at these gatherings. Tonight's event was the second annual World Pelmeni Eating Championship (pelmenis are a Russian pasta—think tortellini crossed with pierogi), one of the year's biggest contests, with a modest media presence and a semirespectable cash prize, and George wanted everyone present mega-early and ready to cram.

So Badlands had driven the hour from his house in Copiague, Long Island, in wrist-slitting rush-hour traffic and by successive miracles had found a parking spot two blocks from the Atlantic Oceana Ballroom in Brighton Beach, Brooklyn, parallel-parked his mammoth SUV in two beautiful, for-the-record-book turns, and lumbered through the Oceana's clouded glass doors, slightly out of breath and major-league agitated, right on time.

That was at six P.M. Now it was eight, and it had been early morning since he'd last eaten. Nothing all day, not even a Slim Jim.

After a circumnavigation of the Oceana's sprawling insides, I found Badlands slumped in a chair near the kitchen, its swinging doors divulging an anthill-like scrum of waiters while offering a glimpse of the boiling madness inside, a war zone of grease-strewn men and crashing metal. Badlands looked sedated. His eyelids sagged; a meaty sliver of tongue was clamped between his teeth; and his hands were clasped across his broad belly. A 420-pound, six-foot-five-inch semivegetative Black Goliath.

I revived him with a knuckle punch to the bicep. SMACK! His eyes shot open; his size fourteens flew off the floor; and his massive body lurched forward.

Blinking, frowning, he struggled to his feet.

"You alright?" I asked.

"Yeah, yeah. I'm feeling good," he said. "My stomach is stretched and I'm ready to go."

"You looked half-dead."

"Aw man, I was visualizing."

One of Badlands' precontest rituals entails visualizing the eating of whatever food is at hand, like a skier might imagine slipping through a slalom course prior to a race. It's akin to meditation: a cleansing of the chakra bowels to achieve unobstructed intestinal harmony.

Badlands's jeans rode low off his waist, hitched up his thick shanks, and his 5-XL black Sean John jersey had an ironing board look to it, the sleeves coming to points at the shoulders like a kite. He also wore a matching baseball cap, the brim flattened and flipped to the back. Despite his fervent attempts to keep the jersey clean, in about thirty minutes it will be streaked white down the front from the soupy extract of pelmenis.

"I guzzled a half gallon of water before I left home," he said. "Just a little something to keep myself stretched. I haven't had anything to eat since breakfast, and I'm worried how that'll affect me. Plus, my bladder is about to go, man."

A few days earlier, Badlands had explained to me one of the pillars of his gurgitational philosophy, namely, that with every food comes an ideal strategy for attack, a strategy to be measured against an eater's individual speed and capacity. Over the past couple of weeks, Badlands had been searching for his pelmeni strategy, guzzling gallons of water and plowing through bowls of ravioli and pierogi at his kitchen table while his eleven-year-old son, Brandon, timed him on the microwave.

"Pelmenis are a relatively easy food to speed-eat because they're soft," Badlands had told me, "but the pasta gets tough after a while and is hard on the jaws." To address this problem, he'd been chewing a wad of Big Red—twenty-one sticks at a time—for an hour a day. "You gotta have strong jaws in this game," he'd said. "You cannot come to the table with weak jaws and expect to go the distance. A lot of people don't realize that, and they try to take shortcuts."

The grand prize at the Pelmeni Championship was fifteen hundred dollars, and Badlands hoped tonight would be the payoff for all his Chef Boyardee workouts. The standing record, held by Oleg "the Russian" Zhornitskiy (who's actually Ukrainian), was 244 pelmenis in six minutes. Badlands thought he could do at least 250.

"I'm through with this fasting stuff, though, man," he said, rubbing his stomach and arching back on his heels. "It's wrecked my energy level."

A few other gurgitators milled around nearby—Ed "Cookie" Jarvis, "Hungry" Charles Hardy, "Gentleman" Joe Manchetti, Sabatino "the Great" Manzi, "Krazy" Kevin Lipsitz—all of them big, big dudes. Sabatino had a cartoonishly oblong gut, like a yoga ball held in suspenders, and a swinging, bovine double chin. Cookie packed most of his extra weight in several intimidating saddlebags fore and aft of his waistline. And Hungry seemed to hold his spare pounds primarily in his neck and shoulders, which appeared as solid as armor. Despite this awesome display of flesh, Badlands could easily claim Fat Bastard supremacy over them all.

Above: Badlands at the first annual Dumpling Eating Contest, Columbus Park, Chinatown, New York City, June 2003. Badlands came in second, with 85 pork dumplings. Ed "Cookie" Jarvis won with 91. PHOTOGRAPH BY JOHN O'CONNOR © 2003

In fact, Badlands's sheer bulk is a little intimidating at first. On instinct I tend to be wary of people who are taller than me, let alone 250 pounds heavier. And Badlands not only looms over me; he looms around me. When I hug him (we always greet each other with a soul brother handshake) it's a little like being in the arms of a grizzly, except, I imagine, gentler. But his liquid brown eyes, pudgy shaved head, and cylindrical jowls give him the sublime and placid mien of the Buddha. It also helps that he's possibly the nicest person I've ever met.

From the looks of them, none of the other gurgitators had eaten much that day either. That is, aside from Cookie, who was inhaling a sweating pastry he'd boosted from a passing tray. The tables around us were swamped with steaming platters: smoked fish, roasted chickens, mystery-meat patties, and what looked like some sort of eggplant-squash hybrid. All of which was off limits. The gurgitators had only a short while till the Pelmeni Championship got underway, and they'd all apparently resolved to channel their hunger into the competition.

George Shea materialized, perspiring liberally in a black tuxedo, a clipboard jammed in his armpit, his hair moist and delicately slicked back in the Pat Riley manner. He started barking instructions.

"We're going to introduce you individually! Remember when you come out to space yourselves! Don't bunch up! And make a little show for the crowd!"

From what I could gather from George's harangue, gurgitators were supposed to emerge single file through a cloud of dry ice at the top of the stage, which was set in the back of the ballroom, and then descend a short, deceptively steep flight of stairs to a narrow platform, which would maybe (maybe not) hold all twenty of them shoulder to shoulder—an imposing phalanx of whoddling flesh and bone—before they again had to descend another short flight of stairs to a large U of banquet tables assembled along the periphery of a parquet floor. In other words, what sounded like a catastrophe in the making.

George wrapped things up—"Everyone backstage, pronto!"—and then sprinted off into the darkness. Gurgitators dispersed slowly, knocking back drinks and rubbing out cigarettes. I turned to Badlands and swung a crisp right hook through the air, bringing it down squarely on his wide shoulder. WHACK! He feigned injury, stumbling backwards. I went to find a seat. A few minutes later I looked over and saw him standing right where I'd left him, talking to a newspaper reporter. He'd once told me that interacting with the media used to terrify him. He'd get tongue-tied, worried about saying the wrong thing, offending someone. Now he craved the attention. Everything about contests—the cameras, the hot lights, the revolted audience—he found totally irresistible. Here, sprung from the anonymous masses, Badlands was a star, and he absolutely lived for these moments. Now he was lingering, however, and George reemerged from the shadows to give him a last pleading look to get a move on.

Competitive eating has gained a small measure of notoriety in recent years almost entirely because of George Shea and his younger brother Rich, who together constitute the IFOCE, which they formed in 1997 to promote eating contests, half tongue-in-cheek, as "the sport of the new millennium." Today the IFOCE oversees more than 150 events a year and has over 3,000 registered gurgitators. The sport's pinnacle is the Nathan's Famous Hot Dog Eating Contest held on Coney Island every July Fourth, which is attended by thousands and carried live on ESPN. The five-time Nathan's champ and undisputed gurgitational hegemon is twenty-seven-year-old Takeru Kobayashi, a 132-pound Japanese eater who holds the record of 53.5 hot dogs and buns in 12 minutes and who is said to earn around $150,000 a year from contests in Japan and the United States.

Badlands, by comparison, is the number-five-ranked gurgitator in the world, with major victories in burritos (15 in 8:00 minutes), corned beef hash (4 pounds in 1:58 minutes), peas (9.5 one-pound bowls in 12:00 minutes), onions (8.5 ounces in 1:00 minute), and *hamantaschen* (50 traditional Purim cookies in 6:00 minutes), among others. While his winnings are nowhere near Kobayashi's, he earns enough from contests to make occasionally lavish upgrades to his home entertainment center. The pelmeni cash prize would help in this regard, and the three-foot-high trophy would be a welcome addendum to the glinting metropolis of gurgitating honors already buckling his mantelpiece.

The Oceana was jammed to fire-hazard capacity that night, mostly with Russians from the surrounding Brighton Beach neighborhood, which is just down the road from Coney Island. Everybody looked related, or at least as though they shared a tailor. The men all wore Soviet-era double-breasted suits and had moustaches like fat caterpillars, while the women labored under mountains of hair and wore sequined evening gowns, all thighs and wilting cleavage. It was like a politburo reunion from the class of 1979. The fifty-dollar cover bought you a Pantagruelian smorgasbord and several stage performances, of which the pelmeni contest was the finale. There was *way* too much food, an unfathomable amount of food, in fact, and whole tables of it went untouched.

After the cabaret acts, George and Rich Shea appeared onstage. Rich is a half-foot shorter than George, his hair almost reflective, like George's, from the generous application of hair products, and his bottom lip is held permanently in a subtle pout. Together they gave their standard carnival barker introduction, expounding on the illustrious history of competitive eating and extolling the sport's "physical poetry." Then, as Guns N' Roses' "Welcome to the Jungle" rumbled out of the PA system, gurgitators began plodding through the dry-ice fog at the top of the stage. There was confusion at first as the blinding luminescence of the strobe lights immobilized them. A cluster of eaters crowded at the precipice, toeing the shadowy top stair and shielding their eyes as George waited expectantly below. At last, a cooperative leap of faith was made, and those in front started gingerly down, arms outstretched, fear in their eyes. The rest soon followed, and free of the stairs, they swaggered and chest-thumped one another onstage as though they were part of a college bowl game introduction.

Oleg the Russian had come first (given pole position as defending champ), followed by Cookie, Hungry, Krazy Kev, Crazy Legs, Sabatino, Dale "The Mouth from the South" Boone (who claimed to be a descendant of Daniel Boone), Gentleman Joe, Don "Moses" Lerman (carrying replica cardboard tablets), two guys wearing military-style *ushanka* hats and black leather boots who Rich said were members of the Ukrainian National Eating Team, and a few others.

Badlands came out second to last, waving a white hand towel in circles above his head, his underarm flesh wagging like a hammock. He appeared to be growling. An arc of spittle flew from his mouth and was briefly illuminated by the backlighting, flickering out like a dying sparkler. As Axl Rose squealed, "Feel my…my…my serpentine!" Badlands paused at the foot of the stage between George and Rich and, with the hand towel clenched between his teeth, flexed Mr. Universe style. The audience ate it up. When the applause reached its crescendo, Badlands's scowl vanished, and his face blazed into a quarter moon of teeth: his signature entrance.

A COUPLE OF WEEKS BEFORE the Pelmeni Championship, I met Badlands for lunch at a diner in lower Manhattan. A gray slab of sky hung over the city. Rain was coming down like sprayed buckshot and created little rivers that spilled along the curbs, overflowing the drainage grates at the corners and forcing people to leap over the sprawling puddles. Despite the weather, Badlands was in a good mood, and before we'd even sat down, he launched into a monologue on his favorite topic: the future of competitive eating in the United States.

"It's a sport. I definitely think it's going to be in the Olympics one day, if not as a main event then as an exhibition sport. I mean, look, right now you got ballroom dancing as an exhibition sport. What the hell *is* that? Some guys twirling ladies around? C'mon, man! The thing is, everyone can relate to eating. There's a fascination there. Rich Shea calls competitive eating 'the sport of the everyman,' because in America we're big eaters, and everyone

Above: A training session for the 2004 Nathan's Famous Hot Dog Eating Contest at Jason "Crazy Legs" Conti's apartment. From the left are Badlands, "Hungry" Charles Hardy, and Crazy Legs. PHOTOGRAPH BY JOHN O'CONNOR © 2003

likes to pig out once in a while. Eating contests have the same things that people look for in other sports. Mainly, they're fun to watch, and they also make you wonder, how can that guy or girl eat so much, so fast?"

Badlands looked formidable across the small Formica table. I imagined it was how Gulliver appeared to the Lilliputians, and I wasn't inclined to disagree with him just then. Besides, his logic sort of made sense. Americans *do* like to pig out. I could personally attest to that. Plus, adding ballroom dancing to the Olympic pantheon did seem to widen the criteria for how you defined "sport." Chess was an exhibition event at the 2000 Sydney Olympics, and the mind-numbing Japanese board game Go was being promoted as a possible addition to the 2012 games. Where, after all, do you draw the line with this sort of thing?

Our waitress arrived, and Badlands ordered the ten-ounce "Colossal" hamburger with onion rings and a Sprite. Not wanting to seem abstemious, I got the Colossal too, with bacon and cheese, plus fries and a Coke. Badlands flipped open his wallet and pulled out a wrinkled photo of himself and his wife, Gina, on their wedding day. They got married right out of high school and now have three sons, ages eleven, fourteen, and seventeen (the oldest is from Gina's previous marriage). In the photo Gina is wearing a cream-colored gown and holding a bouquet, her hair in a spire of curls that tilts slightly over her forehead. Badlands is in a black tux with a white corsage, a high-top fade, and a thin goatee cut around his lips. He's thinner by probably 150 pounds.

When our waitress returned, she dropped our plates on the table with a heavy clunk. My Colossal, which stood a little taller than my soda glass, looked as if it had been buffed and polished. Gleaming curls of bacon jabbed from its sides, the twisted fat resembling entrails. The burger leaned against an arc of fries that seemed to have been strategically positioned to prevent it from tipping over and spilling its contents on the table.

Before we dug in, I asked Badlands if he ever worried what effect, if any, his hobby might have on his health.

"My doctor says as long as I don't eat too much during the off-season I'll be okay," he said.

"When is the off-season?"

"Whenever there's no contest."

As we laid siege to our Colossals, I was tempted to ask whether he considered today part of the off-season, but I chickened out.

"There's a theory that says the skinnier you are the more food you can eat," Badlands went on, "because your stomach can stretch more." He held his hands out in front of his stomach to illustrate this. "I want to see if that's true. I'm planning on losing some weight. It sounds crazy, but you really have to be in shape to be competitive in these contests. I mean, I want to be around for my kids, too, you know? But secondly, I want to be in top form for contests."

With an onion ring poised to slither through his lips, Badlands said he'd been trying to cut red meat and fried food out of his diet.

I let Badlands ramble as we ate, and ramble he did, a great meandering tangent that eventually wound back, as most things do with him, to competitive eating.

Born in 1969 in Jamaica, Queens, Badlands attended high school in Brooklyn, where he played basketball and football and got decent grades. Later, he dreamed of making it as a rapper, and in the early 1990s he recorded a rap album in a friend's basement. Nothing came of that, but in December 2004 Badlands self-released the album *Hungry & Focused*, his autobiographical ode to competitive eating.

"I wanted to do something positive and with a competitive eating theme, like the Fat Boys," Badlands explained, "but more about what I do and how I got into this and where I am in the sport."

Twelve years ago, Badlands landed a job as a subway conductor with the Metropolitan Transit Authority. Five nights a week he rides the Number Seven train its twenty-one stops from Flushing, Queens—one stop past Shea Stadium—to Times Square and back again, three round-trips total. He has to stand the entire shift crammed into the conductor's booth, a coffin-like space in the center of the train from which he flips a switch to open and close the doors. Seeing Badlands's haunches roll off his chair in the diner, I guessed that the conductor's booth couldn't be too cozy—all 420 pounds of him stuffed into that airless, shuddering closet, hurtling under the East River and through the bowels of Queens and Manhattan in near pitch blackness, inhaling the tunnels' horrid stench while the squeal of the train's brakes broke his eardrums apart.

I started to ask him if he ever got tired of his job, but he didn't want to talk about work.

"In Japan, competitive eating is huge," he said. "It's like baseball or hockey is here, and the eaters make a pretty good living from it. Look at Kobayashi. It'll be like that here eventually. Just watch." Badlands jabbed the tabletop with his finger for emphasis, rattling the ice in our glasses. "It'll get to the point where the type of money that's available to Japanese eaters will become available to us. It's just a matter of time."

In the past few months Badlands had competed in practically every eating contest in New York City and a few others around the country, he said. Pickles, matzoh balls, cannoli, corned beef hash, doughnuts, and cheesecake. The pelmeni would be his third in three weeks.

"How do all of these contests affect you digestively?" I asked.

"I used to feel the aftereffects when I first started," Badlands said. "Basically, a lot of gas and stuff, but my body has gotten used to the rigors of the sport. Now I feel like a person after a big Thanksgiving meal. I get back into shape by taking a laxative the night after a contest, and I'm back to normal by morning."

He appended an apologetic smile to the end of this sentence and then ripped away another bite, his jaws opening menacingly and clamping down on his Colossal like Jaws on Robert Shaw.

"Why put yourself through this?" I asked. "Why compete in these contests for other people's amusement and for little or sometimes no pay?"

Badlands paused, eyes skyward and head askew, as if considering this question for the first time. "I just loved it from the first day I tried it," he said. "Just being able to know that I can eat this food faster than anyone in the world, it's a great feeling."

This wasn't exactly the response I was after, but it would have to do for now. We'd finished our Colossals, and Badlands had to go.

As we were getting ready to pay, a boy of about thirteen approached and said he recognized Badlands from the Nathan's contest, which he'd seen on TV. He asked for an autograph. After the kid scurried off, Badlands said to me, "That happens more and more. People recognize me in the subway, in the street, wherever. When they appreciate what you do, it's really something. And you gotta show them love."

The pulse at the Pelmeni Championship had flat-lined through the cabaret acts, but by the time the contest rolled around, most people were out of their seats and swarming around the parquet floor, armed with DV recorders.

Gurgitators were spread out along the U of banquet tables with large white oval plates of pelmenis in front of them, waiting for the start whistle. Badlands was seated in the middle of the U. He'd draped dishtowels across his lap and tucked a few in his jersey and even laid them under his chair. He was doing some precontest rituals: neck rotations, arm and jaw stretches, a massive cracking of knuckles. This routine varies depending on the circumstances. At Nathan's, for instance, where gurgitators stood at waist-high tables, he warmed up by pumping his arms like a sprinter, arcing invisible hot dogs into his mouth in mock eating motion. Tonight, he would use his hands to shovel the pelmenis into his mouth, and when he'd finished his warm-ups, he sat with his face inches away from his plate, his hands twitching beside it like a gunslinger's.

His mental approach is always the same, though. "What I do is I try to get a rhythm going and not worry too much about my speed or what other eaters are doing," he'd told me. "You've got to stay focused. If you let yourself get distracted and start worrying about the guy next to you, you're in trouble. The main thing is to concentrate." To help him concentrate, Badlands listens to his MP3 player during contests. The style of music varies, though recently he'd been leaning toward techno.

From my seat I caught sight of Rich Shea on the other side of the tables, waving for me to come forward. When I'd snaked through the crowd to Rich, he said he'd volunteered me, along with three others, as a judge for the contest. With the lights from DV recorders winking at us, Rich had us raise our right hands and swear to uphold the rules and regulations of the IFOCE, so help us God. We'd be responsible for counting the empty plates of pelmenis as they left the tables, he explained, and for monitoring the gurgitators to ensure there was no cheating.

"Be especially vigilant with urges contrary to swallowing," he said, employing his euphemism for puking. "That's an automatic disqualification."

Onstage, George was itching to go. He bobbed back and forth on his toes, pursing his lips and lobbing a microphone from hand to hand. Then suddenly he screamed, "Gentlemen! Start your engines!" And before I knew it, they were off.

Right away, Rich started jogging among the tables, delivering color commentary with one hand held aloft, an index finger pointing to the rafters, screeching into his microphone.

"Ladies and gentlemen! Oleg Zhornitskiy has just finished his first plate!" "Ladies and gentlemen! Dale Boone is positively RAGING!"

I'd been assigned a table with Hungry Charles and the two guys from the Ukrainian National Eating Team. The Ukrainians started strong but slowed about midway through their second plates. Hungry lost steam around his third. I've dubbed Hungry's eating style the "Crouching Tiger, Hidden Cram," because he bends his body over and folds his arms around his plate, almost concealing it completely, and then shoves the food into his mouth hand-over-fist until he is spent. Occasionally, this is a deadly technique, and early in his career it earned Hungry a string of impressive victories. But tonight he'd reached his limit far before the rest of the field, and he looked devastated, leaning with his elbows on the table and shaking his corn-rowed head, his gold crucifix dangling in his plate.

A couple of tables away, Dale the Mouth and Badlands were setting the pace. A mass of crazed Russian youth mobbed their table, shrieking and waving their arms, and a few leaned over to shout encouragement/obscenities at the two gurgitators. One commented to Dale the Mouth, who had his face mashed into a plate of pelmenis, his jaws pumping like pistons, that he was eating like a mad dog.

Badlands's eating rhythm was predictably cadenced as he nodded along to his music and swayed his body laterally. He didn't seem to notice the swarm across the table or Dale frothing next to him. He ate deliberately, not particularly rushed, pausing occasionally to take sips of water. Yet by the looks of it, he was consuming a staggering number of pelmenis.

Finally, George blew the whistle and called for the gurgitators to cease and desist. As the turmoil subsided, the audience members lowered their cameras and gazed blankly about. The crowd had worked itself into a frenzy during the contest, yowling, thrashing, dispensing with any pretense of restraint. But everyone quickly recovered themselves and began filing sheepishly back to their tables.

Once the dust had settled, a sobering scene emerged on the parquet floor. Twenty panting, corpulent men, slathered jowl to jowl in butter and pasta fragments, stumbled around in a daze. The Shea brothers scurried from table to table, sifting through plates, sorting leftovers, hurrying to count the remaining pelmenis and declare a winner. The Pelmeni Championship has a history of controversy. Almost every year someone demands a recount or alleges fraud or protests a disqualification. So George and Rich were anxious to have the results decided as quickly as possible before things got ugly. We judges stood aside as the Sheas did all of the tallying, scribbling on scraps of paper and conferring with one another at the foot of the stage.

Then George trod up the stage steps and, a little hoarsely, declared Dale the Mouth the winner with a total of 274 pelmenis. Badlands was second with 271, and Oleg the Russian, with 267, was third. Sure enough, Oleg's brother, Alex, who bore a striking resemblance to Peja Stoyakovich of the Sacramento Kings, pulled George aside to argue for a recount. But after a long night, George wasn't having it, and the results stood.

Dale the Mouth, clad in a coonskin cap and denim overalls, received his winning trophy onstage, a delicate dribble of pelmeni stuck in the corner of his mouth. Overcome with emotion, he grabbed the microphone out of George's hand and screamed, "This is for the victims of September 11 and for New York City!" George wrenched the microphone back and, with just the slightest touch of irony, said, "Ladies and Gentleman, we are in the midst of competitive eating's best. And Dale Boone, my friends, is a true athlete."

Badlands received a trophy, a bouquet of pink roses, and a check for one thousand dollars. A horde of kids and little old ladies converged on him, clamoring for autographs and pictures, to which he happily obliged. A few days earlier he'd confided to me that there were a lot of big egos in competitive eating but that he wasn't one of them.

"I know the same way I got these fans I can lose 'em," he'd said. "If you don't sign an autograph for somebody and treat 'em like you don't have the time, it's the same thing like if you're a musician, and they're not gonna buy your record. Besides, I'm not like that. I'm not conceited. I just try to stay grounded and be myself." ◉

Summer 2006, volume 6, number 3

r. marie griffith |

"Don't Eat That"

The Erotics of Abstinence in American Christianity

We are all now gastropornographers.

—British celebrity food writer Nigella Lawson

MONKS FASTING IN THE DESERT, saints beating their bodies and sleeping on nails, apostles renouncing all pleasures and subsisting on the charity of benefactors, pious men and women starving their senses in emulation of Christ: It is by now a truism to note that devout Christians of earlier eras displayed profound ambivalence about food and flesh. For both patristic and medieval followers of the faith, the body was felt to be a burden that must be suffered resignedly during earthly life while yet remaining the crucial material out of which devotional practice and spiritual progress were forged. Thus the body, cultivated as an instrument for salvation, was to be endured, subjected to the scrutiny of the spirit, and strenuously disciplined.

Such discipline would take many forms, one of the most recurrent of which was extreme abstinence from food. The discipline of fasting, well established in the Mediterranean world long before Christianity emerged, became especially important in Christian communal practice during the early fourth century C.E., used variously as a method of baptismal preparation, a means of purification, a sign of grief, a work of charity, or an expression of penitence and the desire for God's mercy. Over the next several centuries, as Caroline Walker Bynum has richly documented, both the meaning and the practice of Christian abstinence changed significantly, so that by the thirteenth and fourteenth centuries preachers and theologians urged "spiritual more than physical abstinence," meaning general restraint or moderation in all areas of life. Yet many Christians of the later Middle Ages, particularly women, decried this perspective as a dangerous compromise with the world and chose the path of extreme asceticism, imitating and deeply identifying with the broken flesh of Christ on the cross through rigorous sacrificial fasting. For those such as Catherine of Siena, who died of self-induced starvation at the age of thirty-three, true nourishment came only from Christ, and to rely too heavily on earthly food was to commit the terrible sin of gluttony.[1]

Prescriptions and practices of nutritive abstinence fluctuated in subsequent eras, and scattered examples of intense food refusal among Christians, again mostly though not exclusively women, have continued to dot the historical record. Since the transformative religious revolutions of the sixteenth and seventeenth centuries, Catholics and Protestants alike have participated in the ascetic tradition, though always in very particular, localized ways. Martin Luther condemned extravagant forms of self-denial that destroyed the body; yet he urged moderated fasting both to curb distracting physical desires and to take care of the body so that it might minister to others' needs. John Calvin held more strictly to fasting as a necessary discipline for appeasing God's wrath, a view echoed in later groups like the English Puritans. The Churches of England, Rome, and the Eastern world followed fixed calendrical times for fasting—such as Lent, Ember Days, Rogation Days, Fridays, and Vigils prior to certain holy festivals—but varied in the precise meaning given to "fasting" per se.

Meanwhile, medical and devotional writers on both sides of the Atlantic increasingly recommended a sober and temperate diet for the health of the body as well as the glory of God. In fact, since the Colonial period, American Christians have wrestled with questions about bodily asceticism and gluttony in ways that would arguably feel increasingly unfamiliar to their patristic and medieval forebears. While critiques of gluttony—articulated variously by Puritans and Social Gospelers, radical Catholics and Holiness adherents—recall themes expressed by earlier Christian ascetics, an evolving fixation on health and perfection (chiefly among Protestants) represents a stark departure from the older emphasis on corporeal acts of penitence. Even more discordantly, the contemporary obsession with slender, toned bodies and the ideal of extreme thinness bear only a distorted resemblance to rituals of purification and self-denial that occupied Christians in earlier periods. Somehow, it seems, the kinship between body and soul has become dramatically reconceptualized, with significant help from men and women professing Christianity but focusing as much on the "promised land of weight loss" as on the eternal Kingdom of God.

How did this happen? What exactly is the relation between Christianity and the modern American diet obsession, the compulsive anxiety felt by so many women, men, teenagers, and increasingly even children toward their weight, food intake, and body size? Our knowledge of Christianity's profound impact on diet in prior historical periods, including the antebellum body reform movements inspired by figures such as William Alcott, Sylvester Graham, and Elizabeth Blackwell, helps us see how Protestant morals were transformed into somatic disciplines, such that dietary correctness became central to the larger reform project of forging a Christian nation.[2] Many people would nonetheless argue that religion is so attenuated in the modern world as to have little if any tangible connection to, say, contemporary food refusal. Some, like Joan Jacobs Brumberg in *Fasting Girls*, have promoted a fairly standard model of secularization, arguing that religious fasting was transformed into secular dieting sometime during the nineteenth century (though neglecting to show just how and why this change occurred). Others, most notably Hillel Schwartz in *Never Satisfied*, have argued that modern dieting is itself a central ritual in what has become *the* predominant religion of late twentieth-century America: the worship of the body beautiful, lean, and physically "fit." But though religion plays an important—albeit mostly speculative—role in such accounts as a Foucauldian disciplinary apparatus to be resisted and rejected, its appreciable impact has not been clearly elaborated. So the problem remains unsolved: what relation might a specific tradition such as Protestantism have to modern American bodily practices and food obsessions?[3]

This was one of the questions that led me into my book, *Born Again Bodies: Flesh and Spirit in American Christianity*. The project explores the recent trajectory of religious struggles with food and the body, historicizing the links between varied dietary regimens and devotional practice. Included are such topics as the trajectory of fasting from an act of mortification into a masculinized therapeutic practice; sundry quests for physical vigor, purification, and immortality among such groups as Methodists, Pentecostals, and proponents of mind cure; the rhythms of hygienic discipline and celebratory abundance in organizations like Father Divine's Peace Mission Movement; the advent of evangelical dieting in the postwar era; and the persistent ideals of corporeal beauty and "fitness" in contemporary Christianity. American culture's treasured doctrine of the perfectible body is deeply indebted to Christian currents that have perceived the body as central for pushing the soul along the path to progress. And nowhere is that relationship more evident than in the deeply contested arena of the appetite, where desire and pleasure, once associated with excessive food intake, now more typically inhabit the realm of strict abstinence.

"Sculptors of Our Own Exterior": Modern Quests for Physical Perfection

The modern chapter of Christianity's struggle with the appetite begins with the New Thought movement of the late nineteenth and early twentieth centuries. New Thought was a Protestant offshoot whose proponents were intensely preoccupied with metaphysical questions and with uncovering the relations between mind and matter, the soul and the body. A cousin of Christian Science, it was a movement whose impact went far beyond the bounds of its own institutional structures to inspire the traditions of positive thinking, the self-help movement, so-called New Age philosophies, and the therapeutic ethic that has permeated virtually all major manifestations of twentieth-century American Protestantism. Its participants tended to be well educated and were interested in Eastern and occult traditions. They believed that "thoughts were things," that is, that mind power could secure wealth, health, and happiness through techniques that would now be called "creative visualization." New Thought leaders were deeply concerned with healing bodily illness and with attaining prosperity, and they described God not as an authoritarian father but rather as the "immanent, indwelling Spirit," Mind with a capital M, the All-Supply or Universal Supply of power that any human being could access with the right skills. And while New Thought writers often seemed to be saying that this power was accessed by means of mind energy alone, a closer look reveals clearly that, for many at least, the *body* was the real source of might. That is to say, while New Thought disciples frequently displayed an apprehensiveness toward materiality and doggedly insisted upon the ultimate power of Spirit, they also gave strenuous attention to the flesh and to the food that sustained it, paying meticulous attention to dietary regimens and systems of physical culture as a way of suggesting that physical development was the primary source of mental and spiritual development.

Prentice Mulford (1834–1891) was one well-known New Thought writer who considered matter essential to the life of the spirit. Mulford took care to note that as faith increased, the

Despite her best intentions, Pam Parnell failed diet after diet—until her faith in God replaced counting calories

spirit would call in "many material aids" to aid in personal renewal, including the selection of foods. Elsewhere Mulford explained his view more thoroughly:

It is not a good sign for a person to say that he or she doesn't care what they eat... It is the spirit that demands varying dishes and flavours. The spirit has reasons we cannot now explain for such demands. When the palate becomes indifferent in these respects, and one flavour is counted as good as another, it proves there is a deadening or blunting of the spirit. The higher the spiritualisation of any person the more vigorous and appreciative becomes the palate. It is the spirit that receives the pleasure of eating through the physical sense of taste.

Above: "My Faith Helped Me Lose 45 Pounds!" (after success on the Weigh Down diet). From *First for Women* magazine, October 28, 1996, p.34. PHOTOGRAPH BY BOB SCHATZ

The pleasures of eating, like other physical pleasures, were to be savored and taken very seriously, in Mulford's view, lest one fall into gluttony. "The glutton does not eat," Mulford observed. "He swallows. Proper eating dwells on every morsel with relish, and the longer it can be so dwelt upon, the longer it serves as the physical medium for the conveyance of life to the spirit."[4] Readers were urged, then, to eat what most pleased their taste, rather than eating merely for health from a sense of duty.

Paradoxically, the advice to eat only such foods as were individually pleasing was followed by a lengthy exposition of the proper and most spiritual diet. Topping the list were fresh meats, vegetables, and fruits, said to "contain the most force" (though meat was noted to be "grosser" and "coarser"). Products that were salted or pickled had reduced force, since the preserving process depleted them of life. Reduced intake of food in general, and of meat in particular, was unambiguously associated with higher spiritual attainment. This Mulford attributed to the fact that the fear and helplessness implanted in animals at the time of slaughter (and even in plants at harvest) was, through ingestion, transferred to the human eater. Other New Thought teachers similarly urged their hearers toward vegetarianism, many holding out the hope that the day would eventually come when humanity would be so spiritually advanced as to live on air alone. A good number of these approached that goal through rigorous, extended fasting, a devotional technique that had fallen out of many branches of mainstream American Protestantism by the mid nineteenth century, only to be reborn some decades later as a system for obtaining perfect health, happiness, longevity, and beauty. According to this "New Gospel of Health," nearly all diseases and illnesses could be attributed to excessive eating, to gorging oneself on immoderate quantities of food out of habit or "morbid hunger." A vast and diverse parade of apostles soon entered the scene, expanding and popularizing the gospel of fasting to a degree that its ancient practitioners could scarcely have imagined. Most were Protestants who had been inspired by New Thought optimism and preached a cheerful gospel of health and wealth into which fasting fit quite nicely. Few sang the joys of austere living, instead arguing that brief periods of fasting were pleasurable in and of themselves, not to mention their results. Rather than glamorize ascetics and mystics, these gospelers defended fasting from the so-called epicuric point of view: food would be relished more thoroughly, rest would be sweeter than before; in short, fasting opened the way to a richer enjoyment of all life's embodied pleasures, perhaps most especially controlled ingestion.[5]

By the early decades of the twentieth century, Anglo-American diet reformers had achieved colossal success in their quest to demonize corpulence and preach thinness as necessary to personal salvation, condemning the wayward appetite even as they elevated the role of proper food in the life of the spirit. While these ideas were nurtured at the fringe of Protestant culture in their own time, they were steadily gaining ground, eventually coming to look downright conventional. Christian piety and diet reform first enthusiastically reunited in the mainstream avenues of mid-twentieth-century America, disseminating to the hungry populace an updated equation of thinness with godliness that has only grown stronger over time. By the middle decades of the twentieth century, with religion firmly ensconced as a "this-worldly" and therapeutic enterprise, Christians could reclaim their concern with beauty and health, conveniently packaged as a scripturally sanctioned matter of holy discipline. Weight loss would prove its robustness as a vital and highly lucrative theme in Christian literature and practice for decades to come.

Praying the Weight Away: Scripture and Devotional Practice in Service to Weight Loss

"We fatties are the only people on earth who can weigh our sin," wrote Presbyterian minister Charlie W. Shedd in 1957.

> Evil thoughts don't come by ounces; vile temper, hatred, unbridled passion, censorious words, selfishness, these do not measure in pounds. But your sin does, and mine! Stand on the scale. How much more do you weigh than you should weigh? There it is: one hundred pounds of sin, or fifty, or eleven.

Shedd's book, published when the author was in his early forties, was aptly titled *Pray Your Weight Away*. Here Shedd, who professed having lost one hundred pounds himself, announced his "new truth" that was "glorious news for the obese." Writing to an audience rather less jaded by diet books—and far more unfamiliar with combining spirituality and weight loss—than later readers would be, Shedd promoted a gospel of slimness that condemned fat bodies in the explicit language of sin and guilt while guaranteeing weight loss by means of sustained prayer, devotion to the Bible, and unshakeable faith in thinness as a sign of sanctity.[6]

To claim that "reducing," in the parlance of the day, was a "spiritual problem" rather than merely a medical one echoed older themes rehearsed in the Jacksonian and Progressive Eras while replaying them in a new key. Since at least the 1920s, Protestants in the old-line churches had been importing and absorbing New Thought notions of health and healing into their practice, including under that rubric both emotional and physical well-being. The Pentecostal tradition, which spawned such widely influential preachers and healers as Aimee Semple McPherson, William Branham, and Oral Roberts, further contributed to the increasingly accepted belief that good health was at the heart of God's plan for all believers.

At the time that Shedd wrote, however, there had been very little public attention paid to overweight as something that itself required healing from divine hands. Although the postwar period was a time of increased consciousness about weight and an upsurge in diet, the religious literature remained mostly silent on the issue. Shedd argued that such diseases as were associated with obesity—from diabetes to heart problems to flat feet—were all in opposition to God's design for humanity. Moreover, because fat preceded and in some sense seemed actually to cause these and other maladies, fat in any amount could not logically be part of God's plan. "When God first dreamed you into creation," he chided his heavy readers, "there weren't one hundred pounds of excess avoirdupois hanging around your belt. No, nor sixty, nor sixteen."[7] In this way, Shedd shifted the discussion surrounding

religion and health by insisting that fat itself, and not simply the medical illnesses it helped create, could be—and should be—subject to God's healing, slimming power.

During the following decades, other Christian diet books began to emerge on the scene, until by the mid-1970s and carrying on well into the 1990s and beyond, this had become a visible and well-publicized genre that promoted slim bodies for the sake of God's Kingdom in highly individualized, thoroughly modern terms. Older theories of the body as sinful and dirty yet ultimately perfectible were joined anew with condemnations of fat and flabbiness, in a discourse that distinguished the righteous from their sinful brethren with implacable seriousness. Representative and best-selling titles in the early years included *Help Lord…The Devil Wants Me Fat!* (1977), *God's Answer to Fat* (1975), *More of Jesus, Less of Me* (1976), *Slim for Him* (1978), *Jogging with Jesus* (1978), and *Free To Be Thin* (1979), which itself sold more than a million copies worldwide and spawned a virtual industry of diet products

Above: The Triumphant Dieter. Cover of Patricia Banta Kreml's *Slim for Him* (Plainfield, NJ: Logos International, 1978).
JACKET DESIGN BY CYNTHIA A. SAHLMAN

marketed by the Pentecostal author, including an exercise video and a low-calorie, inspirational cookbook. These were later joined by an outpouring that included titles from *Greater Health God's Way* (1984, 1996) to *The Bible Cure for Weight Loss and Muscle Gain* (2000), *Fat-Burning Bible Diet* (2000), and *The Bible's Seven Secrets to Healthy Eating* (2001). Nor has this been solely a genre produced by White Christians: in 1997, African-American evangelist T. D. Jakes published *Lay Aside the Weight*, replete with before-and-after photographs of himself (from 338 to 228 pounds) and his wife, Serita (from 210 to 169 pounds).

In concert with this escalating literature have arisen biblically based diet groups, which had emerged in scattered fashion during the 1950s and 1960s as prayer-diet clubs only to bloom into full-blown organizations during the 1970s and 1980s. This trend expanded into the 1980s and swelled still more in the 1990s, as growing numbers of Christian diet groups emerged locally and went national. Some, such as Jesus Is the Weigh and Step Forward, enjoyed only modest success, while others, such as 3D and Overeaters Victorious, grew by leaps and bounds, at least for a time. The two most successful organizations (numerically and financially, at least, if not demonstrably in terms of weight loss) have been the Texas-based First Place (1981), whose curriculum is now owned by the Southern Baptist Convention; and the Weigh Down Workshop (1986), headed by Gwen Shamblin from her corporate headquarters in Nashville. First Place was founded by twelve members of Houston's First Baptist Church who wished to form their own Christian weight-loss program. It peaked during the 1990s with groups in approximately 12,000 churches in the country, including some in each of the fifty states and abroad.[8] Throughout these Christian counterparts to national weight-watcher programs, the message seemed apparent: God expects His children to strive for perfection in this life, and the most visible index of one's progress along that path is the size and fitness of his or her body.

The largest devotional diet program, by far, has been the Weigh Down Workshop, a twelve-week Bible-study program founded by nutritionist and fundamentalist Gwen Shamblin in 1986 and, by 2000, offered in as many as thirty thousand churches, seventy countries, and sixty different denominations.[9] The program gained national attention with the publication of Shamblin's first book, *The Weigh Down Diet* (1997), which was published by Doubleday and distributed at chain bookstores across the country. As the book quickly reached sales in the millions, Shamblin's program received national press coverage, on television programs such as CNN's "Larry King Live" and ABC's "20/20," as well as in print venues such as *Good Housekeeping* and most recently *The New Yorker*.[10] Shamblin has become well-known for her insistence that there are no "bad" foods and that dieters can eat anything so long as they do so in strictly limited quantities. If one remains in doubt about how much should be eaten, Shamblin counsels prayer, advising her audience that God will answer them in no uncertain terms. Advertising herself as a "size 4–6" in her midforties (at 5′4″ she weighs 115 pounds), Shamblin is an advocate of extreme thinness and denounces body fat as a sign of unholy disobedience to God's spiritual laws. Putting her program in more positive terms, Shamblin echoes other popular diet writers in her descriptions of overeating as the misguided attempt to fill what is instead a spiritual hunger for God.[11]

How successful are these programs at helping their members lose weight and maintain a slimmer physique? No one knows, though we do know from the research of Purdue University sociologist Kenneth Ferraro that churchgoing Christians (and especially southern evangelicals) have high rates of obesity, well above those of any other American religious group.[12] Not surprisingly, Christian leaders contend that their plans assist dieters in achieving their goals to a far greater extent than non-Christian programs, but there are no studies to support this claim. Promotional materials typically put a positive spin on this sparse data by presenting the program's leaders as exemplars of the victory others can expect from following their regimen. Gwen Shamblin avoids talk of statistics by placing the burden of failure directly on the hopeful dieter. To the question, "What is the average weight loss for people attending the Weigh Down Workshop?" Shamblin responds: "God has made each of us wonderfully unique. Some people take the program only to lose five or ten pounds, while others need to lose one hundred pounds or more. It doesn't matter how much weight you have to lose; being obedient to the way God created the body to maintain itself will allow everyone to achieve their weight loss goals."[13] Those who do not lose or maintain their losses, in other words, are simply disobedient to God's will.

This religious concern for diet and thinness has not been strictly limited to Protestants: alongside guides by evangelicals, fundamentalists, Pentecostals, charismatics, and mainliners have also emerged Mormon diet books such as *Joseph Smith and Natural Foods* (1976, 2001) and *The Mormon Diet* (1991), and at least one religious Jewish text on weight loss, entitled *Watching Your Weight...The Torah Way* (1989).[14] Even Christian Scientists, still denying the materiality of the body and declaring that the true nature of human beings is nonmaterial spirit, addressed the problem of excess weight and diet control in a special 1997 issue of the *Christian Science Sentinel*, where readers were encouraged to pray about what foods to eat.[15] Yet the vast majority of energetic disciples working in this arena of religious weight-watching have been Protestant; in fact, not a single book of this type seems to have surfaced from the pen of an American Catholic writer, though there exists at least one Catholic weight-loss program (The Light Weigh, based in Kansas). On the whole, leaders and participants involved in these and countless other Christian fitness enterprises in America have agreed that God commands human beings to glorify their bodies as God's own temple, and they have dieted vigorously to keep healthy. As one author put it, in a bubbly reformulation of Christian theology, "Think of your 'promised land' as a thin body."[16] Whether all would express it this crudely, this promise permeates the wider Christian diet culture.

In Bondage to Boston Cream Pie: Food as Taint and Transgression

And what about the means employed, the attitudes inculcated about food in this culture? The practice of dieting, of "watching what one eats" in service to particular ideals of health and weight, subsists on the rhythms of restraint and excess. Like other acts born of desire piled on necessity, eating can be an act of passion and anticipated satiation, while also carrying live possibilities for regret and shame. For American Protestants, for whom sex, alcohol, dancing, and other bodily behaviors have often been restricted or eschewed altogether, eating has long carried dense and contradictory meanings.[17] Those contradictions have been nowhere more richly evident or expressive than in modern Christian diet culture, where food has everywhere been the object of desperate longing as well as embittered loathing, of ambivalent attitudes toward pleasure no less than sin.

As in earlier historical periods, latter-day religious diet reformers have promoted a variety of messages, some advocating fasting as a useful means of weight control and others urging against it, several advocating vegetarianism while opponents uphold the benefits of meat, growing numbers recommending special vitamin supplements to fight toxins while the more conservative proffer basic dietary variety mixed with exercise. As in the wider diet culture of which Bible-based writers have been part, there is no general consensus as to the most proper and righteous way to eat (indeed, authors often seem to thrive on denouncing each other's programs), but few if any authors question the belief that following God means taking a deeply suspicious stance toward food.

Food, in fact, has consistently remained an evil temptation in this literature. Most authors have echoed the idea early suggested by Deborah Pierce in *I Prayed Myself Slim* (1960), that while they were once taught to say grace for their food, they now pray for the grace to stay away from food.[18] For decades, Christian diet writers have likened love for food to idolatry. "Did you know," write Marie Chapian and Neva Coyle in *Free To Be Thin*, "that you stifle God's working in your life when you habitually overeat?" They approvingly cite one man's admission of how a divine voice intervened to prevent him from eating a particularly sinful food: "I wanted to eat a fattening dish—it was spareribs soaked in greasy tomato sauce. Ugh! Anyhow, just as I was about to order it, the Lord spoke to me and said, 'Don't eat that.'" God will always be there to advise His children about the proper amount to eat; in fact, His instructions are far more important than any humanly constructed diet plan, say the authors, who provide no calorie-counting plans for their readership. God, in fact, "is more concerned with your weight than anyone else you know. Let Him speak to you and direct *every morsel you eat.*"[19]

For Chapian and Coyle, as for most other writers, particular kinds of foods have been evil and others virtuous, in much the way that these divisions have structured the food plans of nonreligious diet instructors. In *Free To Be Thin*, victuals are divided as "World Food vs. Kingdom Food," while the authors argue, "The foods that have defiled our bodies are foods that have appealed to our flesh, not our spirit." Tootsie rolls, pizza, candy, and cookies, as well as the low-calorie substitutes and artificial sweeteners marketed as diet products, all come under fire as being "fattening" and hence "worldly" foods. Foods from the Kingdom of God, by contrast, consist of lean meats (steamed, water-packed, skinless), dairy products ("lo-cal," not processed), fruits and vegetables (raw or steamed, without butter), and whole-grain breads and cereals. The authors recommend the daily food guide published by the U.S. Department of Agriculture, which they advise adapting to individual daily calorie limits. And they urge readers to pray with them: "Dear Lord, help me to develop an interest in nutrition and what my body needs to function beautifully for your glory.... I renounce the lusts for those foods that are harmful to my body. I refuse to be a friend of the world's system and foods. I choose to eat Kingdom food to the glory of God. In Jesus' name, Amen!"[20]

The anticonsumer-culture strain evident in such refrains against "worldly food" has rarely been taken very far by diet writers—certainly not the most popular ones, who have benefitted handsomely from the rising consumer ethos within American evangelicalism witnessed powerfully in the publishing industry (among other places). Yet a persistent lament against processed foodstuffs rings strong, with evil heaped in correlative increments upon the more "commercialized" types. Good foods are plainer in their packaging and preparation, unembellished by sauces, dressings, or immoderate spices. The biblical figure of Daniel has provided the ideal model for this system of austerity and renunciation, inasmuch as he rejected the rich food and wine of King Nebuchadnezzar in favor of simple vegetables and water. Quoting Daniel, Chapian and Coyle note that his spare diet was a choice against "defiling himself," according to the scripture. They conclude on a dismal note: "Think of the last time you binged on some rich or fattening food. By eating that food, you were actually making your body filthy, unclean, unfit, desecrated." The authors also try to appeal to their readers' personal revulsions, observing, "You wouldn't want to eat a hair, a roach, or a rat, but that éclair or those greasy french fries may be just as defiling."[21] Authors such as these have worked hard to upend readers' own food hierarchies and unhealthy tastes, here and elsewhere utilizing disgust in an attempt to turn tempting treats into aversions.

Mab Graff Hoover's 1983 book of "meditations for munchers," inspired by Chapian and Coyle's best-selling volume, cites Paul's letter to the Colossians as proof of the need to put lust for food to death, which she herself attempted to do by recalling the corpse of her own mother.

> When mother died, the body looked like my mother, but it wasn't she. Mother liked to eat, but that body never grew hungry. Even though her body had no appetite, I knew mother was still alive—hidden from me, but alive in Christ. The apostle Paul says that my life also is hidden with Christ; because I have died to self, I am commanded to kill my earthly nature![22]

Like the lifeless body that no longer hungers, so should living Christians adopt indifference toward food. Those who care too much about food, Hoover notes, make a "god" of the stomach (another reference to Paul) and are hypocrites as she herself has been: "I see myself sitting in church, hands folded over the Bible, innocent eyes on the pastor, but with my mind on waffles, sweet rolls, pancakes…"[23] Heavy, sweet food could be tempting as a fantasy no less than as victuals actually partaken, for they drew her mind away from God's Word to the evil things of this world.

Hoover mocks her own struggle to choose righteous foods over wicked ones, writing, "Can I imagine myself picking up a grease-filled, chocolate-covered donut, and saying, 'I eat this in the name of the Lord Jesus?'" Indeed, she laments, "When I look at chocolates or a beautiful birthday cake or Danish pastries, it's hard for me to believe they are being offered through the Evil One. But I know from Scripture that Satan continually tries to ruin the temple of God, the church, (my body!)." Instead of giving in to her temptation to eat such foods, she resolves to emulate Paul and Jesus, eating sparingly as she presumes they did. "Today, I will eat one piece of chicken (without the skin), a lot of salad (chewing it well), some vegetables, fruit, and one small slice of bread! I will imitate the Lord." Yet the struggle continues, admits Hoover, and perpetually she must "come to the place where I am totally convinced that sugar, chocolate, and fat are also [with alcohol and nicotine, her former vices] dreaded enemies."[24] As fitness writer Pamela Snyder later taught in *A Life Styled by God*, "We have a choice to make: living within the *bounds* of Christ or living in *bondage* to Boston cream pie."[25]

That liberal Protestants have been as subject to this mode of thought as their conservative counterparts was made clear early on in a 1981 *Christian Century* article by Unitarian Universalist minister Bruce Marshall. Noting that, "in this age salvation by diet seems easier to conceive of than salvation by grace," Marshall gently lampooned what he called "the Protestant approach to eating" as "purification through sacrifice."

> Virtue is won through deprivation. The faithful are warned against the lure of pleasure. If you enjoy what you are eating, chances are that it's bad for you. Your menu has been formulated by the devil to tempt you to ruin…. If I don't drink wine, I'll be a more virtuous person. If I don't eat sugar, if I don't eat meat, if I avoid cream sauces and rich desserts, God will shower his blessings upon me. Salvation is earned by not eating things.

Arguing that this theology, like other contemporary theologies of eating he outlined, was "sacrilegious," Marshall sought to promote a more joyous, less constricted notion of divine feasting. Yet he spoke for many of his ilk in noting that his own occasional indulgences in such "illicit" foods as doughnuts sparked an inner voice warning of the torment soon to follow this pleasure.[26]

An example of the occasional Christian diet book aiming to promote a more positive view of food is Edward Dumke's *The Serpent Beguiled Me and I Ate: A Heavenly Diet for Saints and Sinners* (1986). An Episcopal priest and licensed counselor in the state of California, Dumke taught "seven lessons" about food as taught in the Bible (and, he argued, religions more generally) that included "food as a symbol for the sacred," "food as a symbol for love," and "food as a symbol for community." Dumke titled another section "Enjoy Your Food," recommending the benefits of eating slowly for enjoyment as well as eating less; and he urged readers at one point to "Eat the foods you really like. Many people associate dieting success with deprivation. It doesn't have to be this way. Remember, if you enjoy what you eat, you will not need to eat as much and you won't get bored with your diet." Yet the very title of Dumke's book, evoking the biblical theme of temptation and the transgressive dangers of eating, conveys a primary equation of food with sin—or, in the book's more nuanced passages, a line demarcating foods into opposing categories of virtue and indulgence. Intermittently in the text, as in his "Ten Commandments of Good Nutrition," Dumke instructs readers in religio-scientific terms: "Thou shalt consume sufficient protein but thou shalt limit the amount of animal protein…. Thou shalt create a diet in complex carbohydrates…. Thou shalt create a diet low in saturated fat…. Thou shalt limit the amount of chocolate thou eatest." His test at the end of this section has readers attempt to distinguish between the "good" and "not" good foods in a list of pairs that include such combinations as chocolate cake and grapefruit, fried chicken and boiled chicken, steak and fillet (*sic*) of sole, pastrami and tofu. "Remember," he concludes, "you are what you eat."[27]

Stories of failure abound, though, for while the knowledge that certain foods and ways of eating are sinful may be simple to grasp, the life change that is supposed to follow such awareness is surely more difficult. At one point, Hoover admits her problem to being, deep down, "not totally convinced that eating chocolate, sweets, or even overeating is all that bad, much less sin." Discouragement combines with her flesh, "a hungry tiger, always ready to break out of the cage of discipline and gobble everything in sight." But the Bible teaches that gorging is sin, according to Hoover's interpretation, as is overindulgence of any kind. Hence, she advises herself sternly, "Participating in food orgies (even at church!), helping to plan unhealthy dinners, or offering junk foods to my loved ones is sin. As long as I overeat or poison my body with chemical additives, I shall not become the righteousness of God."[28]

Poisoned Bodies, Blemished Souls

The poisoned body: the notion hearkens back vividly to health reformers of earlier eras, who similarly equated gluttonous eating with contamination and filth. Naturalists and alternative health advocates have long deplored the toxins and impurities allegedly infecting the body ignorant or blasé about its intake, and they have counseled abstinence as an indispensable therapy for this sad situation. Even mainstream Christian diet books that oppose the alternative health culture have imbibed many of these ideas about bodily poisons, as seen in Hoover's concern about chemical additives or this passage in Jewish convert Zola Levitt's *How To Win at Losing*: "God has, in a sense, already committed himself on the matter of eating. The foods found easily and naturally on the earth are the ones that do you no harm. The weird combinations made by men—the processing and drying of grains, the 'enhancing' of foods with sugar—are the ones that got you where you are today."[29] Chapian and Coyle repeat the belief that fasting "giv[es] the overworked internal organs and tissues of the body a good rest and time for rehabilitation. Fasting (over six days) flushes out toxic matter and poisons from the body system. Fasting improves circulation and promotes endurance and stamina. Fasting renovates, revives and purifies the cells of the body."[30] Twentieth-century technological innovations in food production and pest control have, of course, only given new force to these fears, making for a much expanded list of sinful foods than those that are simply "fattening."

The most publicized and widespread of the Christian programs of this kind has been the North Carolina–based Hallelujah Diet. Conceived by Baptist minister George Malkmus after he allegedly cured himself of colon cancer in 1976 by eating only "natural" foods, the Diet consists mainly of raw fruits and vegetables and is grounded in Genesis 1:29: "I give you every seed-bearing plant on the face of the whole earth and every tree that has fruit with seed in it." On that early diet, Malkmus argues in *Why Christians Get Sick* (1989), people lived over nine hundred years, but once meat and cooked food were added to the human diet sickness came into being and radically reduced the life span. Whereas raw fruits and vegetables are "good" foods, junk foods are bad and to eat them morally wrong. The partition of the world into such stark classifications of good and evil provisions once again points to a conflicted, ambivalent stance toward food and ingestion, though of a profoundly different sort than that proffered by more mainstream dieters like Coyle and Hoover—or Gwen Shamblin. The tensions among these programs over which foods to demarcate as "good" or "evil" represent, in a sense, larger disagreements over which parts of secular culture to appropriate and which to reject.[31]

Shamblin, the reigning queen of the Christian diet industry, has been especially direct in teaching that food is something to be transcended and sometimes avoided altogether: it is a devilish lover, tempting human beings to betray their covenant with God and enter a lascivious relationship with food. In her words:

> We fell in love with the food by giving it our heart, soul, mind, and strength.... We obeyed it. It called us from the bed in the morning, and we used our strength to prepare it. We also used our strength to force more of it down into the body than the body called for. We gave it our mind all day long by looking through recipe books and discussing the latest diets with our friends, asking, "What do you get to eat on your diet?" We lusted after the foods that were on the menu, and we gave our hearts to the 10 o'clock binge.[32]

Shamblin's explicit identification of food with sex contains the corollary that to over-eat—regardless of one's weight—is a sin closely aligned with adultery. Though she notes that food can be enjoyed if it is not desired too much, her teachings throughout suggest a deeply embattled relationship with food and a strict regimen of asking God for guidance at each and every bite. Shamblin's image of food as a seductive lover who entices the overeater away from her true husband, God, is unusually graphic for this literature; yet the overriding distrust of and loathing for food is widely shared.

Human beings must eat to live, however, and since conservative Christian theology assumes God to be the author of all things, food cannot be unredeemably evil. In fact, authors often linger at great length on the subject of food, which they claim to enjoy more now that they are liberated from obsession with it. Gwen Shamblin writes about food with erotic abandon, in sensual language that makes her experience of it sound as lush in its ordinariness as that of celebrity "gastroporn" writer Nigella Lawson.

> As soon as I get to the movie theater, I can smell the popcorn and the hot dogs. I like to make sure I am hungry when I arrive, so most of the time I won't eat supper before going to the movies.... I find the best kernels of popcorn with just the right amount of butter and salt on them. I like to eat one kernel at a time so I can savor the combined flavors of the popcorn, salt, and butter.... Keep in mind that I still have my box of candy, so I do not want to fill up entirely on the popcorn.... If the candy comes in a variety of colors or flavors, I will eat my favorite colors and flavors first. I take a bite, savor it, and take a sip from my diet drink.[33]

(Heavy breathing, courtesy of Jujubes and Diet Coke.)

Sometimes Shamblin's descriptions of her food habits, which conclude all but one of *Rise Above*'s fourteen chapters, seem as obsessive as any overeater's:

> My friends and I love to celebrate a special occasion with a wonderful steak dinner. I may skip lunch to make sure that I am really, *really* hungry! When the meal arrives at the table, I eat the best morsels while they are hot, remembering to save room for my favorite dessert. Plenty of real butter and sour cream for my baked potato assures that I can create the perfect combination.... I then move on to the medium-rare filet mignon. I cut until I reach the center, which has the juiciest pieces.... The filet that is cooked right will just melt in your mouth.... This occasion calls for the ultimate brownie topped with hot caramel, chocolate fudge, whipped cream, nuts— and several spoons for sharing! Again, I search for the perfect bite before the towering dessert begins to melt.[34]

It is easy to forget, when reading such passages that practically moan with ecstasy, that they come from a text that denounces Christians for loving food to the point of idolatry.

But for Shamblin, unlike so many of her predecessors, food itself is not sin (there are no sinful foods in Shamblin's world, only sinful worshipers of it); *fat* is sin, and so long as one can eat blissfully within the limits set by God's hand, no rules have been broken. The ideal attitude toward food is a kind of thoroughgoing indifference combined with exhilaration and a sensual basking in the pleasures of eating. Achieving this delicate balance is not difficult, in Shamblin's view: God wants people to enjoy food, after all, and as soon as one's will is fully submitted to his, he will restore the joy of eating that remains unavailable to the person obsessed with food. Those who greedily keep hold of their bodily desires will fail to find contentment or satisfaction, but those who surrender will be blessed with the immeasurable bliss of a thin body and a guilt-free way of eating. Set free from enslavement to food, the truly Christian eater may revel in all good things and inhabit a kind of succulent paradise on earth. Where other devotional diet programs teach followers that they must restrain their appetites for the rest of their lives, Shamblin promises complete emancipation and libidinous fulfillment.

Christian authors have clearly differed on the finer points of righteous eating. Still, the loud chorus of voices propounding abstinence has left most churchgoers with little doubt as to the value of eyeing food through a religious lens. For virtually all who have bothered to write on the subject, moreover, that lens has been acutely focused on discerning transgression, defined from a wide variety of angles. Zola Levitt early made a typical point when he noted that bad eating was a theological problem. "Eating wrongly is a matter of conforming to this world and denying that we can forego temptation," he warned. "It's a doubting of the power of God, in whose perfect image we are all made."[35] By citing scriptural precedents for eating well—from Adam and Eve to the exiled Israelites (who ate only manna and meat), Daniel (who fasted on vegetables and water), John the Baptist, and Jesus—Christian authors may well elude criticism that their instruction conforms too closely to the body standards of American popular culture. At the same time, they provide biblical justification for their readers' desire to be lean and appealing, for although the material rewards of slenderness offered by the secular world have been repeatedly decried in this literature as superficial, Christian diet writers appeal to them unremittingly.

The biggest sell by far, though, seems to be Shamblin's promise of carnal gratification for those who repent of gluttony and surrender to the master genius who created all foods, from brownies to Fritos (two of Shamblin's frequent examples), and who is also a romantic husband for those who love him. The desert monks and medieval fasting women would hardly find all aspects of Shamblin's pleasure theology recognizable, however rapturous their own ascetic practices. Her fusion of sin and salaciousness, austerity and consumerism, disciplined submission and delicious seduction, captures the profuse contradictions within American Christianity (not to mention the wider culture shaped by and shaping it), offering more than a few clues to the ever intensifying eroticization of food and appetite within a devotional culture once based on abstinence. ⊕

NOTES

Epigraph: Nigella Lawson, "Gastroporn," *Talk*, October 1999, 153–154; cited in Elspeth Probyn, *Carnal Appetites: FoodSexIdentities* (London: Routledge, 2000), 59.

1. Caroline Walker Bynum, *Holy Feast and Holy Fast: The Religious Significance of Food to Medieval Women* (Berkeley: University of California Press, 1987), 42 and passim.

2. For the medieval and patristic periods, see especially Bynum, *Holy Feast and Holy Fast*; Rudolph M. Bell, *Holy Anorexia* (Chicago and London: University of Chicago Press, 1985); Teresa M. Shaw, *The Burden of the Flesh: Fasting and Sexuality in Early Christianity* (Minneapolis: Fortress Press, 1998); Veronika Grimm, *From Feasting to Fasting, the Evolution of a Sin: Attitudes to Food in Late Antiquity* (London and New York: Routledge, 1996); and Walter Vandereycken and Ron van Deth, *From Fasting Saints to Anorexic Girls: The History of Self-Starvation* (New York: New York University Press, 1994 [published in Germany as *Hungerkünstler, Fastenwunder, Magersucht: Eine Kulturgeschichte der Ess-störungen*, 1990]). On the nineteenth-century health reform movements, see especially James C. Whorton, *Crusaders for Fitness: The History of American Health Reformers* (Princeton: Princeton University Press, 1982); Stephen Nissenbaum, *Sex, Diet, and Debility in Jacksonian America: Sylvester Graham and Health Reform* (Westport, CT: Greenwood Press, 1980); and Robert H. Abzug, *Cosmos Crumbling: American Reform and the Religious Imagination*, especially chapter 7, "The Body Reforms" (New York: Oxford University Press, 1994), 163–182.

3. Joan Jacobs Brumberg, *Fasting Girls: The Emergence of Anorexia as a Modern Disease* (Cambridge: Harvard University Press, 1988); Hillel Schwartz, *Never Satisfied: A Cultural History of Diets, Fantasies, and Fat* (New York: The Free Press, 1986).

4. Prentice Mulford, "Grace Before Meat; Or, The Science of Eating," in *Essays of Prentice Mulford: Your Forces and How To Use Them*, 4th Series (London: William Rider & Son, 1909), 34–47; 38.

5. See R. Marie Griffith, "Apostles of Abstinence: Fasting and Masculinity during the Progressive Era," *American Quarterly* 52:4 (December 2000), 599–638.

6. Charlie W. Shedd, *Pray Your Weight Away* (Philadelphia and New York: J.B. Lippincott Company, 1957), 11–12, 14.

7. Shedd, *Pray Your Weight Away*, 14, 15, 40.

8. The story of First Place's founding is recounted in Carole Lewis, *Choosing to Change: The First Place Challenge* (Nashville, TN: LifeWay Press, 1996), 7–17; testimonial quote from p.89.

9. Statistics obtained from the official Weigh Down Web site: http://www.weighdown.com/home.htm (January 11, 2001).

10. Laura Muha, "The Weight-Loss Preacher," *Good Housekeeping* 226:2 (February 1998), 26; Rebecca Mead, "Slim for Him," *The New Yorker*, January 15, 2001, 48–56.

11. Shamblin's clothes size is listed on the Web site for the Weigh Down Program, http://www.wdworkshop.com/wdw/wdwfaq.asp#Q1 (accessed January 22, 2001), under the question headed "Who Is Gwen Shamblin?"

12. Kenneth F. Ferraro, "Firm Believers? Religion, Body Weight, and Well-Being," *Review of Religious Research* 39:3 (March, 1998), 224–244.

13. Obtained from Weigh Down Workshop Web site: http://www.wdworkshop.com/wdw/wdwfaq.asp#Q9 (accessed January 23, 2001).

14. John Heinerman, *Joseph Smith and Natural Foods: A Treatise on Mormon Diet* (Manti, UT: Mountain Valley Publishers, 1976; Springville, UT: Bonneville Books, 2001); Earl F. Updike, *The Mormon Diet: A Word of Wisdom: 14 Days to New Vigor and Health* (Bayfield, CO, and Orem, UT: Best Possible Health, 1991); Ethel C. Updike, Dorothy E. Smith, and Earl F. Updike, *The Mormon Diet Cookbook: Easy Permanent Weight Loss: Fat Free, Cholesterol Free, High Fiber* (Bayfield, CO: Best Possible Health,

1992); Moshe Goldberger, *Watching Your Weight…The Torah Way: A Diet That Will Change Your Life!!* (Staten Island, NY: M. Goldberger, 1989. (Updike later altered his books and published them under the title *The Miracle Diet: Easy Permanent Weight Loss* [Phoenix, AZ: Best Possible Health, 1995]. See also Colleen Bernhard, *He Did Deliver Me from Bondage: Using the Book of Mormon and the Principles of the Gospel of Jesus Christ as They Correlate with the Twelve-Step Program to Overcome Compulsive/ Addictive Behavior* [Orem, UT: Windhaven Publishing and Productions, 1994].)

15. *Christian Science Sentinel* 99:36 (September 8, 1997). See also David M. Wilson, "Overeating Can Be Checked," *Christian Science Sentinel* 86:24 (June 11, 1984), 1003–1005.

16. Marie Chapian and Neva Coyle, *Free To Be Thin* (Minneapolis: Bethany House Publishers, 1979), 17.

17. For a different take on these matters, see Daniel Sack, *Whitebread Protestants: Food and Religion in American Culture* (New York: St. Martin's Press, 2000).

18. Deborah Pierce, as told to Frances Spatz Leighton, *I Prayed Myself Slim* (New York: The Citadel Press, 1960), 19.

19. Chapian and Coyle, *Free To Be Thin*, 21, 27, 31, 33 (italics in original). Neva Coyle, who eventually gained all her weight back, has thoroughly recanted her own earlier views about God's desire for Christians to be thin; see, for instance, Coyle, *Loved on a Grander Scale* (Ann Arbor, MI: Servant Publications, 1998). However poignant and noteworthy such later retractions, however, her earlier promotion of Bible-based dieting remains far more influential (as she herself pensively realizes).

20. Chapian and Coyle, *Free To Be Thin*, 107, 109, 115.

21. Chapian and Coyle, *Free To Be Thin*, 60, 64. This story comes from the first chapter of the Book of Daniel in the Hebrew Bible.

22. Mab Graff Hoover, *God Even Likes My Pantry: Meditations for Munchers* (Grand Rapids, MI: Zondervan, 1983), 20.

23. Hoover, *God Even Likes My Pantry*, 56.

24. Hoover, *God Even Likes My Pantry*, 24, 29–30, 26, 110.

25. Pamela Snyder, *A Life Styled by God: A Woman's Workshop on Spiritual Discipline for Weight Control* (Grand Rapids: Zondervan Publishing House, 1985), 22 (italics in original).

26. Bruce T. Marshall, "The Theology of Eating," *Christian Century* 98 (March 18, 1981), 301–302.

27. Edward Dumke, *The Serpent Beguiled Me and I Ate: A Heavenly Diet for Saints and Sinners* (New York: Doubleday, 1986), 109, 110, 82–85. Episcopal authors generally seem more positive about food than their evangelical counterparts. Episcopal priest Victor Kane, author of *Devotions for Dieters*, had earlier taught his readers that Jesus was no ascetic but rather a lover of food; yet Kane also distinguished between "good" and "sinful" foods (Kane, *Devotions for Dieters: A Spiritual Life for Calorie Counters, with a Touch of Irony, by a Fellow Sufferer* [Old Tappan, NJ: Fleming H. Revell Co., 1967]).

28. Hoover, *God Even Likes My Pantry*, 95, 96.

29. Zola Levitt, *How To Win at Losing* (Wheaton, IL: Tyndale House Pub.; London: Coverdale House Pub., 1976), 83–84.

30. Chapian and Coyle, *Free To Be Thin*, 40.

31. George Malkmus, *Why Christians Get Sick* (Eidson, TN: Hallelujah Acres Pub., 1989).

32. Gwen Shamblin, *The Weigh Down Diet: Inspirational Way To Lose Weight, Stay Slim, and Find a New You* (New York: Doubleday, 1997), 149.

33. Shamblin, *Rise Above: God Can Set You Free from Your Weight Problems Forever* (Nashville: Thomas Nelson Publishers, 2000), 196.

34. Shamblin, *Rise Above*, 81.

35. Levitt, *How To Win at Losing*, 15.

Fall 2001, volume 1, number 4

richard wilbur |

A Shallot

French translation by Jean Migrenne, illustration by Julio Granda

A SHALLOT

The full cloves
Of your buttocks, the convex
Curve of your belly, the curved
Cleft of your sex—

Out of this corm
That's planted in strong thighs
The slender stem and radiant
Flower rise.

RICHARD WILBUR

Summer 2004, volume 4, number 3

the family table

Delicacy | *Paul Russell* **54**

The Unbearable Lightness of Wartime Cuisine | *A. Marin* **60**

One Year and a Day: A Recipe for Gumbo and Mourning | *James Nolan* **75**

The Prize Inside | *Toni Mirosevich* **87**

Messages in a Bottle | *Barbara Kirshenblatt-Gimblett* **89**

dinner, 1933 | *Charles Bukowski* **100**

paul russell |

Delicacy

I AM PERUSING THE MENU with all the sense of serious purpose a ten-year-old unaccustomed to restaurants can muster. It's 1966, a restaurant called The Passport in the brand new, sleekly modernist terminal of the Memphis International Airport. What catches my eye is dolphin. I have never seen dolphin on any menu, never heard of anyone eating dolphin, and I am seized by an urgent need to taste this dolphin whose allure is, like the new terminal itself, the beautiful promise of a future in which we shall all travel effortlessly to distant places, dine nightly on marvelous dishes.

When it comes my turn to order, I speak with a trembling voice, trying to sound as if it is a perfectly ordinary thing I am doing.

My words fail to slip past my mother. A cautious eater, she's inclined to instill caution in her children as well.

"Are you sure?" she asks. "Do you know what a dolphin is?"

I nod my head vigorously—a curious fifth grader's head full of ancient Greek myths. I see graceful, leaping sea creatures, familiars of trident-brandishing Poseidon, and riding their cavorting backs, bronzed sea-sprites.

"Oh, let him try it," my father tells her. "It's good for him to be curious."

"I don't think I could bring myself to eat dolphin," my mother mentions quietly, but to no avail. Already I've slipped past the carefully guarded perimeter and am stumbling into the unknown. Already I am on my way to the future.

The dolphin, when it arrives, is a rather ordinary-looking fish fillet—redeemed, a little, by the pat of butter in the shape of a scallop shell that accompanies it. What is even more enchanting, the scallop shell of butter is itself nestled into a real scallop shell. No one else's dish comes with anything remotely like that, I note with quiet delight, and as I take my first expectant bite, I tell myself that dolphin will be the most exquisite food I have ever tasted. Like those sea-sprites, I too shall be laughingly transported.

But the dolphin is not exquisite; it's only an ordinary fish—pallid, soggy, bland. I eat slowly, trying to savor each mouthful, hoping somehow to discover a clue that will unlock dolphin's marvelous but thus far hidden essence. I close my eyes. Ancient sunlight starkly illuminates the scene. I am waiting for Achilles and Patroclus to join me at the feast. On the banquet table, dolphin has been set out on great platters. In the distance beckons the wine-dark sea, thick with the proud ships of the Greeks.

But none of this gets me anywhere at all; I can discover nothing except the dreary truth. I'm ten. I'm trapped. I will never get out of here.

"How is it?" my mother asks.

"Wonderful," I report breathlessly. At least there is the scallop shell, which I persuade her to wrap in a paper napkin and put in her purse, so I can carry it home as a souvenir of the meal that might have been.

Beyond the restaurant's grand, panoramic windows—The Passport's real attraction, I suspect, and not the food—jet planes roar down the runway, lift into the clear blue sky of early evening.

My family seldom dined out. When we did, we'd go to restaurants that more or less duplicated the fare my mother cooked at home. There was Bill and Jim's, whose most daring offerings tended toward trout almondine and liver with bacon and onions, or the family's favorite, Shoney's Big Boy, where we'd all enthusiastically order the Big Boy, a splendid double-decker hamburger and fries. Other, more suggestive restaurants I had never actually set foot in lurked at the fringes of my young imagination: Joy Young's, a Chinese restaurant downtown where my parents would sometimes go for special occasions (as a child, my only experience of Chinese food was chicken chow mein from a can, poured over crunchy dry noodles); and the Luau, which served Hawaiian food and was said to feature tables set out on small islands in an indoor lagoon. There was Pappy and Jimmy's, intriguingly advertised by a neon sign showing the grinning faces of Pappy and Jimmy attached to the bodies of lobsters; and Anderson's Oyster Bar, with its green-tiled facade and large, heavily curtained windows—but my parents didn't care for seafood, so I knew nothing of what went on inside those mysterious precincts.

My mother subscribed, more or less, to the notion that cooking was something you did to kill the germs—a chore to be undertaken conscientiously, but with little enthusiasm. I remember dry meatloaf and gray pot roasts and endlessly chewy pork chops. She had evolved, in the course of raising three children, an updated, more efficient version of the foods she'd grown up with. In this suburban shorthand for the richer, deeper, older cooking her own mother daily lavished so much time and effort on, commercially canned vegetables replaced the home-grown beans and tomatoes and corn my grandmother sealed away in mason jars; toast from a toaster substituted for the flaky buttermilk biscuits my grandmother could be found rolling out before dawn each morning in her kitchen; grape jelly muscled aside homemade damson and blackberry and pear preserves. My mother refused to be a slave to the kitchen, and shook her head at the way her mother, whenever we'd visit, would persist in organizing the entire day around the production of meals whose homespun bounty—country ham and fried chicken; mustard greens, black-eyed peas, sweet potato casserole; creamed corn and mashed turnips; those heavenly buttermilk biscuits— never ceased to amaze and even confound.

"We can't eat all that food!" my mother would exclaim, confronted by memories of her childhood, when she'd been what she called a "picky eater," her appetite no doubt crippled by my grandfather's propensity to dose her with a vast variety of patent medicines, especially cod liver oil—hence her adult aversion to seafood.

The meals my mother visited on us nightly were strictly routine—ordinary food about which one never gave a second thought. The ordinary may be dependable, but it holds no mystery, not even the possibility of mystery. Everything in my family was perfectly visible in the flat glare of the ordinary, and since, early on, I saw in myself the shadow of unfathomable urges, I knew with a secret whisper of nausea that sooner or later I would have to be found out.

Into my mother's cautious cooking, I suspected, an ingredient like myself would never be allowed.

I AM IN THE EIGHTH GRADE, eating lunch in the school cafeteria; the meal on my plate resembles beef stew in the way that every meal in the school cafeteria resembles some food or another. I've been eating this stuff for years; I have no illusions (See? If I turn the bowl of so-called peach cobbler upside down, the congealed mass clings to the bowl and can't be shaken loose). Nonetheless, I am intrigued by a cube of beef lying in gummy brown sauce. A few nights earlier, I have seen on television an episode of *Star Trek* in which the logical and adamantly vegetarian Mr. Spock, through some accident of time travel, finds himself plunged ten thousand years into the past. Stuck in the ice ages, thrown together with a convenient cave girl, he begins to revert to the atavistic practices of his ancestors; when the cave girl offers him a succulent hunk of barely cooked woolly mammoth steak, he eats with relish, luxuriating in the forbidden taste of animal flesh. A passionately illogical kiss with the comely cook soon follows.

As a thoroughly alienated eighth grader, I fancy myself another Mr. Spock, exiled among the earthlings with all their messy emotions (which I fear as much as he). So I pretend, for the moment, staring at my cube of beef, that I too am about to taste forbidden pleasures. I glance around to see that no one is watching, and, with my fingers, pluck the meat from its viscous sauce. I raise it to my lips, imagining its tender, juicy texture, throw back my head, and drop the morsel into my mouth. But the luscious explosion of flavor I expect does not happen; the meat—its dreary simulacrum, rather—is dry and stringy, bland as anything my mother might cook. Still, in that brief moment before I actually tasted it, my imagination registered the poignant possibility of an altogether different reality.

How, THOUGH, TO FIND THAT other reality I glimpsed from time to time? Often it took the form of an aimless, painful longing—for distant landscapes, people I did not yet know, musics I had discovered on my own. All my life I had been vaguely aware of the existence of what my mother called "delicacies"—foods she herself would never eat, but that other people, inexplicably, took great pains to seek out and consume. General currency had handed me several more or less abstract instances of what she was talking about: caviar, which I could barely imagine; oysters and champagne; truffles; frog legs. For me, they were not so much actual comestibles as emblems of the lives that attached themselves to such unholy meals.

To none of these foods, of course, had I any access. But there were other items closer to home, an eclectic and mostly accidental array of opportunities with which I proceeded to stock my imaginary larder: shrimp, for instance, breaded and deep-fried, which I rebelliously began to order whenever my family would eat at Shoney's Big Boy, till one day I managed to correlate those meals with nights of feeling utterly, alarmingly strange, and reluctantly concluded that I was, in fact, allergic ("I told you so," I could hear my mother say, though she never actually did; she didn't have to); the greasy canned tamales wrapped in corn husks that I bought every noon from the vending machine in the high school canteen (I remember trying to figure out how to eat them, not quite understanding for some time that the corn husks weren't meant to be eaten); kippered herring that came in a little flat tin that had to be opened with a key (anything that came in a tin rather than a can—anchovies, smoked mussels, sardines in mustard sauce—was practically guaranteed the status of delicacy). Had my mother discovered my predilections—at that point, almost entirely imaginary— she would simply have stared at me and wondered aloud, But why would you want to eat something like that? And I'm not sure I could have answered her; but I wolfed down my delicacies every chance I got, on the theory, I suppose, that if you are what you eat, then by consuming these rogue pleasures that ranged so far from the predictable orbit of my mother's cooking, I could somehow succeed at last in becoming someone other than the thwarted, unhappy creature I seemed destined to remain.

I HAVE ORDERED THE AVOCADO SALAD. Never mind that I've never in my life tasted avocado, and have scarcely any notion even of what an avocado is.

I'm fourteen; my mother and I are visiting my aunt in Atlanta, a city, it seems to me, of enormous sophistication, unlike shabby, backwater Memphis. We are in a restaurant in a complex of shops in the glittering, modern downtown.

"Are you sure?" my mother asks, almost, at this point, by rote. "Have you ever even tasted avocado? What if you don't like it?"

I know by now there is no logic to this. Perhaps I am merely drawn to the word "avocado," which sounds foreign and humid and passionate, so unlike the unimpeachable sobriety of my family. I say the word to myself, drawing out its rich vowels. I am pretty sure I have never even seen a picture of an avocado; certainly my first encounter with guacamole lies years in the future.

"I know what I'm doing," I insist.

"You're very brave," my aunt tells me. "Trying new things like that."

"Don't encourage him," my mother says with a sigh. "It's bad enough his father does." She has not raised me to be curious like the poor proverbial cat. My curiosity seems to her, in fact, vaguely disobedient, a perverse streak running through me that will no doubt, sooner or later, land me in some kind of trouble, not so much legal as metaphysical, since in most respects I am still an extraordinarily well-behaved kid. She has tried to protect me from my riskier instincts, but is beginning to suspect that no one, not even a mother, can save another human being from himself.

The waiter places my salad before me. On a bed of romaine lettuce, in itself mildly, pleasingly exotic, lie beautiful strips of avocado, a delicate yellowish green, not unlike cantaloupe slices, I tell myself, but certain to be far more exquisite.

"Is that what you were expecting?" my mother asks. "Are you going to have enough to eat? You can have some of mine if you're still hungry." She and my aunt have ordered hamburgers, a fail-safe choice.

"This is exactly what I want," I tell her bravely. With my fork I cut off a bit of avocado, surprised by how easily the fork slides through it. I spear the piece and slide it into my mouth, prepared for a wonderful surprise.

I have never tasted anything quite so disconcerting. The texture is soft, buttery, slick. I chew warily, I force myself to swallow. To my immense relief, my mother and aunt are more interested, at the moment, in their hamburgers. My second and third bites do not make my task any easier—if anything, my disgust grows with the alarming realization that this avocado salad contains a very generous amount of avocado, every last bit of which I will have to work my way through.

"How's your salad, honey?" my mother asks, as I have known she must.

"Delicious," I tell her. "Would you like a bite?"

"Oh no, not for me," she demurs, making something of a face.

When I have successfully downed that last slimy morsel I feel vaguely sick, though the last bite, I have to admit, has not been as dreadful as the first. A subtle change has wrought itself in me. Neither my mother nor my aunt can see this; at the time I can scarcely see it myself. But I am on the way to becoming a person who will eat avocado, for whom avocado is ordinary, no longer a delicacy but the stuff of everyday. For the day will soon enough come when I forsake the south and head north to college, when I taste my first caviar and drink my first champagne, when I make love to another man. Unimaginable feats, irretrievable losses. I am beginning the journey toward that person I will one day be, the adult my mother will no longer entirely recognize anymore as her son.

FOODS I NEVER ATE AS A CHILD still draw me; I delight in eel and Bulgarian feta and the dozens of varieties of olives, none cored and stuffed with pimento like those of my youth. I still long for the exotic, the unexpected, the strange, and though I no longer depend on the as-yet-untasted delicacy to transform my life, I nonetheless understand the part those foods, either real or imagined, played in provoking change of a profound and irrevocable kind. On my mother's cooking I look back with a certain melancholy fondness: all those ordinary nights of comforting sameness now utterly vanished, that quiet decent family scattered to ashes and the far ends of the earth. My father is long dead, my grandparents more recently so, the secrets of my grandmother's country recipes—her dash of this and pinch of that— irretrievably lost. My mother lives alone in our old house in Memphis. When I call her from time to time (I have not visited in years), I usually seem to catch her at dinner.

"What're you eating tonight?" I ask.

Our conversations are guarded, bland, polite. She has never forgiven me my many betrayals, I think, though she tries not to give any of it a second thought. The shadows are too dark, the mysteries too daunting. We maintain a delicate truce.

"Oh," she says. "I'm just having some cheese and crackers. A glass of milk."

She hasn't cooked in years. "I hardly even remember how anymore," she admits. "Anyway, there's no reason to these days." The supermarkets abound with frozen pizzas, microwavable dinners of every sort—though most evenings, I think, she just snacks.

I don't tell her that a handsome, interesting man I have recently met is coming to dinner tomorrow night, and that already I am contemplating what to cook that will impress him. I tell her virtually nothing of my life, and that is fine with her since the alternative is far worse, but as I grope for something to say about the weather, I am remembering some nice-looking fillets of monkfish I saw at Gadaletto's Seafood this afternoon. If they have some tomorrow, I think I'll buy a couple. I know a pretty good recipe for monkfish with mango chutney. ◉

Winter 2001, volume 1, number 1

a. marin |

The Unbearable Lightness of Wartime Cuisine

The world has always been imperfect. I just didn't pay much attention, like so many people who go about their lives ignoring atrocities, war, hunger as if such things happened only in books or films. And even when I found myself in the middle of the chaos of war, for a long time I thought that I would awaken into a beautiful spring morning and realize it was all a bad dream.

In those years, my life spun around one word: survival. *That meant coping with existence without water, electricity, and with very little food; queuing in lines for hours under incessant shell and sniper fire to get basic things that are normally taken for granted.*

"THE BEST FOOD I'VE EATEN in my life was in Chechenya," said a veteran UN official. "Well, and in Bosnia, of course," he added quickly so as not to offend me. I was hosting a party for a friend's sixtieth birthday in my loft in Sarajevo, Bosnia. It was 1993, the second year of the four-year-long war and siege of the city. The guests were "internationals" (the term we used for foreign aid workers and journalists, war zone veterans) and a few friends who were still around. Most of my friends had left at the beginning of the war. The ones who stayed became my family. The loft where I lived with my (then) husband and two children in the heart of the old town was a meeting place where we shared every morsel of food, where we built a semblance of normal life, interrupted only by regular explosions.

The food the official referred to was delicacies of my war cuisine, a full array of "something-from-nothing" dishes. By then I had mastered the art and craft of this healthy cooking style, and I was more than happy to show it off in exchange for instant friendship and favors, for cigarettes and chocolate or a piece of fruit. I remember them well—each foreigner and each act of kindness. They helped us survive. But I also remember hunger, despair, and humiliation.

Food and I

My maternal grandparents were religious and very concerned about all living creatures. Consequently, they would never throw food out but would try to feed as many mouths as possible with it. Leftovers were eaten the next day; bones were distributed to neighborhood cats and dogs (yes, there were times when pets just ate leftovers). Extra bread was dried in the oven, packed in big white cloth bags, and used for dinner and snacks. My grandmother even went so far as to "save" rotten fruit from the market. Even though they lived comfortably, she would buy basketsful of rotten apples or peaches and spend the evenings salvaging the good parts. The smell of rotten apples catapults me back to my early childhood, when my grandparents would sit in the living room and tell me stories or sing old folk songs while peeling piles of rotten apples. Now I can proudly say that my grandmother was the first person I met who composted, as the rotten parts would be buried in the garden among her geraniums.

If, by any chance, a piece of bread would somehow get moldy, my grandmother would kiss it and wrap it in a newspaper, as if it were a gift for someone, before throwing it into the garbage. "This is God's gift," she would say, "and I have to apologize for throwing it out."

On the other hand, "excess" is the word I'd use to describe my paternal family's relationship with food. My grandparents were well-to-do and considered that being well fed (and feeding everyone else around them) was the best indicator of wealth. Their cupboards and fridges were filled to the brim with all kinds of foods. I remember huge greasy breakfasts—liver, brain, steaks—early in the morning. Lunch would last for hours, and dinner was planned carefully as soon as the lunch was over. Bosnian cuisine is quite heavy. A meal consists of several courses, starting with appetizers, followed by soup, an obligatory meat dish with potatoes or rice, salad, and several kinds of dessert. "What would you like to eat?" was the only communication we had in the family, except for gossip and jokes about other people. My grandparents' lives revolved entirely around food.

I acquired my own need for excess in opposite directions—either to starve myself for days to prove how different I was from them or to succumb to the delicacies around me and eat until I couldn't open my mouth, admitting masochistically: *I am one of them, and there is no escaping it.* I can safely say that they never threw food out either—there were never any leftovers, because the ritual of eating would continue until everything had disappeared.

My parents incorporated a bit of both attitudes. As if afraid of hunger, they always piled food in the house. (Or was it simply my father's proof that he was a success?) We had two fridges and two freezers full to the brim, and our garage shelves were lined with jars full of wonderful preserves. As the vegetables and fruits in my childhood were seasonal, with almost nothing available in wintertime, we would carefully prepare for the "dry" period. Jams of all kinds, fruits in heavy syrup, pickled vegetables, tomato sauce, vegetable spreads, and sauerkraut were prepared, labeled, and shelved. My mother is an amazing cook, and we always ate well. She prefers lighter cuisine, so there was no danger that we would all end up getting sick from excessive fat, as most of my father's family members did. The only rule in my family, which I dutifully passed on to my children as one of their heirlooms, was not to leave a single crumb on the plate, because "there were so many hungry children in the world." Later, I learned that my friend's father had a different philosophy: You should always leave a bite on the plate for a hungry child. I stick to the first one, and my children accept it as a house rule. They have never tried to be logical and ask themselves or me, How exactly does the food we eat or leave on the plate get to the hungry children? I guess their acceptance of rules without questioning their logic is what is called tradition.

The Beginning

As the war was getting closer (and I ignored the signs), my parents tried to talk me into leaving, or at least stocking up on food. I refused both—the first by insisting that there was never going to be a war in my country, let alone my cosmopolitan city, and that if I needed food, I could get it from them, as I had so many times before in the (very different) times of need. Namely, my (then) husband and I had chosen a bohemian life, which meant that we were quite careless with money and would often turn to our parents for help.

In general, I refused (and still do) to stockpile anything except spices and teas, which are more like souvenirs I bring, or ask my friends to bring, from their travels. I insisted that if I ran out of sugar, I'd simply buy some in the supermarket. I was adamant that my children should eat only fresh food, bought daily at the market. Of course, I could always count on getting anything I needed from my parents.

In April 2002 the war did start in my country, and my city was surrounded by enemy soldiers, who had, until recently, been neighbors and acquaintances. The siege lasted almost four years, and the statistics say that over two million shells fell on the city. My parents' food supplies remained in the occupied territory. They had to leave everything they had behind. They left the apartment in a hurry, thinking that they'd be back in a few days, and instead of family photos and valuables they packed two packages of pasta, a liter of cooking oil, and a bunch of carrots, thinking that this would last us those few days they'd be visiting. My parents never went back to their apartment. Even when the siege was lifted and that part of the city was liberated, they couldn't bear to look at the empty walls and rooms. The only thing left in their apartment was the bidet. Their whole life was stolen from them. But that's another story.

My own food supplies consisted of half a chicken, a jar of honey, half a kilo of sugar, a kilo of wheat flour, half a liter of vegetable oil, a liter of olive oil, vinegar, some pasta, and rice, and my collection of spices and teas, which oddly enough steadily grew in the first months of the war as more and more people left the city and brought all their edibles to the ones who were staying. Not having any food in the freezer proved to be a good thing because the electricity was cut off right away. People who were hopeful that it would come back and didn't share their food with the neighbors ended up throwing it out in the end. The stench of rotten meat was in the air for days. I gave the chicken to a cousin who had contracted hepatitis B and needed something other than bread to recover. So, with no supplies and two children to feed, we became miracle workers.

War Diet

In my letters to friends, I joked about how quickly I was getting thin and how the war diet was the first one that worked for me—I had lost twenty pounds in the first few weeks, as had everyone else. The fitness schedule was so strict that it would have been impossible to keep any fat: three to five rounds of water carried in ten-liter canisters (one in each hand) up the stairs (no elevators) every day, running from the snipers at crossroads (at least one person a day wouldn't make it), and walking everywhere (no public transport).

But there was no fat to keep. The food was hard to find. And even when we did find it, we had to share it: children first, then the sick, then the less fortunate. I don't remember ever eating alone during the war.

At the very beginning of the war, finding food was an exciting challenge, since we thought that "the whole thing" would be over soon. This illusion lasted a few months, until the food became more rare, until the shellings became more frequent, and until it became impossible to leave the city. There was no electricity, no water, no phone lines to the outside world.

The humanitarian aid delivered by the United Nations High Commissioner for Refugees (UNHCR), as often as was possible to get it into the besieged city, consisted mainly of beans, rice, wheat flour, sugar, and oil. Occasionally, we would get something different, like soy flour, powdered milk or eggs (a sulfur yellow powdered egg substitute), feta cheese, canned mackerel or meat, or an American army lunch package. So, our basic diet consisted of bread, beans, pasta, and rice. Everything else that we could on rare occasions add to this was a luxury.

Above: "This is milk and chocolate soluble in cold water. Fuck an empty letter!" When parcels didn't work, friends would sneak something in a letter. COURTESY OF A. MARIN

Bread

"You bake your own bread?" my Canadian friends ask me. Yes, I still do it sometimes on Sundays. My children love it when they wake up and the whole house smells of freshly baked bread.

There were three things still produced in Sarajevo for most of the war—bread, cigarettes, and beer. Each person was entitled to 250 grams of bread a day. This wasn't enough to keep us going, and there were many days when the city bakery would be closed. So, those of us who were fortunate to have a solid-fuel stove baked bread. When our next-door neighbors left the city, they gave us their stove, which we had shared before. Having a stove in the house was like having gold. But it did require something to burn in it, like coal or firewood, or lacking those, books, tires, or old shoes. It was easier when shared with neighbors. In the first months of the war, until we got our own stove, we used the one set up for the whole building, where all the neighbors would bring their pots and pans and stand around the stove with spoons and ladles, dishcloths and lids in their hands as if in some long-ago time, sticking their noses into each other's pots and gossiping if anything out of the ordinary should show up in somebody's pot.

Wheat flour was a priority on my food list, and I would trade anything for it. I made sure always to have enough flour for a few loaves of bread. Having less made me anxious because it was our essential food; having more was dangerous because of the mice and rats that happily proliferated in the chaos of war. I baked many loaves in those years, very often for other people, and I connect kneading with calm thoughts, friendship, and sharing. In the first months of war, we would go to the basement during the shelling. Later, we learned that death in war had no rules, and we stopped leaving our apartment. The fear was still there, but we would all pretend that it was just an ordinary day and go about our business. I remember a scene (and this surely happened more than once) in which, with a tense expression on my face, my lips pressed tight, my fingers masterfully knead the dough, and beside me my daughter practices the piano (playing études), part of her lost in music and the other part fighting fear and listening to the gun on the hill above the city and the whizzing shells. In our invisible shields (bread and music) we were protected from evil, or at least that's what we liked to believe. I decided that I couldn't get killed while making bread for somebody else. We were eating my fear. Developing my own superstitions to be able to cope with the war, which is still beyond my understanding, was a very helpful exercise. I assuaged my fear by cooking, and what more comforting, familiar food is there than bread?

There were many people who didn't even have bread—elderly people living on the top floors of high-rises, who depended entirely on the kindness of strangers, or on what they could find in the garbage. One day, I met my mother's friend looking for food. The bakery hadn't been working for days, and she and her husband had nothing to eat. The market was empty. The next day I baked a loaf of bread for her, small and round. No special efforts, no extra fuel: the oven was big enough for more than one bread, and I baked it together with ours. A few days later she brought me a small package. She cried quietly. She is the type of person honest to her bones who is not used to asking for favors, only doing them. She was absolutely lost and helpless in the war. Such people survive only by miracle. I am aware how desperate she must have been when she swallowed her pride and told me, her friend's child, that she was hungry. The package contained a bottle of an expensive perfume: Madame Rochas. Many times I used to spite death with it, putting a drop on my temples before going to fetch water under the rain of shells.

I can say that we shared the daily bread not only with humans but with felines as well. The first cat we had adopted during the war ate only bread and water. It had been somebody's pet, a beautiful gray Siamese, deserted by its owners, like the thousands of cats and dogs that roamed the city and starved, unused to having to provide for themselves. She ran away from us when she realized how much grief she had caused, leaving behind thousands of fleas that found shelter on our bodies and stayed there for months until we managed to get a special powder from abroad. Our second cat ate only mice (there were plenty of those). One evening as we were eating dinner with some friends, he proudly brought us his most recent catch to share. He was very disappointed when we refused to add the mouse to our dinner menu and a few days later walked out of the house for good. The only food that our third cat liked was pigeons. Every day we would find just a few feathers on the floor. Only once did I actually witness the struggle, both the bird and the cat fighting for their lives. The cat won and was happy to offer me some feathers. One day he broke his spine by falling from the roof while chasing a pigeon. He was in such pain that we had to put him to sleep.

Pasta was just a variation of bread, made of flour and water. When cooked, it's gray and sticky. With no cheese on top or sauce, it is completely tasteless. But, like bread, it fills the stomach.

Beans

We celebrated New Year's Eve 1993 with an all-bean dinner: bean pie, bean salad, bean pâté, and bean cake. Beans were the main part of the humanitarian aid brought to the city by the UNHCR after they took over the airport a few months into the war. There were months when the airport was closed because of fighting, and the food couldn't be delivered. In those months old people starved to death and were buried in wooden boxes functioning as coffins, in the soccer field substituting as a graveyard. These were not recognizable beans—they were war beans, possibly left over from some other war, just like the cookies from the Vietnam War we once got, white and hard and dated 1969. There was only one kind of bean—small, round white ones, often broken and so old that tiny flies would soon emerge and we would have to face a difficult question: to cook them and eat the flies or to throw them out.

I've read somewhere that beans have such impressive nutritional benefits that you could live on them for six months and get all the nutrients you need. They are an excellent source of fiber, high in folic acid, a B vitamin, and mostly fat free. But eating them almost daily for three years, cooked in water, only every now and then with an onion or a carrot, or a pinch of paprika or Tabasco, can cause some serious psychological resistance. I remember talking to the beans one day, "You are so gray, and I can't stand you any longer." But I did continue eating them, at least as long as I was living in Sarajevo.

Although we did not get lentils as frequently, the similar taste and color make me shrink, and I cannot bring myself to eat them now. But I will always sing praises to beans, the most versatile of all foods. They kept us alive and healthy.

Rice

One of our daily dishes was a soup consisting most often of rice and a few drops of oil and water, with nettles, when available, or green onion from our roof garden. I had been under the impression that the soup was quite tasty until I read an account by a foreign journalist who wrote about having lunch with us and eating the "tasteless watery soup." I was angry with him for saying something that may have been true but that he had no right to say, let alone write for the whole world to read. We had to like what we ate. We built a life that seemed normal to us, and some visitors were sensitive enough not to point to the absurd. War is a self-contained universe whose rules cannot be understood by an outsider. And a very important rule was to enjoy every minute of life and every bite of food. And to see color in the grayness surrounding you, including the food. The proximity of death helped us cherish the illusion of normalcy in a completely surreal existence.

Then there was rice cheese, a really terrible substitute for cheese, and rice wine, fermented at home with a little help from (obviously) rice, then some sugar, water, and a drinking straw. For our exhausted bodies and minds, it was strong enough to blur the world around us for a few moments and help us forget how miserable we were. I even tried to make rice brandy once but failed and stuck to the wine.

Nettles

The use of nettles dates from the ancient Egyptians, who made oil from it; the Greeks and Romans used it as a vegetable, as mentioned by Hypocratus and the Heretics. Pliny recommended nettles as a tasty and healthy food that protects from all kinds of diseases. Nowadays you can find nettles in the markets of the healthy-lifestyle capitals of the world. They are quite popular at the Granville Island Market in Vancouver.

The fear of death instilled in children the need to listen to everything their parents said. The fairy tales I told my children were about the outside world and life after the war. I also told them stories about food, how privileged they were to eat nettles, how nettle soup was a delicacy that had been served in the European courts before fancy balls. "There would be a whisper in the room, and not because the emperor was arriving, no, my darlings, but because the servants were bringing in the nettle soup. The nettle-pickers would go early in the morning into the fields, without gloves, and pick the pale green leaves, their fingers red, their palms stinging. But no pain could prevent those brave souls from bringing this unique food to the royal chefs, who would then pull out their secret recipes and cook the famous nettle soup. Yes, my lucky darlings, think of other poor children in the world who have never had the opportunity to eat this dish of the emperors. Yes, other children have chocolate and hamburgers and hot dogs. But have you ever heard a story about an emperor who ate hamburgers? Or a princess who ate hot dogs? No, the princess would eat the nettle soup and it would give her strength to dance all night. Now eat your soup today and Mummy will cook you some beans tomorrow. And what a story I have for you about their magical powers!" And they believed me and never complained.

Chocolate and Sweets

All the wish lists my children made during the war consisted only of food items, mainly sweets. My son wrote to the tooth fairy, "Please bring me a can of Coke, a few candies, a small chocolate, and an apple." Children swarmed around UNPROFOR troop carriers and trucks or ran after them, pointing at their mouths and shouting, "Hungry, hungry." The soldiers tossed them little packages of sweets. I wanted to protect my children from humiliation and strictly forbade them to do that. But survival instinct (and peer pressure) prevailed in this case. So my five-year-old son continued to run after soldiers until one day he was almost run down by the carrier. When the neighbors brought him home, he was frightened to death. He stopped running after foreigners, but he invented other ways of getting what he wanted. He became a businessman. His most precious possessions were glossy magazines (waiting to become fuel). He clipped pictures of models and cars and sold them to teenagers or exchanged them for chewing gum or sweets.

One day my son came home from school and said, "I want to be a Muslim." I was surprised by his declaration. My children were brought up as atheists, and religion was not a topic of conversation. None of our friends were religious, and we didn't really feel that we belonged to any nationality. Perhaps it was a result of our communist upbringing, or our cosmopolitanism. But the war imposed divisions. Again, not among our friends, but among neighbors and people on the streets. And, as always in difficult times, people turned to religion for comfort. Missionaries used the opportunity to attract more people into the folds of their respective religions. Sarajevo, which during the war lost about half of its citizens (from six hundred thousand it was reduced to less than three hundred thousand), swarmed with various religious groups posing as NGOs, who offered food in exchange for a commitment.

So it was quite easy to find out where my son's religious drive originated. A humanitarian aid organization from Saudi Arabia came to his school and made lists of Muslim children. They were getting packages with dried fruits and notebooks and colored pencils. It turned out that my son was the only one who didn't declare himself a Muslim, and he was the only one who didn't get a package. I was tempted to tell him to be whatever he wanted, but I was also trying to raise the children as human beings who wouldn't exchange their own beliefs for a package of dried fruits. That was hard, because very often I myself had similar dilemmas and thought I would sell my soul to the devil for food. Luckily, I didn't have to, but the very fact that I did think about it makes me believe that there could have been circumstances when I would have done it.

Catholic priests were knocking on people's doors and making lists of Catholics. In exchange for having your house blessed, you would get on the list of your local church and receive food packages. The Jewish community was also active, and people were digging out the death certificates of their ancestors to prove that they had Jewish blood. The Orthodox Church consisted of one old priest who managed to gather quite a big flock, attracted by prospects of food. My son had befriended a young man who was a Seventh Day Adventist, and he would get toys and sometimes chocolate from him. It is unbelievable how many missionaries risk their lives to spread their faith, choosing the most dangerous parts of the world where people are most vulnerable and inclined to embrace religion, sometimes for comfort and sometimes just for food—another kind of comfort.

Both my (then) husband and I belonged to the weirdest sect of all—the sect of artists and intellectuals. We also had our missionaries, some well intended, without whom we wouldn't have survived, like Susan Sontag, who collected money for artists among her friends and organizations like PEN and Human Rights Watch and risked her life many times to bring that money into the city. Some came to use our stories to advance their careers. They usually didn't do any favors.

We gave many interviews and sometimes got food in return. The stingiest were the big American networks. Unless we asked, they wouldn't even bring a chocolate for the children. When a very famous TV personality came to our loft to interview us, he was preceded by a crew of ten people who rearranged our furniture and lit hundreds of candles (what a waste that was, apart from the fact that it wasn't authentic—we could use one candle for a few days). They brought bags of chips, sweets and fruit, wine and juices. My children's eyes were wide open in shock. I was so happy with the prospect of sharing all that with my friends who were there. But by the time the interview ended several hours later, the crew had eaten and drunk all of it. My kids each got a peach.

I didn't really care about giving interviews. At first, I thought it would be good for the country; I thought that if people in the outside world saw how "normal" we were, they would lobby their governments to help us. After the disappointing false signs that we would be saved, I didn't believe that my words had any impact on anyone. They were probably edited anyway, in whatever fashion suited the network. So, after many interviews that were all the same—the same superficial questions and false compassion—I started doing them only in exchange for food. I would ask ahead of time, "Okay, but what's in it for us?" and negotiate a food package in exchange for an interview.

A Fair Exchange

As I was sitting on a beautiful sandy beach, playing with waves in a summer resort in the south of Italy where I spent a year as a refugee after leaving Bosnia, I noticed beside me a small plastic bag. A familiar brown thick plastic bag with the contents listed on one side in black letters. It was the American army lunch package, the same one we used to get occasionally in humanitarian aid during the war. The same one we could buy on the black market for DM 15 (ten dollars) each. It was odd that I of all people should come across this bag when it arrived at the Italian shore of the Adriatic Sea, having come all the way from the Mediterranean where American ships were stationed.

I tried to recall the contents. There were five or six different types. But there, on the beach in Italy, I could remember only the tiny bottle of Tabasco sauce, its drop or two the most precious supplement to our bean dish or rice soup, the only color added to the same food we ate almost every day. How did it get there? To tease my memories, to tell me that I couldn't run away.

American lunch packages consisted (are they still the same?) of one or two brown packages with an "entrée" and smaller plastic bags with coffee, sugar, salt, toilet paper, matches, and dessert—usually a small chocolate bar. These delicacies would cause our hearts to beat faster. The contents were listed on one side in black letters. The entrée would be divisible into as many portions as we needed. A meal that fed one American soldier could feed a whole family and their friends. Four meatballs could easily become eight or sixteen pieces of meat. A small chocolate bar would be shared among children.

Markets are among my favorite places—the buzz, the colors, the smells. In wartime a market is as drab as its surroundings. In Sarajevo it was also a favorite shelling target. I went almost daily to look for food, for something green and fresh. That particular day I had a few worthless coupons in my pocket. They were printed by the government instead of money, and salaries were paid in coupons. You could buy your monthly bread supply with them, or a few packs of cigarettes, or sometimes a thing or two at the market. I managed to buy some nettles, happy that I had found them so late in the day, noon already, and that the vendors agreed to take my coupons. I walked home slowly. Since losing all of that weight and having to do hard menial jobs every day, I was quite exhausted. We hadn't seen fruit or vegetables or juice in almost a year. We were among the lucky ones because we had enough to eat. But it was always the same, and I had to force myself to eat. I sometimes added something green, a few dandelion leaves, vine leaves (which we also smoked when we couldn't find cigarettes), or nettles, and invented different shapes to make the food appealing for the children. Did they just pretend to be fooled by my castles, trains, and boats made of rice or flour and salt and water and some grass or herbs?

Walking home from the market with a few green leaves in a plastic bag, I imagined bringing home a bag full of apples and oranges and cheese; I imagined the faces of my children opening the bag. "Would you like to give blood for the wounded?" a man in a white coat woke me from my daydreaming that day. Of course not, I wanted to say. Ashamed to say no and yet selfishly thinking of my exhausted body, I just stopped and stared at him, speechless. What if I faint? What will happen to my children if I end up in a hospital? What if the needles aren't sterilized? Does this blood really go to the wounded? How much blood will they take? Squeezing the white plastic bag with nettles I silently communicated my questions to this man in the white coat. If I faint, somebody might take my bag. This is war.

He noticed my hesitation and added: "You'll get the American lunch package and a juice." But I have two children, I thought. As if reading my mind, he casually added: "Actually, I can give you two juices." That was enough to persuade me. I was easily bribed, with food especially, in those days. I entered the former toy shop turned clinic where I used to buy birthday presents for my children and for my friends' children: colorful wooden blocks with which they built castles, trains, boats. There was a hospital bed, and beside it a metal stand with the infusion bag and a table with a rack of test tubes on it, some empty, some filled with blood. I lay down and rolled up my sleeve. He smiled. I closed my eyes and imagined the faces of my children when they opened the bag and saw those two small juices. I imagined them unwrapping the tiny straws and sucking the juice slowly, rolling each swallow in their mouths, gargling with the sweet liquid, trying to keep it as long as possible so that the taste would stay until the next juice, slurping it at the end, then opening the tops of the boxes carefully, at the edges, to stick in their tongues and lick the last drops. "Would you like some?" they would offer as they always did, and I would say, "No, thank you, this is yours," as I always did. "It's done," said the man in the white coat, and he handed me the package and two juices. I stuck them under the nettles. I wanted to see my children's surprised faces. For almost two weeks my hand was blue and it hurt. But it was worth those meatballs we had with rice that day. And the small chocolate and peanut bar that was in the package. And the tiny bottle of Tabasco sauce. It took me a long time to realize that the event was not a mere exchange of blood for food but that it was supposed to result in saving someone's life.

French army food packages were different, much smaller than the American ones. It was difficult to make a lunch for four or more people out of one, but the dishes were much tastier. Luckily, we did not get them in humanitarian aid, but they turned up on the black market. Somebody brought us one, and I remember only that everything was tiny. They looked like airplane meals with more wrapping than food, and they contained white tablets for heating the prepared dish. Since the instructions were in French, which they couldn't understand, some people thought that these tablets were vitamins and swallowed them. There was a warning printed in our daily paper: "Citizens of Sarajevo are kindly asked not to eat the tablets from French food packages. They are merely to be used as a food-heating device. Consuming them can harm your health."

A Parisian Affair

Our next-door neighbors were among the few lucky ones who immediately got jobs as fixers for foreign journalists. We had met them only when they moved into the loft beside ours a few months after the war had started. Our former neighbors had left with thousands of others as soon as the war started. The brother-and-sister team employed by CNN regularly threw parties to which very few locals were invited. There was no curfew for foreigners or for those who worked for them. Everybody else had to be home by nine o'clock.

We lucked out one night around Christmas in the second year of the war and found ourselves among the privileged. On the menu that night was a turkey flown in directly from a famous restaurant in Paris. The children were asleep. We left the door open in case they woke up, or screamed in their sleep. They often did. I brought my nettle pie, always exotic enough to bring accolades.

The first thing I noticed was fruit, some that I hadn't seen in two years. And, quite naturally, I started following it with my eyes as it disappeared into people's mouths, thinking of my children asleep in the next-door apartment, angered that they wouldn't get any. My husband was drinking whiskey, and he took a soda from the table. I did not say anything, certain that there was a silent agreement between us that whatever we were offered except liquor we would put in our pockets and keep for the children. It was the nastiest look I had ever given him when I realized he had opened the can.

Apart from our hosts, we were the only "locals" at the party. Despite a few drinks, my food antennae were on the alert: Will there be anything left? A Spanish journalist noticed I wasn't eating anything. She took a banana and offered it to me. I said: "No, thank you. I have children. And they love bananas." She seemed to understand what I meant by my odd answer; she collected the rest of the bananas from the tables and gave them to me. "Take these to your children."

Ashamed and happy, I hurried to take the bananas home with the excuse of checking on the children. I did the same with my share of turkey. When it was time to go home, I could not help noticing that there was still some turkey left. What will they do with it? To be certain it would not end up in the garbage, or rather, to be certain it would end up in my friends' stomachs, I offered to clean up the apartment. The hostess accepted because she had to work early the next day. Playing the part of a good neighbor gave me a good excuse, and the next day I scraped bones from dirty plates until there was not a single shred of meat left. My heart was beating as if I were stealing something, happy that no one saw me. I managed to fill a plate with meat. I invited all my friends the next day and shared the turkey from Paris, bananas, and humiliation with them.

Monde bizarre

The loft I lived in with my family had become a drop-in place. Old friends, new friends, foreign journalists, UN officials, diplomats came by. The door was always open throughout the whole war, and we were never alone. I think that in some odd way I felt that we were safe as long as there were people who cared around. They would bring food, cigarettes, liquor, presents for the kids, and I would feed them my war specialties or freshly baked bread. Or caviar. A friend from New York came to visit one morning and brought a British journalist along. I offered them breakfast. "I don't want to eat your children's food," she said. "But they don't like caviar." I opened the fridge, which was empty, having been disconnected more than a year before because there was no electricity. And there it was, on the shelf, an open jar of caviar. When Marc, a French soldier, had brought the jar to the party the previous night, neither of us could believe it. A kilo of caviar! My friends, at least those who liked caviar, and I had eaten some, but it was impossible to eat the whole kilo.

It was cold enough in the house to keep it for a day or two. I brought out the freshly baked bread and spread a thick layer of caviar on slices. My friend said, laughing, "I haven't had caviar in a long time."

Fruits and Vegetables

As we grew accustomed (?!) to living under siege, we became more and more inventive. We created balcony and roof vegetable gardens. Plots in city parks were used to bury the dead and to grow vegetables. Seeds don't take up too much space and can be sent in a letter. What a joy it was to receive a rustling letter; it meant that it contained seeds. I managed to grow onions and parsley. Carrots never grew big enough to be taken seriously. But anything green and fresh was a little miracle. A friend of mine grew cherry tomatoes, the sweetest I've ever tasted.

In the first year of the war, you could find nettles, vine leaves, and dandelions at the market. Locally grown fruits—plums, apples, and cherries—were too expensive. We didn't have any money in the first year (my resistance to stockpiling applied to money as well). So the only way I could get something at the market was by exchanging the canned food that we would get with humanitarian aid. Bargaining with black marketeers had never been my forte, but you can do anything when you have two hungry children at home.

Much later, we started getting money from friends abroad, from PEN and similar human rights organizations. Our currency was the German mark, and prices were astronomical. There was a period when sugar was DM 100 (sixty-seven dollars), a liter of oil DM 120 (eighty dollars); a piece of fruit or vegetables smuggled into the city, or an egg, went for DM 15 (ten dollars). The black market was flourishing. There were times, later in the war, when the tunnel out of the besieged city was built and black marketeers traded even with the enemies, when you could find anything on the market. There were people who could afford it. During one of those periods, for the first time in two years, I saw an eggplant on sale for DM 30 (twenty dollars). Eggplant is one of my favorite vegetables. I started crying, partly because it was beautiful, partly because I couldn't have it.

The first fruit my children had were cherries. A soldier who used to be a waiter brought bags full of cherries from an orchard on the front line. He went door to door giving cherries to children. They had had a few apples in the fall and two oranges, distributed once with humanitarian aid to the elderly and to children. Then, after a while, they got bananas. And then in the late summer of the second year of the war, a friend showed up at the door with a huge watermelon. An American journalist was going to enemy territory to do an interview, and she asked him to bring it for my kids. We had a camera and snapped their faces at the moment when we brought the watermelon. It is hard to describe the joy one feels when seeing food.

My children's nightstands were full of peels and pits—mementos of fruits they had eaten—and candy wrappers.

Parcels

The city was under siege, but trucks with parcels were regularly (once every few months) allowed to cross enemy lines. The most successful in this venture were the Seventh Day Adventists and the Jewish community. Somehow, both armies allowed them to go back and forth. When word got out that a convoy had arrived, thousands of hopefuls would gather to look for their name on the lists taped on a downtown bulletin board. We were often among the lucky ones whose friends did everything to send parcels whenever possible. Often I would discover that even people we hardly knew felt the need to help, like my colleagues from the British Council, where I had started working just before the war.

Seeing your name on the list was just a first step. Then you had to choose a relatively calm day, which was always unpredictable, to walk for an hour to the warehouse, usually followed by sniper fire. Then you had to wait in line for hours to get the parcel, and lines of all sorts were a shelling target. Then you had to walk back with the parcel for another hour or carry it home using one of the improvised carts made of prams or roller blades or anything that had wheels. But it all paid off the moment you got home, with your family and friends waiting. Opening a parcel was utter bliss. Our friends became experts in sending exactly what we needed, and sometimes even what we didn't, like brandy sneaked in a dishwashing detergent bottle. Once we got a whole wheel of cheese. But since it was wrapped in a plastic bag and the parcel had traveled three months, it was rancid and stank terribly. But we ate every bite, including the outer layer.

Above: My children and their friend seeing a watermelon for the first time in two years. The fridge in the background was covered with pictures of food from magazines, since it was empty. COURTESY OF A. MARIN

A friend of mine who was living in Germany as a refugee had been into macrobiotic food, so her parcels were the best because they contained nuts and seeds, soybeans, and all the healthy supplements for our monotonous diet. But she did send us sausages once, and we had a real German feast. The parcel that moved me the most was from a family in France. We got it through another friend whom they had asked to find a family in Sarajevo to whom they could write. The parcel came for Christmas. It was full of beautifully wrapped chocolates and candies, coffee, and cookies and had a big Christmas card and a letter with a picture of the family. It felt just as if we were receiving a Christmas present from close friends.

Epilogue

The world is still imperfect, wars are still raging, and children are dying of hunger all over the world. Only now I pay attention, and with this experience that I never really asked for, I know what they are going through. I live in Canada now, and I haven't started stockpiling yet. There are grocery stores at every corner, and we can afford lots of fresh fruits and vegetables. My children now make different wish lists. But, if by any chance we have some leftover bread that goes bad, I still follow the same ritual that I inherited from my grandmother, replacing the newspaper with a sandwich bag. Well, and I also kiss the bread only in my mind. ◉

Spring 2005, volume 5, number 2

james nolan |

One Year and a Day
A Recipe for Gumbo and Mourning

GUMBO TAKES THREE DAYS TO MAKE, if you do it right, although in a kitchen piled with greasy pots and smelling of shrimp heads, it may appear more like a year. According to Hebrew law, a body takes one year and a day to decompose inside a casket. In many cultures the mourning period corresponds to this biblical measure. Here in New Orleans, a corpse buried in an above-ground tomb may not be "disturbed," as undertakers call it, or shifted below to make room for another burial for one year and a day after it has been sealed inside. Making gumbo and the decomposition of a body have little in common except that, like grief, both take time.

In Louisiana we have plenty of time, time to make a twenty-minute roux, to simmer a soup stock, to peel shrimp and time to rock and chat, to chop and mourn, to stir and sway over cauldrons of memories. A Creole good-bye may take hours, as inching toward the door we kiss good-bye then talk some more, kiss again then come back to add what we forgot to say all evening, then kiss good-bye again, and so on.

Making gumbo can be a Creole good-bye for the dead.

Here we don't talk about dying but passing, a euphemism that reflects our superstitious cosmology. People who emphasize passing to the other side, rather than dying to this one, treat death as a celebration. And people who believe in passing also believe in ghosts and hauntings, and in the dead supervising the affairs of the living. We live with the dead as vertical neighbors, not those on either side but those down there, where the bones go, and those up there, where the spirit resides. We say the dead look down, although I'm not sure from where. Perhaps this voyeuristic perch is an atavistic memory from when our ancestors lived in trees. All I know is that from somewhere on high, my mother directed the vigil that marked the one-year anniversary of her passing.

I had been trying to come up with some way to commemorate the occasion, which signaled the end of the traditional mourning period. When I was a child, powdery great-aunts with flowery French names still observed mourning by wearing dark clothes during the year and by not playing the Victrola or Motorola, as they called the phonograph and TV. From an earlier era, I have a brooch mounted with a tinted photograph of my great-great-grandfather Numa Landry that contains a lock of his hair soldered inside and was probably pinned to my great-great-grandmother's dress during the year his family spent shuttered inside their house on rue Bourbon. At one time in New Orleans wearing ornate jewelry fashioned from the hair of the deceased was a common mourning practice, as were black armbands, black

wreathes hung on the front door, black-bordered calling cards, special novenas, and votive candles lit at Mass and on bedroom *prie-dieus.*

All of this seemed hopelessly fuddy-duddy to my mother, a modern career woman who sported a pink pantsuit to my father's wake. The only mourning custom she maintained was cemetery visits to place flowers on the family tomb in the St. Louis cemetery every All Saints Day, Christmas, Easter, and on dead family members' birthdays. So after her passing I was cut adrift as to how to mourn, when and for how long. The dead linger with us for a while, then move away. In a recurring dream I am astounded to come across my long-deceased grandparents living in a dilapidated cottage in some lost neighborhood of the city. Perhaps their neglected house reflects my own neglect of their memory, and they've become what the Chinese call hungry ghosts, begging for morsels of food and attention.

Recently, I ran into a friend who was on her way to Australia carrying half of her mother and a sixth of her grandfather in Ziploc sandwich bags. Not body parts, of course, but ashes. People die the way they live, and Americans are a rootless people. But the paucity of grieving rituals in the United States strikes me as part of a deeper denial, a childish refusal to acknowledge death that often masquerades either as hard-boiled pragmatism or new-age pantheism. The pattern now is a sensible cremation, the upbeat memorial service, democratically divided ashes, a check to charity in lieu of flowers, releasing pastel balloons, holding hands in a circle, a little sentimental "Kumbaya" borrowed from scouting jamborees, then chin up, back to work, as though nothing had happened. This is followed months later by sudden paralysis, depression, medication to get you "back on track," as if grief, that most ancient of emotions, the inspiration for so many of the heart-rending laments of world literature, were nothing more than a chemical imbalance. Yes, sadness does follow death, as it must. But depression is something else: a numbness, an inability to grieve, to experience that sadness. Deep feeling, like a river, needs banks, channels, levees, and locks, or the water will not flow but dam up and stagnate, or overflow and destroy.

How to mourn is something I worked out on my own, with candles, cemetery visits, flowers, solitary strolls through familiar places, going through papers and photographs. But you can walk only so far with the dead, and then you must let them go. Here some of us sing and holler and dance our grief second-lining during a jazz funeral. As the year-and-a-day marker approached, I decided to cook my grief, to end mourning by making gumbo—that togetherness dish—and by inviting the friends and family who had supported me during my sadness to gather once again and—I don't know what to call it—suck crab claws to glory.

Start with a carcass, if you have one.

In this case I used the remains of the Thanksgiving turkey roasted at my cousin Karen's house, where we had gathered for a large family-cooked meal a few months earlier. The dinner was the sort of warm, woozy affair the dead hunger for: children watching cartoons on TV while adults sip wine in the kitchen, arguing about whether the giblets go in the

Left: Helen Partee Nolan in the early 1940s. COURTESY OF JAMES NOLAN

dressing or the gravy, old folks reminiscing on a couch, card tables added at the last minute, a dish forgotten, a missing chair. All of this ended up in my mother's gumbo. Karen lives in the attic apartment of a refurbished orphanage, where you can sense the spirits of orphans in bloomers and knickers skipping along the wide wrap-around verandas, presided over by nuns in starched sailboat wimples. How fitting, I thought, to spend my first Thanksgiving as a fifty-year-old orphan at an orphanage.

The frozen turkey carcass goes into a covered stock pot of boiling water along with bay leaves, several halves of peeled onions, a few carrots and stalks of celery, salt, thyme, crushed garlic, and red peppers. As the rich-smelling steam rises, lower the heat to a simmer, and leave the pot there for about three hours. Like mourning, cooking is the art of transforming the dead into the living, of wringing out a present from the past, constructing what is from what used to be. That Thanksgiving turkey, last picked over by children looking for leftovers, was still gobbling in a bubbling soup stock, memories swirling with the pungent holiday smell.

I had baked the turkey for our last Christmas together at my new apartment in the French Quarter crammed with packing crates, to which my mother brought not only a portable oxygen tank on wheels but a bedside potty. The winding staircase to my second-floor bathroom would have been too much for her to climb.

"I feel like a walking hospital," she complained, trying to untangle the yards of clear tubing that snaked into her nostrils. Should the need arise, my sister and niece had volunteered to hold a sheet around the potty, stashed in the living room next to the nativity scene. "That stable is where the Virgin Mary would have to go to the bathroom," I reminded my mother. She was stoic but humiliated by the paraphernalia, the immobility imposed by the final stages of congestive heart failure. She wouldn't be here long, so I'd hung spruce garlands and put on her beloved, scratchy LP of Handel's *Messiah* that skipped. We sang along to the Hallelujah Chorus, which I conducted with a wooden spoon from the kitchen. As usual, her eyes watered at the solo "I Know That My Redeemer Liveth" as I was bringing in the caramelized yams. "That's my favorite part," she said. The next week she turned seventy-nine, and two weeks later she was gone.

She had refused hospice care. "It makes me feel so...I can't think of the word." Five minutes later she called me back. "Doomed," she blurted into the phone just as I picked up the receiver. She needed that precise word, its thump of Faulknerian finality. So rather than at home, as I'd hoped, she died in an ICU ward connected to beeping monitors, besieged by white coats with clipboards and name tags.

"My name Dr. Goo," said one in faltering English. "How long been sick?"

"Look it up on her chart, if you can lift it," I thundered, and ordered Dr. Goo from the room.

In the reptilian cortex of the brain, our bodies scamper to survive against all odds, in spite of any mammalian concerns with comfort or lofty ideals of dignity. Survival is like walking a Great Dane on a leash, dragging us down the grimmest of streets, especially that last one where we thought we'd never venture.

"Doomed" *is* the word.

"At least I'm here," I told my mother, taking her boney hand in mine, "and not in Timbuktu." That's where she always swore I'd be at this moment. A few months earlier I had moved back to New Orleans from Madrid after my mother had been rushed to the hospital for the third time in two weeks. Whole pages in her address book were devoted to my exotic whereabouts, each neatly scratched out. She thought of me as being "away at sea," like her merchant-marine uncle.

"Like you say, we all have to die sometime." The Great Dane's leash had broken, and she looked up at me, amazed at where she was.

I broke down. "When you get to the other side, send me a sign, a flower, a purple one…."

"Even if it's from Hell?" she rasped, a smile playing across her face.

Meanwhile my stormy sister—let's call her Cynthia—was speed walking the corridors, grilling everybody in a uniform she could buttonhole about our mother's prognosis. Dying must be somebody's fault, and Cynthia was going to get to the bottom of it. Occasionally she would burst red faced into the room, ranting about upping the doses or lowering the doses because this stupid doctor says this and that stupid doctor says that.

Mother would just turn her face and sigh.

"Honey, I'm just not up to all this commotion," she confided to me, barely audible. Graciousness has its limits, and the deathbed may be one of them.

"Look," I said, "they're going to kick us off the ward at nine. I'm going home, and Cynthia says she'll get a room in the hospital hotel to be near you."

"Tell her I won't pay for it." Mother pursed her lips. They call it Creole thrift, and hers was intact until the end.

And those were the last words my mother ever spoke to me, except for a mysterious comment she made as I was leaving the room. "It's so crowded in here," she marveled in a little girl's voice. Nobody else was in the room. What she saw were spirits coming to take her home, her own mother, perhaps, holding out a tiny lavender windbreaker: *Hurry up, Helen Alice, it's time to go.*

She passed that morning at six. My sister, who spent the night on a sofa in the hospital lobby, claims she was with her, but I'm afraid her presence was less palpable than the soothing shapes my mother witnessed filling her room like vapor.

It's time, Helen Alice.

Death does leave a carcass, and all you can do with it is to make soup. Don't waste your grief: use it to add flavor to your living. And after three hours the turkey stock should be ready. Let it cool, and then pour the contents from one pot into another through a colander, draining out bones, bits of flesh, vegetables, and spices, those earthly remains. The pure, milky broth is the essence, separated by fire from the residue: what continues, and what does not. Throw the boney, melted mash away, and place the stock in the refrigerator overnight.

Try to get some rest. You'll need it for the wake.

ON THE SECOND DAY, gather the ingredients around you like old friends: onions, green bell peppers, and peeled celery, diced; a bunch of parsley and a few cloves of garlic, minced; some seasoning ham, cubed; two pounds of okra, sliced; sautéed andouille sausage (any smoked sausage will do); three pounds of chicken thighs and drumsticks, skinned; a large can of tomatoes; flour and oil. This is a long process, so you had best put on some gospel or blues, and have a beer or glass of wine first, before you start dicing, cubing, mincing, slicing, sautéing, and skinning. Kick up a few dance moves around the kitchen to get started.

My friend Kim and I thought we would be the first to arrive at the funeral home on Canal Street an hour before my mother's wake was to begin. Preparations were in order, and we were burdened with trays of sandwiches and tins of cookies from Winn-Dixie, as well as bottles of wine, liquor, and soft drinks. I was also lugging envelopes of family photographs to display on bulletin boards mounted on pedestals around the rooms, and photo albums to leave open on coffee tables. Soon scores of people would gather not only to mourn a death but to celebrate a life, and if they couldn't remember the stages of that life, I meant to remind them.

Crossed by early evening shadows, the plush parlors were already brimming with purple, lavender, and violet flowers, not only the ones I'd ordered but those sent by friends and family. Anyone who knew my mother knows she loved purple, so the color scheme was a given. Balancing a tray of sandwiches in one hand and a bag of clanking bottles in the other, I was steeling myself to the shock of seeing my mother's body in a casket, for that gut-level acknowledgment of my own flighty fate. From this I came, to this I shall return, I thought, stepping forward through the gauzy light.

Only I couldn't see past my sister standing in front of the coffin screaming.

"Look how they botched the job," Cynthia screeched without preamble, arms flailing above her head like Medea. "They're just going to have come back down here and embalm her again. And I mean NOW. She didn't look like that."

Of course, she didn't, I thought, bracing myself to peer at the rouged, parchment face above the ruffled violet blouse, an old-lady doll tucked inside its box. But now she's dead. Once again, this was somebody's fault, and Cynthia was going to get to the bottom of it.

A parent's death dredges up whatever lurks in the profundities of our murky souls. Looking around, I was amazed to discover that at the depths of mine were ham sandwiches and bottles of Beaujolais, old photographs and floral wreathes. And at the core of my Vesuvian sister was what I had recognized years ago as a boiling rage, the intractable kind that you give up trying to understand and just want to get away from.

Send her to a therapist? Sorry, but she *is* a therapist.

So I did the only thing I knew how to do. I sicced my sister on the undertaker, a mousey man with a stutter who launched into a rambling monologue about fluids, and started to redecorate. I shifted flowers, arranged bulletin boards, positioned the harpist, set up a bar, and spread out the food in a separate room with a Mr. Coffee that the morticians called "the kitchen," far out of earshot of my sister.

Speaking of things that boil and turn red, let me mention crabs, the only ingredient you may have to kill yourself. The shrimp and oysters are best bought the morning of the third day, when the gumbo is served, and added at the last minute. But one of the first ingredients to be thrown into the simmering stock are the crabs, broken in half. I use two pounds of gumbo crabs, those small Gulf crabs that are precleaned and sold either frozen or submerged in icy vats at seafood shacks. I was raised never to buy a dead crab, and I'm not sure why gumbo crabs merit a special dispensation to this writ of Creole catechism, but they do. If they aren't available where you live, you will have to boil half a dozen live crabs, remove the shells, clean them, break them in two, and just pretend you're in New Orleans.

When you take the turkey stock from the refrigerator, skim off the thick yellow fat congealed on top. When the stock begins to simmer, toss in bay leaves, salt, and a few pinches of cayenne. At this point, you may add the skinned chicken parts to the pot. Remove them when the meat is cooked, cool, debone, chop into chunks, and reserve in the refrigerator for the third day, adding them to the gumbo along with the shrimp and oysters. Chicken cooked too long in gumbo turns stringy, ruining the velvety texture.

Now add the crabs, bring to a boil, and let the pot simmer. Meanwhile, heat cooking oil in a huge skillet, wok, or paella pan to sauté the garlic with what we call the Holy Trinity: onions, bell pepper, and celery, adding them in that order. Pour yourself another glass of wine or beer, change the music to Aretha or B.B. King, and get ready to work it.

When the onions have cooked clear, add the okra and seasoning ham, stirring, stirring, stirring until the okra becomes gummy. Add three teaspoons of Chef Paul Prudhomme's Seafood Magic or Tony Chachere's Original Creole Seasoning ("Good on Everything"). Authentic Creole seasoning is a delicate blend, like an Indian curry or Mexican molé, and there's no need to reinvent the wheel, especially when it's already rolling around town.

Into this gooey mixture go several heaping tablespoons of flour, stirred until it turns brown and smells toasty, like a roux. To this add a large can of peeled tomatoes chopped in strips, juice and all, and stir some more, until the mixture begins to bubble. Then scoop out every last bit of this sticky goulash into the simmering pot of turkey broth and crabs. Add slices of smoked sausage, after the sausages first have been pierced with a fork, fried for a few minutes, and drained on paper towels. Bring to a boil, and simmer for several hours, until most of the vegetables have disappeared into the primordial funk of the gumbo.

The mourners have begun to mingle, and the wake is underway.

BEFORE THE ADVENT OF FUNERAL PARLORS, the dead used to be laid out on their dining room tables the night before they were buried, and family, friends, and neighbors gathered around to eat, drink, and mourn. This cannibalistic detail of the dining room table as the last resting place before the tomb shouldn't be missed. Like food, death draws people together. Dying constantly feeds living so that it produces yet more life, although this may not be the most appealing way to think of a lost loved one or a chicken-salad sandwich. In their ritual preparations of flesh, morticians have much in common with cooks.

Once mortuaries replaced private homes as the site of the wake, New Orleans funeral parlors had bedrooms upstairs where bereaved families camped out all night, stumbling up and down the stairs to tearfully greet visitors. These days few families spend the whole night, although the funeral director invited us to use the facilities as we wanted, noting some families even bring in Cajun bands. But now families seldom even have wakes, holding only spooky-sounding visitations the morning before the funeral. I made the undertaker scratch out the word "visitation" and insert "wake" in the obituary he was preparing for *The Times-Picayune*. My mother had prepaid her funeral, insisting on a real wake with food, booze, music, and lots of people. She'd also given me the model number of the lavender-lined oak coffin she picked out so that the funeral home didn't pull a fast one on her.

"Sometimes they substitute one of those cheap ones," she complained, "that look like they're made out of dryer lint." The day she went to pick out her coffin, a friend dropped her off, and not wanting to waste money on a taxi, she bummed a ride home in the hearse. "Might as well know what it feels like," she said, "since I won't be around to see what I paid for."

She got her money's worth. Even though we have scant family left in town, my mother's many friends attended, and droves of my own, and it turned out they all knew each other. We say there is only one degree of separation between people in New Orleans, and all evening I was surprised by the unlikeliest combinations. My uptown Jewish writing student greeted my sister's Catholic ex-husband from Cajun country like an old friend: they had worked together in the same law office. At one point, I was standing in a circle of women, some my mother's friends, some mine, who had all acted in the same production of *The Women* at the Gallery Circle Theater in the French Quarter in 1964. My friend Lynn's boyfriend knew my cousin Roy from painting circles across the lake. Antonio, the husband of Mother's housekeeper, recognized her close friend Marta from their childhood in Nicaragua.

And those who didn't already know each other soon got to, rather quickly. I realized the wake was a success when I came upon my retired-colonel uncle from Mississippi, married to my mother's sister, drunkenly pawing my cousin Karen, a hip young Buddhist to whom I'm related on my father's side. My uncle then swiveled his gallant attentions and thick black bifocals toward my Korean friend Kim's aunt, an imposing, elderly actress in a mink coat. "One little detail I need to find out," he drawled, taking me aside in the kitchen. "I know she's one of your friends and don't get me wrong, hear. But is she really a woman?"

My mother had visited me only once during the many years I lived in San Francisco and wasn't familiar with the term "multicultural." But one friend looked around and commented, "She sure had a wide variety of people in her life, know what I mean?" Dressed to the nines, several black staff members from her assisted-living home were perched on couches with their daughters, and the Central American interpreters from her hospital job were chatting in Spanish while the drunk Choctaw uncle was chasing an actress in a mink coat and my beret-wearing bohemian friends were scarfing up all the sandwiches. The harpist was playing celestial strains of Mozart, but all I could think of was Harpo.

During the past year I've heard people refer to each other as "someone I met at your mother's wake." Which brings me back to that aromatic pot of gumbo simmering on the back burner in the kitchen, crab blending with sausage, tomato with okra, turkey with ham.

Gumbo began as a poor man's dish: you threw in what you had. *Gombo* is a West African word for okra, and one legend has it that slaves hid seeds in their hair so they would have something to eat in the New World. Gumbo is the African cook's improvisation on French shellfish bouillabaisse, cooked with Native American seasonings such as cayenne and sassafras. Out of the death and suffering of whipped slaves, massacred Indians, and French and Spanish settlers, who dropped by the thousands during cholera and yellow-fever epidemics, comes this regal concoction, this Creolized tribute to a mixture of bloodlines, languages, and cultures, this culinary wake, thick and dark as the swamps we spring from.

The final touch of the second-day preparation is to make a roux the shade of bayou mud, the color gumbo should resemble. While the gumbo simmers, you must stir it every fifteen minutes to keep the ingredients from sinking and charring at the bottom of the pot. Meanwhile, heat a cup of cooking oil in a cast-iron skillet until it begins to bubble, and then slowly blend in two cups of flour over a medium flame. With a wooden spoon stir and stir and stir this mixture in a counterclockwise direction for about twenty minutes, until it has turned thick and dark. You must give your undivided attention to making a roux, involve your whole body and soul. If the telephone rings, let it. While stirring I sway to blues or gospel, often tipsy, lost in reveries, weeping or chuckling at memories, as the rich nut-brown aroma of sautéed flour rises to fill the kitchen. But mourning is never finished: when the mixture turns bayou colored, turn off the heat, and then stir and sway a few minutes more, to keep the hot skillet from scorching the flour.

Then standing back, throw in a bunch of minced parsley. The roux will sizzle and sputter to a standstill, braking at the moment of its perfection. Ladle in broth from the simmering gumbo until you have a paste, and then scrape it all into the gumbo pot. Bring to a boil, and then simmer another half hour or so, stirring regularly and checking the spices.

Cool.

The wake is over. Refrigerate overnight.

"AFTER GREAT PAIN," writes Emily Dickinson, "a formal feeling comes / The nerves sit ceremonious, like Tombs." This is the best description I've ever read of the benumbed formality of a funeral. I recalled these lines the next day as my "Feet, mechanical" went round, greeting guests, organizing pallbearers, choosing music, making sure the organist, singer, and minister were cued and positioned, that everyone sat in the right pew and stepped into the right limousine, that certain flower arrangements were taken, or not taken, to the cemetery, that everyone received prayer cards and signed the guestbook and found the bathroom. The minister intoned his canned homily, and we squirmed; the singer belted out "May the Circle Be Unbroken," and we wept. At some point somebody slipped me my mother's glasses in their frayed purple case, which I carried in my pocket all day, and the last photograph ever taken of her, which I lost.

> This is the Hour of Lead — / Remembered, if outlived — / As Freezing persons, recollect the Snow — / First — Chill — then Stupor — then the letting go

Mourning is the thawing of everything that must be frozen inside to lumber with any degree of grace through the intricate waltz steps of a formal good-bye.

Two hours before your guests are to arrive, slowly reheat the pot of chilled gumbo over a low flame, stirring frequently to keep the heavy mixture from sticking. Simmer an hour, until the very woodwork is impregnated with its smell. Then just before the gumbo is to be served, throw in several dozen raw oysters, the chicken chunks, and three pounds of shrimp, which your first guests can help to peel, rolling up their sleeves to tell you about who fell down at their own mamas' wakes. Bring to a boil, and then simmer for five minutes. Ladle the gumbo steaming hot into bowls over small scoops of white rice.

Death makes everybody hungry, so after my mother's burial I gathered with friends for the repast at Mandina's, a classic neighborhood restaurant across Canal Street from the funeral home. My mother had instructed me not to eat there after her funeral, as we had after my father's and my grandparents'. "It's too noisy and smoky," she admonished, "and the string beans are canned."

We didn't order the string beans, and I don't think she minded.

Seated at three tables pulled together, we spooned dark, pungent turtle soup laced with sherry into our mouths, teary-eyed, weary, but oh so alive. The memories of everyone's death we had ever loved melted into that one moment. Mandina's was crowded that afternoon, crowded like my mother's hospital room with spirits. But we fed those hungry ghosts through spoons rising to our lips, swaying together for a while, until the fried oysters and soft-shelled crabs arrived, and then we dug in to feed the living.

LIKE A WELL-PLACED PUNCTUATION MARK, death further unites those already close, or forever separates those who are not. Several days after the burial, my sister and I were to meet with the lawyer at my mother's assisted-living apartment to sign the succession papers. I arrived early with a few cardboard boxes, planning to begin organizing my mother's belongings. I opened the door to find Cynthia already in full cry, heaving everything within reach into a supermarket shopping cart parked in the middle of the room. My mother labeled hat boxes, sorted clothes by the season, and alphabetized her files, and for the rest of my life, I will wheel around a vision of this tidy lady's possessions being tossed in a roiling heap into a metal shopping cart, as if she were being sent homeless into the universe. I quickly filled a few boxes with what I planned to take and then disappeared down the corridor. Cynthia came charging after. Finally she had gotten to the bottom of dying and death. No stupid doctors or undertakers were left to blame for her loss: now it was my fault. "I hate your guts," she screamed, doubling over and pumping her fists like a three-year-old in a tantrum.

"After I'm gone you're going to have one heck of a time with that sister of yours," my mother would tell me with a rueful chuckle. She pictured our fate as a common scenario from her downtown childhood: the aging siblings connected at the pocketbook like Siamese twins, living in either side of a shotgun-double, infirm, alone, and cranky, not having spoken a single word to each other in over thirty years. To avoid broken crockery, I didn't invite my sister to the one-year vigil, although in many families a feud begun during one funeral often ends at another.

At the vigil I placed a framed photograph of my mother behind a votive candle next to where the gumbo was being dished out. I added three Bartlett pears as an offering, unsure if spirits like fooling with gumbo. Guests brought lavender tulips and purple orchids to fill vases around the photograph, and from this perch Mother presided as the guest of honor, finally more out of the tomb than in it.

In New Orleans the whitewashed tombs are designed like little brick houses with steps, porches, alcoves, and slanted roofs, and cemeteries are laid out like cities of the dead. Newborns with just-opened eyes are photographed in their beaming mother's arms in front of the family's little houses, just so the babies know where they come from, and where they're headed. A marble tablet bolted in place, inscribed with names and dates, serves as a door to the shelves on which the coffins rest. As a boy, I was fascinated by our dollhouse of the dead and in tracing the weathered lineage of names, engraved with dates preceded by *né* and *décédé*, back to the immigrant French great-great-grandfather who purchased the tomb in the 1880s. Although I'm the last in the family to still speak Creole or what I call "kitchen French" (which is where I learned it), I've continued the *né* and *décédé* tradition with the inscriptions. To my ear, my mother is not exactly deceased. She is *décédée*, which, like an honorary degree, confers many more privileges.

To complicate the matter, through marriage many families have several such tombs. I'm not sure why, but these tombs inevitably pop up in conversation when we're eating boiled seafood. Whenever a pile of crab shells, shrimp peels, and crawfish heads began to mount on top of newspaper obituary pages spread across our kitchen table, that was when our family hashed out "who wanted to be with who," swilling beer and gesturing our allegiances with sticky, seafood-smelling fingers. My mother wanted to be with her family in the French tomb, my father, with his in the Irish tomb, and I wanted to be with my mother, usually because I'd just argued with my father about some explosive topic such as who really owns the Panama Canal. My grandfather insisted he didn't want to be in the French tomb if his sister-in-law Mercedez was buried there. "The way that woman yaks," he'd say, "I'll never have any peace."

Tombs are not engraved immediately after a burial. The dead are not quite gone yet but still linger on the tomb's shallow marble porch, putting on their jackets and saying their Creole good-byes. The last image I have of my mother comes in a dream, eight months after her death. She has moved to a ramshackle shed on a barrier island off the Pacific coast, facing west. Isolated on the windy rim of the world, the one-room cabin is painted a dull red. She is seated on an aluminum patio chair on the wooden back porch overlooking the pounding surf, the pink plastic kerchief she wore to protect her hairdo knotted '50s-style under her chin, her tiny body calm and accepting as she stares straight ahead into the tremendous force of sunlight and sea spray surrounding her. Then in a flash, she has passed, every hair in place.

On an overcast January afternoon the day after the gumbo vigil, I brought the lavender tulips and the purple orchids to the tomb where my mother's names and dates had been inscribed since All Saints Day. After placing the flowers on the tomb, I joined my friend Joanna at nearby Café Dégas for a cup of coffee. I felt a year of obligations sliding from my shoulders, as if I'd been pallbearing the weight of that oaken coffin all year. I was ready to put it down. Suddenly, a friend of Joanna's burst through the café doors and exclaimed, "I just buried my mama. And you know something? She directed the whole thing."

"I don't know your name," I told the woman, "but sit down. We've got to talk. I just left the cemetery, and today is one year and a day since I buried mine."

We locked eyes and exchanged stories, both convinced that our mothers, looking down, had been in charge of their wakes and funerals. Joanna's friend liked my idea of the gumbo vigil and promised to try it for her mother's one-year anniversary.

"Did you use your mother's recipe?" she asked me.

"No, my grandmother's."

"Bet your mama is jealous." She flashed me a wink, sure of a set-to inside our tomb.

"You know, my mother never really made gumbo. She always said it was too much trouble." I stared down at fingers still redolent of garlic, shrimp, and cayenne. That familiar kitchen smell, almost impossible to scrub away, was all I had left of the year my mother passed. ◉

Winter 2005, volume 5, number 1

toni mirosevich |

The Prize Inside

THE RECIPE WENT SOMETHING LIKE THIS: Get a fish; snapper or ling cod, mackerel or halibut, an everyday fish, a regular fish, not a special fish, not albacore or swordfish or salmon, too fancy for this common dish. Put the fish in a soup pot, cover with water, let it come to a slow boil, like your mother's slow boil as she waits for your father's fishing boat to come in, for his ship to come in, for him to make good on his promise to fix the leaky gutters this time he's in port. Cook until the juices of the fish are released, then simmer. The simmering goes on for minutes or hours or days, for weeks or months or years, fish is simmering on the stove forever, from cradle to grave, the fish simmers and simmers and at some point is done. Lift the fish out to place it on a platter. As you lift the meat falls away from the bones, millions of bones, the ribs, the spine, the long bones, the short, the flat bones, the small bones around the cheeks, like lacework, the intricate system of delicate, delicate bones, and now the need to pray to St. Blaise, patron saint of things caught down the wrong pipe, and now the need to go to church and have the priest draw two white candles across your neck and bless your throat, so the bones won't get caught and choke you to death. And once blessed, tell me, your mother will say, how can you swear like you do, like your father swears, how can you say *jebem*, fuck, so easily that foul language rolls off your tongue.

What remains in the pot is fish stock, golden broth, that can cure all, a sore throat, a sore life, a salty cure, and now add potatoes, cubed, or rice and peas like the Italians, *reeezi beeezi*, that's what you say, and simmer until the rice is cooked and puffed up, and the air again smells salt sweet, perfumed by the sea.

Place the platter on the dinner table, on display. You listen, with your sisters on either side, while your father talks about the other Slavs, about the lack of money, lack of fish, about who's getting screwed, *jebem, jebem, jebem*. Hear your mother slip in something about the weather, the forecast for rain, the gutter. See your father gaze out the window at the horizon, just outside, calling him, though he's only been in port one day. Today in school you learned about Christopher Columbus. Did he too have the same look standing at the helm, on the lookout for the New World? You play around with what's left of your meal, why does it take them so long to eat, and *finish everything on your plate*, she'll say, and then you sit. And then you wait.

On the platter all that is left are the bones, the backbone like the one you see in the cartoons, where the cartoon cat tips over the trash can in the alley and pulls out the fish spine, with only the head and tail intact. Here there's no escaping the face, the open mouth, the eye looking upward, toward heaven or the ceiling light, it was living and now it's dead, and you focus in on the white eye, like the pupil-less eyes of the zombies you saw in the science fiction film *The Night of the Living Dead*, zombies who looked just like regular townspeople the day before—the mailman, the neighbor, the school nurse—then the next day were walking with their arms stretched out in front of them, coming to claim you, coming your way. You look at the eye, covet it, think to yourself, it's not a crime, what's about to happen next: the fish no longer uses its eyes to evade the net, the hook, to see whatever it is a fish sees. The fish is blind to what will happen next, the soul already gone, as we are blind to what will happen, tomorrow, the next day and the next, blind to what lies just around the bend.

And now the arguing, the fight every time, who gets the prize and who got it last, and *you always get your way* and *you're a lying cheat*, for the fish has only two eyes and there are three daughters and someone will be left out. Someone always gets left out.

But tonight I'm the lucky one. Tonight I get an eye.

When I put the eye in my mouth it tastes salty and fishy and good, and when I chew it's a little chalky (*remember*, she says, *don't tell your friends at school about the eyes*). I chew and chew, it's not the taste I covet, it's the prize inside the eye, inside where we cannot see. When the white is gone, there it is, the clear round center as tiny as a small glass bead. If you hold it up and look closely it's like looking inside a clear globe and there you'll find a sea and sky, and there, I spy a boat, and there, a sea full of fish, and in this world the sea is always calm and the sky is always clear, and if I could vault this life, into the world inside the eye, my vision would expand, I could see into the future, I could see beyond the kitchen table, beyond the house, to the world past this life.

And what's that out there, Captain, just around the bend? And what's that out there, Christopher Columbus, just beyond the horizon's edge? ◉

Spring 2007, volume 7, number 2

barbara kirshenblatt-gimblett |

Messages in a Bottle

First thing in the morning or last thing at night, alert or tired, I release myself into the uneventfulness of my ordinary days. I do not normally keep a diary or journal or write personal letters. What made writing so urgent on this occasion—what made the ordinary luminous—was my sister. I was in New Zealand. She was in Canada. Late at night, when pain would not let her sleep, she would look for me in her electronic mailbox. Like messages in a bottle, my words would wash up on the shores of cyberspace. Writing armed me for the imminence of death, and I found myself writing into its face.

Auckland, New Zealand, 1994

Talked to Lina this morning. She was born in Scotland, in a small fishing village outside of Aberdeen, and came to New Zealand as a young woman. At eighty-six, Lina and her friends keep close track of each other with calls and visits and intimate knowledge of each other's routines. Any deviation spells trouble. But, she's quick to explain, "We don't live in each other's pockets, you know." Her telephone life, a web of voices emanating from the receiver, a switchboard of her friends and relatives, sustains her. I call Lina around 9:30 each morning. Sadie, her sister, calls her at 9:00. She calls Sadie at 6:00. It is all very precise and regular.

Lina is Max's aunt, his mother's sister. I first met Lina in 1972, when Max took me to New Zealand to meet his family. I have returned many times since then. This time Max returned to New York before me. I stayed in Auckland for another five weeks, and Lina invited me to eat with her once a week. The night arrived. Lina was waiting with dinner. The front porch light was on and the door open. I brought her a few lemons from my tree for a Delicious Pudding, a very lemony pudding with grated peel that I adore. The mixture bakes in a Pyrex dish, set in a pan of water. The miracle of Delicious Pudding is that it starts out as one batter but ends up in two layers, the bottom a lemon custard and the top almost a meringue. She has been planning my birthday meal. We'll have Delicious Pudding and pizza.

Lina's pizza is an archeological wonder, a virtual time capsule of New Zealand history in food. She starts with scone dough. Since it's wasteful to turn the whole oven on just to make scones, the day she makes pizza Lina also makes scones from the same dough. The scones are also a way to use up some extra cream. We would have those scones with a cup of tea for dessert. Now that Max has left, she explained, there were to be no more puddings. Not good for us. She never makes them when she is on her own. But for Max, that's different. As for scones, she usually wraps up a few for me to take home for the morning and saves a few for the next day, no doubt to take to Sadie. She tells me that if they dry out, just run them under the tap and tuck them in the oven and they'll be as good as new.

To continue with the pizza. On this scone dough, which has been pressed into a little round pan with holes in the bottom, she spreads a tin of Wattie's Spaghetti in Tomato Sauce and on top of that a finely chopped onion, fresh cherry tomatoes halved, grated yellow cheese, and, on her half, two kinds of bacon. Some people add a layer of creamed corn and even pineapple. The pie tin goes onto a cookie sheet, and the pizza bakes in the oven till it bubbles and develops a lovely golden top. It is a perfect meal for two, because what is left can be heated up the next day. Lina always sends me home with a slice and saves a slice for Sadie. Weeks later, when I gave Sadie the focaccia I made, she cut it into wedges, toasted it, and ate it with marmalade for breakfast, the dried tomatoes and rosemary topping notwithstanding. Instantly localized. It was her first encounter with focaccia and she immediately knew what to do with it.

Tonight, for a change, Lina's making fresh fish. She hates fish, but feels challenged to come up with meatless meals for me. Her head thrown back, nostrils flaring, she gestures with her hands in the air to show me how she washed the fish several times and patted it dry with paper towels. The fish recipe came from Muriel, her friend nearby. Lina prepared the trevally in the oven with a little sherry and dried mushroom soup to season the sauce—the recipe is written out on a scrap of paper that she keeps with her essential recipe collection in a plastic bag in a kitchen drawer.

Dinner gets dished up with mashed kumaras, imported fresh green beans, broccoli with a little grated cheddar cheese—all the vegetables boiled, the water poured off—and a fresh hothouse tomato. Kumaras are sweet potatoes, for centuries a staple of New Zealand's Maori people. They have bright purplish skin and creamy sweet flesh. Lina chills a glass of water for me that she has covered with a little plastic shower cap so it will not pick up any smells from the refrigerator (really, a glass of thoughtfulness). We always debate whether the veggies are done. Lina says I like them with "a bone in," which means still somewhat crisp. And then, with good appetite, we tackle this beautiful food, the steam rising from the plates, which she has run under boiling water to warm.

Food has to be piping hot, the kitchen windows all steamed up, our faces flushed. Partly that's because there is no central heat, so people find ingenious ways to warm the little spot they feel—their beds, their food, the little space in which they are sitting, their skin. And for older people with false teeth, they will not feel the warmth of the food in their mouth if it is not very hot.

We sit at this lovely table, set with a clean cloth. Place mats with scenes of old English cottages protect the table from the hot plates or any wetness. Fresh flowers (camellias, daisies, freesia, rosemary, lavender) from my garden stand in an old vase. The space heater's coils glow incandescent orange. There is also a basket covered with a white cloth napkin. Partway through our piping-hot meal, Lina suggests that I peek. Rock cakes. Lovely, golden

Right: Max Gimblett and Matt Jones, *Delicious Pudding*, 2001. Digital montage.

EXER

Delicious Pudding.
Cream cups of sugar
Tablespoon Butter a
Y ablesp. Flour juic
grated Rhind of larg
or 2 small lemon
add 1 cup of milk

FOWLE
VACO

FOWLAWLER'S FOWLER
WLER'S N?

FOWLER'S
METHOD or
BOTTLING
FRUITS AN
VEGETABLE

rock cakes. With currants and bits of candied peel. She made them yesterday. We finish up with a hot cup of tea. Always, she remarks that she pays a bitty more and that this tea is specially good. We talk about the food as we eat. About the pleasure.

We talk. She hasn't been doing well at bridge for the last two months, after winning steadily, and is feeling discouraged. Cards are her divinatory medium. She reads human character at the card table. She reads life's lessons in the hand she's dealt. She lives out her life's principles in the way she plays the game. Her partner has diabetes and her eyesight is very bad—"Their eyes do go," she explains. Even with heart trouble and several hip operations, her friend takes two buses to come to play bridge, so keen is she on the game. With a mixture of fury and compassion, Lina tells me that "Flo makes a terrible lot of mistakes." The issue is not so much the game as the fear of senility. Cards exercise and test short-term memory. This time there was an added factor. Her neighbor's husband had just died, and Flo was upset. "We must be tolerant of one another," Lina bites her tongue. She plans for their next game. Flo will play to the west, with her back to the window. The light will fall on the cards. Lina remembers compassion and patience and the cardinal principle of never hurting someone else.

Lina reads the obituaries in the *New Zealand Herald* every day without fail. She was shaken to learn that one of her bridge friends had died just a few hours after getting home from their last game. "Oh," she said, "I wish I could go like that." She hoped that at the next bridge game, all the players would stand for a moment of silence. The doctor tells Lina how proud he is of her good health. She is, he says, his best patient, and is sure to live many more years. Lina confides to me that she tried to hush the doctor up. A week after a doctor gave her brother Bill a clean bill of health and projected a long life, he promptly died. Nonetheless, Lina now feels confident she'll make it to ninety and is thinking about the celebration. She casts back over each marker—Betty made her a birthday party for her sixtieth, seventieth, and eightieth, and for the years between, Lina took out all her surviving siblings for a birthday smorgasbord.

The topic turns to family. Lina recalls her mother's death. It is not the first time she has described it to me. The body releasing itself from within, expelling its contents from the mouth and the bowel. Lina and her siblings gathered round the bed. The doctors were not of much help. Lina was the one who cared for her mother, right to the very end. When she and her husband, Reg, went on vacation, Lina took mother with. She confessed, "You know, I always put mother first." To Reg, she would say, "We'll have plenty of time on our own when mother is gone." That was not to be, for Reg passed away before his time. Life's lesson in all of this was the shame of illness, the secrecy, and the inability, the unwillingness, to seek medical attention, something that worries Lina today when it comes to her sister Sadie. Some time after mother died, she appeared by Lina's side—a phantom. Just once.

Then there is the long period of caring for Max's mother, who had decided to die years before she was taken. Lina knew Dora was declining the moment she could not see well enough to do her crochet. Crochet was Dora's mandala, a geometry in thread, whose loops repeated themselves endlessly to form a perfect pattern. Crochet everywhere, on the backs and arms of chairs, on tables—place mats and coasters and runners and whole tablecloths. Ecru cotton, a single thread twisted and curled and knotted into lacy webs, makes a soft, perforated skin for the furniture. Whenever Dora made a mistake, which became more frequent, she would rip out all the work she had done. The frustration became unbearable.

But it was on the matter of scones that Lina finally put her foot down. Dora loved to make scones, girdle scones, on an old cast iron girdle—a flat disk of black iron from which arose a semicircular wire handle attached at either side. This girdle, what I know as a griddle, now sits on a shelf under the sink. Lina was thinking of getting rid of it. Someone had given it to Dora when she first came to New Zealand in the 1920s. Knowing how much I would love to have it, Lina will save it for me. Lina's great fear was that Dora would set the place on fire making scones. Her eyesight was failing. She was no longer able to crochet. She was no longer able to make scones. Her sense of smell gone, food lost its taste and much of its pleasure. Death took its own good time in coming, and Dora was impatient for its arrival.

Max makes our evening. His call from New York arrives just as we are having tea. Nine o'clock and time for me to go. Lina seems a little tired tonight. She hasn't slept well the last few nights. I call Alert Taxi and within minutes a Samoan driver is there to take me home. Lina tucks gifts of food into my basket—tree tomatoes (my favorite fruit), five rock cakes (all that are left), and two oranges from a friend's tree.

I'm feeling bad about not bringing more than three miserable lemons from my tree. Last week I brought flowers from my garden, and they are still fresh and looking lovely on her table. Lina has been cooking meals for me for months. And, way back at the beginning of my visit, she remembered the one meal I cooked for her and for Max's mother, many many years ago, when they still lived downtown. It was my very first visit to New Zealand—Max and I had been married eight years at that point and had finally saved enough money for the fares. Wracking my brains to think of what these two wonderful cooks would enjoy, I came up with a cheese soufflé (copied out from a Julia Child cookbook that I read in a used-book shop) for the miracle of its aerial performance, glazed carrots—sweetness is always appreciated—and a crusty baguette swathed with sweet butter, fresh garlic, and parsley. I do not recall the other elements.

This visit I proposed to cook a few dinners, starting with a repeat of the original one. Lina was delighted with the proposal. She wondered if I had forgotten my offer to cook the original dinner again. I don't believe I've made another soufflé since that fondly remembered one. Dinner is set for next week. Lina's sister Sadie, who is seventy-nine, will join us, and possibly her son Ross. Lina reminds me that Ross never passes up a game of canasta and, with four of us, we could play canasta after dinner. That would make the evening more like a party.

Over dinner tonight, I ask Lina about what she likes to eat, just so I can bring her appropriate gifts of food. Women constantly circulate food gifts—from their kitchen, their garden, or from shops, where they purchase items they know to be favorites. The ultimate gift is a full meal. Food trails make tangible the web of their relationships and mark out their histories in the most personal and material ways. Food exchanges literally embody those relationships each time a gift passes the body's portal, the mouth. Yvonne, a beautiful Maori woman who lives next door, has been bringing grapefruit for weeks. She just gave Lina a big jar of soup. Lina gives the grapefruit to me. I make candied peel and marmalade and give them to friends who do not make their own. Lina makes a hot meal for Stuart when he comes to cut the lawn. She knows his favorite foods. Each person has a distinctive food print, its clarity an indication of the close fit between the recipient's general preferences and the cook's forte. The relationship is defined by this repertoire and performed in food exchanges.

Sadie sometimes withholds the pleasure of gifting by refusing to receive. She insists that Lina have lunch at her place, but is sometimes reluctant to receive Lina's food gifts. When they play canasta now—Bruce and Betty will come by on a Monday and Sadie will join them at Lina's—they have a cup of tea and one dry biscuit. Not like the old days, when melting moments, rock cakes, scones and pikelets, shortbread, tutti-frutti, and other sweets would make their way out of jars and from under tea towels. Now, everyone is watching their diets and their hearts. Why make rock cakes, as Lina did for me, when everyone will refuse them? "I didn't come down in the last shower," Lina demurs. Reconnaissance complete, I fall asleep and wake up the next day thinking about the meal. The main act will be the cheese soufflé—its magical inflation never fails to stop the breath. Lina has a Teflon pan with high sides, a gift she has never used. I think it will work. Flavorful carrots freshly dug and glazed. Garlic bread. Lina offers to cook some sausages for Ross. Or to take a piece of corned beef out of the deep freeze and boil it in its own plastic bag. A soufflé would never be substantial enough for a man. As for veggies, she murmurs, "Potatoes." I'll surprise them with potatoes roasted with olive oil, garlic, and fresh rosemary till they are golden and crisp, the centers like cream. Broad-bean shoots, steamed and dressed with lemon and a little butter, will be our green vegetable. I found them at the Kelmarna Farm around the corner. Lina offers to do the pudding—either her apple pie in short biscuit crust or, my preference, Delicious Pudding.

Oddest thing, sitting here in New Zealand planning a meal for these old Scottish women and reading Elizabeth David explain French cooking to British readers in the fifties—anticipating their likes and dislikes, what they can find, and how they might respond to the cuisine she presents. Through this little meal, Elizabeth will speak to Lina and Sadie.

We wash up the dishes, and as the water gets sucked down the drain with a big noise, threatening to take us with it, Lina nods approvingly, "Good suction." Then, at precisely 8:00 P.M., we turn on the TV to check the Lotto numbers, buoyed by the promise of millions of dollars for the winner. Very intense concentration, great hope, crushing disappointment, resignation, and a few phone calls, regular as clockwork, to a sister and cousin, both of them advanced in years, to compare results. Turns out my birthday gift is to be a $5.00 Lotto ticket tucked into a beautiful birthday card, placed beside my plate at my birthday dinner.

I've planned my food gifts for the occasion of my meal for them. Everyone gets: six big brown organic eggs with deep orange yolks; one hundred grams of locally made rich blue vein cheese; a lettuce freshly pulled from the ground; a lemon from my tree (Meyer lemons are so hard to get in New York), dried persimmon slices, and a jar of Potage Bonne Femme from the recipe in Elizabeth David's *French Provincial Cooking* that I picked up today in a used-book shop. The centerpiece is my candied grapefruit peel.

Citrus. Abundance beyond ingenuity. The trees strain under the weight of grapefruits. Lemons are so plentiful that you cannot give them away. In the absence of an abundance of oranges, all citrus, it seems, aspires to the status of an orange. Even their names say so. Poorman's Orange is an old grapefruit variety, the first type to be grown in New Zealand. Morrison's Seedless, an improved version of Poorman's Orange, is what many people grow in their gardens. Meyer lemons are prolific here, too. Gillian Painter, a New Zealand food writer, says they were discovered in China and may be a cross between an orange and a lemon. The Meyer lemons and Poorman's Orange grow prodigiously in the cool temperate rainforest climate of the North Island.

A few weeks ago, when Max and I visited Babich Winery outside Swanson, near Auckland, there was a box of lemons at the door for visitors to help themselves. I'm lucky I can pass my lemons along. Several people told me that in the past the Lion's Club used to do a grapefruit drive. Their members collected grapefruit in vast quantities, brought them down to a big woolshed, and sorted and packed them for shipping to orphanages and old folk's homes in the South Island, where the climate is too cold to grow citrus. But these days the costs of shipping are prohibitive.

So, the fruit hangs on the tree till it falls off. It lies on the ground, neglected. Piles of grapefruit on the ground are a sign of defeat. Even the most ingenious and thrifty house-holders cannot keep up with their refusal to stop coming. When I was getting a newspaper at the local dairy, the woman ahead of me brought three kilos of sugar to the counter. As he rang up the sale, Harry, the Indian proprietor, commented, "Marmalade, eh?"

For years, Max's mother used to give us jars of marmalade. We wrapped them carefully, carried them by hand onto the plane, and brought them all the way back to New York. Savoring every morsel, we eked them out so they would last till our next visit. Though I knew marmalade was made with citrus from the trees in people's gardens, I had no inkling of its place in the ongoing battle to beat the abundance.

Marmalade keeps moving around in little jars. Everyone makes it and passes it along. It turns up on the table at church sales. Personality in a jar, it is as different as the women who make it. Some make a clear marmalade, with the thinnest shreds of peel in suspension. Others coarsely grind the whole fruit—the quick method—for a chunky marmalade, somewhat opaque and rough. There are solid marmalades that stand upright on the spoon—assertively. There are marmalades that weep. Mine is dark and very concentrated and almost like a citrus caramel. More an essence of marmalade, it slinks out of the jar, reluctantly, so tightly has it been packed in. Marmalade is the wine of the kitchen, with its vintners and vintages and distinctive qualities, each batch a snapshot of the season and the maker. I occasionally open the refrigerator door. There they all are, the jars lined up on the shelf, the light passing through them, each one a link to someone who compressed this overflow of citrus into a jar and to someone, maybe someone else, who set the jar moving along a path of gift exchanges.

Gretchen, my painter friend, brought me a jar of chunky marmalade a few weeks back. She spotted me right away. Someone without a supply of marmalade is a valuable trading partner, for what good are gifts if they cannot be received? One night she proudly showed me a jar of candied grapefruit peel that she had made. Fat wedges of peel coated in white granules of sugar. The peel inside the sandy sugar coating was translucent and soft—the very essence of grapefruit, much of the bitterness gone. It was as if the peel had sucked the marmalade into itself. I left her house that night with a big bag of grapefruit from a neighbor's tree, whose branches reach over the fence into their garden. The grapefruit that falls on their side is more than enough for their needs, she explained. And so I too entered a vortex of citrus. I was sucked into the challenge of its abundance. All those yellow orbs hanging from the lemon tree in my garden just called out.

Citrus peel is such a luxury. Peel in New York City is a lethal blotter for dyes and fungicides and waxes. Such fruit belongs to the undertaker, for it is dead food, the supermarket the funeral home, our body its cemetery. It cannot be trusted, even for a few slivers of lemon peel. Not with all the rites of purification in the world can it be redeemed. Here citrus is clean—no fertilizers or pesticides. There was no resisting the compulsion to tackle the citrus avalanche.

That night I began. Water in a big stainless steel pot simmered on the gas burner. A three-kilo bag of Chelsea white sugar and a can of Chelsea golden syrup (since 1884) on the counter, I removed the peel from nine grapefruit of various sizes, none of them huge. The fruit aside, I boiled the peel to reduce the bitterness. Leaving a mixture of peel and sugar to stand overnight, I went to sleep with the volatile oils of grapefruit in my hair.

The next morning, I headed directly from my bed to the pot. Radio New Zealand filled the air. My first cup of coffee steamed on the counter. Rain was spitting, and two snails kissed the glass window with the suction of grey muscle. Still in my long black nightgown and barefoot on the cork floor, I reheated the mixture just enough to loosen the syrup and lift out the peel, which I tossed in sugar. Gifts of peel are a wrinkle on the jars of marmalade. Few people bother anymore, and when they do, it is candied orange rather than grapefruit peel that they make.

Despite the fruit salad I made for breakfast, there was no way my body could absorb the fruit of nine grapefruits. What was to be done with all that fruit? And the syrup left in the pot. I found myself in the marmalade business. Into the pot went the chunks of grapefruit. I boiled lemon and orange peel, their fruit going in with the grapefruit. Lots of juice and sugar to bind it all, a few fresh bay leaves and sprigs of thyme. I'll take these jars—dark and syrupy and intense—back to New York with me.

As I write this I am listening to a recipe on the radio for Banofee, which calls for boiling an unopened tin of condensed milk in a pot of water for two hours. An Irish recipe. Listeners are cautioned. Be sure the can is covered with water at all times so it does not explode. The dish is later assembled with 150 grams of butter, two bananas, and a package of digestive biscuits.

I talk to Lina morning and night each day. When I tell her how happy I am here, she says, "Max must be so pleased that you like the land of his birth."

That's it for the message in this bottle.

IIMBLETT 1967

Postscript

A week after I left New Zealand, Sadie waited for Lina's daily phone call at 6:00 P.M. The call never came. Sadie rushed over to Lina's flat. There on the living room floor was Lina, felled by a massive brain hemorrhage. She lay in a pool of vomit. The impact of the fall had knocked her false teeth from her mouth. They rested a few feet away. Lina died a few hours later in the hospital without regaining consciousness. This was the swift death she wanted. She would be ready for it, whenever it arrived. From time to time, she would sit quietly in the funeral home.

Three months later, my youngest sister, Annie, the person to whom I was sending these messages electronically, fell into a deep coma. Defeated by breast cancer at the age of forty-two, she died in Toronto. Unwittingly, I was the designated emissary between Lina and Annie during the last months of their lives. These are the messages I transmitted. Both loved to cook and were endlessly fascinated by conversations about food.

Above: Max Gimblett, *Anne*, 1967. Drypoint etching, 17.5″ × 11″.

While Annie was dying, Max was in New Zealand putting Lina's flat in order. Lina communicated with him after her death, first in New York and then in Auckland. A few days after she died, Max found a brand-new playing card, a three of spades, outside our front door on the Bowery. This was her ultimate trump card, taken from the games of whist we used to play, a sign that she had passed to the other side. On his return to New Zealand, several months later, Max could feel her presence in the flat. She returned every night. Max was awakened just after midnight when Lina's alarm clock, packed away in a box just after she died, mysteriously went off. Possessed by a very strong feeling, he took a flashlight and searched each room. He did not find her, but he told her to calm down. "Everything is O.K.," he reassured her. The next morning, he told Yvonne, "Lina's in the flat. She came during the night." Yvonne replied, "She's very angry." "Yes," Max confirmed. Yvonne went on, "She's really angry you're doing the laundry. That's her job." Through her window Yvonne could see Lina's laundry line and would read it for indications that Lina was all right. Two or three days later, when Max returned to the flat after a heavy rain, he found the laundry dry and neatly folded, on a ledge near the front door. Lina had been there.

I sent a fax to Max, as Annie lay in a coma, asking him to bring the plastic bag of Lina's recipes to me. I wanted to include them in this tribute, which I revised at Annie's bedside in the intensive care unit of the hospital.

Lina's Delicious Pudding

Cream 1 cup sugar with 1 tbsp butter. Add 2 tbsp flour and the juice and grated rind of 1 large or 2 small lemons. Add 1 cup milk and two beaten yolks. Fold in stiffly beaten whites of 2 eggs. Pour batter into a deep dish. Set dish in a pan of hot water. Bake slowly (300 degrees Fahrenheit) for ¾ hour. Serve warm, but not hot. Serves 4.

Muriel's Fish Casserole

Cut 250–300 grams fresh fish fillets into large chunks and place in casserole. In a saucepan, mix 3 tbsp soup powder (mushroom, chicken, or asparagus) and ¾ cup milk and simmer till thickened. Add 1 tbsp sherry and 2 tbsp chopped parsley. Pour sauce over fish. Cover casserole and bake at 300 degrees Fahrenheit for 20 minutes. Serves 3–4.

Rock Cakes

Rub ¼ lb butter (at room temperature) into 1 cup flour with your fingers. Add 3 tbsp sugar, 2 tsp baking powder, 2 tbsp currants, and 1 tbsp chopped candied peel. Dampen with a beaten egg (optional) and enough milk to make a stiff dough. Break off pieces with a fork to form rough "rocks." Place onto a greased cookie sheet. Bake 10–12 minutes at 400 degrees Fahrenheit.

Scones

Sift together 2½ cups flour, 1 tsp soda, 2 tsp cream of tartar, ½ tsp salt. Rub in 2 tbsp butter. Add just enough milk or cream going begging (about ⅔ cup) till it pulls away from the sides of the bowl and forms a ball. Knead lightly on a barely floured board. Handle as little as possible. Form half the dough into a sheet ½″ thick. Cut into rounds with the rim of a floured tea cup. Bake on an ungreased cookie sheet for 10–15 minutes at 425 degrees Fahrenheit. Best served warm, with sweet butter, and tea. For dessert scones add raisins and sprinkle scones lightly with sugar before baking. Reserve the remaining half of the dough for pizza, which will bake in the same oven at the same time.

New Zealand Pizza

Press the reserved scone dough into a pie tin. Cover it with a layer of tinned spaghetti, a finely chopped onion, a tin of creamed corn (optional), slices of fresh tomato, grated sharp cheddar cheese, and slices of side and back bacon. Bake at 425 degrees Fahrenheit for about 30 minutes, or until the pizza bubbles. Serves 4.

Dora's Marmalade

Wash and quarter 12 Poorman's Oranges and 6 large lemons. (If American citrus, use 12 oranges, 6 grapefruits, and 6 lemons.) After removing the seeds, slice the fruit finely. Place fruit and 6 quarts water in a large pan and let stand 24 hours. Bring to a boil, stirring occasionally, for 2 hours. Let stand overnight. Next day, bring to a boil and add 6 lbs of sugar. Stir well until sugar is dissolved. Boil hard for 10 minutes. Add another 6 lbs of sugar. Boil 20 minutes. Stir well to prevent scorching. Simmer, stirring, until the marmalade sets when dribbled onto a cold saucer. It is ready when it wrinkles as the saucer is tipped. I like to add bay leaves and sprigs of thyme and rosemary to the marmalade. ☻

NOTE

A version of this essay appeared in *Kulturanthropologinnen im Dialog: Ein Buch für und mit Ina-Maria Greverus*, edited by Anne Claire Groffmann, Beatrice Ploch, Ute Ritschel, and Regina Roemhild (Koenigstein/Taunus: Ulrike Helmer Verlag, 1997), pp. 233–246.

Winter 2002, volume 2, number 1

charles bukowski |

dinner, 1933

when my father ate
his lips became
greasy
with food.

and when he ate
he talked about how
good
the food was
and that
most other people
didn't eat
as good
as we
did.

he liked to
sop up
what was left
on his plate
with a piece of
bread,
meanwhile making
appreciative sounds
rather like
half-grunts.

he *slurped* his
coffee
making loud
bubbling
sounds.
then he'd put the cup down:
"dessert? Is it
jello?"

my mother would
bring it
in a large bowl
and my father would
spoon it
out.

as it plopped
in the dish
the jello made
strange sounds,
almost fart-
like
sounds.

then came the
whipped cream,
mounds of it
on the
jello.

"ah! jello and
whipped cream!"

my father sucked the
jello and whipped
cream
off his spoon—
it sounded as if it
was entering a
wind
tunnel.

finished with
that
he would wipe his
mouth
with a huge white
napkin,
rubbing hard
in circular
motions,
the napkin almost
hiding his
entire
face.

after that
out came the
Camel
cigarettes.
he'd light one
with a wooden
kitchen match,
then place the
match,
still burning,
onto an
ashtray.

then a slurp of
coffee, the cup
back down, and a good
drag on the
Camel.

"ah that was a
good
meal!"

moments later
in my bedroom
on my bed
in the dark
the food that I
had eaten
and what I had
seen
was already
making me
ill.

the only good
thing
was
listening to
the crickets
out there,
out there
in another world
I didn't
live
in.

Fall 2001, volume 1, number 4

FROM *THE LAST NIGHT OF THE EARTH POEMS*, ©1992 BY CHARLES BUKOWSKI, REPRINTED BY PERMISSION OF HARPER COLLINS.

social constructs

Otto Horcher, Caterer to the Third Reich | *Giles MacDonogh* **104**

The Cooking Ape: An Interview with Richard Wrangham | *Elisabeth Townsend* **116**

How Caviar Turned Out to Be *Halal* | *H. E. Chehabi* **129**

"La grande bouffe": Cooking Shows as Pornography | *Andrew Chan* **139**

Recipe for S&M Marmalade | *Judith Pacht* **149**

giles macdonogh |

Otto Horcher,
Caterer to the Third Reich

AMONG THE FINE RESTAURANTS OF EUROPE, Horcher claims an unparalleled status. From 1904 to 1943, it was *the* place to be seen at in Berlin, and from 1943 until quite recently, Horcher was *the* place to go in Madrid. There is no other restaurant in the history of the twentieth—or indeed any—century that has relocated from one European capital to another without losing a jot of its social exclusivity.

Horcher was the creation of Gustav Horcher, who hailed from the Black Forest, still the source of much of Germany's best ham, cheese, game, and fish. When he opened the restaurant in 1904, he injected vitality into Berlin's restaurant scene. The oldest luxury establishment in the city at that time was Borchardt, where the sinister diplomat Fritz von Holstein invented the veal escalope that still bears his name. Borchardt was in the city center. Horcher situated his restaurant in the Lutherstrasse, the more fashionable west end. The younger members of the Prussian royal house—Crown Prince William, in particular—could be glimpsed at its plush leather banquettes. And so, for a middle-class boy with social pretensions like Hermann Göring, who had attended the cadet school in Berlin-Lichterfelde, eating at Horcher would have been a dream night out.

Horcher specialized in game dishes, a repertoire that flattered its customers, who associated hunting with an aristocratic lifestyle. This choice proved useful during the periodic outbreaks of rationing that marked the first half of the twentieth century in Germany. You never needed ration coupons for game or fish; you just needed land—or connections to those who possessed it. Thanks to game, Horcher limped through the lean days of World War I, when Germany slaughtered its entire porcine population.[1] The potato harvest failed on account of the British blockade, and supplies of food all but dried up. But according to Gustav Horcher, the founder's grandson, the restaurant never closed its doors.

Despite the seesaw swings of the German economy, the restaurant prospered throughout the 1920s. In 1923 it was mentioned in the English-language edition of Baedeker's guidebook for northern Germany, although without a star. That honor was granted by the time the German edition came out in 1936, when the food was described as "excellent."[2] In "The Irony of the Flesh" (1929), a story by Gina Kaus, a popular feminist writer (and,

incidentally, wife to my great-uncle Josef Zirner), a visit to Horcher is described as a milestone on the path to seduction.

If Horcher was without question the smartest restaurant in Berlin, it owed its international dimension to Hermann Göring. The former airman arrived in Berlin in 1927, hoping to win a seat in the Reichstag. Broke and hungry, he made a beeline for Horcher, where Gustav senior and his son Otto knew the flier from his glory days when he had commanded the JG1—the Richthofen Squadron (postcards were printed of Göring with his *pour le mérite*, Germany's top military distinction, suspended around his neck). Those seated at the future Reichsmarschall's table included such distinguished pilots as Ernst Udet and Bruno Loerzer. Dressy and fond of his food, red wine, and eau de cologne, Göring cut a particularly dashing figure in that crowd. The present Gustav Horcher shrugs his shoulders at the idea, but his grandfather almost certainly extended Göring credit.

Before his arrival in Berlin, however, Göring had known moments of dejection and humiliation. On November 9, 1918, the Kaiser had abdicated at Spa in Belgium and fled into exile in Holland. Two days later the Germans signed an armistice in Compiègne, north of Paris. Revolutions and mutinies had broken out behind the lines, and the German officer's uniform—once the badge of social acceptability in the parvenu German Reich—lost all credibility with the man in the street, who felt that the officers had betrayed him and his country. Those officers who ventured out frequently had their epaulets ripped off, and Göring felt this loss of status acutely. He refused to believe that Germany had been defeated in the field. He crashed his plane into the ground rather than let it fall into the hands of the French.

After the war Göring desperately needed to find a source of income. He represented aeronautical companies but did not make much money doing that. The Reichstag seat, for its part, meant guaranteed income and privileges. Eighth on the list of Nazi Party candidates, Göring was on the way up, so it would have been natural for Gustav Horcher to extend him credit. When Hitler allowed Göring to run in the spring of 1928, Göring celebrated at Horcher, along with Pilli Körner, later a Nazi civil servant; the future field marshal Erhard Milch; and his first wife, Karin. In the event, the Nazis won twelve seats, and Göring was home safe and sound.

Horcher's restaurant suited Göring's plans. Hitler had provided him, the socially acceptable war hero, with a specific brief: to make friends in high places, reassuring the upper classes and the captains of industry that the Nazi Party was made up neither of revolutionaries nor of common thugs, but that it was sufficiently broad-minded to encompass them, too. Göring courted the crown prince and his more susceptible brother, Auwi; he entertained princes, counts, and barons, as well as top industrialists. Much of this wining and dining was done at Horcher.

Gustav Horcher did not need to give Göring credit for long, as money soon came rolling in. In 1932, when the Nazis became the largest party in the Reichstag and Göring was made president of the Reichstag, he finally had a decent salary. On January 30, 1933, the Nazis achieved what had once seemed impossible: power. Adding to his list of portfolios, Göring took over Prussia's top job to become minister president, the prime minister of the federal state that made up three-fifths of Germany.

One of Göring's many offices was as director of the Forschungsamt, or research department, of the air ministry. This position allowed him to tap telephones and read transcripts in the form of *braune Bogen*, or "brown sheets." His manservant, Robert, brought him these papers each morning with his breakfast. Göring's early biographer Willi Frischauer wrote that this was the best moment of the day, for he found out the secrets of his rivals. Occasionally, however, Göring read something about himself that displeased him, such as Ernst Röhm calling him "that pig" and referring to his second wife, the actress Emmy Sonnemann, as "his sow." He would have read other jibes from the left wing of the party. He knew, too, that the party had to make itself *salonfähig*—socially acceptable—if it was to continue to enjoy the support of the middle classes and the army. Göring's response was the Night of the Long Knives on June 30, 1934, during which he suppressed unruly elements on the left and a few on the right. Among the victims were the Strasser brothers, Gregor and Otto (Otto escaped), and the *Sturmabteilung* (storm troopers), as well as General Kurt von Schleicher and leading conservatives such as Edgar Jung and Erich Klausener, who had written a critical speech for the former chancellor, Franz von Papen. Hundreds of people, possibly as many as a thousand, were killed. The Night of the Long Knives was a reminder that Göring could be totally ruthless. He celebrated the success of this evening at Horcher with a meal for his lieutenants, Heinrich Himmler and Werner von Blomberg (the minister of war), and his cronies Milch and "Pilli" (Paul) Körner. They dined on crab.

Von Blomberg was satisfied. The threat from the SA had been nullified: no popular revolutionary force would replace the traditional officer corps. Not all the soldiers were happy, however, and a regime that began in an outpouring of blood continued to shed it by the bucketful in its concentration camps. Certain segments of society began to worry that Hitler's cause was not their own, that his ethics flew in the face of Prussian virtues, and that indeed he had none. Military intelligence—the Abwehr—under the command of Admiral Wilhelm Canaris, also became increasingly distrustful. Matters came to a head when Hitler had the commander in chief, Werner von Fritsch, dismissed on trumped-up charges of homosexuality. The real reason was von Fritsch's reluctance to agree to Hitler's requests to draw up plans to invade Austria and Czechoslovakia.

From that moment the rebellious factions grew in importance. The general staff and the Abwehr, as well as elements within the German foreign office, met every two weeks to discuss the situation and to conspire to remove Hitler. These meetings took place at Horcher. It must have been a curious scene: In one corner, the Duke of Windsor and Mrs. Simpson being entertained by Himmler and Joachim von Ribbentrop (this took place in 1937); in another, Canaris, Ludwig Beck, and Ernst von Weizsäcker, the secretary of state at the foreign office (and father of the recent president), plotting Hitler's overthrow. With his little dog at his feet, Canaris raised his glass: "We drink to our beloved Führer's…," and in a whisper, *"elimination."*[3]

Four years after the Night of the Long Knives, Göring arranged another of the Third Reich's set pieces, the Anschluss, which "connected" Austria to Germany. Göring was no stranger to Austria, as he had been partly brought up there, and after the 1923 Beer Hall Putsch in Munich, it was to Austria that he had fled. Many members of his family lived there, including his anti-Nazi brother, Albert. Hitler followed Göring's troops, stopping at Linz on March 12, 1938, to make his first great speech, crowned by another on the Heldenplatz in Vienna on March 15.

The Nazi takeover of Austria was the cue for Horcher to expand his empire beyond the city limits of Berlin. A series of events allowed him to take over Zu den drei Husaren, the ultrafashionable Hungarian restaurant run by Count Paul Pálffy. Then, as now, the restaurant was in the Weihburggasse, the former carriage drive and stables of the Palais Arnstein-Pereira. The palace had been built on the site of a convent, and the present owner, Uwe Kohl, says the restaurant's thick columns date from the time it was a religious building.

The story goes like this. My great-great-aunt Ella Zirner owned the palace and the department store next door. In 1933 she had rented the space out to three former hussars: Count Paul Pálffy, his uncle Peter Pálffy, and a Baron Sonjok. Sonjok had his hand in the cash drawer, so Paul Pálffy removed him, returned his uncle's investment, and took over the running of the restaurant himself.[4] He furnished the restaurant from his own home with the necessary porcelain, glass, and chandeliers and provided the atmosphere expected from a Hungarian magnate by installing his collection of military prints along with a gypsy band conducted by Béla Berkes. Pálffy still needed efficient management, however, since a man of his station could not be expected to perform that function himself. As it happened, Anna Sacher had just died, and her family sold the famous hotel of that name (where the Sachertorte was born) to the Gürtler family, who brought it down-market. Pálffy was therefore able to hire the entire disgruntled staff of the Sacher hotel, led by the old bar manager, Ignaz Diener.

The Golden Book of Zu den drei Husaren—a guestbook in which distinguished diners could comment on their meals—reveals the sort of customers Pálffy attracted in the early days. There were visits by the British Duke of Windsor ("who scarcely ate anywhere else"),[5] who had reigned briefly as Edward VIII until being forced to abdicate for wanting to marry the American divorcee Wallis Simpson and make her queen. The book's pages are peppered with Liechtensteins and Rothschilds, Hungarian magnates, and the stars of screen and sports. After the Anschluss, however, the Golden Book changes dramatically. On the day the Germans prepared to march, Maria and Friedrich Frankau from Montreal expressed their pride in having been in the restaurant on the big night (their Teutonic name perhaps gives them away): "We both were very happy to have been in Vienna the very day Austria became a part of the greatest country in the world. God be forever with the Austrians."[6] Four days later Hitler was in Vienna, and more-sinister names began to appear in the Golden Book. Some sycophants from the German state railway inscribed the page with a swastika, and Edmund Veesenmayer, the Nazi diplomat who was later responsible for the deportation of Hungary's Jews to Auschwitz, trilled that it was the "loveliest day of his life," adding that there was unfinished business: Germans were calling for help from the Sudetenland across the Czech border.

On March 27 some of Göring's closest friends, World War I fighter pilots Ernst Udet and Ritter von Greim, graced the banquettes of Zu den drei Husaren. There is no trace of Göring himself, who was elsewhere in Vienna at the time. (Udet would later commit suicide after falling out with him. Greim replaced Göring as head of the Luftwaffe and eventually took his life in Allied custody.) More bigwigs follow: storm trooper chief Viktor Lutze on April 3 and Albert Kesselring, later field marshal, two days later.[7]

Pálffy had been, at best, a reluctant restaurateur. When the Nazis arrived, he had no desire to continue; besides, Ignaz Diener was a Jew. In his memoirs Pálffy was pleased to report that he had been able to ship Diener out "with all his possessions, wife, child and piano."[8] Diener went to Britain, where he became the proprietor of a restaurant in Reading called the Green Monkey.[9] Pálffy then went in search of a white knight to take the business off his hands. His membership in the Green Mafia, the international hunting confraternity, proved fortuitous. In 1937, when attending the World Hunting Exhibition in Berlin, he had been invited to a reception at Göring's country house, Karinhall, a few miles east of the city. Göring, too, was fond of the hunt. One of his multitudinous titles was Reichsjägermeister, imperial master of hunts, and he added the Lobau—Lower Austria's famous game park—to his hunting grounds.

Otto Horcher was at Göring's the night Pálffy was there. Since the Nazi takeover, his business had gone from strength to strength. He had a catering company on the outskirts of town and was able to supply food for all of Göring's banquets. It was Horcher, for example, who prepared Göring's feast for the 1936 Olympiad. Because Hitler was a vegetarian who scarcely inspired confidence among gourmand diplomats and heads of state, they went to Göring's if they wanted to eat well. Horcher was in charge of the catering the evening Pálffy visited Karinhall. Dressed in a blue velvet tailcoat, breeches, and white stockings, he stood behind Göring's chair. According to Pálffy, Horcher couldn't take his eyes off Göring. Pálffy paid him a compliment: he had never tasted better food, not even in France.

With Diener safely out of the country, Pálffy called Otto Horcher on March 26 and offered him the restaurant for a pittance. They were two of a kind, after all: they had the best restaurants in Berlin and Vienna. Horcher agreed, and Pálffy retired to his family estate in Slovakia. On April 6, Horcher renewed the restaurant's lease with my Aunt Ella. But in July the laws forbidding Jews from doing business came into force, and Ella was obliged to offer not just the space but the bricks and mortar of the restaurant to Otto Horcher as well. Pálffy never owned the building, but Horcher did.

Göring had delayed his first visit to post-Anschluss Austria until March 26, so he had not yet enjoyed Zu den drei Husaren under new management. He contented himself with a vitriolic speech against the Jews, whose numbers he overestimated at three hundred thousand souls.[10] From his estate in Slovakia, Pálffy heard that his restaurant had sunk to the level of a middling gathering place for Nazi apparatchiks and that a giant bottle of eau de cologne had been set up at the entrance to show what a distinguished place it was.[11] But that was not everyone's experience. According to some surviving Viennese who knew the restaurant at the time, it did not remain a Nazi stronghold for long. Under the management of a certain Herr Heck, Zu den drei Husaren reverted to what it had been: the best place in the city to eat. The kitchen could do wonders for food coupons during the war, turning a simple potato soup into a dream, and there was always game—some of it, perhaps, from the Lobau.[12]

It is not known whether Göring was a frequent visitor, but it is hardly likely that he did not show his face in Otto Horcher's new establishment. After all, Göring liked Austrian food; we have Hitler's word for that. In the first weeks of 1943, following the German defeat at Stalingrad, Hitler ordered extra food to be prepared for a visit by Göring. "They can cook something extra for him: his favourite dish, for example, [Viennese-style] fried chicken [*Backhendl*], and an apple pie for pudding."[13]

The persecution of the Jews reached fever pitch with the Reichskristallnacht on November 9, 1938. Even Zu den drei Husaren was witness to bloodshed when Leon Liebesny, one of Aunt Ella's tenants in the Palais Arnstein, was savagely beaten. He died two days later. Like most of Vienna's Jews, Liebesny had been trying to escape. To that end he had converted to Anglicanism in the former embassy church, in the hope of obtaining a precious visa to Britain or one of her colonies.

Vienna served as the model for the expansion of Horcher's empire. Even before World War II Horcher had been the culinary ambassador for Germany. He catered for the German Pavilion at the 1925 World's Fair in Paris, and until aryanization, his takeover of Zu den drei Husaren had been aboveboard. Legitimate, too, was the concession he took out at 3–5 Burlington Gardens in London's Mayfair, although this London Horcher seems to have flourished for only a few months in 1938.[14] So it is not surprising that, when the Wehrmacht crashed into Paris in 1940, Horcher rolled in behind the tanks and took over the city's most prominent restaurant, Maxim. (Coincidentally, the building housing the restaurant on the rue Royale had once been sacked because of its pro-German leanings. On July 14, 1890, passersby had reacted with their feet and fists when they saw a German flag in the window.) Now, Otto Horcher possessed the best restaurants in Berlin, Vienna, and Paris. He was the culinary czar of the Third Reich.

But the takeover of Maxim was not what it seemed on the surface. Maxim was owned by the Vaudable family. Octave Vaudable had been a friend of the Horcher family from Gustav's time, and every year the Frenchman and the German exchanged wine and schnapps. When the Wehrmacht arrived, Louis Vaudable asked Otto Horcher to manage his place. During the war, therefore, Maxim was protected by Otto Horcher. When the Vaudables returned in 1944, everything had been properly paid for, and their money was in the bank.

Gustav Horcher the younger says his father, Otto, never met Hitler. There was no reason why he should have: the Führer was not interested in food. The relationship between Otto Horcher and Göring was one of mutual back scratching; they were never friends, and Göring always used the formal *Sie* when addressing the restaurateur. People said he had a financial interest in the business, but Göring laughed off the suggestion, saying he was not that versatile. Göring undeniably supported Horcher's business, however. Not only did

Horcher provide food for the Reichsmarschall's many parties, but as the war went on, he set up Luftwaffe clubs, where Göring's fliers were furnished with decent food and drink. There were clubs of this sort in Tallinn and Riga, as well as two others in Oslo that were open to the general public.

In his unpublished memoirs Prince Willy Thurn und Taxis offers a snapshot of the main Horcher restaurant in Oslo, which was actually one of the Luftwaffe clubs. After all princes had been expelled from the German armed forces, Thurn und Taxis spent two days living it up in Oslo: "I always ate in Horcher's restaurant. He was the former owner of the aryanised 'Zu den drei Husaren' in Vienna, who was in Madrid after the war. Herr Horcher greeted me with great joy and issued instructions that I was not to receive a bill."[15]

As long as Germany was successful on all fronts, Otto Horcher's several establishments were able to get around any problems imposed by rationing. Food was brought in from Denmark, while wine was bought in France and paid for in "occupation francs." Göring provided Horcher with caches of drink that he found on his travels. When Otto himself discovered nearly six thousand cases of port, probably thanks to a secret tip, Göring secured the fortified wine for the Luftwaffe—but only after skimming off ten thousand bottles for Horcher and a few cases for himself. German officers had a seemingly unquenchable thirst for champagne, and the Wehrmacht retained a permanent representative in Reims to procure it. Even at Stalingrad some of the last planes to get in were delivering champagne to the stricken officers. Göring ensured that Horcher's cooks and waiters were exempted from military service, and the Reichsmarschall tripled the gas ration for Horcher's trucks.

Such favoritism could not counterbalance the relentless Allied bombing of Germany, however. It was only a matter of time before Horcher was bombed out of his restaurant in central Berlin. The restaurant moved to a cozy villa on a sand ridge above the Havel Lake in Wannsee, between Berlin and Potsdam.[16] After February 1943 the Russian advance could hardly be contained. Gauleiter Joseph Goebbels's answer was to declare "total war"—*la guerre à l'outrance*—imitating Danton's answer to the threat posed to revolutionary France in 1792. This declaration afforded the Gauleiter the opportunity for an added pleasure: shutting down the frivolous luxury restaurants that upset his more austere ideology.

Horcher headed the list. Hans-Georg von Studnitz, the gourmand press secretary at the foreign office, was eating at another restaurant a few days after Goebbels's announcement. The waiter asked him, "Will the Russians grind to a halt if we close Horcher's?"[17] Göring was furious with Goebbels: during a forty-five-minute harangue on the telephone, he informed the Gauleiter that he would reopen Horcher as a Luftwaffe club. Goebbels responded with one of the "spontaneous demonstrations" he had stage-managed on Reichskristallnacht: one of the restaurant's windows was smashed. When the Nazi thugs returned the next day to cause further damage, however, they were thwarted by a Luftwaffe picket.

Horcher was stuck in the middle. Göring won a stay of execution, and the restaurant limped on, but by the autumn of 1943, it was clear that there was no place for grand restaurants in bombed-out Berlin. The last of Berlin's luxury restaurants—Quartier Latin, Neva Grill, Pelzer's Atelier, and the Tuskulum in the Kurfürstendam—had closed. Studnitz recorded their demise: "Although the more recherché dishes have long since disappeared from their menus, these restaurants have nevertheless remained a refuge and an oasis, thanks to the elegance of their appointments and the excellence of their service." He praised the "occasional coupon-free piece of game or poultry" and the wine cellars, which had not been plundered to the degree that they had been elsewhere.[18] Although it remained open, Horcher had changed: the classy old clientele had been replaced by officials, above all from the air ministry and the aircraft industry, and a few diplomats and intimates of the general director of the ministry. Procuring a table took an entire day. Otto Horcher remained active; he was also in demand for all state functions. He had a bevy of waiters at his command, as well as the use of the New Palace in Potsdam. "As the favourite chef [sic] of Hermann Göring, Horcher has risen to become the foremost restaurateur of the Third Reich," noted Studnitz.[19]

When aristocratic diarist and intimate of the July 20 Plotters Princess Missie Wassiltchikov went looking for Horcher in January 1944, she found the villa boarded up. The Horchers themselves had vanished. Gustav Horcher tells the story as he heard it from his father: Otto had gone to see the Reichsmarschall, but Göring had told him that he could do nothing for him in Berlin. Otto had another idea. He wanted to move his premises to another place, where it would be safe from Anglo-American bombs. Göring agreed. He provided a train and a safe conduct pass. During the first week of November 1943, the chefs, managers, waiters, and entire batterie de cuisine of the seven Horcher establishments left Germany together. Two weeks later, on November 18, Horcher opened in Retiro in Madrid. It has been there ever since.

Madrid was a tabula rasa. The civil war had only recently ended. There were tascas, where you might eat an olla, and a few grand hotels, but Horcher was the city's first formal restaurant. Initially, Otto Horcher had too much staff. The Berlin chef, Puccini, had taken over the kitchen. There was a superabundance of headwaiters, all treading on one another's egos. The managers Heck (from Vienna) and Hirschfeld (from Berlin) jostled for power. Eventually, Dubois (who had worked at both) left to start another branch of Horcher in Lisbon, but it was not a success.

When the war ended, it was natural that well-groomed Germans resident in or passing through Madrid should pay their respects to Otto Horcher. After all, they had known him in his glory days. An exile community gathered in Madrid and in Marbella around Prince Alfonso zu Hohenlohe.[20] There were not only bad Germans but good ones, too. With no extradition treaty between Germany and Spain, however, many ex-Nazis prospered, like spy chief Walter Schellenberg. The daredevil Otto Skorzeny, who had liberated Mussolini and stormed the Bendlerstrasse army headquarters in Berlin on the night of July 20, 1944, was frequently in Horcher. He was in business selling tungsten to Scandinavia, while claiming to head the Odessa Organization, which took Nazis to safety in South America.[21] Gustav is wary of people who mention Skorzeny, although he remembers seeing him in the restaurant. Although Skorzeny's memoirs refer to Horcher, they are riddled with errors.

According to Gustav, Otto Horcher did not actually sell Zu den drei Husaren until 1950, when it became the property of Baron Egon Fodermayer. Between 1945 and 1950, it had

served as a private restaurant for Karl Renner, first chancellor of the second Austrian republic and president from December 1945; the negotiations that led to Austria's first postwar government are said to have taken place there. By 1947 the Zirners had effected the restitution of half their estate: they got Modehaus Zwieback department store back, but not the Palais Arnstein-Pereira. Why the Horchers were able to retain Zu den drei Husaren—an aryanized windfall—is not easy to explain (or excuse). A letter from Pálffy to Ignaz Diener dated May 30, 1948, shows that the original owner was also hoping to get his restaurant back—despite the fact that he had *sold* it to Horcher.[22]

The Madrid Horcher rapidly became a mirror of what it had been in Berlin: frequented by grandees as well as the political upper crust of Franco's Spain. An English journalist eating there in the late 1940s found it filled with government ministers and businessmen trading with Germany. Horcher told him that he got the very best produce—his fruit and vegetables, it seemed, came from the royal gardens at Aranjuez,[23] where the Horchers later opened a small restaurant that was patronized by Juan Carlos and other members of the Spanish royal family. Once again, Horcher enjoyed protection from the highest strata of society. When Franco died in 1975, the country underwent momentous change, and Horcher's cachet declined. Otto Horcher died in Marbella the next year. When Gustav Horcher took over the reins of the restaurants in Marbella and Madrid, he was to cater to a new Spain.

Above: Horcher's restaurant in Madrid. PHOTOGRAPH BY DANIEL ZARZA © 2006

Although no one draws attention to it, Horcher remains a very German restaurant, and Gustav Horcher has remained faithful to the dishes that brought the restaurant fame: smoked eel with horseradish sauce, potato salad with Pommery mustard and a poached egg, lentil soup with frankfurters, *Kartoffelpuffer, Wiener Schnitzel*, and goulash. These dishes are not at all Spanish. The restaurant still specializes in game and uses a silver-plated duck press that was once the pride of the Berlin restaurant. When I ate in the restaurant with Gustav Horcher, he recommended a pancake called *Sir Holden* that he knew had been on the menu in Berlin in the 1920s. Also carried over from Berlin are the Meissen figurines and the Prussian military prints. At the bottom of the left-hand page of the Horcher menu today, obscured by the Spanish words *pollo de grano a la Vienesa*, is none other than *Backhendl*, the Viennese version of fried chicken—although Horcher's recipe is clearly much more than that. The inclusion of Göring's favorite dish on the menu is an unwitting tribute to the man who protected the Horchers as long as he could.

Gustav Horcher would obviously prefer to forget his father's association with Göring. It would be absurd to imply that Göring was harmless, a John Falstaff of the Third Reich. He could be as brutal as any of the Nazis. For Göring, however, there were always exceptions, instances where the law might be bent a little. The line "I decide who's a Jew" is often attributed—falsely—to Göring, who was capable of protecting a Jew when it suited him. He believed in an Austrian idea of a *Freundlwirtschaft*, an economy of half nepotism, half jobs for the people he liked. He chose to think of himself as a decent guy, even when he was nothing of the kind.

Himmler and Goebbels took a different view of the Jewish problem. Both failed priests, they were fanatical in their ideological commitment to National Socialism. Goebbels stuck to his guns, and as Germany's situation became ever more dire, his mettle increased. He was with Hitler to the end, taking his own life and that of his wife and six children in the bunker in Berlin.

At the end of February 1945, Goebbels fulminated against Göring, the Reichsjägermeister who had hunted bison while Berlin burned. He was "no National Socialist, but a sybarite."[24] It was Goebbels who encouraged Hitler to arrest his fat friend in the last hours of the Third Reich, using the example of Frederick the Great, who had relieved his brother of his command. Göring and Goebbels represented the same two schools as Danton and Robespierre. Here was a conflict of ideology that reveals the heterodoxy of National Socialism. Brutality they may have had in common, but thanks to Horcher, you ate better *bei* Göring. ◉

NOTES

This article is based on two interviews with Gustav Horcher conducted in Madrid on February 10 and 11, 2005. The fruit of the interviews was *The Reichsmarschall's Table*, produced by Dennis Sewell and first broadcast on BBC Radio 4 on March 14, 2005. My first attempt to unravel the Horcher story, "Grand Restaurant with a Past," was published in the *Financial Times*, January 30, 1992.

1. Giles MacDonogh, *The Last Kaiser, William the Impetuous* (London: Weidenfeld & Nicolson, 2000), 377.

2. Quoted in Giles MacDonogh, *Berlin* (London: Sinclair-Stevenson, 1997), 286–287.

3. Josef Müller, *Bis zur letzten Konsequenz—Ein Leben für Frieden und Freiheit* (Munich: Süddeutscher Verlag, 1975), 120.

4. Paul Graf Pálffy von Erdöd, *Abschied von Vorgestern und Gestern* (Stuttgart: Schuler, 1961), 209.

5. Ibid., 210.

6. The Golden Book is in the possession of Uwe Kohl, present owner of Zu den drei Husaren.

7. Ibid.

8. Pálffy, *Abschied*, 210.

9. It was very probably Diener, who in 1948 cooked for the cast of *The Third Man*, which was largely filmed at Shepperton, some twenty minutes from Reading. Information from Brigitte Timmermann, who organizes the successful Third Man walks in Vienna.

10. There were around 160,000 members of the Kultusgemeinde, but nonreligious Jews may have accounted for half again as many.

11. Pálffy, *Abschied*, 211.

12. Interview with Hans von Kienast, Vienna, 2 February 2005.

13. Henrik Eberle and Matthias Uhl, eds., *Das Buch Hitler* (Bergisch Gladbach: n.p., 2005), 188; translated by Giles MacDonogh as *The Hitler Book: The Secret Dossier Prepared for Stalin from the Interrogations of Hitler's Personal Aides* (New York: PublicAffairs, 2005).

14. The restaurant was in the Bristol Hotel, 33 Old Burlington Street and 3–5 Burlington Gardens. It appears in the telephone books for 1938 but not for 1939. Horcher was presumably also the proprietor of Horcher's Wines & Spirits in Old Bond Street, which survived only as long as the restaurant.

15. Prince Willy Thurn und Taxis, unpublished memoirs, 8, in the possession of HSH Daria Maria Gabriele Princess von Thurn und Taxis, Munich.

16. Ian Goodhope Colvin, *Canaris, Chief of Intelligence* (Maidstone: Mann, 1973), 150–151.

17. Hans-Georg von Studnitz, *Als Berlin brannte* (Bergisch Gladbach: Bastei-Lübbe, 1985), 21; translated by R.H. Stevens as *While Berlin Burns: The Diary of Hans-Georg von Studnitz, 1943–1945* (Englewood Cliffs, NJ: Prentice-Hall, 1965).

18. Ibid.

19. Ibid., 10–11.

20. Marbella had also started out as a colony for dispossessed central European aristocrats after the war; the impetus had come from Alfonso zu Hohenlohe, and Bismarcks and Metternichs were among the first residents. One of the Kaiser's great-granddaughters still lives there.

21. Christopher Moorsom, unpublished memoirs, 14, in the possession of Lord Norreys, Sorn, Scotland.

22. Pálffy had been told that the government would look favorably on his suit because he had been consistently anti-Nazi. Although he had been offered the chance to re-create Zu den drei Husaren in New York, he told Diener that he would not consider taking up the offer unless Diener consented to be his partner. Letter in the possession of Uwe Kohl.

23. Moorsom, memoirs, 15.

24. Joseph Goebbels, *Tagebücher 1945: Die letzten Aufzeichnungen* (Hamburg: Hoffmann und Campe, 1977), 55.

Winter 2007, volume 7, number 1

elisabeth townsend |

The Cooking Ape
An Interview with Richard Wrangham

PRIMATOLOGIST RICHARD WRANGHAM might be best known for the 1996 book he coauthored with writer Dale Peterson, *Demonic Males: Apes and the Origins of Human Violence*, where he used his research on intergroup aggression in chimpanzees to reflect on combative male behavior. Wrangham's twenty-five years of research have always been based on a deep interest in human evolution and behavior, and recently he's shifted his focus to the evolution of cooking in humans.

An anthropology professor at Harvard University, Wrangham, fifty-six, was first mesmerized by Africa when he spent a year working in Kafue National Park in western Zambia before going to college. There he assisted a research biologist in studying the behavior and ecology of the waterbuck, falling "in love with the excitement of finding out about African habitats and species." He's been back to Africa every year since then, with only one exception—the year when his first son was born.

That first year in Kafue determined Wrangham's course of study at Oxford University and in his life. After Oxford, when his plans to study Ugandan mongooses fell through, his advisor suggested he contact Jane Goodall about working with her and the chimpanzees in Gombe National Park in Tanzania. As her research assistant, he spent a year recording the behavior of eight siblings, choosing one each day to observe. Later Wrangham returned to Gombe to do his doctoral research on the behavioral ecology of chimpanzees, and he has continued to collaborate with Goodall.

Eventually, using money from a MacArthur Foundation fellowship, he launched his own chimpanzee study in Kibale, Uganda, where it took six years to get the chimpanzees habituated enough to get good observations. At Kibale, spending from two to seven months a year with his six Ugandan field assistants and several graduate students, he has focused on both chimpanzee behavior and the way their behavior has been affected by the exploitation of the environment—from finding food and escaping from predators to forming social relationships. He has also analyzed how their social organization has evolved, especially female social relationships and aggressive male behavior.

Though Wrangham has made his reputation explaining the similarities and differences across species in primate social organizations, he expects that his work on cooking will have the broadest impact because cooking affects many human behaviors—such as those associated with food choice, familial relationships, and food production that can satisfy a huge world population. His favorite part of the day is when he can steal an hour from teaching to

analyze chimp data or to work on his book *The Cooking Ape*. But Wrangham is happiest at his Ugandan research site, enjoying those quiet moments alone with the chimps, watching their relationships and catching up on the social gossip. He hasn't eaten a mammal since 1976 because of his profound empathy for the ones he has enjoyed and spent so much time with in the wild. Occasionally, his vegetarianism makes life a bit harder, as when a host offers him meat, but he'll never turn down seconds on a chocolate roulade. Wrangham spoke from his home in Weston, Massachusetts.

Elisabeth Townsend: *What prompted your research into how cooking affected human evolution?*

Richard Wrangham: As a primatologist, I am often asked to think about human evolution. I sat one evening in my living room preparing a lecture for the next day, thinking about the standard story that involved hunting being important around two million years ago. As I was staring at the fire, I had an almost ghostly experience where I just allowed my eyes to be drawn deep into the fire. I could feel around me the presence of hominids, from up to one million years ago, sitting in the African bush.

I started thinking about the fact that fire is something that has been on the Earth ever since there's been plant vegetation and how when I'm in the bush there is no way that I'm going to spend a night without sitting next to a fire. I was thinking about the impact of fire on the "cookability" of food.

Above: Richard Wrangham. PHOTOGRAPH BY JIM HARRISON

Then I thought, "Well, would there really have been a fire for our early ancestors—a million years ago, say?"

I realized I didn't know the answer to the question. But I also realized that it was extremely difficult to imagine that they did not have cooking, because even as long as 1,500,000 years ago humans looked incredibly similar from the neck down to humans living today. Even our heads are very similar—though we have larger brains and we don't have quite as big a mouth or teeth as they did. So surely, if those million-year-old ancestors were generally like us in the size and shape of their bodies, they should have been eating cooked food. After all, cooking has this huge impact. It changes so much about how we relate to the natural environment: it changes the ease with which we digest the food; it changes the availability of calories; and it changes the distribution of food.

If cooking has such a big evolutionary impact, in other words, and we haven't changed much, then there are only two possibilities. Either we somehow managed to adopt cooking without it affecting us very much, which would be very mysterious, or it happened so early that cooking had already been adopted by a million years ago.

ET: *What's an example of how changes in the food supply affected primates and how that led you to think cooking had a significant impact on humans?*

RW: If you compare chimpanzees to gorillas, they eat very similar things. They both like to eat fruits when fruits are available. They both eat more leaves and stems when there aren't many fruits available. But there's one relatively small difference: when there's a shortage of fruit, gorillas will switch entirely to eating leaves and stems, whereas chimpanzees absolutely insist on finding their daily ration of fruits before they go bulk up on leaves and stems. That's why gorillas can live entirely without fruit—in the mountains of Uganda, for instance—whereas we don't know of any place where chimpanzees can live entirely without access to fruit.

That small difference in food supply between chimps and gorillas can account for the fact that the gorillas are three to four times the body size of chimpanzees and that they live in more-stable groups. Therefore, gorillas have an entirely different set of sexual relationships, with males being enormously bigger than females, and so on. This is just one example where a relatively small difference in the food supply creates a big difference in the way that two species look and behave. And to shift from eating raw food to eating cooked food is a much bigger change!

ET: *How did cooking change calorie intake and thus the human species?*

RW: Amazingly, we still don't have a good picture of the most important ways in which cooking changes food. There are different effects on plant foods and meat, though. One impact on plant foods is probably to increase digestibility. That means that our food has a relatively low proportion of indigestible material; in modern surveys you see that 10 percent or less of what we eat is indigestible plant material (fiber, in other words). Whereas in chimpanzees, for instance, fiber is over 30 percent, which therefore seems a reasonable guess for what it might have been like in our raw-food-eating ancestors. Well, if we ate 30 percent fiber, compared with 10 percent now, that 20 percent of the food our ancestors were eating was just bulk material passing through the gut. So, they simply absorbed less energy.

That 20 percent figure is a lot. When we compare the actual rate of energy expenditure in human foragers, which is between 1.5 and 2.2 times the basal metabolic rate, as compared with 1.4 times for chimpanzees, we're getting a lot of extra energy from somewhere compared to the chimpanzees. Where are we getting it from? I think it's because the food that humans are eating is more digestible. Instead of spending all day with our guts holding a high proportion of indigestible material, we're able to have a higher continuous stream of calories going through our guts.

What's the result? Maybe it explains why humans used so much energy, starting around 1.9 million years ago. First, that's when we got our bigger body, made by the greater amount of energy. Second, it means that we can have a relatively large proportion of expensive organs, such as brains (they're expensive in the sense of using calories at a particularly high rate). For a long time people have been interested in the notion that, since the brain is unusually expensive, our ancestors needed to have some way of getting more energy in order to afford having a bigger brain. At 1.9 million years ago, you have arguably the largest increase in brain size in evolution. Third, there's the opportunity for longer travel distance per day because you just got more energy to put into traveling. Chimpanzees are quite long-distance travelers at 2.5, 3, 4, 5 kilometers a day, but humans, males in particular, are traveling 9, 10, 15, 20 kilometers a day—a lot more than chimps.

This extra energy probably comes from the fact that, as a result of cooking, we're able to eat a relatively compact food that is full of calories. And then at the same time, of course, the food has become softer, and that enables us to have smaller teeth and smaller jaws, a flatter face, and less prognathous jaws. At the same time we, in fact, have smaller guts and a shift in the arrangement of our guts that reflects the fact that we're eating food that is relatively highly digestible. So we have long small intestines, the part of the gut that absorbs the products of digestion, and we have short large intestines, where fermentation goes on when you retain food that takes twenty-four hours or more to be fermented under the action of bacteria. We have relatively little food that comes in that needs to be fermented. All of these changes are easily explained by the adoption of cooking.

ET: *How much did our brains and bodies change as a result of eating cooked food?*

RW: The standard estimate is that female bodies increased in weight by about 60 percent around the 1.9-million-year mark. So, if you compare the body size of about 125 pounds for an average woman with the average range of 70 to 80 pounds for a chimp, it's really quite a big increase. And the brain size is going up....It might be 60 percent.

ET: *You've said that cooking and meat eating are the only two proposals for what transformed the ape into a human. Why couldn't the changes just be from eating more raw meat rather than cooking?*

RW: We don't know too much about what it's like to chew raw meat because people don't do it. But chimpanzees are a good model because they have teeth that are just about the same size in relation to their bodies as those of our early ancestors 1.9 million years ago. When we look at chimpanzees eating raw meat, it turns out that they're eating it so slowly that it would just take a tremendous amount of time to rely on eating nothing but raw meat. And that would be a problem.

Think about how many calories our early ancestors would have needed at that stage, estimated at somewhere in the low 2000s. This would take five to six hours a day of simply chewing *without* going out and finding more meat, cutting it up, and looking after your babies and so on. And they would have had to develop some kind of tooth arrangement that was sharp and enabled them to chop it up quickly and swallow it in the manner of a carnivore.

It just seems very unlikely that, at any time since 1.9 million years ago, our ancestors were chewing for half the day, because animals that chew a lot have got deep jaws and robust bones in the mouth to accommodate the stresses of the chewing. That's not what you see—our ancestors' jaws have been built relatively lightly ever since 1.9 million years ago. So, it's not that I think that meat is unimportant; it probably was eaten a lot. It's just that to become important it had to be tenderized to allow it to be eaten easily. The tenderizing could have begun in a physical way by someone hammering it with stones, maybe, but cooking would have solved the problem much more efficiently.

ET: *When did humans learn how to master fire and then use it for cooking?*

RW: No one knows for sure. But there is such good evidence from caves in southern Europe that humans controlled fire by 400,000 years ago that essentially everyone accepts that fire was controlled by then. So the conservative view is that we started our control of fire then. The 800,000-year date recently published by Goren-Inbar and colleagues in *Science* (April 2004) is perhaps the best evidence yet for an earlier date for fire. It's particularly nice support for the notion that control of fire must have started before we can see it, because around 800,000 years ago even less happened in human evolution than at 500,000 years ago. People rarely lived in caves before 400,000 years ago, so the remains of earlier campfires can't easily be found. But the more radical view, which seems right to me, is that bits and pieces of archeological evidence for control of fire at earlier dates, all the way back to 1.9 million years ago, are right. In other words, I believe our species started to control fire at 1.9 million years ago.

Then, the question is, what's the relationship between control of fire and cooking? Some people imagine a period when our ancestors had fire but ate raw food. But, once we had control of fire, I think that we would have started cooking very soon, maybe within a week, maybe within ten generations—but waiting 1,000 or 10,000 or 100,000 years? It's unthinkable. Modern primates, such as monkeys in captivity, allow foods to cook in fires before they take them out. It's obviously just not a big cognitive step from controlling fire to cooking.

So, if humans were cooking by 800,000 years ago, it seems likely that they had been cooking since 1.9 million years ago, because that's when our modern frame evolved. Basically nothing happened in human evolution between 1.9 million years ago and 800,000 years ago to suggest any improvement in the diet—certainly nothing as radical as being able to shift from raw to cooked food.

ET: *Who was the first cook?*

RW: It was not fully human. It was one of these prehuman hominids around the 2-million-years-ago mark, living somewhere in Africa, perhaps an australopithecine or a species like *Homo ergaster* [an early form of *Homo erectus*].

Whenever cooking evolved, we've got this problem of how on earth the first cook managed to solve the problem of getting to use fire and controlling it rather than running away from it.

One fantasy that I enjoy is the notion that there was something like the chimera that we now see in western Turkey. In western Turkey you've got a mountain, Mount Olympus, where there are several holes in the ground, quite small, just a foot or two across, with fire coming out of them. This fire has been going for at least 2,700 years, judging by the fact that Homer recorded its presence.

To call it permanent fire is too exaggerated, perhaps, but it's said that an earthquake was a cause of some release of gas that's been seeping out ever since then and that has been burning all that time. There are several places around the world where you get little patches of permanent fire burning like this. So it doesn't seem unreasonable to imagine that there was some permanent fire in Africa somewhere.

We know that chimpanzees can learn to be happy with fire. Kanzi is a captive bonobo (pygmy chimpanzee) who goes for walks with Sue Savage-Rumbaugh in the forests of Georgia (United States). When she asks him to go get firewood and to use matches to light a fire and then to cook up some sausages, he does so. These things are not that difficult for a species as big-brained as a chimpanzee.

So, it's relatively easy to imagine an australopithecine who keeps coming back, sees these flames roaring out of the ground, and starts playing with them. Then it wouldn't be long before they see what happens to one of the roots they have been eating when it is heated by the fire. That may not be the way it happened, but at least it gives a sense of the possibility of the transition. You don't have to be fully human, I think, to imagine that you could tame fire. So, if indeed you were prehuman and started being able to use fire, then that knowledge could be passed on from generation to generation in the many, many years before these species would have actually been able to make fire.

ET: *How do you imagine they were cooking?*

RW: The cooking would have been very, very simple. Once you've got a campfire, then it's the way that people cook nowadays. In the bush the main plant food would be roots— African versions of carrots or potatoes often dug from the edge of swamps or lakes. Many would be tough and leathery, pretty nasty in the best of times, but improved enormously by being heated. You'd just rest these on the coals next to the dying flames. After twenty minutes and occasional turning, the roots change from something that is extremely fibrous into something that is a lot softer and easier to eat.

Very often the way that people eat meat is they throw a small animal on the flames and that singes the hair off. Then they cut it up. We know that at 1.9 million years they were capable of cutting meat up because there are cut marks [made by stone knives] on fossil animal bones that go back 2.5 million years. So they could have laid strips of meat onto sticks above the fire. Well, maybe it would have taken a little time before that happened. But it doesn't seem very difficult if they had already been cutting up meat for 500,000 years to imagine that they could put small chunks on the embers next to the fire or next to the flames themselves. And all you need to do is heat meat to 170 Fahrenheit, and it reduces enormously the problems that make meat so difficult to eat when it's raw, which is the toughness. Heat coagulates the collagen fibers that make meat tough and turns them brittle. Suddenly, you've got something that you can eat pretty quickly.

ET: *How did humans make the transition from cooking over an outdoor fire to hearths and then to earth ovens?*

RW: No one knows. I imagine that the way things started is that the first kind of controlled fire would be simply sticks on the flat earth. Then at some point you'd start digging a little pit and you might surround it with some stones that would protect it against the wind a little bit further, and maybe other ways I don't know about making the fire more efficient.

An earth oven is a little hole that has been dug in the ground. Hot stones are put into the hole, and the food that you want to cook is put in with those hot stones. Then you stop the hole with earth, and the heat from the stones combined with the moisture of the earth leads to a sort of steaming effect, and you get a rather nice, gentle, slow cooking. That's practiced nowadays in various parts of the world, such as New Guinea and India.

There are other complicated kinds of hearth arrangements in sites in southern Europe, for instance in France in Pech de l'Azé II, that go back 250,000 to 300,000 years. At the entrance you have one kind of hearth arrangement, rings of stones where probably there was some kind of lighting arrangement to scare off predators from coming into the cave. And then inside the cave, in addition to something like an earth oven, there was apparently a cooking area more than a yard across, indicated by flat stones whose red and black colors indicate repeated burning.

But to assume that earth ovens start very quickly seems to me to be an unnecessarily optimistic assumption. Earth ovens look like a pretty complicated kind of technical achievement. I had assumed that this was just a signal that cooking had been going on so long at that point that they had been able to devise various rather ingenious ways of making cooked food even nicer.

ET: *Did humans start cooking to be able to defrost frozen raw meat?*

RW: According to Loring Brace, a physical anthropologist from Michigan who has been the main person suggesting that cooking was important in human evolution, the reason that cooking was adopted was to defrost meat. He said this because the early earth oven sites in southern Europe in the 300,000- to 400,000-year range were made at a time when the glacial ice sheets from the Arctic were covering Europe. So, his notion was that we needed to be able to have fire in order to defrost hunks of frozen meat. But it was defrosting, nothing more than that. I suppose even Brace would allow that, once you start defrosting it, then you would probably go all the way to cooking it, but it was defrosting that he emphasized.

ET: *Why is cooking often considered unimportant in human evolutionary biology?*

RW: There are several reasons. One is that there is just an implicit and sometimes explicit assumption that cooking was late. This is a result of the Balkanization of our field, because once you look at the archeological evidence from about 400,000 years ago, it's very difficult to imagine cooking was late. And yet you have a great expert like Katherine Milton, a leader in the field studying primate and human nutrition and the evolution of the digestive system, who says she assumes that cooking happened too late to have had the opportunity to have any biological effect—that would have meant we invented cooking less than 10,000 years ago!

After all, we know that biological effects happen within a few thousand years. The lactose tolerance example is one that speaks directly to the diet. We know from archeological evidence that people have not been herding cattle and therefore drinking milk of other species for more than about 8,000 years. In the areas where adults do drink milk, they've got a very high, say 95 percent, proportion of genes that make them tolerant of the lactose in the milk. It means there's been very rapid selection for this specific phenomenon. So the question in my mind is, "If cooking was adopted, was it adopted in such a short time that it wouldn't have had a chance to make us dependent upon it in the way that people who now drink milk are able to do so as a result of their biological adaptations?"

So, that's when you go for the really secure archeological evidence: we *know* that 20,000 years ago people were eating things that they could not have eaten unless they were cooked because you can see evidence in the fossilized feces. And if you look at the archeological sites back to 60,000 years ago, you've got people with *huge* piles of thousands of bones, many of which are burned in a pattern that is exactly the same as you find in extremely recent sites from hunter-gatherers in North America just 500 years ago. So, this is strong evidence that people were cooking in an essentially modern manner as far back as 60,000 years ago.

Well, this is enough time for three species to evolve in turn. Evolution is not that slow a process. There would have been plenty of time for cooking to have had major effects on our biology, if in fact it had been adopted as recently as 60,000 years ago. But as we've seen, we've controlled fire for much longer than that.

ET: *So there is more evidence of humans cooking earlier than most anthropologists would agree to?*

RW: Yes, my strong sense is that people just haven't put the evidence together. In addition to the long history of control of fire and the lack of any recent correlated change in our jaws and teeth, there's the question of whether cooking is an option or a necessity. You often find people accepting the notion that cooking was adopted without having a big effect on us. Okay, theoretically that's true. But in practice it's a tough argument to make.

Cooking would have dramatically changed our ability to take calories from the environment, so it would completely increase the rate at which we can use energy. It would completely change our food distribution and therefore change our social system.

So it just revolutionizes our relationship to the natural world. Simply to say, "Oh, by the way, we started cooking at some point," and then not say it didn't do anything to our bodies and social relationships is to ignore a very important question. How could we start cooking and not be changed by it? I think there's a clear answer. We couldn't do it. Any animal that learns to cook becomes a new kind of animal. So cooking didn't start during one of these phases when humans were just doing the same thing and not changing their frame. It started *way* back and it changed everything.

ET: *How did cooking affect the social structure?*

RW: I think the social structure is a *really* interesting question because this is in many ways the biggest gap in the way anybody has thought about cooking so far. Everyone's aware that cooking would have improved the quality of the food, so it's not that big a deal to think about it affecting our energy and our teeth and so on. But there's been amazingly little thought given to this question of what cooking did to social structure.

My colleagues and I made the following argument in a paper that we wrote in 1999 proposing that cooking lay at the base of human evolution: The huge problem that cooking presents is that it changes a species from feeding as it picks the food to forcing a species to keep its food for some time, which will be at least twenty minutes to probably several hours during the period when it is gathering it and going to cook it. That means for a period of time there is individual ownership, and once you have ownership, then there is the possibility of competition over those owned goods.

In other words, just as with any other animal where somebody gets a piece of food that is relatively valuable, others will try to pinch it. Female lions bring down the antelope; the male lion comes and takes it away. The low-ranking male chimp kills a monkey; the high-ranking chimp comes and takes it away. The female baboon digs for some roots; the male baboon watches, and just as she reaches to get the results of her labor, he says, "I'll take over, thank you." And in a similar way it seems impossible to imagine that when our ancestors first started cooking there wasn't pressure by which the hungry high-ranking individuals would not have taken advantage of the low-ranking individuals who had done all the hard work to get some meat or dig up the roots and get it cooked. And that problem seems to me to be really severe. We need to think about how we solved it.

ET: *How do you suppose humans solved this problem?*

RW: The human species is the only one, in all of the animals we know, in which there is a thing we call "sexual division of labor." I think it is a slight misnomer because it underestimates the extent to which there is a bias in favor of the male. It implies that the male and female are equal, doing equally well under the sexual division of labor. But women are always the ones that get to do the least favorite tasks, and women are the ones who predictably have to take responsibility for producing a meal in the evening.

Men are free to do what they want. A man can go off every day and hunt for three weeks and never get anything, and still he's going to get food, given to him by his wife in the form of a cooked meal when he returns in the evening. But if a woman goes off and tries to dig for food and never gets anything, she's in big trouble. A man knows that he can rely on a woman to produce food for him. A woman has nobody to rely on; she has to do it for herself.

So a woman is more like a chimpanzee, as it were: she is producing for herself, and then she has the problem of somebody who's taking some food away from her. A man is an entirely new species of animal, because a man is relying on others to feed him every evening. Now it's true that he will often produce foods that he will give to his wife, and the relationship can be beneficial. But some men don't. Some men are lousy producers, and they are still able to take advantage of the system. The problem is not so much why men and women divided and then cooperated. We should be asking this question instead: "Why is it that men are able to get away without having to be responsible for their own food supply?"

ET: *Why aren't men responsible for their own food supply?*

RW: I put these two observations together: on the one hand, there's the fact that you know that there's going to be pressure to steal the food of low-ranking individuals. On the other hand, there's the fact that only in our species is there a sex that doesn't have to collect their own food every day. Among hunters and gatherers, men are able to get away with not feeding themselves. The solution is that males have developed a relationship with females in which they protect a female's food supply from everybody else in the community. And in exchange, she feeds him.

The way I imagine it working in the past was something like this. Around the ancient campfire you have females getting their own food. Then you find males who are coming back in the evening, having been unsuccessful in hunting or getting any other food. Maybe they were off chasing other women instead of trying to find honey. So now they've got nothing to eat, and they bully a female into giving them some of her food.

And that kind of social pressure creates a situation in which it pays every female to develop a friendly relationship with a male who will protect her from being bullied by a whole herd of males. Better to have one male to protect your food supply and predictably feed him, if he can keep everybody else off, than be a lone female who is exposed to the possibility of theft from many other individuals. The male is an effective protector of her food supply because he's part of a system of respect among males. In a sense, he pays other males to stay away because he's part of a food-getting system in which whenever he does get food, he shares it on a predictably culturally agreed equal basis with other males. So, all the males are in an arrangement whereby they agree not to interfere with each other, and the female is in a relationship with the male whereby he agrees to keep all the other males off. It seems to make sense.

ET: *How has cooking affected human life history—how fast we grow, for instance?*

RW: These are areas that still haven't been well explored. But of course one of the most dramatic things about human life history is the fact that we have children that are dependent. This is different from chimpanzees, for instance, where the infants are weaned at about the three- to five-year stage and then they're independent. The only way chimpanzees feed each other is through nursing.

Whereas with humans, the child is being fed until it's an early adolescent. Children make some contribution to the domestic work and food gathering and so on, but nevertheless, the net flow of energy is definitely from the parent to the child, not just until weaning but all the time until at least 10 to 12 years old. So, childhood (a period of economic dependency beyond weaning) is normally regarded as a special human feature.

And childhood is made possible by cooking, because a species that cooks can easily overproduce. A chimpanzee that spends six hours collecting and chewing her own food doesn't have time to collect extra food to give to her children. But a foraging woman can collect and cook enough food to feed her family. Instead of spending six hours a day eating, she spends only about one hour eating. That leaves enough time to gather and cook for others.

Then, earlier in the life span, for at least 20,000 years, babies have been given cooked mush so they can abandon nursing very early. The result is that the mother has less energetic strain on her body, so she's able to a have a relatively quick interbirth interval of three to four years, whereas in chimpanzees it's more like five to six years. That is presumably because even though the women still have children with them, they're able to feed them by cooking and still get enough food themselves to return to a high rate of ovulation.

So, cooking gives us big families—dependent children, produced relatively quickly.

ET: *What effect does cooking have on the human mortality rate?*

RW: Well, it's very interesting that humans have a very low rate of mortality. If you compare humans and chimps, at every age humans are dying more slowly than chimpanzees. This is not because of predation, because most of the chimp populations have not been subject to predation. It's just something inherent about their bodies. The implication is that the immune system or other systems of defense are less effective in chimps than they are in humans. I don't want to suggest that this is well known, but I think it's an interesting speculation. Part of what's happening as humans are able to acquire more energy as a result of cooking and eating superior food may be that they're able to divert a proportion of that energy into the kinds of defenses that enable us to live a long time.

ET: *If cooking evolved as a women's task primarily, why are the majority of professional chefs men?*

RW: I'm sure cooking is biological in many senses, such as the fact that we have adapted to need cooked food. But it's clearly not biological in the sense of being a cooking instinct. It's not that women automatically just moved to a fire and said, "I want to cook, I've just got this inner feeling that makes me want to cook." Actually, it's the opposite probably; most women would probably *prefer* to have the man cook.

We know perfectly well that men can cook in all sorts of circumstances. If there are ceremonial foods, they cook; if there are communal foods to be prepared, they cook; if they are bachelors who have some kind of rule that means they can't have contact with women for years at a time, in some societies, even in hunter-gatherer societies, they cook. If it pays in terms of profession, again, then they cook. I think the existence of professional chefs just reminds us that the reason that women cook is essentially because of the unfairness of the sexual division of labor. It's not because cooking comes in an automatic package with childcare and nursing. It's because the social arrangement fits women and men best, but it particularly fits men.

ET: *Is it possible for humans today to live on raw food alone?*

RW: Many people would still dispute whether there really is an answer. I've become convinced that all of the little subtle references that you get about the notion that people can live by raw food alone are in fact fictional conjectures. When I talk about subtle references, I'm thinking about *The Lord of the Flies*, where William Golding's boatload full of boys are on an island and are surviving quite happily by finding and eating raw fruit. It is as if, through that sort of cultural reference, we get the idea that this isn't a problem. "Yeah, sure, we can eat raw food if we want." But I have found no cases at all of people surviving on raw food in an ordinary world. Even the most prolonged cases of eating raw food are extremely unusual. One example is the Tartar or Mongol warriors of Genghis Khan who could live for up to ten or eleven days at a time by drinking just the blood of their horses before they stopped and with great gratitude had a cooked meal.

ET: *Why can't humans live on only raw food now?*

RW: Well, actually, people in industrial society who choose to eat raw food can survive pretty well. But even so, we're so badly adapted to eating raw food that if you study these urban people who by choice live on it, you find that many of them end up underweight. There's a German study by Corinna Koebnick and colleagues from 1999 in which 25 percent of the women were chronically undernourished as a result of living on raw food. These are women who live under the very best conditions: they don't have to take much exercise compared to the very hard physical work of being a forager; they're eating foods that have been domestically selected for thousands of years and are therefore relatively low in fiber and high in soluble carbohydrates, so it's high-energy food; the foods have even been extensively processed, such as by sprouting, drying, and pressing; and they're eating food that is available at high quality all year, in contrast to the inevitable food-poor seasons in the wild where people always starve and lose weight even under the conditions of cooking.

That alone makes it very difficult to see how people could survive on raw food in the wild, where people would have hard physical labor and their foods would be tough, high fiber, and low energy. But then you add the fact that in the Koebnick study 50 percent of the women who were eating 100 percent raw food were completely amenorrheic. They had no reproductive activity at all. Another high proportion, perhaps 25 percent or more, would have been severely subfecund; so this means that even under ideal conditions a raw-food diet is not producing sufficient surplus energy to be able to maintain an effective reproductive system. So that says to me that humans are just not adapted to eating raw food. What exactly that means in terms of our failure to be adapted is not clear, but it probably means that our guts are now too small to allow us to survive on raw food, and too high a proportion of the gut is devoted to absorption rather than fermentation. The most important conclusion, however, is that we know remarkably little about the constraints on our digestive system.

ET: *Are there problems with humans today eating too much or only meat?*

RW: Nowadays, people can eat a tremendous amount of meat because there's a lot of fat to go with it. But if you're eating meat from the wild, which has very little fat and is mostly protein, then there is a problem with getting rid of the urea that is produced by digestion of excess protein. Urea poisoning can result. So too much meat can definitely be bad for you.

Of course, people in rich countries eat too much of everything. Indeed, the irony is that although cooked food has been so important for human evolution, raw food might be one of the healthiest diets for today. A raw-food diet is possible in rich countries today because of our low level of physical activity, the high agricultural quality of foods that go into a modern raw-food diet, and the extensive processing that makes raw foods palatable and easily digested. Even so, it takes a tremendous amount of determination to stick to a raw-food diet, because you'll feel hungry so much of the time. If you can do it, however, you'll bring your caloric intake nicely down, and maybe you'll have the philosophical satisfaction of imagining what the lives of our prehuman ancestors were like in those distant days before cooking was invented. ◉

Winter 2005, volume 5, number 1

h.e. chehabi |

How Caviar Turned Out to Be *Halal*

WHEN THE SHIITE CLERGY acquired control over the Iranian state in 1979, they found themselves in a position where, in addition to enunciating the prescriptions of divine law (*shari'a*), they also had to supervise the actual enforcement by the state of the religious injunctions it comprises. Islamic law contains detailed rules about food, drink, and culinary etiquette,[1] and although the actual practice of Muslim societies has never fully conformed to these rules,[2] the obvious importance of food and drink in the daily lives of people confers upon religious dietary laws a subjective importance for Muslims that helps define the boundaries of their community.[3] An Islamic state, as defined by modern-day Islamists, must therefore be a state in which Islam's dietary laws are legally enforced.

The Koran explicitly forbids the consumption of only three things: pork, alcohol, and carrion. The consumption of pork and alcohol was indeed outlawed soon after the revolution of 1979, there being no need to prohibit carrion since Iranians are not particularly fond of it. Caviar, however, posed a delicate problem. Shiite jurisprudence considered it *haram* (forbidden), but since its production and export were a state monopoly, caviar procured the Iranian treasury millions of dollars in revenue. Trading in what is forbidden being equally forbidden under the *shari'a*, the Islamic Republic faced the alternative of either reneging on its promise of applying divine law or depriving itself of valuable export earnings. Moreover, caviar is the epitome of luxury and culinary refinement in Western culture,[4] which alone must have rendered it suspect in the eyes of the populists who took power soon after the revolution. To find a way out of this dilemma, the status of caviar under religious law was revisited. At the end of a laborious process involving both clerics and fisheries experts, the traditional ruling was reversed, and caviar was declared *halal* (permitted).

Seafood in Muslim Dietary Law

The various juridical schools of Islam differ on which animals Muslims are allowed to eat. As a general rule, Hanbali, Shafi'i, and Maliki Sunnis are more liberal, with Malikis being the most liberal of all. Hanafi Sunnis (who constitute over half of all Sunnis) and Shiites are more restrictive, with Twelver Shiites (the main branch of Shiism, dominant in Iran and Iraq) being the most restrictive of all.[5]

Regarding seafood, the three liberal Sunni schools permit all aquatic animals, often justifying this by reference to Koran 5:96: "Permitted to you is the catch of the sea and the

food of it." Hanafi Sunnis and Ibadis (the third branch of Islam, adherents of which live mainly in Oman) permit all fish but no other aquatic animals. Shiites as a rule consider only fish with scales to be *halal*, and they are guided in this by the traditions of the Imams.[6] Fish without scales were already singled out as unfit for sacrifice to the gods by Numa, Rome's legendary second king,[7] but the Shiite prohibition of nonsquamous fish is more probably related to the injunctions contained in Leviticus 11:9–12, where we read: "Of the various creatures that live in the water, you may eat the following: whatever in the seas or in river waters has both fins and scales you may eat. But of the various creatures that crawl or swim in the water, whether in the sea or in the rivers, all those that lack either fins or scales are loathsome for you, and you shall treat them as loathsome. Their flesh you shall not eat, and their dead bodies you shall loathe. Every water creature that lacks fins or scales is loathsome to you."[8]

For contemporary Twelver Shiites the standard law text where this ruling is explained is the *Lum'a*, written in the fourteenth century by a scholar known as the First Martyr (Shahid al-Awwal). In its chapter on food and drink, "Kitab al-at'ima wa l-ashriba," fish and roe are actually considered at the very beginning, before land animals. The first rule concerns fish: "Among sea animals, a fish that has scales is permitted, even if its scales have fallen off, like the *kan'at*....Nor are turtles, frogs, crabs, and other sea animals permitted. And a fish that feeds on impurities is not permitted, unless it is cleansed by feeding it clean food in the water for a day and a night."[9]

The one nonichthyic water creature allowed by Twelver Shiism is shrimp, which in Iran is eaten mixed with rice (*meygu-polo*), in an herb stew with cilantro and fenugreek (*qallieh meygu*), or salted and dried as a snack.[10] The licitness of shrimp derives, depending on the sources, from its being considered either fish or fowl. The first classification appears in a number of recent and contemporary Shiite "manuals of practice" for the faithful, which base themselves on an old eastern Arabic convention that knew shrimp as *samak al-irbiyan* (Irbiyan fish).[11] Another, probably related, account has it that a man from Basra took a shrimp to the Sixth Imam, Ja'far al-Sadiq, and asked him to rule on its status. The Imam responded that it was a kind of fish, asking the man: "Do you not see how it wiggles in its *qishr*?"[12] The Arabic word *qishr* denotes an outer cover or husk, and in an aquatic animal this, by implication, qualifies as fish scales, the usual word for which is *fals* (usually pronounced "fils"). The second line of reasoning uses a syllogism. It posits that the shrimp is an aquatic locust and argues that since the locust is a bird, the shrimp can also be considered a bird, rendering it *halal*.[13] Spelled out laconically in a self-help manual for Muslim travelers to the lands of the infidels, this demonstration invites ridicule, but it should be remembered that it is premised on the isomorphist theory, which is attested in classical sources and rests on the idea that aquatic and terrestrial animals can be paired off and that an aquatic animal is *halal* if its terrestrial counterpart is.[14] This bodes ill for the sturgeon, the most prized

Left: Fresh out of the warehouse, the tins are opened at a small tasting session for the few exporters authorized to sell Iranian caviar. PHOTOGRAPH © F. RAEVENS / THEREPORTAGE.COM

variety of which is called *sag-mahi* (dog-fish)[15] in Persian, although it is more commonly known by its Turkish name *ozun borun* (long nose).

Sturgeon and Caviar

Caviar is the roe of sturgeons, fish belonging to the order of Acipenseriformes, which comprises more than two dozen species.[16] Sturgeon was once the dominant large fish in every major river system on all three continents of the temperate northern hemisphere, but its range has been reduced by overfishing, and many species are now extinct.[17] In the Caspian Sea the sturgeon is still found in large (but rapidly declining) numbers, and in Iranian waters three species have been fished: the beluga, the Russian (or Persian), and the stellate sturgeon, called in Persian *fil-mahi*, *tas-mahi*, and *sag-mahi* (*ozun borun*), respectively.[18]

According to the *Lum'a*, as far as permissibility is concerned, "the eggs of the fish follow the fish itself. And if there is suspicion, the hard eggs should be eaten, not the soft."[19] This means we have to ascertain whether sturgeon have scales or not. Acipenseridae is such an ancient family that even the modern species within it have been traced as far back as the Upper Cretaceous, 100 million years ago.[20] For this and other reasons, naturalists have had difficulty placing sturgeon on the fish family tree. For the purposes of this article, suffice it to note that according to taxonomists "it has few scales, and these are not round and thin like a salmon's, but rhomboid, with peg-like extensions overlapped by the adjoining scale."[21] The technical term for these lozenge-shaped bony scales is *ganoid*. Do they render a fish *halal*? Since Shiites, as we saw earlier, follow the Levitic code in matters of seafood, one place to start looking for an answer is Jewish dietary laws. In one guide to these, we read: "'Scales' are defined as ones that can be scraped from the skin without tearing the skin from the flesh. These are cycloid (round) and ctenoid (comblike) scales. Other types of scales such as placoid and ganoid (platelike, armorlike) are embedded in the skin, and it is necessary to remove some of the skin or flesh in order to remove them….The lumpfish, sturgeon, sharks, swordfish, and some of the turbots (European flatfish) are examples of fishes with types of scales that are not of the kosher variety."[22] But the subject apparently lends itself to ambiguity in the Jewish tradition as well, for in a different book we read: "Bony tubercules and plate or thorn-like scales that can be removed only by removing part of the skin are not considered scales in this context. Some fish that have such scales, such as eels, lumpfish, shark, sturgeon, and swordfish, are not kosher. Only the eggs of kosher fish, such as fish roe or caviar, are allowed."[23]

Assuming that observant Shiites had a close look at the sturgeon in the centuries before the Iranian revolution, the answer seems to be that, like Jews, they did not consider ganoid scales to be *fals* in the religious sense. Traditionally, the sturgeon was considered *haram*, as was its roe. This suited the Russians, who began exploiting Iranian fisheries in the Caspian Sea in the middle of the nineteenth century (the Iranian government granted concessions to both the Russian [1876] and Soviet [1927] governments). Article 3 of the 1927 agreement established different regimes for *halal* and *haram* fish and explicitly placed sturgeon in the latter category. The Soviets were entitled to all the *haram* fish caught in Iranian waters,

and any *haram* fish caught by local fishermen had to be sold to them at prices the Soviets determined. By contrast, local fishermen could keep the *halal* fish they netted but were free to sell it to the Soviets.[24]

By the mid-1950s only 10 percent of Iran's fish and caviar production remained in Iran, the rest being taken home by the Soviets on terms that were quite unfavorable to Iran. And so when the 1927 agreement expired, the government of Mohammad Mossadegh did not renew it and in fact nationalized Iranian fisheries in the Caspian Sea.[25] To exploit these fisheries, the government established a state-owned company, the Shilat company. But for the time being, two-thirds of the company's sturgeon catch and half of its caviar production were still being exported to the Soviet Union.[26] Gradually, the words *mahi khaviari* (caviar fish) came to be used for sturgeon, perhaps to distract from the fact that the Iranian state was now dealing in *haram* fish.

Very little of Iran's sturgeon and caviar production was actually consumed in Iran. This was not only because of its being *haram* and a big earner of foreign currency but also because the inhabitants of Iran's noncoastal regions have little taste for seafood in general, especially if it tastes like fish. Caviar was thus an acquired taste for the happy few who could afford it, its acquisition hugely facilitated by its being a status symbol much appreciated by sophisticated Western palates. None of the many Iranian cookbooks, for instance, include any recipes using caviar.

Even in the Caspian province of Gilan, whose inhabitants are generally more open-minded and whose culinary culture differs greatly from the rest of Iran's,[27] the various dishes incorporating roe (*eshpil/ashbal*) use mostly the roe of *mahi sefid*, a kind of surmullet.[28] Some

Above: With a certain degree of solemnity the sturgeon is carried to the laboratory for preparation. PHOTOGRAPH © F. RAEVENS/
THEREPORTAGE.COM

locals considered the sturgeon a rare delicacy and deemed it an exception to the rule that only fish with scales could be eaten, arguing that if the Prophet had known how delicious it was, he would have allowed it.[29] But the vast majority of the population considered it *haram*. In the mid-1960s, for instance, an Irish traveler who had managed to find a black marketeer in Bandar Anzali to grill a sturgeon for him observed that "pieces of fish were portioned out among ourselves and the boys, but the women refused it on the ground that it was unclean."[30] In Tehran an Armenian-owned restaurant on Ferdowsi Square in the capital's central business district, Leon's, was famous for its *ozun borun* kebab among foreign residents, local Christians, and Muslims who were not "*halal*-fussy," to use a South African term.

On Iran's southern shores Sunnis (and, one suspects, quite a number of Shiites) eat such delicacies as octopus and shark,[31] and the postrevolutionary state has, to the best of my knowledge, made no effort to prevent that. But sturgeon and caviar were different: they constituted a state monopoly now exercised by an Islamic state, and besides, the Iranian constitution in its article 12 guarantees Iran's Sunnis application of their own *fiqh* in areas where they predominate.

Khomeini's 1983 Ruling

After the revolution, production of caviar continued, but much of it was stored at the state-owned warehouse, with some of it being sold illegally on the black market, much to the delight of the few foreign and domestic gourmets who remained in the country. After the ouster of President Abolhasan Banisadr in June 1981, the fundamentalists consolidated their rule over the state, and from then on, all policies had to conform to the *shari'a*. Caviar had netted Iran millions in export earnings before the revolution, and the loss would be keenly felt. Shilat officials therefore decided to ask the clergy to give a ruling on whether sturgeon was *halal* or not. The Shiite clergy had traditionally shied away from giving such precise rulings, preferring to state the general rule ("only fish with scales can be eaten") and leaving the actual application of the rule to a specific case ("the sturgeon has scales") to the individual believer. But upon taking control of the state, they in fact assumed legislative powers since the very *raison d'être* of the Islamic Republic was to bring state policy in line with the religious injunctions the clergy knew best. Under these new conditions, general rules were no longer sufficient, and the clerics had to make concrete statements that would inform policy: the exact status of sturgeon and caviar was now an affair of state.

On September 27, 1981, one specimen of each of the three varieties of sturgeon was taken to Khomeini's office in Qom (the center of the Shiite clergy of Iran), and Shilat officials asked that it be made clear whether the three fish could be consumed inside Iran.[32] There, on September 28, four clerics, Ja'far Karimi, Azari Qomi, Rasti Kashani, and Abtahi, had a close look at the fish and found that near the tail as well as "under and near"[33] the fins they had an extra covering in the form of appendages, which, they concluded, was sufficient proof that the sturgeon had scales,[34] there being no a priori geometric form that extra coverings of fish must have in order to qualify as "scales."[35] Upon being informed that there was no impediment to fishing for these three types of sturgeon and trading in them, Khomeini was asked for a *fatwa*, and he wrote: "If it has scales, even if it is in the region of the tail, it is *halal*."[36] On May 12, Shilat officials wrote letters to experts and asked them to give their scientific views on the matter. The collected views were then sent to Sadeq Ehsanbakhsh, Khomeini's representative for Gilan province and leader of Friday prayers in Gilan's capital, Rasht, to whom the matter was referred by both Khomeini and Grand Ayatollah Golpayegani. Proceedings were slowed down somewhat when an assassination attempt injured Ehsanbakhsh, but after his convalescence he convened a seminar to finalize the new policy. On February 5, 1983, clerics from Qom, Tehran, and the two Caspian provinces of Gilan and Mazandaran, as well as university professors, fishermen, and representatives of the local population, met in Bandar Anzali, the main port city of Gilan, and "most of the brothers present" gave written testimony that the fish had scales.[37] The minutes of the seminar and the individual testimonies of the fisheries experts were shown to Khomeini, who was again asked for a *fatwa*. Below the request he wrote: "On the matter of the fishes in question, the views of trustworthy experts are valid, and should be acted upon."[38] A new document was now prepared, containing the *fatwa* and the individual testimonies, and this was made public by Ehsanbakhsh. On September 5, radio and television reported the news, as did newspapers on September 6.

Between the convening of the seminar in Bandar Anzali and the final declaration about the permissibility of eating sturgeon and caviar, the work of the experts and clerics came under repeated attack by traditionalists.[39] It was to defuse this criticism, no doubt, that officials also bothered to ask Grand Ayatollah Golpayegani, the most conservative of those traditional clerical leaders who maintained friendly relations with the revolutionary regime, for a *fatwa*. He, too, opined that the issue of whether a fish has scales should be determined by two just experts.[40] Outside Iran the ruling must have seemed doubtful to some, for a request for a *fatwa* was addressed to Khomeini in Arabic, asking explicitly whether caviar was permissible or not. Khomeini's response had a hint of ambiguity, perhaps a forward defense to forestall future contestation: "If it comes from a fish with scales, or if there is uncertainty whether it is from a fish with scales or *from a fish without scales*, it is permitted. Otherwise, it is not."[41]

The *fatwa*s notwithstanding, the new state policy was ascribed to economic necessity alone and spawned the following joke: A man dies and enters Hell. There he sees that a group of Hell's denizens are leaving, suitcases in hand. He asks about them and is told that these are people who had eaten caviar. After a while he comes across another group of people, and this time they have packed their suitcases but are not going anywhere. When he inquires about them, he is told that these are people who had drunk vodka with their caviar.

It was perhaps in response to reactions like these that the newspaper of the Revolutionary Guards, published in Qom, took the trouble of explaining the genesis of the new ruling. In an initial article the events that led to it were chronicled, and the prohibition of sturgeon and caviar was ascribed to a Russian conspiracy aimed at depriving Iranians of an important food source.[42] In two subsequent articles Ja'far Karimi, a scholar who had returned to Iran from Najaf with Khomeini and who, in his capacity as a member of Khomeini's *fatwa* office in Qom, had taken part in the consultations, explained the genesis of the ruling in jurisprudential terms. Quoting classical authors, he demonstrated in the first article that only fish with scales were permitted.[43] In the second article he quoted from the Imams themselves to prove that, first, scales did not have to cover the entire body of the fish and that, second, they need not have a particular shape.[44] He ended his demonstration with a "warning to compatriots":

> At this point I have to issue a warning to [my] dear compatriots: they might unwittingly be fooled by the enemies of the Islamic Republic of Iran and say: "How come this fish that was *haram* until now has now become *halal*?!" It is not that something was *haram* in the past and has now become *halal*, but [the fact is] that since until now no research had been done on these fishes, perhaps because there was no need to do so, we were fooled by the Russians, who wanted to keep this God-given delicacy for themselves without us benefiting from it. They told us: "It is *haram*! Do not go near it!" Now that we have thought of doing some research ourselves, we know that there is no reason to deem this *halal* fish *haram*.
>
> If you brethren have determined that these fishes have scales, you will naturally conclude that they are permitted. And if you cannot determine the matter yourselves, you have to defer to two just experts who know the criteria of Islam, and act according to their testimony. Did you know that if at your own discretion you render *haram* [what] God [has made] *halal*, you have sinned?[45] Therefore, do not unwittingly echo the enemies of Islam by saying: "How come the Islamic Republic made *halal* what God declared *haram*!!" The Islamic Republic has come to revive the tradition of the Prophet of God, P.B.U.H., and to rescue people from ignorance.
>
> I thank those brethren who have gone to a lot of trouble on the matter of caviar fish, for they have rendered a great service to the economy of Iran and to our beloved nation....May God grant success to all those who serve Islam and the Islamic nation.[46]

After Khomeini's *fatwa* caviar consumption inside Iran took off dramatically.[47] The breakup of the Soviet Union in 1991 had a nefarious effect on sturgeon fisheries in the Caspian Sea. Poachers overtook legitimate fishermen, catching ever smaller fish, and the catch went down so much that by the late 1990s Iran had overtaken Russia as the world's largest caviar producer, its hatcheries being more modern and efficient than those of the Soviet successor states.[48] But fish stock have continued to dwindle, and in September 2005 the United States Fish and Wildlife Service announced that it would ban the import of caviar from the Caspian region, as the sturgeon is faced with extinction.[49] A few months later the Convention on International Trade in Endangered Species announced a ban as well.[50]

While the decision to declare sturgeon to be a *halal* fish broke with tradition, this break was not as cynical as critics of the Iranian theocracy made it out to be at the time. Although admittedly motivated by practical considerations, the reasoning was precise and honest, and the final conclusion that ganoid scales meet the criteria laid out for *fals* represents a legitimate use of the power of *ijtihad*, i.e., interpreting (and, if necessary, updating) Islamic law, claimed by the Twelver Shiite clergy. Unless, of course, somewhere in the collection of traditions from the Imams there lurks one to the effect that to qualify as *fals*, scales must be detachable from the fish's flesh without tearing bits of it out, which is not for me to determine. Be that as it may, it would seem that, in a theocracy, necessity is the mother of, if not invention, then at least *ijtihad*. ☉

NOTES

I would like to thank Shademan Akhavan, Guive Mirfendereski, and Hossein Modarresi for their help.

1. *Encyclopaedia of Islam*, 2nd ed., s.v. "g̲h̲id̲h̲ā" and "k̲h̲amr." See also Mohammed Hocine Benkheira, *Islâm et interdits alimentaires: Juguler l'animalité* (Paris: Presses Universitaires de France, 2000).

2. See, for instance, Rudi Matthee, *The Pursuit of Pleasure: Drugs and Stimulants in Iranian History, 1500–1900* (Princeton, NJ: Princeton University Press, 2005), 37–96, for the consumption of wine in Safavid Iran.

3. The power of dietary practices to help define communities is of course not specific to Muslims. Already in Leviticus 20:26, we read that God had separated the Jews from other nations by instituting their dietary laws. See the various articles in *Identité alimentaire et alterité culturelle* (Neuchâtel: Institut d'Ethnologie, 1985).

4. Cf. Grant Richards's immortal novel *Caviare* (Boston: Houghton Mifflin Company, 1912), whose hero "would sit by the hour and discuss wines and salads and dishes with famous maîtres d'hôtel," on which occasions he "sometimes…would capture the rare feeling that he was not living in vain" (p.5).

5. See Michael Cook, "Early Islamic Dietary Law," *Jerusalem Studies in Arabic and Islam* 7 (1986), especially the table on p.259. As Philippe Gignoux has pointed out, Shiite prohibitions are very similar to those of pre-Islamic Zoroastrian Iranians. See his "Dietary Laws in Pre-Islamic and Post-Sasanian Iran: A Comparative Survey," *Jerusalem Studies in Arabic and Islam* 17 (1994): 30–31.

6. Ibid., 237–240. Cf. Benkheira, *Islâm et interdits alimentaires*, 68–73.

7. Pliny the Elder, *Historia Naturalis*, 32.9.

8. Cf. Deuteronomy 14:9–10, whose wording is almost identical. For a study of the relationship between Jewish and Muslim dietary laws, see Brannon Wheeler, "Food of the Book or Food of Israel? Israelite and Jewish Food Laws in the Muslim Exegesis of Quran 3:93," *Food & Judaism*, Leonard J. Greenspoon, Ronald A. Simkins, and Gerald Shapiro, eds. (Omaha, NE: Creighton University Press, 2005), 281–296.

9. Shaykh Abi Abdallah Shams al-Din Muhammad ibn Jamal al-Din Makki al-Amili, "Shahid-e Avval," *Tarjomeh-ye Lom'eh-ye Dameshqiyyeh*, Ali Shirvani, trans. (Tehran: Dar al-Fikr, 1996), 2:180. The Persian translation explains that the *kan'at* is a fish that rubs against sand, thus losing its scales.

10. The intriguing question of whether that other delicious crustacean, the lobster, sometimes called *shah-meygu* (king-shrimp) in Persian, can also be fit into one of the two Procrustean categories and hence be considered *halal* has, to the best of my knowledge, not yet been settled.

11. See, for instance, Abu l'Hasan al-Isfahani (d. 1946), W*asila al-najat* (Qom, 1385 AHL), 2:180; Ruhollah Khomeini, *Tahrir al-wasila* (Najaf, 1387 AHL), 2:55–156; and Ayatollah Sistani, *Minhaj al-salihin* (Beirut, 1996), 2:291.

12. *Wasa'il al-Shi'a*, vol. 16, ch. 12, as quoted in Ayatollah Seyyed Ja'far Karimi, "Tahqiqi darbareh-ye mahiyan-e khaviari," *Pasdar-e Eslam*, no. 28 (Farvardin 1363/Jamadi II 1404), 17.

13. Mohammad-Hosein Fallahzadeh, *Ahkam-e feqhi dar safarha-ye khareji* (Qom: Nashr-e Ma'ruf, 1378/1999), 117. For the avian nature of locusts, the author refers the reader to Imam Khomeini's *Towzih al-masa'el* (problem no. 2622), which does indeed pronounce locusts to be *halal* but nowhere mentions birds. In the *Lum'a* cited in endnote 9, we read, however, that a locust is permitted only if its wings have developed sufficiently so that it can fly (p.178). This, incidentally, is congruent with the Levitic code, which states (11:21–22): "But of the various winged insects that walk on all fours you may eat those that have joined legs for leaping on the ground; hence of these you may eat the following: the various kinds of locusts, the various kinds of grasshoppers, the various kinds of katydid, and the various kinds of crickets." For recipes see Julieta Ramos-Elorduy, *Creepy Crawly Cuisine: The Gourmet Guide to Edible Insects* (South Paris, ME: Park Street Press, 1998); and Peter Menzel and Faith D'Aluisio, *Man Eating Bugs: The Art and Science of Eating Bugs* (Berkeley, CA: Ten Speed Press, 1998).

14. Cook, "Early Islamic Dietary Law," 238, 242–245. As the author notes, however, "isomorphism was not adopted systematically by any classical law-school, and attestations of it are accordingly fragmentary" (p.238).

15. What is called *dogfish* in English is actually a small shark and is unrelated to the sturgeon.

16. Inga Saffron, *Caviar: The Strange History and Uncertain Future of the World's Most Coveted Delicacy* (New York: Broadway Books, 2002), 32.

17. Richard Adams Carey, *The Philosopher Fish: Sturgeon, Caviar, and the Geography of Desire* (New York: Counterpoint, 2005), 3.

18. *Encyclopaedia Iranica*, s.v. "caviar," 99. For a photo showing specimens of all three lying next to each other, see Axel von Graefe, *Iran: Das neue Persien* (Berlin: Atlantis-Verlag, 1937), 31.

19. See note 9. "Soft eggs" probably refers to soft roe or milt, the semen of male fish. Islamic jurisprudence is not alone in juxtaposing roe and milt. See Wilhelm Eilers, "Kaviar: Eine Wortstudie," *Iñānamuktāvalī Commemoration Volume in Honour of Johannes Nobel*, Claus Vogel, ed. (New Delhi: International Academy of Indian Culture, 1959), 51–54.

20. Carey, *The Philosopher Fish*, 3.

21. Ibid., 6.

22. Rabbi Yacov Lipschutz, *Kashruth: A Comprehensive Background and Reference Guide to the Principles of Kashruth* (Brooklyn, NY: Mesorah Publications, 1988), 47–48. For further conditions that scales must meet, see Rabbi Binyomin Forst, *Kashrus: A Comprehensive Exposition of Their Underlying Concepts and Applications* (Brooklyn, NY: Mesorah Publications, 1993), 39.

23. Rabbi E. Eidlitz, *Is It Kosher? Encyclopedia of Kosher Foods Facts & Fallacies* (Jerusalem: Feldheim Publishers, 1992), 154.

24. Guive Mirfendereski, *A Diplomatic History of the Caspian: Treaties, Diaries, and Other Stories* (New York: Palgrave, 2001), 125–128.

25. For details see Wolfgang Lentz, "Der iranische Fischfang im Kaspischen Meer," *Zeitschrift für Geopolitik* 24 (1953): no. 3, 171–172; Mirfendereski, *A Diplomatic History*, 158–159; and *Dar'erat al-Ma'aref-e farsi*, s.v. "Shilat."

26. Mirfendereski, *A Diplomatic History*, 171.

27. Christian Bromberger, "Eating Habits and Cultural Boundaries in Northern Iran," *Culinary Cultures of the Middle East*, Sami Zubaida and Richard Tapper, eds. (London: I.B. Tauris, 1994), 185–204.

28. See *Encyclopaedia Iranica*, s.v. "caviar," 101, for recipes.

29. Poopak Taati (a native of Rasht), e-mail message to the author, 18 January 2006.

30. Peter Somerville-Large, *Caviar Coast* (London: Robert Hale, 1968), 143.

31. Personal observation of the author, Bandar Abbas and Qeshm Island, January 2004.

32. "Tahqiqi darbareh-ye mahiyan-e khaviari," *Pasdar-e Eslam*, no. 26 (Bahman 1362/Rabi' II 1404), 65.

33. Cf. the Jewish dietary code, which states that "a species of fish that develops only one scale must have this scale located near the jaw, fin, or tail." Lipschutz, *Kashruth*, 48–49.

34. Ayatollah Seyyed Ja'far Karimi, "Tahqiqi darbareh-ye mahiyan-e khaviari," *Pasdar-e Eslam*, no. 28 (Farvardin 1363/Jamadi II 1404), 18–19.

35. Ayatollah Seyyed Ja'far Karimi, "Tahqiqi darbareh-ye mahiyan-e khaviari," *Pasdar-e Eslam*, no. 27 (Esfand 1362/Jamadi I 1404), 22. The section is titled *Dar fels, shekl-e hendesi-ye khassi mo'tabar nist*, meaning "for scales, no specific geometric form is mandated."

36. "Tahqiqi darbareh-ye mahiyan-e khaviari," *Pasdar-e Eslam*, no. 26 (Bahman 1362/Rabi' II 1404), 65.

37. These are reproduced in ibid., 67.

38. *Keyhan*, no. 11,959, 6 September 1983, 18.

39. "Tahqiqi darbareh-ye mahiyan-e khaviari," *Pasdar-e Eslam*, no. 26, 66.

40. *Keyhan*, no. 11,959, 6 September 1983, 18.

41. *Estefta'at az mahzar-e marja'-e taqlid-e jahan-e tashayyo', za'im-e howzehha-ye elmiyyeh, Hazrat-e Ayat Allah al-Ozma Emam Khomeini*, vol. 2 (3rd printing; Qom: Daftar-e Entesharat-e Eslami, 1375/1996), 504. Emphasis added. Unfortunately, the *fatwa* is not dated.

42. See note 34.

43. Ayatollah Seyyed Ja'far Karimi, "Tahqiqi darbareh-ye mahiyan-e khaviari," *Pasdar-e Eslam*, no. 27 (Esfand 1362/Jamadi I 1404), 20–23.

44. Ayatollah Seyyed Ja'far Karimi, "Tahqiqi darbareh-ye mahiyan-e khaviari," *Pasdar-e Eslam*, no. 28 (Farvardin 1363/Jamadi II 1404), 16–19.

45. A reference to Koran 5:87, 6:119, and 16:115.

46. Karimi, "Tahqiqi," no. 28, 19.

47. See *Encyclopaedia Iranica*, s.v. "caviar," 100, for numbers.

48. Saffron, *Caviar*, 138.

49. Felicity Barringer and Florence Fabricant, "In Conservation Effort, US Bans Caspian Beluga Caviar," *New York Times*, 30 September 2005. On 2 January 2007, however, the Convention on International Trade in Endangered Species (CITES) lifted its year-old embargo on the caviar trade and said that it would allow ninety-six tons of caviar to be sold in 2007.

50. "Conserving Caviar," *Economist*, 7 January 2006, 72.

Spring 2007, volume 7, number 2

andrew chan |

"La grande bouffe"

Cooking Shows as Pornography

TV COOKING SHOWS TODAY ARE, in a word, pornography.

As in the contemporary pornographic film industry, the modern TV cooking programs appeal to our hidden or perverse side. They seduce us to desire the virtual, while complicating our relationship to what is real (or desired). Media outlets such as the Food Network cable TV channel provide special insight into the perversity of contemporary American culture, yet the genealogy reaches further back, as brilliantly visualized in Marco Ferreri's 1973 film *La grande bouffe*, in which four men eat, screw, and fart themselves to death.

Today's TV cooking shows arouse our senses not only through the material shown but in the way it is presented. Food preparation is a form of foreplay in which the ritual of cooking is announced with sensory cues: the sizzle of oil in the frying pan, pots bubbling away, the crescendo of chopping, dicing, and slicing. The chef starts building the viewer's expectations and hunger by his cleaving, stirring, and whisking—every gesture, raised eyebrow, and licked lip a sign of what is to come.

The idealization of cooking is subtly evident in the surreally colored foods, anatomically perfect chickens, and super-sized "vertical" displays of cooking shows, comparable to the cosmetically altered, human sex-toy actors in porno films. Contemporary TV cooking shows create a gap that separates the viewer from the reality of actual cookery. This gap is evident in the setting itself, an environment far removed from the real goings-on of either a professional restaurant kitchen or the everyday domestic kitchen of the viewers. In the TV program's fantasy kitchen there is copious space and ventilation; there are also no dishes to wash, no mounds of trash to throw out, and no impatient waiters checking on orders. Everything has been carefully planned and prepared beforehand to appear spontaneous and effortless on-camera. Everything has also been meticulously edited and orchestrated, often to the strains of classical music, so that the master chef and his happy minions can sauté and garnish to the melodies of Vivaldi or Mozart.

Yet these programs only tease us, since the complete steps involved in cooking have been omitted, just as the bedroom scenes in post–Hays Code films only hint at intercourse.[1] The viewer is left to imagine what has transpired between scenes—or commercial breaks—after which the chef and/or host can be seen *à table*, metaphorical cigarette in hand, the detritus of a partially consumed meal strewn on the table like tousled bedsheets. We are physically unable to taste the meal the host presents to us; thus, for us, the relationship between the chef's exertions on the program and the resulting by-product is never consummated. We are always left wanting more, so there is a reason to tune in again.

If television audiences really knew what went on in kitchens during the preparation of food, would they be so receptive to the allure of the visual representation of a recipe? If they saw the pig being slaughtered and butchered prior to the making of the stuffed pork loins, or the fresh lobsters being drawn and quartered, then—claws still twitching—boiled alive, would they be as enticed by the televised demonstration of the meal? Classic cookery often involves every part of the animal—the entrails, hoofs, tongue, liver, tail, brain, heart—so that nothing is wasted. Indeed, the more aesthetically ugly, the more challenging to beautify. Hence, by its nature, the cooking program is deceptive, because the primary nature of food is disguised or excised.

And the same goes with real life: our sense of reality is always sustained by a minimum of disidentification. Thus the viewer is not only spared the real-life, violent aspects of food prep-aration, but also cheated of the full extent of the work and the physical exertions required to accomplish the results. Often, these shows are edited so that the viewer sees a simplified process, which then cuts to the chef pulling out an already-cooked version of the same dish from a hidden oven.

As in pornography, the abbreviated preparations parallel the brief or non-existent use of foreplay during sexual intercourse before getting to the climax in a porno film, where the usual *modus operandi* is "Wham, bam, thank you, ma'am." But in real-life cooking or lovemaking, foreplay is perhaps the most important part of the process, with the completed dish serving as almost an anticlimax. For many people, sex is predicated on the ability of the participants either to "successfully" achieve orgasm (singularly or simultaneously), or, at the very least, to stave off ejaculation for as long as possible. In essence, TV's cooks are demon-strating how to fornicate or fuck, and not very well at that, whereas real chefs are engaged in making love—or art, which is how many chefs view their passion and profession.

That they get paid for making meals many times a day does not make professional chefs prostitutes. The television cooking show, however, can be viewed as the illegitimate love child, or even the prostitute, of the real world of gastronomy. Each show offers a virtual form of fast food or a "quickie" instead of a real meal or mutually satisfying experience. This, of course, fulfills the producers' and the networks' needs—leaving viewers unsatisfied or still hungry makes them keep coming back for more.

The demonstrative aspect of contemporary TV cooking shows is, in effect, a rehearsed and studied performance. With slick production values, the program itself has less to do with food and cooking and more to do with the manufacture and packaging of the host/ chef himself or herself—and the manufacture of emotions surrounding eating. In the BBC's long-running TV series *Gourmet Ireland*, for instance, Jeanne and Paul Rankin—a married couple who are also professional chefs and restaurateurs—travel around Ireland in a Range Rover to visit their homeland's most picturesque landscapes. When the show finally cuts to the studio (which resembles a high-tech disco more than a serious cooking environment) for their recipe demonstrations, the viewer gets to watch the couple "do it," as it were. We watch them banter and chuckle in a type of foreplay as he prepares the meat and she the vegetables and the dessert, reinforcing stereotypical male/female dominant behavior and sexual role-playing as they argue and tease each other over the preparation methods.

Another popular type of cooking show portrays the chef as pioneer or, dare I say, missionary, venturing out into the great wide world in order to evangelize the surrounding profane worlds and reveal the culinary secrets of foreign lands. In the BBC series *Far Flung Floyd* the eponymous chef/host goes off on a series of culinary adventures in remote locations, such as cooking on board a sampan in Bangkok's floating market. The viewer marvels at his virile confidence, dash, and flair as he dares seemingly impossible feats, such as cooking with a saucepan in each hand while enduring driving rain, howling winds, or sub-zero temperatures. In a sexy, breathy touch, the steam from his pots inevitably fogs up the camera lens while a bewildered penguin or local looks on. The inherent message: enjoy the spectacle but don't try this at home! Similarly, pornographic movies filmed in nature offer similar bemusing intrusions of the real—be it ants crawling up the actors' legs or sand clinging to the creases of their flesh.

One of the more recent incarnations of the cook as missionary is New York chef Anthony Bourdain. On his show *A Cook's Tour* he is a chef on a quest, traveling the globe in search of new memories and experiences. He will try anything, risk everything…and he has nothing to lose. In contrast to Floyd's bringing the message to the natives, Bourdain never actually cooks and is the willing guinea pig—almost a stand-in or surrogate—for cross-cultural experimentation for the viewer.

This voyeurism seems almost kinky, as though Bourdain is living out our darkest desires and fantasies by dining off the carcass of some freshly slaughtered beast or sucking the flesh from deep-fried spiders in a market in Thailand or Vietnam (and that's only breakfast). It is visceral, covert television at times. In the grainy, blurry footage, we see our intrepid chef on the move and in possible danger—venturing into parts unknown and meeting someone he doesn't know, every image caught in a steamy, pseudo-wildlife-documentary style.

At the beginning of each episode we get a taste of the cult of the chef in his kitchen. Bourdain's persona as the head chef of Les Halles is that of a foolish, romantic man who is a "leader of cooks, a wrangler of psychopaths, the captain of his own pirate-ship."[2] He makes it look cool as he reinvents the classic French chef as a sexy stud, paddling down a river in Southeast Asia in search of food to the bemused looks of locals. Bourdain cuts quite an image in his sleeveless khaki army fatigues, somewhere between battle-hardened war correspondent and the Marlboro Man as chef. On his home turf of Manhattan, we see the virile silver fox with his curly hair, sinewy body, bad-boy stud earring and tattoo (even if it is tastefully small). Bourdain dares the viewer to keep watching as he revels in breaking taboos, testing his toughness and manliness in feats of eating and wanton consumption where cigarettes and alcohol are always involved in each feat of derring-do. In the safety of our living rooms, we eat this up (via TV) as he tests his virility. Testosterone oozing from every pore, Bourdain eats and partakes in what the locals do…and as in hardcore porn or bondage films, he constantly ups the ante while doing what we deem unthinkable.

Another British series breaks our cultural taboos—against fat, butter, and daring to enjoy one's food without watching the waistline. One of the highest-rated and critically acclaimed cooking shows in recent years, *Two Fat Ladies* features Clarissa Dickson Wright and

Jennifer Paterson. They are enormously watchable because they represent the antithesis of what is nowadays considered appropriate food for a healthy diet. Their cooking is an extension of their corpulent bodies, their physical beings emblematic of their approach and attitude toward cooking and life.

Of all the culinary TV series in recent years, *Two Fat Ladies* perhaps comes closest to embodying a philosophy of cooking and living. The Fat Ladies gleefully and emphatically say "no" to the food police and foist on an unsuspecting world (i.e., the audience) some time-tested truths about basic cooking skills. They announce and then proceed to act out a series of forbidden fantasies, showing that it is not only permitted but downright delicious to dally with off-limits substances such as cream, that adding a little bacon to a dish won't kill you. The Fat Ladies are exotic, eccentric, and naughty, exhibiting an almost sexual pleasure in debunking the no-carb/no-fat food fetishists.

By breaking rules they are transgressors; by watching, observing, and leering at their wares, we play the role of pervert and thus become the inherent transgressor par excellence along with them. Their favorite lubricant for their act, one which they apply with quivering squeals of delight, is that much-maligned ingredient in most other cooking shows and homes: butter. Most TV chefs today would apply it sparingly, if at all, or recommend substitutes. To the Fat Ladies, however, butter is everything. "*Monter au beurre!*" (or "Lay on the butter!") is their rallying cry against a commandment from the law books of today's kitchen and lifestyle police that viewers love to observe being violated, but dare not disobey in their own homes.

We drool and leer because we want to see how far they will go and what they will do next. Their grand operatic voices, their garishly inappropriate nail polish, their thick, fleshy hands performing dainty little tasks…with their ridiculous appearances they don't seem to be cooking professionals, although they are professional chefs and cooking writers (or were, as Jennifer Paterson has since passed away; the fact that reruns are still shown attests to the show's popularity). Instead, the Fat Ladies seem to take great delight in appearing on-camera as culinary prostitutes of sorts, kitchen dominatrixes who enact their viewers'/ voyeurs' fantasies.

Whether they cook for a group of nuns, a troop of bare-legged Boy Scouts, or the muscle-bound champion rowing team at Oxford, their on-screen audiences (the more innocent the better) also fall willing victim to their pots and pans. In a typical episode, the Fat Ladies double the cream, rub in some oil, add lard to their blood sausages, set sail to icebergs of meringues in a sea of chocolate and—if that weren't enough to make the viewer's arteries shudder—each episode climaxes with a post-performance cigarette and drink.

Most engaging of all, the Two Fat Ladies are complete naturals in front of the camera, cooking pros who are polar opposites of the usual polished, coiffed, and thin hosts of most television shows. Their bodies are imperfect, yet they love what they do and are proud, feisty performers of their art. This parallels the way in which the most popular pornographic videos in recent years have been produced by and star non-actors—"real" people such as housewives and husbands—or are "never-before-seen" celebrity home sex videos taken via hidden camera.

Another cheeky British series, *The Naked Chef*, promises erotic cookery, when actually the title is a metaphoric displacement, or perhaps transference, governed by the pleasure principle for the stripped-down cooking style of Jamie Oliver, the young chef whose antics the series follows. With the title as a teaser and a come-on, our imaginations run amok. Sexual scenarios become manifest with every gesture, as when Oliver pokes at some meat he is preparing, or verbalizes his desires and preferences for certain combinations of ingredients. This sense is further reinforced when the viewer realizes that the chef is not directly addressing him but an interviewer who is just off-camera and offscreen.

Not only is the action mediated in the guise of a cooking program, but we are complicit agents—we actively stalk the chef as he leaves work, eavesdrop on his private conversations, and check out his friends when they drop in. The camera's point of view is always at a distance, jerky, and moving—as though we were on a police stakeout, playing the role of an international spy, or observing Oliver's moves as a sexual predator might. This further heightens his image as an object of desire and the viewer's role of voyeur. The frustrations of not exactly seeing everything he is doing, the jump cuts, different film stocks, hip-hop music, etc., are necessary obstacles that sustain our desire in our own desperate attempts to attain the object of our desire. The idea of nakedness is further reinforced in the sense that the chef is perceptibly vulnerable and does not know we are there.

Nigella Bites is the natural successor to *The Naked Chef*. If *The Naked Chef* is about "stripping down food to its bare essentials," as stated in the introductory promotion at the start of each episode, then in *Nigella Bites*, the emphasis is on stripping down our lives. *The Naked Chef* retains an element of the professional chef: we can admire Oliver's knife skills or the deft way he handles a saucepan. Nigella Lawson, on the other hand, jokes about her inadequacies with a knife or her weakness for licking the bowl and then sensuously licks her fingers. As the naughty (and seemingly unfulfilled) housewife and self-declared amateur cook, she embodies the premise (and promise) that at home—or at least in her TV home—we can and indeed should all get down and dirty. She assures the viewer that it's perfectly natural and not shameful to cook like she does, or at least to watch her cook—and like spectators at a nudist camp, we buy in to her libertine ways.

The beautiful and curvy Lawson seems to have it all—another fantasy for the viewer. She appears able to juggle career, kids, husband, and three-course meals including dessert and still look fabulous. In reality, her husband was dying of cancer while she shot the first series, and she was struggling to keep her family on track while making extra money on television for her children's (and her own) future.

The TV Nigella appeals to both sexes. She's seemingly problem free, except for her constant bemoaning of her weight—which just points out her voluptuousness and love of food. Men are attracted to her like naughty schoolboys with a crush on their teacher; women love her because she is their virtual girlfriend, a confidante. Nigella presents herself as just as vulnerable as they are, and no better or worse in the kitchen (or presumably bed). Her life is a (sex) object lesson—if she can do it and enjoy herself, so can the viewer. She makes mistakes but laughs them off with a toss of her hair, for the fun is in trying.

She becomes our sultry food-as-sex therapist, confidently dispensing advice and offering opinions, but always with a recipe/prescription for every woe. There is no problem that cannot be cured with the perfect dessert. If you are going through a breakup—or, as she states in one of her shows, "when you've been chucked"—she advises making and devouring a dark chocolate cake with double-whipped cream. She is a kitchen goddess presenting food as salvation, eating as therapy. Indeed, one of her books is titled *How to Be a Domestic Goddess*; it presents page after page of tempting tarts, cakes, and pastries.

Nigella leads by example, exuding passion and emotion as she handles food, which she fondles and caresses before voraciously devouring it in front of our eyes. She flirts with her unseen audience as the camera plays up her physicality. Her dark, northern Italian looks are coupled with knowing and suggestive actions. She winks as she sucks on an oyster, licks cream from a spoon, or spills a little food as she eats, the crumbs bouncing off her too-tight sweater—every move captured in a mute, pale, soft focus or startlingly revealing close-up. In the show's promos we are teased by a full-lipped and soft-focused siren, her dark, curly locks cascading over her ample bosom as she deftly holds a cooking implement. She appears enticing but dangerous—coolly beyond reach, but ours to watch at will.

Nigella constantly reminds us that she is a real woman who is on a quest—fighting society's notions of the ever-decreasing dress size (we'll soon be in the negatives, as she says). Nigella plays up her common-sense attitude that you don't have to starve yourself to look good. By promoting a healthy attitude and appetite for food, she is empowering. Her sense of "love thy food as thyself" fits right in with the talk-show or self-help-book craze of modern times. She accepts the way she looks but reaches out to her viewers. Her problems are shared problems, for they are our problems. She is not perfect, she struggles with her weight, yet she doesn't hate herself—and that's a turn-on. At times she comes across like a type of fertility goddess, not only in the more traditional sense of having full-figured, child-bearing hips and sensual lips, but for the glimpses we see of her off-screen life. The show is filmed in her large house in a trendy London suburb, which is full of running and laughing children and happy friends. The kitchen pantry is always fully stocked with food, and she boasts a cookbook library that occupies a whole room. But her producers also take pains to stress the ordinariness of her life so that she isn't too remote or inaccessible—or a turn-off. We see her pick up the children from school, take them to the park, give them a bath, and then read them bedtime stories—all staged for the camera, as this isn't a reality show where cameras are supposed to live with her family. As we spy on her busy, full life, the message is that even we TV-watching schlumps at home should be able to find some time to cook in our own busy lives.

During the course of a half-hour show, Nigella typically zips through preparing breakfast, lunch, dinner, and often a midnight snack on the side. With the filming done at her home, using her family recipes and stock of ingredients, she makes us feel like one of her visitors or even part of the family, touching a memory of sitting around the kitchen watching or helping our own mothers cook. This sense of intimacy and the feeling that we are watching a real person who is providing for her family is a crucial ingredient that drives the success of the show—and perhaps separates it from the normal fluff of many cooking shows. But, of course, it is all fake and staged for our benefit.

Such British cooking shows touch on the archetypal brand of British humor and attitude toward sex, which features naughty and lascivious tempters and temptresses who don't take themselves or their efforts that seriously. Indeed, laughter is part of the turn-on and recipe for manufacturing desire. To be truly dominated and not just teased, we have to look across the Atlantic, to the visual and physical affirmation of masculinity: Emeril Lagasse.

Lagasse is seemingly the master of his domain, a larger-than-life human phallus. He's large and in charge: loud, testosterone-driven, cocky. This burly, verbose chef is a consummate entertainer, driving viewers into a frenzy of oohs and aahs and emotional responses. The mostly female audience sits on the edges of their seats, leaning forward toward the action. Even the introduction of the ingredients is a performance in itself, with a loud exclamation of "Bam!" every time Emeril adds a handful of spice to a dish, which acts like a laugh track to cue the studio audience and work it up into a frenzy.

The audience serves as an exulting Greek chorus, standing in for the at-home viewer's wishes and desires. Whether the on-camera emotions are genuine or not doesn't matter— there's a winking knowledge that it's being done for the at-home viewer. The audience gets giddy with anticipation and excitement as Lagasse throws in a whole clove of garlic or a dash of paprika. The purpose of the show is not to produce the perfect bouillabaisse, coq au vin, or shrimp gumbo, but to facilitate Emeril's role as that of primitive Pietà.[3] The camera lingers on his contorted face as he feigns ecstasy while stuffing a chicken or caressing its skin as he seasons it. His actions are in marked contrast to the usually sober instructions in cookbooks that typically tell us what to do and when to do it, not *how* to do it.

Emeril is the king of the culinary come-on, dramatizing every aspect of the compressed cooking process with excessive gestures and theatrical pauses while he sighs and groans at his own performance, whether he is whisking an egg, frying bacon, or whipping up some cream. The audience shudders in anticipation whenever he exclaims his signature "Let's kick it up a notch!" before adding even a hint of spice to a pot. They squeal in delight and unison when he garnishes a dish with a bold flourish punctuated by the ubiquitous "Bam!" (which can't help recall the above-mentioned "Wham, bam, thank you, ma'am!" abbreviated sex act).

As the camera jumps from workstation to workstation, from sous-chef to waiter to panting kitchen hand, the viewer is teased, tantalized, and titillated by the unfolding spectacle. Each dish is an act that culminates in the meal, and every finished plate in the succession of acts in each course is like the "money shot" in a pornographic film, providing a mini-climax before we cut to the next act in the show.

"Money shot" is the commonly used descriptor in pornographic films for the scene containing the climax/orgasm scene, i.e., when the male actor ejaculates for the camera. As Susan Faludi noted in "The Money Shot," her 1995 *New Yorker* essay on Los Angeles's pornographic film industry, "The on command male (erection) orgasm is the central convention of the industry: all porn scenes should end with a visible ejaculation. There are various names for it: the pop shot, the payoff shot, the cum shot; most resonant is 'the money shot.'"[4] Hence in porn the (usually male) viewer is aroused by the on-screen ejaculation as a trigger for his own. Whether or not it confirms his own masculinity, there is a reciprocity of some transferential kind through his own off-screen ejaculation.

In cooking shows, the money shot is the achievement and presentation of the finished dish, which magically appears at the end along with the dish that was cooked on-air. In TV shows that are based on performance, the actual presentation of the dish needs an accompanying rider or exclamation marks. The money shot as the signifier, like Emeril's exclamatory "Bam!," prompts the audience in the studio (and presumably at home) to issue its own groan or sigh in a collective virtual orgasm with the chef/presenter that is the hook, presumably, to keep everyone "coming" again. Sometimes the money shot comes when the chef tastes the meal or invites a member of the studio audience (as in *Emeril Live*) or "real people" (as in *The Two Fat Ladies*) to taste along. These TV cooking and dining scenes are usually edited to show partial glimpses of food and consumption in soft focus with lots of laughter, paralleling the voyeurism in *Playboy*- or *Penthouse*-style videos.

In contrast, the Japanese show *Iron Chef* presents the cooking program like a reality show—the ultimate in gustatory voyeurism. It combines exotic, hard-to-get ingredients with colorful and foreign cuisines and the incessant chatter of the presenters, which is reminiscent of the patois of sports commentary. *Iron Chef* represents a kind of mythological fight between Good and Evil, a carefully constructed spectacle of excess. The public is aware of the obviousness of the roles of the participants, whether through their physical traits or their over-acting.

The voyeurism aspect is embodied by a panel of amateur judges, who are never professional chefs or foodies. The group usually includes a handsome young athlete, a pretty (and naïve) starlet, an aging spinster, and an elder-statesman type, such as a lawyer, politician, or some other power wielder. They are like stock characters in a soap opera, except their plot lines revolve around cooking, eating, and judging food. Like Emeril's audience, they are stand-ins for the at-home viewer, sampling and judging the food—and squealing and oohing at the culinary feats of derring-do. The spinster is always expected to make advances to the young sports star and reprimand the young starlet or put her in her place.

In front of this absurd group, the two dueling chefs must prepare four courses with one ridiculous ingredient, such as monkfish head, octopus, or a rare spice. The whole spectacle is carried out in borderline chaos—will the chefs finish their cooking by the one-hour deadline? The challenger is always represented as the underdog, with video vignettes showing his humble upbringing in a small village in Japan or an earlier humiliating defeat by an Iron Chef. The Iron Chef champion, in contrast, arrives in some grand spectacle, such as striding on-camera through mist, with a clap of thunder, dramatic lighting, or ominous music. This further heightens and/or exaggerates to almost mythic proportions what the challenger has to overcome in order to beat the Iron Chef.

Like soft-core fantasy or 1970s porn films, which rely not on what is genuine but more on an idealization of sex, *Iron Chef* operates on a level of heightened imagery to simulate passion. However badly written and/or cheesily acted, it is fictional, and the viewer is aware that these are not real feelings or real emotions. As viewers and consumers we revel in the substitute for real life. With the intervention of cosmetic surgery, porn actors today look more virtual than real, human approximations of inflatable sex toys. The porn film helps viewers maintain a comfortable distance from the inadequacies in their own appearance or sex life. While cooking shows or porn videos don't actually replace the real experience of eating or having sex, they do at times distort our perceptions of what constitutes real food and sex. We may eat TV dinners, frozen food, or takeout foods while watching a cooking show, and we may consider ourselves gourmets for doing so.

The popularity of the cooking show as fantasy is paralleled by the real-world decline of culinary culture in America. According to Harvard University nutritionist Dr. George Blackburn, the average meal in this country is consumed in less than seven minutes and in one of four ways: alone, watching television, on the run, or standing up.[5] Blackburn also notes that because it takes at least twenty minutes for the brain to register that food has been consumed, the body is cheated of its natural mechanism to warn the eater when the stomach is full, and when it is time to stop.

Recent figures from the American Medical Association also show that one in five Americans is clinically obese, and more than half are overweight, statistics that represent a 12 percent increase since 1990.[6] The evidence is all around us: people slouch along the street eating fast food or have pre-cooked meals delivered to their homes—all because they don't cook. (A recent *New York Times* article featured a Manhattan couple who had their stove removed to make room for a bigger fridge—to store their takeout and delivered meals.)[7]

And when modern TV viewers do not eat at home, where they usually eat standing up or in front of the television, they can be found gobbling food at their desks or while in transit. Not only do they claim they have no time to shop and cook, but they're too stressed to care about what they consume, factors that not only rationalize why Americans don't make meals but are also used to explain why they don't get regular exercise.

This might be the downside of TV cooking shows: rather than increasing and improving the viewer's joy of cooking, they might make viewers feel inadequate or unconfident in their own culinary prowess (just as porn might create unrealistic expectations or depression about one's own sexual skills). Cooking shows and porn tap into our primal needs. We are all hungry for love, comfort, passion, gusto, and communal experiences, and we are curious about forbidden pleasures—even if we don't act on our curiosity. These are all experiences and needs that can be vicariously acted out, fantasized about, and observed via both cooking shows and porn.

Just as most clients of prostitutes are lonely men looking for more comfort and understanding than sex, so, too, are cooking-show viewers looking for more than a little distraction from the exigencies of modern living, such as preparing food. While viewers may not have a naughty Nigella or cheeky Naked Chef to whip up a little love on a plate at home, they can make a date to catch up with them in a lip-licking saucy mood. These video sirens can be found at most hours, somewhere on the tube, with no complaints, excuses, or headaches to impede the pleasure of their company. Culinary pornography? Perhaps, but why not… especially if it leads us to enjoy and partake of such pleasures in our own lives. ☻

NOTES

1. In April 1930, faced with threats of censorship by the federal government, the Motion Picture Producers and Distributors of America created a movie production code, commonly known as the "Hays Code" after Will H. Hays, the organization's first director. An excerpt from the Hays Code states: "No picture shall be produced which will lower the moral standards of those who see it. Hence the sympathy of the audience shall never be thrown to the side of crime, wrong-doing, evil or sin. The technique of murder must be presented in a way that will not inspire imitation. Brutal killings are not to be presented in detail. Adultery and illicit sex, sometimes necessary plot material, must not be explicitly treated or justified, or presented attractively....Excessive and lustful kissing, lustful embraces, suggestive postures and gestures are not to be shown. Complete nudity is never permitted. This includes nudity in fact or in silhouette....Undressing scenes should be avoided, and never used save where essential to the plot. Details of crime must never be shown and care should be exercised at all times in discussing such details....There must be no scenes, at any time, showing law-enforcing officers dying at the hands of criminals." In 1968, the Hays Code was replaced by a rating system similar to that in effect today. The Hays Code was designed to make all films suitable for any audience. The new rating system was designed to restrict children and adolescents from seeing "mature" films. For further information see www.cinema.ucla.edu/collections/Profiles/pre.html and http://www.artsreformation.com/a001/hays-code.html.

2. Anthony Bourdain, *Kitchen Confidential: Adventures in the Culinary Underbelly* (New York: Bloomsbury, 2000), 247.

3. Emeril's exaggerated expressions evoke the Pietà as the archetypal image of lamentation; the comparison conveys the impression of Emeril's status among his audience as a Christ- or God-like figure.

4. Susan Faludi, "The Money Shot," *New Yorker*, 30 October 1995, 64–86.

5. Michael D. Lemonick, "Will We Keep Getting Fatter? That's What We're Programmed to Do—Unless We Find Some Genes That Will Switch Off Fat Metabolism," *Time*, 8 November 1999, 88.

6. "Wider Waistlines, More Diabetes in US Each Year." This Reuters article dated 31 December 2002 refers to an article in the *Journal of the American Medical Association* (JAMA) 289:76–79 (2003).

7. Amanda Hesser, "So You Think Your Kitchen Is Too Small?," *New York Times*, 24 January 2001.

Fall 2003, volume 3, number 4

judith pacht |

Recipe for S&M Marmalade

Blood oranges
should be eaten
naked,
blushing,
cupped
in the palm.
Easily entered,
fingers
separate skin from flesh,
carefully pulling flesh
segment by segment,
opening the ruby-orange,
rosy-wet.

Ignore
the rest:
the bitter Sevilles,
Hamlins
the under-ripe
green-tinged,
the rusty orange.
Mottled.
Rough.
Sour.

Leave them
to the flash
of a newly whetted blade
sharp and cold
cutting into skin and flesh.
Slice.
Soak.
Turn up heat.
Boil until flesh melts
and bubbles blister
thick deep orange.

Think only of the end,
the mouth-feel,
the stew of dark sweet
and juice
and thickened pulp

to swallow.

Fall 2002, volume 2, number 4

the art of food

Man Ray's *Electricité* | *Stefanie Spray Jandl*   **152**

Food + Clothing = | *Robert Kushner*   **158**

Vik Muniz's *Ten Ten's Weed Necklace* | *Vanessa Silberman*   **170**

Zhan Wang: Urban Landscape | *John Stomberg*   **174**

The First Still Life | *Lawrence Raab*   **178**

stefanie spray jandl |

Man Ray's *Electricité*

IN 1931 MAN RAY CREATED a portfolio of photographs for an unlikely patron, a French electric company. The client, la Compagnie Parisienne de Distribution d'Electricité (CPDE), had recently launched a campaign to increase the domestic use of electricity and wanted a special gift for its "art-minded" customers that would give visual expression to its marketing efforts.[1] They boldly commissioned the avant-garde American photographer Man Ray, living in Paris and well-known for his portrait studio and his innovative "rayographs." Man Ray delivered a stunning portfolio entitled *Electricité*, which consisted of ten photogravures of original photographic works. Five hundred copies of *Electricité* were produced, most of which were given to the CPDE's shareholders and preferred customers. These lucky recipients were visually dazzled by a suite of arresting images that described the infinite reaches of electricity, and the benefits and conveniences it brought to every facet of the home. Two of the photographs, *Salle à Manger* and *Cuisine*, portray the utility of electricity in the kitchen, reflecting a larger campaign to promote domestic appliances. A successful union of the commercial and the avant-garde, Man Ray's *Electricité* offers a modern, and at times witty, vision of an electrified home and world.

When *Electricité* was commissioned, French electric companies were aggressively trying to establish their markets. In doing so, they were competing with gas, a more established form of energy. In 1920s Paris, a small number of private electric companies existed, which provided energy primarily for industry; domestic usage was largely confined to wealthy households that could afford electric power, which cost several times more than gas. By the end of the decade, however, Parisian electric companies were trying to expand into the middle-class domestic markets. New generating facilities were constructed while domestic rates were lowered. Customers, however, were not convinced of electricity's advantages and were reluctant to pay steep prices, causing domestic demand for electricity to stagnate.[2] When the Depression began in France in 1929, industrial demand was no longer stable, increasing the disparity between supply and demand. The CPDE, like some of its competitors, responded to this crisis by focusing on the development of its domestic market even more aggressively.[3]

Meanwhile, the appliance industry was rapidly emerging, offering a range of new electrical devices that would save time and ease labor for the housewife. Tapping into the aims of the domestic science movement, appliance manufacturers advertised their products as

---

Right: Man Ray, *Salle à Manger* (from *Electricité: Dix Rayogrammes*), 1931. Photogravure. COURTESY WILLIAMS COLLEGE MUSEUM OF ART. © 2009 MAN RAY TRUST / ARS, NY / ADAGP, PARIS. PHOTOGRAPH BY JOHN LE CLAIRE.

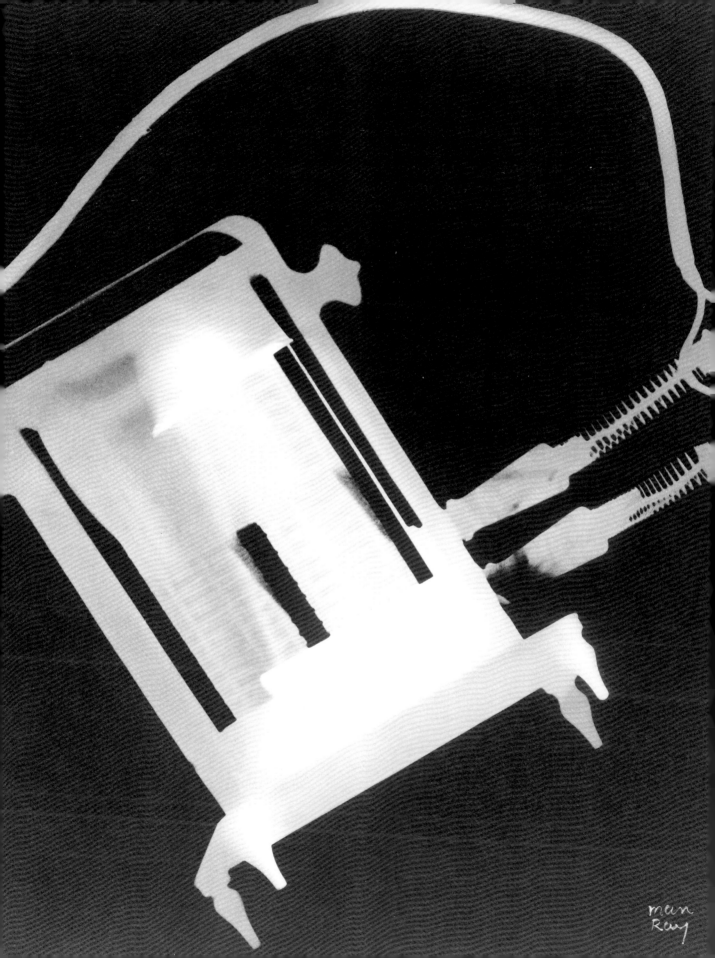

efficient, time-saving, versatile, economical, and hygienic.[4] French women were offered numerous electrical wonders for the kitchen: kettles, mixers, coffee pots and grinders, grills, stoves, waffle irons, toasters, and more. These appliances were often promoted by images of a modern, fully electric home outfitted with convenient appliances, a vision that was shared by both the appliance and the electricity industries.

The promotional efforts of the appliance manufacturers and the Parisian electric companies, including the CPDE, converged at the annual Salon des Arts Ménagers. These popular home shows, begun in 1923, provided a forum for bringing together consumers, manufacturers of domestic goods, and, of course, electricity and gas providers. Just as the electric companies were expanding beyond industrial customers and eyeing the middle-class market, the Salon and the many appliance manufacturers who exhibited there were focused on middle-class housewives. Visitors to the Salon received information on both electricity and gas, the latest appliances, kitchen and bathroom design, home décor, and domestic management.[5] Historian Robert Frost has shown, however, that this newly targeted French middle class was not as well developed as perceived, and the consumer goods industry correspondingly failed to grow significantly.[6]

It was against this backdrop of crisis and competition in the electricity industry and the domestic appliance industry in which its future was so entwined that the CPDE commissioned Man Ray to create the portfolio of photographs. One of the founders of the New York Dada group, and later an associate of the surrealist movement, Man Ray moved easily among different media as he independently followed his creative impulses: he painted, sculpted, and made films in addition to taking pictures. In 1922 he began making "rayographs" or "photograms," camera-less photographs created in the darkroom by placing objects directly onto photographic paper and exposing the arrangement to light. With this process, which he dubbed "rayograph" in reference to the action of light as well as to his surname, everyday objects—a pipe, cotton wool, keys, a comb—are dramatically transformed into mysterious, shaded silhouettes. Although not the inventor of the photogram (it was known in the nineteenth century but not widely used), Man Ray greatly expanded the possibilities of the process with his creative explorations.

A progressive, independent-minded American artist seems an unlikely match for a French electric company's art commission. The CPDE, however, pursued Man Ray quite deliberately, even though another photographer had already taken what Man Ray described as "wonderful technical photographs of the interior of powerhouses" for the project.[7] Man Ray was finally persuaded by the CPDE and Lee Miller, his studio assistant and lover at the time, to accept the commission. In hiring Man Ray, the CPDE affiliated itself with the artist's reputation for invention, modernity, and—by association—American ingenuity.

Salle à Manger (see image p.153), the first of two photographs in the portfolio relating to cuisine, depicts one of the most common appliances of the era, a toaster. Its title, "Dining Room," reminds us that a toaster was not strictly confined to the kitchen: it was often placed in the dining room, within reach of the breakfast table. Using the rayograph technique, Man Ray captured the appliance floating weightlessly against a charcoal haze, its structure revealed in muted tones and shadows, its cord looped in gentle undulation over the top. This mundane appliance, though still recognizable, has been transformed into an ethereal, haunting X-ray of itself.

The toaster Man Ray used to create *Salle à Manger* was an early twentieth-century design popular for several decades. Manufactured by a number of different appliance makers, this type had no sides to encase the heating elements, leaving them dangerously exposed. In 1926 the revolutionary "Toastmaster" arrived in the United States, an enclosed toaster that ejected the toast and shut off when finished,[8] soon to be followed by similar automatic toasters in Europe. Man Ray purchased a toaster (and other household items) especially for the *Electricité* commission,[9] and would have been confronted with a choice of new and old toaster models as he selected his props. Why would he take an older style as his subject, especially when his client was an electric company concerned with the latest domestic appliances? Most likely, Man Ray, never subordinate to his clients, chose the older design for simple aesthetic reasons. Under the spell of the rayograph technique, a boxy, enclosed toaster would not have offered the depth and intriguing contours of an open model. This old-fashioned toaster also gave Man Ray the opportunity to create a visual pun: its stubby, tapered legs and platform base take on the distorted likeness of a dining table, something that would have been found in every *salle à manger*.[10]

Cuisine (see image p.156), features a small roast chicken on an oval platter, surrounded by a bed of rice. During the printing of this photograph Man Ray rayographed a coil spiraling over the chicken to suggest the radiant heat that cooked it. This photograph, with its basis in traditional studio photography, stands unique among its *Electricité* peers for being nearly divorced from darkroom manipulations. It is possible that it was taken by Lee Miller, who worked closely with Man Ray on the creation of *Electricité*. Tony Penrose, Lee Miller's son and director of the Lee Miller Archives, has pointed out that this "was just the sort of photograph she would have taken."[11] Miller, herself an accomplished photographer when she began working for Man Ray, had considerable commercial experience. But it was probably the irreverent Man Ray who then rayographed the coil over the chicken, giving this commonplace dish a silly, pseudo-cosmic aspect as well.

The choice of a roast chicken over a more sophisticated dish was probably a deliberate one. It made a tidy, affordable meal, one that would have been familiar to the middle-class customers that the CPDE and its competitors, as well as appliance manufacturers, were courting. Under the bright, focused studio lighting, the crisp skin of this chicken glistens with the promise of deep, rich flavors slowly coaxed out in the roasting process. But is this bird really appealing? With its hardened, caramelized skin, the chicken, on second glance, looks rather over-cooked and dry. Nonetheless, in the context of the *Electricité* portfolio, this decidedly roasted appearance was probably meant to counter the then-popular perception that gas is better for roasting, while electricity is best for baking,[12] declaring an electric oven equally suitable for preparing a traditional French meal. Man Ray and Lee Miller, however, may have shared a private laugh when this photograph of an overcooked chicken was submitted.

The *Electricité* portfolio is a smartly packaged, cohesive statement of a French electric company's marketing posture. *Salle à Manger* and *Cuisine,* in particular, speak of the significance of the culinary sphere in the early marketing efforts of electricity providers and appliance manufacturers. In creating these images and the eight others in the portfolio, Man Ray was not seeking to deliver easy, literal, commercial photographs to his client. Instead, he drew from his independent Dada spirit to create photographs of the everyday that surprise the eye. Looking through his lens, we find humor and discover the shady alteregos of everyday household appliances. *Electricité,* in the end, transcends its commercial origins to become a compelling artist's portrait of the unseen force of electricity. ◉

NOTES

1. Mario Amaya, "My Man Ray: An Interview with Lee Miller Penrose," *Art in America,* May–June 1975, 57.

2. Robert L. Frost, "Prelude to a Nationalization," in *Alternating Currents: Nationalized Power in France, 1946–1970* (Ithaca and London: Cornell University Press, 1991), 9–39.

3. "Revue financière," *Journal des debats* 5 (September 1930), 407.

4. Martine Segalen, "The Salon des Arts Menagers, 1923–1983: A French Effort to Instil the Virtues of Home and the Norms of Good Taste," *Journal of Design History* 7 (no.4), 1994, 271.

5. See Jacques Rouaud, *60 Ans d'Arts Menagers, Tome 1: 1923–1939, Le Confort* (Paris: Editions Syros Alternatives, 1989). See also *Les Bons Génies de la Vie Domestique* (Paris: Editions du Centre Pompidou, 2000).

6. Robert L. Frost, "Machine Liberation: Inventing Housewives and Home Appliances in Interwar France," *French Historical Studies* 18 (Spring 1993), 109–130.

Above: Man Ray, *Cuisine* (from *Electricité: Dix Rayogrammes*), 1931. Photogravure. COURTESY WILLIAMS COLLEGE MUSEUM OF ART. © MAN RAY TRUST AND ARS PHOTOGRAPH BY JOHN LE CLAIRE.

7. Arnold Crane, Interview with Man Ray, October 1968. In the Archives of American Art, Smithsonian Institution. My thanks to Steven Manford, co-author of the Man Ray Rayographs Catalogue Raisonné Project, for bringing the discussion of *Electricité* to my attention.

8. Earl Lifshey, *The Housewares Story* (Chicago: National Housewares Manufacturers Association, 1973), 258.

9. Arnold Crane, Interview with Man Ray, October 1968.

10. I am grateful to Deborah Rothschild for noticing this visual double-play.

11. Conversation with Antony Penrose over the *Electricité* portfolio, February 11, 1998.

12. Christina Hardyment, *From Mangle to Microwave: The Mechanization of Household Work* (Cambridge: Polity Press; and Oxford and New York: Basil Blackwell, 1988), 134.

Winter 2002, volume 2, number 1

robert kushner |

Food + Clothing =

THE JUXTAPOSITION OF THE NUDE BODY with food has always fascinated me. Don't carrot sticks look more inviting when framing a nipple? And what about a glimpse of hair behind the mesh of a hot-dog apron? Our reactions to familiar foods change entirely when the food is displayed on a naked body. By shifting the context from plate to torso, the food, unsurprisingly, becomes sensuous and eroticized. At the same time, the connotations of each costume are radically expanded.

Sometime in 1972 I began asking myself what would happen if I explored the synthesis of food and clothing by constructing costumes that could actually be eaten. This edible element seemed a natural extension of the costumes I had already been making for several years. An essential component of this performance would be the public consumption of the clothing. First the models would sample each other's clothes, then we would invite the audience to participate. During the course of the performance the elaborate garments would disappear, leaving only memories (and, of course, a few photos). The primary artistic elements would be the ephemeral composition of all the costumes together, the observation of their disintegration through eating, and the lingering sense of gustatory titillation.

The idea of performing nude in public was only slightly provocative in the early 1970s, at least in the art world. Nude performance reflected the counter-culture ideal of the body as a manifestation of the beautiful and a way of questioning the status quo. Of course, there was also a touch of exhibitionism. Still, I was definitely pushing the envelope when I asked my models to wear only food and then allow an audience of strangers to eat their "clothes." To my surprise, many of my friends enthusiastically volunteered.

My first food costumes were presented on June 28, 1972, at the Jack Glenn Gallery in Corona del Mar, California. For *Costumes Constructed and Eaten* I designed a fashion show of costumes that were either totally or partially edible. After some initial experiments, I concluded that the costumes would become visually monotonous if they were 100 percent edible. However, if I were to attach food to net-like structures, then the range of design possibilities would grow. Several weeks before the performance, my mother, Dorothy Browdy Kushner, and I began to crochet one-size-fits-all, unisex foundation garments. The gender dislocation of a man engaged in "women's work" like crochet and food preparation appealed to me. At that time transgressive challenges to gender stereotyping were definitely in the air, and they had already become a motif in my artistic production.

Right: "Pretzel Decolleté with Collard Skirt," 1994. PHOTOGRAPH BY STANLEY STELLAR © 2004

In designing the foundations, I soon realized that the human body has only a certain number of points from which heavy objects, like vegetables, could be attached without discomfort or elaborate dressmaking techniques that were beyond my level of skill. The head, shoulders, elbows, wrists, waist, knees, and ankles provide points of support and connection. As my mother and I crocheted together, usually in the backyard, I began to plan which foods to use with each costume, where they would be attached, and, most significantly, at what point in time they would be applied.

Since I approached the costume designs from the viewpoint of sculpture, I tried to ensure that the garments made an innovative statement in combination with the human form. Did the shapes of the costumes create unexpected lines across the exposed skin? Might they reveal what is usually hidden (crotches, breasts, buttocks) and occasionally obscure that which is usually displayed (the face, hair, hands)? Could each costume, combined with the support of its model, function as a piece of kinetic sculpture?

To plan the various phases of applying the vegetables, I sought models and situations involving food beyond the realm of art. I began by recalling my mother's menu planning and preparation for the large parties she threw every few years. Days before the party, she would construct radish rosettes or slivered carrot and celery sticks, keeping them in jars of water in the fridge, where the vegetables would morph into sea-creature shapes. I remember as a child both how strange they looked and how long they would remain fresh. For my project, longevity was essential. I also considered another worldly source: the Tournament of Roses Parade. Growing up near Pasadena and loving flowers, I was obsessed with the monumental effort of bringing thousands of fresh flowers together for the one sustained moment of the parade itself. Friends of mine helped decorate the floats, so I knew that the decorations all came together in three days, starting with the heartiest flowers, usually chrysanthemums, and ending with the easily bruised orchids at the last possible minute. I applied both of these paradigms.

That summer was a time of rather humorous trial and error. For these first costumes, it seemed a good idea to restrict myself to vegetables, a surprising number of which were unusable for various reasons. Boiled baby potatoes would have been good to eat and would look like enormous pearls, but they tended to crack and fall right off the string at the slightest jostle. Uncooked ziti, barely ingestible at best, cracked and crumbled under pressure. Red or green cabbage leaves, particularly the outer ones, looked great and covered a large surface area, but they were basically inedible. Raw collard greens presented the same problem, but I used them anyway. Most fruits were too squishy or too quickly became bruised and unappetizing. Zucchini was tempting, for both its color and shape, but raw ones split too easily, and cooked ones fell right off the string. Lettuce and spinach would be appealing and palatable—but both wilted far too fast. Raw broccoli and cauliflower behaved well, held on the string, and were agreeable to eat, but they produced a lumpen, leaden look, like rows of rocks. String beans proved surprisingly resilient. Heads of fennel were a graceful choice. Ideas and research marched blissfully and madly on.

I began to formulate a battle plan for the construction of my edible garments. First I would stitch the costumes from the sturdiest veggies: carrots, celery, radishes, and string beans. When this first step was completed, I wrapped the vegetables in wet paper towels, put them in plastic bags, and tucked them to bed in the fridge. Next I strung less perishable foods, such as kumquats, olives, and cranberries. Last of all came the most fragile produce.

The tools for this entire project were classically simple and low-tech: large carpet needles, a variety of thread and string, pliers to guide the needles through the tougher vegetables, and a knife for slicing, paring, and shaping. I used various sewing and embroidery techniques—simple stringing, patterned stringing, blind-stitching, over-stitching, hem-stitching—to create as many different uses of the vegetables as possible.

Our suburban grocery store assumed new relevance. Foods that I would not normally consider eating—Cheez Doodles or Froot Loops—suddenly took on interest for their lurid color and the fact that they could be strung. Even though I was a serious amateur cook at the time, for this first food show the taste of the costumes was regrettably of secondary importance to the overall visual effect. For example, in one costume, I strung several lengths of piano wire with Doodles, Froot Loops, Cheerios, pimento-stuffed olives, red licorice, Twizzlers, and gumdrops. These bouncy kebabs made a lush and colorful but grotesque combination, and I savored the aggressive high brow/low brow confrontation of socially disparate types of foods. I resolved to correct my gustatory sadism in the future. I bought and tasted accessory condiments to enhance the more salady costumes: bottles of Green Goddess or French dressing with their weird colors, or shockingly offensive cans of Eezy Cheese—perfect when held as an evening clutch or when used discreetly to fill the cavity of a waiting celery stalk.

For this show, most of the fifteen costumes were carefully planned; others were more extemporaneously constructed. I made schematic drawings for most of the costumes and followed them rather carefully. I knew that I needed considerable help to finish all the work in time for the performance. Echoing the communal efforts of my friends working on the Rose Bowl Parade floats, I invited the models to an undressed dress rehearsal in my parents' suburban backyard. I had no idea how long it would take to make the costumes or how well they would hold up in performance. On the day of the performance the models also arrived several hours early to help finish and embellish their own costumes.

Before the performance began, the costumes were displayed as inanimate and perishable sculptures attached with pushpins to the walls of the gallery. The audience circled through the gallery, looking at the lush, deflated objects that would soon take sculptural form upon the models' bodies. At a prearranged time, fifteen models dressed in street clothes emerged from one of the gallery's back rooms. Taking our places before our assigned costumes, we stripped and re-dressed ourselves in vegetables. Often we needed to help each other secure the closures of the more fragile and finicky costumes. The biggest surprise was the shock of placing a thoroughly chilled ensemble over my nude torso. After the initial jolt, wearing a well-refrigerated costume became yet another invigorating aspect of performance.

The sudden transformation of the gallery was dramatic. Slightly above the audience's heads floated huge escarole wigs and wire-framed hats. At eye level were gloves, bandoliers, aprons, and all that naked skin. The audience was not particularly shocked. The models were instructed to move about the room and chat with each other or engage the viewers in conversation, but they were told always to maintain a sense of dignity. If they wished, the models could exchange costumes with each other to emphasize the androgyny of the designs. I had instructed everyone to tread a delicate balance between light humor and seriousness, to be sexy but not gross.

There was one unanticipated problem: visibility. The gallery was rather full of a quilt exhibition that blocked an overall sense of vista. However, since the ingredients and design details of the costumes were etched in my mind, it was easy to pull individual models to the center of the room and spontaneously describe what they were wearing in a hybrid of fashion and kitchen terminology. A circle of interested viewers formed as I pointed out the details of each ensemble. For example: "An afternoon hat. A metal grill with green onions, black licorice whips, crookneck squash, strands of Cheerios, Froot Loops, Kaboom, and Sirgrapefellow [all breakfast cereals of the day], worn with a string bean cummerbund— suitable for brunches."[1] The narration was a successful focusing device that allowed me to emphasize the individuality of each costume. Then the performers turned to eating. First the models tasted each other's garments, adding salad dressing and condiments as desired. Soon the audience joined in, with gusto. When the models felt that they had worn their costumes long enough, they were free to return the half- (or more) eaten costume to the wall and put on their street clothes again. True to California at that time, three or four audience members spontaneously stripped and tried on some of the costumes after the models had finished. At the end of the evening, I was pleased to see that a goodly amount of the food had actually been eaten.

The following fall I moved to New York and landed a job as a dessert chef at Food, an artists' restaurant in newly emergent, as-yet-unnamed SoHo. Both the menu and the chefs changed daily, so my knowledge of food expanded radically. By the end of the fall I was co-managing the restaurant and learning a lot about exotic food preparation and a wide range of non-vegetarian ingredients. I was invited to present a revival of the California food show at Robert Stearn's loft, Acme Productions, in association with The Kitchen, a cutting-edge performance space. *Bob Kushner and Friends Eat Their Clothes* was performed on December 10, 1972.

Before leaving Los Angeles, I had removed the remaining vegetable bits from the crocheted foundations, which I brought to New York. I knew I could replicate the California costumes, but I was ready to create new pieces that would taste better and offer greater visual complexity. I created sixteen new costumes for this performance. The California food show had been vegetarian (as was I at that time), with the exception of a hot-dog apron. For the New York food show, I wanted to consider a wider range of ingredients that reflected the broader spectrum of foods I was cooking and eating at Food. In the first food show, I had not considered including cooked vegetables. Raw beets on a string are pretty gnarly and unappetizing no matter who is wearing them. But by cooking them first, I got a wild new food color (fuschia!) and an earthy, mellow taste. Inspired by the beets, I designed a calves-tongue necklace: a kind of choker of three cooked, pickled calves' tongues interspersed

with halved, cooked beets. The necklace was modeled with a kitchen knife, which fit into a home-baked holster of bread. I accessorized the ensemble with a mustard dispenser, a huge escarole wig, and a pair of pita chaps to complement the Western theme of the holster. I don't think anyone ate any of the tongue—in fact, the necklace ultimately looked a little gross, even though my friend Ned modeled it to memorable effect.

"Velveeta Epaulettes" was one of my most successful costumes. Simply picturing the words "Velveeta" and "epaulettes" is enough to conjure the essence of the ensemble. Completing the "Velveeta Epaulettes" was a pita-bread mini-skirt punctuated by a marvelously deflated, baked eggplant codpiece and matching pita bedroom slippers. Footwear made of bread products provided dramatic new design horizons.

A sardine and anchovy necklace was shown with a Jewish rye bread mini-vest. The model's addition of a half-pita Nehru cap over his long, curly hair, combined with the oily residue of the sardines on his chest, created a racy mixed metaphor of hedonism and Salvation Army.

I found that apricot leather, a Middle Eastern snack, is strong and supple enough to substitute for real leather. It can be sewn with either string or long red licorice whips. Its only sartorial drawback is its extreme stickiness, particularly under hot lights. Since I could

Above: "Pineapple Falsies," displayed at *Robert Kushner and Friends Eat Their Clothes*, New York, 1972.

not buy any large pieces of fruit leather, even in Brooklyn's Middle Eastern stores, I made my own. It turned out lumpy, but I was able to work it into a delicious wrap-around sarong, worn with a vast wig of pre-squeezed orange halves (courtesy of the juice bar at Food).

My friend Deborah, an earnest meditator, asked for "something suitable for a woman of serious spiritual pursuit." I thought about her reasonable request and decided that covering her breasts and privates would be the solution. What to cover breasts with? Hollowed pineapples sewn into a bikini would echo the tropical excesses of Carmen Miranda's movie costumes and leave Deborah's personal parts well concealed. What I neglected to consider was how monumentally enhanced Deborah became with a pair of projectile pineapples cantilevered from her rib cage. After the initial shock, she agreed to model her pineapples with a lady-apple off-the-shoulder halter, a chestnut and cranberry tiara, and a skirt of apple and pink grapefruit slices. She looked simultaneously demure and flamboyant.

I managed to enlist as many friends and relatives as possible to help me cut and sew. For three days before the show I took time off from work to buy and assemble as much as I could in advance. The models all came early and assisted enormously. Their improvised additions made the costumes in this performance some of the best I ever showed.

Alexandra Anderson-Spivy described the New York performance:

> Having attended this performance, I can attest that any artist who produced such an event in the 1990s would provoke the wrath of the censorship brigade and the withdrawal of any National Endowment for the Arts funding (which the performance actually received, as did several of Kushner's other pieces). That evening an audience of about one hundred, mostly downtown types, put a dollar apiece into the glass jar that served as a cash register, then wandered into the loft, took seat cushions, and arranged themselves on the floor....Every ornately constructed piece, which the audience was supposed to consume at the end of the performance, illustrated the irreverent attitude toward materials Kushner had revealed in his earliest collages. As each confection emerged, the audience first exhibited blasé skepticism, then charmed surprise, and finally gleeful hilarity....Those who had expected something sexually titillating were treated to inventive humor and gentle Eros in a format that poked fun at artistic pretension while it simultaneously parodied and celebrated the creativity of fashion....Wanting the use of nudity to evoke an empathic recognition from the audience, he chose a range of ordinary body types that were not necessarily "professionally beautiful." Embedded in these performances was the implicit intent to address the meaning of several levels of transformation as well as the hypothetical question of how daily life might be different if people wore such arrays to the store, to meetings, or to parties....Kushner deployed humor as an antidote to cultural disillusionment and used it to subvert the pomposity of the avant-garde.[2]

Thinking I needed to round up an audience beyond word-of-mouth, I made the mistake of calling the *Village Voice*, which was at that time a prime resource for anything new or provocative in New York. They ran a sly, sexy preview about the performance that attracted an overflow crowd: "There'll also be an eclectic collection of broccoli skirts, ravissante dresses of lettuce and cabbage and celery ensembles. For a contribution of $1.00, the audience will see a full-length fashion show, after which the models will begin to devour one another's costumes. And for the piece de resistance, the spectators can join the pique-nique. All in good taste, of course."[3]

Hundreds of people showed up. We accommodated two hundred and turned as many away. The crowd was lively and quite ready to be entertained, but I had underestimated how different the New York audience would be from its laid-back California counterpart. There were many cameras in the audience, and at my invitation a video crew was present. The atmosphere of the room was highly charged. I came out dressed in a scallion mini-skirt and a trio of graduated mushroom necklaces, holding a handful of note cards with my narration. I began to model and describe my costume in the small runway area we had marked off in the middle of the room. The other models followed one at a time. While I read, they walked down the runway, demonstrating the various ingredients and features of their costume. They then took places around the edge of the room until all of the costumes had been shown, after which we gathered in the middle of the room to dine on our clothes.

The eating part of the performance in California had been celebratory and communal. By contrast, with our advance publicity and confinement in a crowded SoHo loft, audience participation in New York took on a slightly carnal edge, and many of the performers beat a hasty retreat to the dressing room. During the performance a lot of food fell to the floor and was wasted. This degree of profligacy disturbed me, and I decided there should be a more responsible endgame for my next food performance. For a while I considered the idea of performing on a runway in a restaurant, with huge pots of broth ready to receive the uneaten vegetables. The audience would then enjoy a delicious soup as the last act of the performance. In reality, I never did such a large performance again. I began looking for ways to continue making food costumes, but not on such a grandiose scale.

Harper's magazine asked for a photo story on one of the food costumes, which I viewed as an opportunity to concentrate on a single costume and make it as detailed and lavish as I could. "Asparagus Vest" consisted of a plunging V-neck blouse of raw asparagus spears with twin chokers of Italian salami and radishes. The vest was accented by parsley earmuffs joined by a string of radishes. The ensemble was completed with a floor-length train of strung scallions. The writer for *Harper's* recorded: "Ten minutes later, Robert is chopping my halter into a large wooden bowl, adding mushrooms and feta cheese and onions and a red wine vinegar dressing and we sit down to eat while he explains his art form."[4] I felt that I had solved the waste problem in an appropriate way.

Not long after, I spent a week at the American Crafts Museum teaching people how to make vegetable and flower jewelry and accessories, and a live, morning talk show, *AM New York*, asked me to appear with some sample costumes. I coerced the reticent host into wearing string-bean earrings I had embroidered with tiny carrot slices and a Mae West boa of spinach tied into big, lush clusters, all the while keeping up a continuous stream of fashion and food patter as I dressed him against his will. I modeled a coordinated spinach boa with a carrot-stick hair band and kept primping my mortified host. The string-bean earrings nearly finished him off. In a form of guerilla theater, food became intimidation.

In March 1974 the downtown art journal *Art Rite* asked me to make six costumes for a cocktail party benefit. With more time and experience and fewer costumes, I was able to construct a rather elaborate ensemble of six costumes to my total satisfaction. It was spring, so one of my models wore rhubarb gauntlets with a pussy-willow hat and mushroom cummerbund. Pussy willows are in no way edible, but they extended the natural range of materials and provided a fine visual contrast to the food. There was a redolent herb coat with bunches of fresh dill, mint, chive, and parsley. Graduated leis of strung artichoke leaves accompanied an escarole wig. Couturiers conventionally end a fashion show with a bridal ensemble, and I followed this tradition. My bridal outfit was designed for both the bride and the groom. I depicted them in virginal innocence, strewn with bananas, strawberries, and daffodils in matching bandoliers and mini-skirts. For this show, the descriptive texts had become more baroque:

> A three piece carrot suit for the first day at the beach. Carrots are quartered lengthwise and double stitched in a classic Chanel rounded neckline interspersed with radishes and falling to a becoming elbow length. A complementing strand of carrots here combined with cross slices of red cabbage hangs low at the waist. The ensemble is completed with a spring day hat of fresh dill in bunches and carrot ear guards. Quelle glamour.[5]

I liked the controlled, finished aspect of each costume. But showing them in a room of suited patrons sipping white wine created a strangely distant experience, as there was no audience interaction. We were separated from our viewers and consequently ended up feeling like the hired help, sampling our own costumes but missing participation from our remote audience. I realized another element of the formula that had made the earlier extravaganzas so successful—a sense of parity between performer and viewer. On more equal ground, the audience can be free to be both voyeuristic and sympathetic, making the performer-viewer contact more open-ended, piquant, and enjoyable for everyone.

In 1980, the Philadelphia Institute of Contemporary Art invited me to create a performance and installation for one of the large corner windows of Wanamaker's Department Store. Nakedness felt too provocative for such a publicly exposed street-corner location. Besides, I was tired of nudity as my performance trademark. I decided instead to explore a different social convention, high tea. At a tea the focus falls equally on what one is wearing and what one is served. For *Hats for Tea*, May 1–8, 1980, I sat in the store window creating hats out of found objects, feathers, a Frisbee, plastic leaves, dried gourds, and other ephemera. I did not use any fresh food items, though in retrospect that would have been interesting. At a certain hour in the afternoon, I set a tea table using food from Wanamaker's gourmet shop, a microwave and dishes from Housewares, and a tablecloth from Linens. All of these objects, even the clothes and shoes I wore from Menswear, bore small signs indicating where in the store they could be purchased. If people were observing me from the street, unsure of what was going on in the normally uninhabited window, I invited them to join me for tea, using a microphone that startled many passersby. To accept my invitation, my guests had to thread their way through a thicket of men's suits. Everyone was required to wear a hat for tea, either one of their own or one of the strange ones I had made that morning. Occasionally, friends and relatives joined me for the high tea, a variety of cookies and pastry, crackers, cheeses, and sardines. It made for a good series of afternoon gatherings, with unexpected and witty conversation, as one would expect at tea.

In 1994 I wrote an article, "Life in the Produce Aisle," for an issue of *Art Journal* that was dedicated to the subject of clothing as art. I realized that my photographs of the original costumes had nearly always been performance documentation. Documentation may capture the energy and ambiance of a performance, but it cannot fully convey the textures, details, and nuances of the costumes. I had always wanted to work with a studio photographer and professional models to see if good lighting and greater attention to detail would make the photos look as ambrosial and irresistible as I knew the costumes to be. So I gradually reconstructed the early costumes, adding many new details, which more time allowed. The hot-dog apron became elaborated to three rows of wieners in graduated sizes. I had time to make an accompanying breastplate from half of a huge bell pepper with small Vienna sausages sewn into the pepper's cavity. I recreated the Velveeta epaulettes by splitting and hollowing a magnificent artisanal whole-wheat loaf and adding a row of pendant scallions to simulate fringes. Cross-sections of an enormous banana squash gave me new forms and structure with which to innovate. The results exceeded my expectations:

> Because of the ephemeral nature of the costumes and because of my budget, I have not paid
> too much attention to documentation. After all, the "art" existed in real time. For years I have
> wanted the opportunity to reconstruct and beautifully document the costumes. It is my good for-
> tune to be friends with Stanley Stellar, my collaborator for these photographs. Through the spring
> [of 1994], on a sequence of Thursdays, I would construct one or two costumes, going into more
> detail than I was able to on the originals but keeping in line with their feeling and directness.
> Stanley would book a model, and we would shoot, improvise, repair the broken costumes—they
> are not only temporal but also fragile. Reworking these ideas twenty-two years later, I still find
> them enjoyable, humorous and totally open-ended.[6]

During this time, I was asked to create a costume for a midnight fashion show to be held on October 11, 1994, at the Dada Ball at Webster Hall, New York. For "Pumpkin Prom Dress" I dressed a model in a robust baby pumpkin bra and buttock cover surrounded by the leafy flourish of a collard-green mini-skirt. I had previously drilled small holes into the pumpkins, and once the model was tightly tied into his outfit I inserted long stems of dried wheat, not literally edible but seasonally symbolic. The ensemble was completed by a squash tam accented with more wheat, an apron of miniature Indian corn, and a dried wheat scepter. It was a savory fall ensemble, perfect for a midnight guest appearance, and my last edible performance costume.

Now, as I prepare this *Gastronomica* article, I have become intrigued by many forgotten, unrealized ideas and designs that I found in my old performance notes. One day, perhaps, I will have the opportunity to construct some of the following costumes: a Jell-O tutu (though I can't yet figure out how it could be modeled except prone); a terribly adult anchovy/olive tapenade necklace; mignon caper anklets; a Swiss cheese and prosciutto vest; a Thai cellophane-noodle braided collar garnished with slivered scallions; string-bean sandals with pretzel spats; a watermelon muff; a chocolate marshmallow cookie tiara modeled with a glass of cold milk; a giant crepe coat; and, for brunch, a blueberry pancake poncho worn and served with pure maple syrup. ☉

NOTES

1. *Art Journal*, Spring 1995: 64.

2. Alexandra Anderson-Spivy, *Gardens of Earthly Delight* (Manchester, VT: Hudson Hills Press, 1977), 23–24.

3. *Village Voice*, 7 December 1972.

4. Joyce Wadler, "Asparagus Tops," *Harper's*, July 1973, 10.

5. Robert Kushner, unpublished performance notes, 1974.

6. Robert Kushner, "Life in the Produce Aisle," *Art Journal*, Spring 1995: 65–68.

Winter 2004, volume 4, number 1

vanessa silberman |

Vik Muniz's
Ten Ten's Weed Necklace

True political ideas happen out of necessity, not theory, and usually become associated with politics only after their execution. The artist simply has to portray the world as he sees it.

—Vik Muniz

WHILE VACATIONING on the small Caribbean island of St. Kitts in 1995, the Brazilian-born, New York–based artist Vik Muniz befriended a group of local children. Taken by their joy and abandon, he captured them in Polaroid snapshots. The children took Muniz to meet their parents, who were weary and embittered after years of trading toil for meager pay as they labored in the island's abundant sugarcane fields. The parents' lack of hope contrasted sharply with the innocent vitality of their offspring.

Back in New York, Muniz thought about the parents and was bothered by the "sad metamorphosis most of my little friends were bound to experience."[1] He impulsively purchased some black paper and began to "draw" the children's portraits by sprinkling sugar on the paper. He then photographed these drawings to create *Sugar Children*, a series of six intimately scaled portraits.

Muniz had frequently made multiple copies of an original image through various media, but *Sugar Children* marked his first use of food as an artistic medium. Since completing the series, he has experimented with a wide variety of edible goods—chocolate, peanut butter, caviar, spaghetti, and black beans—to create works that challenge viewers' perceptions while blurring artistic boundaries. However, *Sugar Children* remains one of his most provocative and fully realized explorations of the historical and political resonance of food. These portraits are powerful not only for their technical mastery but also for their subtle command of the multiple layers of meaning that lurk beneath their sweet surfaces. Muniz's use of sugar, a perishable substance, to represent the children accentuates their precarious future, leaving the impression that they are destined to be consumed, disposed of, and ultimately forgotten.

One portrait, *Ten Ten's Weed Necklace*, is particularly gripping. Unlike the other sugar children, whose playful expressions light up the page, Ten Ten has a gaze that is haunting and apprehensive. He does not look directly at the camera as the others do; instead, he

Right: Vik Muniz, *Ten Ten's Weed Necklace*, 1996. COURTESY OF SIKKEMA JENKINS & CO. GALLERY, NEW YORK. © VIK MUNIZ/LICENSED BY VAGA, NEW YORK, NY.

appears to look slightly past the viewer, as if lost in thought. Ten Ten is the only child whose presence does not seem completely established. Instead, the portrait has a fleeting quality, as though the boy's likeness could easily disappear. At the same time, the sugar itself appears to be swallowing the boy as his arms fade into a white blur, lending Ten Ten an angelic, ethereal air that the other children lack.

Muniz's use of sugar offers a pointed commentary on the connections between its consumption in affluent societies and the plight of the indigenous people who farm the cane from which it is made. Once a luxury good, sugar has become so commonplace that its availability is generally taken for granted, as are the lives of those who produce it under harsh conditions. Millions of consumers add the sweetener to beverages and food without ever questioning where it comes from or how it is made. Indifference to the workers' conditions is similarly true of other commodities that are obtained through the misery of others, such as diamonds, another material that Muniz has used. But unlike Muniz's *Pictures of Diamonds*, in which the subjects (Marlene Dietrich and Elizabeth Taylor) exist thousands of miles away from the source of the commodity's production, the subjects in the *Sugar* series are themselves destined to become the source of production.

More generally, the use of sugar in *Ten Ten's Weed Necklace* serves a narrative function, summoning a tumultuous, bloody history of agricultural colonialism and exploitation on St. Kitts that dates back over three hundred years. Considered the mother colony of the West Indies, St. Kitts was the oldest and wealthiest of the British colonies in the Caribbean. The Portuguese introduced sugarcane to the island from Brazil in 1640, necessitating the importation of thousands of West African slaves.[2] The island's fertile soil and tropical climate were well suited to this labor-intensive cash crop, and sugar plantations soon became the source of fabulous wealth reaped from the sweat and toil of slave labor.

Demand drove the need for greater production and, hence, more slaves. By the eighteenth century there were ten times as many African slaves on the island as Europeans.[3] At the peak of production in the nineteenth century, St. Kitts had sixty-eight sugar plantations, a remarkable number considering the island's modest size of just sixty-eight acres. Although many Caribbean islands became wealthy through sugar production, the cultivation of a single non-nutritional export crop in place of self-sustaining and nutritious crops created an economy dependent on the importation of foodstuffs in a widely fluctuating market.

Slavery was abolished on St. Kitts in 1834, but sugar production continued to dominate the island, with approximately one-third of the workforce laboring in the sugarcane fields. Most of the inhabitants were, and continue to be, descendants of the West African slaves who were forcibly sent to the island. By using sugar to "draw" the portrait of Ten Ten, Muniz confronted the history of sugar production and consumption head on. His use of sugar further comments on the nature of consumption: the portraits consume sugar in a way that underscores its ephemeral quality as an object to be ingested. They also draw attention to the consumable nature of art itself, especially in today's frenzied market, where art has become a commodity like any other.

After documenting the original drawing of Ten Ten with his camera, Muniz destroyed it, a fate he imposes on all of his drawings as part of his transformative "ritual of destruction." The photographs are the end pieces, the drawings the means of achieving them. Given the context of the St. Kitts children's lives, a sense of poignancy and regret surrounds the destruction of their images. Perhaps Muniz felt this, too. After photographing each sugar drawing, he placed the sugar in small glass jars (which he tellingly referred to as "urns") to which he affixed the original snapshots of the children.

This suggestion of sugar transformed into ashes is powerful in its simplicity, recalling both the seasonal burning of the sugarcane and the death of the sugar industry it foretold. In 2005 the St. Kitts government closed down the industry. Since then, many of the former sugar-field laborers have found new employment cultivating a variety of fruits and vegetables and developing the island's tourism industry. Little did Muniz know during his 1995 visit that his sugar children would escape the sugarcane fields. The demise of the sugar industry in St. Kitts suggests that the potential of Muniz's subjects, so evident in his portraits, may yet be realized. ◉

NOTES

Epigraph: Vik Muniz, *Reflex: A Vik Muniz Primer* (New York: Aperture Foundation, 2005), 63.

1. Ibid., 60.

2. Carl and Roberta Bridenbaugh, *No Peace Beyond the Line: The English in the Caribbean, 1624–1690* (New York: Oxford University Press, 1972), 81.

3. Richard Sheridan, *Sugar and Slavery: An Economic History of the British West Indies, 1623–1775* (Baltimore: Johns Hopkins University Press, 1974), 13.

Summer 2007, volume 7, number 3

john stomberg |

Zhan Wang

Urban Landscape

THE ARTIST ZHAN WANG constructs cities, most recently Beijing, from a combination of new cookware and hand-molded rock formations, all made from stainless steel. His installation *Urban Landscape: Beijing* appeals on numerous levels simultaneously, and this multiplicity of meanings and openness to interpretation delights the artist.[1] Zhan knows much of what his work can mean, but he also appreciates that objects and ideas resonate differently in different contexts. When he uses common cooking tools to implement his vision, he removes them from the restaurant or kitchen and attempts to commandeer their meaning—tongs become trains, inverted Sterno frames become ruins, and chafing dishes become modern apartment complexes. In keeping with the example of Marcel Duchamp, who famously exhibited found objects as demonstrations of the artist's ultimate power in designating what qualifies as art, these objects gain their urban identity only through the context of a place that the artist identifies as a city. But Zhan's use of found objects also differs significantly from his predecessor's. Duchamp exhibited bottle racks and urinals as "readymade" art in celebration of their inherent beauty and cultural significance. Zhan allows his objects to remain—almost defiantly—cookware, while simultaneously transforming them into something else through his art. The tongs, for example, are both cookware and trains, and each identity carries with it a multitude of cultural and art-historical references.

Zhan embraces and subverts several other major traditions in modern art, both Chinese and Euro-American. He uses an undifferentiated grid on the floor to define the parameters of his work and to heighten our awareness of the space itself. In this he evokes the lessons of major minimalist sculptors such as Carl Andre, but with a critical twist: like Andre's work, Zhan's grid rearranges our understanding of the space we occupy—acting *as* art—but it also exists as a pedestal—a site *for* art. Where Andre is doctrinaire, Zhan is laissez-faire. Zhan also clearly engages the work of artists such as Haim Steinbach, who uses rows of unaltered, mass-produced consumer products wrenched from their commodity context. The overt appeal of Zhan's material (the shiny, new, stainless steel cookware) locates his work, like Steinbach's, in a critique of consumer culture, but Zhan's embrace of multiple meanings extends this critique. His materials are both objects of desire and physical manifestations of the systems (social, political, cultural, and economic) in which they operate: it is precisely the trade in commodities such as cooking tools that is fueling the booming Chinese economy, which is in turn driving the modernization of China's cities.

For Zhan the manufactured goods (their meaning intact) are important to the range of interpretations he wishes to address with his work. In the same way that one stainless steel, thirty-liter soup kettle is indistinguishable from the next, so too are most of the modern buildings that are coming to define the new Beijing. Furthermore, these pans can be replicated—each one bears the promise of never-ending reproducibility, a sameness that becomes the threat of infinite mediocrity when applied to the modern city. Of course, there are slight variations in the buildings going up in Beijing, but overall Zhan has created a truncated visual vocabulary for the modern section of his city. He uses more variety and detail—right down to the tiny frosting tips that form the tops of some of the pagodas—to represent the older sections of the city. Low serving trays, dishes, and a group of lunch boxes denote the Forbidden City; the Temple of Heaven includes matching serving bowls glued together at their rims to create stackable spheres.

Zhan's work evokes the complicated mix of Western and Eastern that has come to define life in Beijing and instigates discussion on the continued utility of *Western* and *Eastern* as meaningful descriptions. In conversation, Zhan insists that the distinction continues to function but may have a limited shelf life. In China, he says, modernization is associated with the West: when China modernizes, it westernizes. In many cases, especially with urban reconstruction, this process is a zero-sum exchange—that is, Beijing modernizes at the cost of its past. In his construction of Beijing, Zhan uses the inverted Sterno frames to denote the city's ruins, some ancient, fostering the elegiac mood that seems to hover over the work.

Above: Zhan Wang, *Urban Landscape: Beijing*, 2006. PHOTOGRAPH BY ART EVANS

On the outskirts of the installation, Zhan's mountains offer a natural border to the city's expansion. Here the artist transforms a much-loved tradition in China, where rocks have long been used in gardens to represent mountains. Zhan's mountains refer as well to the stunning small rock formations, most of them desktop size, prized in China as *scholars' rocks*. In both traditions the rocks are microcosms of nature—entire mountains encapsulated in a small form—and are meant to stimulate productive reverie. Set in a garden or on a desk, these rocks provide opportunities for beholders to contemplate their relative insignificance in the face of nature's great powers. Poets, painters, and calligraphers in China have long used these rocks as inspiration for their art. The scholars' rocks facilitate introspection; one actually gazes *at* these rocks, but figuratively, one stares *into* them—that is, into nature.

When Zhan creates his mountains, he molds stainless steel around existing rock formations so that the physical form of his work faithfully replicates the original.[2] Through this transformation he drastically alters the way we experience the objects. Zhan's mountains reflect our image, rather than providing an opportunity for reflection. In all their shining beauty, Zhan's rocks become the focus of our attention. This, too, could be a lamentable turn of events: the rapid advance of Western-style modernization and the lifestyle that accompanies it, representing a loss of depth for China in terms both spiritual and historical. But Zhan maintains that his rocks adapt to change more easily than their stone ancestors. Being made of reflective material, his rocks can, chameleon-like, take on the color of their surroundings. For him the mountains promise endurance by virtue of their adaptability to modern China's ever-changing environment.

In a Euro-American context, these issues seem as far off as Beijing itself. The cookware is mostly familiar. It is the good-quality ware found in kitchen shops today. We marvel at the ingenuity of Zhan's transformation of his material— how perfectly kitchen tongs replicate trains and bowls become pagodas. Ultimately, the whole installation evokes that most familiar of Chinese cultural associations: its cuisine. In this, Zhan plays to expectations while challenging his viewers to see beyond the surface familiarity. He alludes to the food we love and gives us the commodities we know, mountains we recognize from Chinese paintings, and even some famous monuments. We recognize all of this, and it adds up to our portrait of China. In a strictly domestic context, this all could be just delightful—the type of audacious display of talent and ingenuity that earns our respect at world's fairs.

Zhan's work, though, ultimately transcends a simple tally of its references. His installation embodies an expansive worldview with subjects ranging from economics, theology, sociology, urban planning, and architecture to formal art issues, such as the use of found objects and the role of the grid. In all this, he challenges, engages, and delights his viewers. We are asked to meditate on the multiple impacts of rapid modernization in China while taking pleasure in the gleaming surfaces of the material. *Urban Landscape: Beijing* evokes both the allure of modern urban culture (typified by fine dining) and the consequences of urban renewal—it offers the sensuous pleasure of modernity and the sting of the price paid. ◉

NOTES

1. This and all references to Zhan Wang's opinions derive from a series of conversations with the author, translated by Wei Ren, 12 to 16 June 2006, in Williamstown, Massachusetts.

2. For more on Zhan's work in this area, see Britta Erickson, "Material Illusion: Adrift with the Conceptual Sculptor Zhan Wang," *Art Journal* 60, no. 2: 72–81.

Spring 2007, volume 7, number 2

lawrence raab |

The First Still Life

The scene at the table wasn't going well,
so he thought, Why not try something
different? Leave Christ out. Do the bread
and wine by themselves. Add a knife.

Or perhaps the weather was bad—
had been for weeks—and the painter
of the first still life couldn't work outside
on his landscapes. Or he's poor

and can afford only small canvases
unsuited to a storm or crucifixion.
In front of him on the kitchen table:
a chipped white bowl and an apple.

He thinks, Take a bite out of it, call
the picture *Original Sin*. Or let the apple
decay, add a couple of flies, call it
Allegory of Life, or *Vanity*.

He understands that vanity and sin
will sell better than an apple in a bowl.
And yet—why not try the thing itself?
So he does. After which: blackberries

and lemons on a blue china plate,
peaches and grapes in a wicker basket,
a watermelon sliced open, then a trout,
then an eel, two glasses of wine

beside a letter on a desk, an egg in a cup.
And spoons and forks, of course, vases
of flowers, cascades of drapery. But first:
the apple in the bowl, a curve

of shadow on the top of the table.
He titles it *Apple in a Bowl*
to say: That's all that is here.
There's nothing you can't see.

Spring 2006, volume 6, number 2

personal journeys

Waiting for a Cappuccino: A Brief Layover along the Spice Trail | *Carolyn Thériault* **182**

Include Me Out | *Fred Chappell* **187**

Evacuation Day, or A Foodie Is Bummed Out | *Merry White* **190**

Ripe Peach | *Louise Glück* **194**

carolyn thériault |

Waiting for a Cappuccino
A Brief Layover along the Spice Trail

As I wait for my cappuccino, I subconsciously but quite mechanically begin to play with the salt and pepper shakers on the vinyl tablecloth—pairing them off as ballroom dancers across the checkerboard design, then transforming them into charging bull and lithesome matador. In its zeal, the salt delivers a deathblow to the pepper, knocking it over and spilling much of its contents. Turning my head slightly, I note that I am being watched in disbelief by the server. Embarrassed, I set the pepper shaker aright, affording it (and myself) a little dignity.

Dignity? What dignity can I offer my spilled pepper—its day is gone, the sun has set on its empire, it has paid for its commonness in a questionable currency of novelty shakers, plastic bags from bulk stores, bins, and unimaginative pressed-glass bottles. If pepper (and the same holds true for all spices) is distanced from its origins, then we are wholly ignorant of them. Do peppercorns look longingly back on an illustrious past when bloody battles were fought, queens seduced, peoples enslaved, lives lost, pirate-infested waters crossed, and worlds discovered for their sake, when their value was such that they were counted peppercorn by peppercorn? If they don't, we should, for the "discovery" of our world was founded upon the rapacious pursuit of these peppers, as well as vanilla and allspice. Our land mass stood inconveniently in the way of those ships seeking direct passage to the "wealth of the Orient," but this diversion was serendipitous if not rewarding: the bounty of the Americas proved to be equally profitable to that of the Far East. Our kitchen cupboards are a living map of trade routes: shelves and racks peppered with spices that have traveled since antiquity along their own routes or hitched a ride along the silk and amber roads of China, India, Indonesia, Africa, and Persia—their distant homelands still evocative of culinary erotica.

My cappuccino arrives, and I note that the cinnamon has burrowed deeply into the foam, leaving rabbit holes in its milky peaks; my nostrils flare at the sharp, aromatic hit of spice. The cinnamon gives me pause. Herodotus, the so-called Father of History, wrote that giant phoenixes, notably called *cinnamolgi*, used cinnamon sticks to make their nests. He goes on to say that in order to harvest the spice, men would lob chunks of meat at the nests, causing them to fall to the ground and break apart. It would be an understatement to say that such bits of arcana intrigue me. In fact, I wish I could fumble with a few mechanical

Right: The vegetable seller, Marrakech. photograph by carolyn thériault © 2006

knobs and not only turn back time but turn myself into a cinnamon stick so that I could travel by camel and tall ship across the ancient world to be traded in Malabar, Cathay, or Babylon, to be lauded in the courts of Kublai Khan, to be put on the "historical" map by the likes of Marco Polo. Since I cannot be that piece of bark, I must use less fantastic means to savor that spice experience and, regrettably, rely upon my memory. Sipping my coffee, I allow my mind to return to the *souks* (or markets) of North Africa in which I have not only spent a great deal of time but become deliciously lost over and over again.

It is in Egypt that I first discover that pyramids of saffron and cardamom can surpass their limestone counterparts across the Nile in both beauty and elegance. Crushing hibiscus flowers underfoot, I meander deeply into the Khan Al-Khalili, the labyrinthine *souk* of medieval Cairo, where I am blinded by color: baskets piled high with spices of vermilion, saffron, ochre, and burnt tangerine. These multihued pylons appear to defy the laws of physics, but it is I who lose balance, reel at the headiness of cloves, turmeric, cumin, and pepper. Here, desiccated pods, roots, fruit pits, stems, seeds, gums, bark, berries, and petals from neighboring continents all coincide in blissful coexistence. These modern *souks* are the heirs of the world's first interracial marriages, gastronomic multicultural harems where Lebanese fenugreek flirted with tamarind from Delhi, where no one raised an eyebrow in horror.

The spice trade was once both a serious and a dangerous business: only a few centuries ago, the English stevedores who emptied spice ships were obliged to sew their pockets fast to discourage theft. Spices traveled thousands of kilometers of inhospitable terrain and wild seas by long camel caravans fraught with brigands and in ships plagued by piracy. Conditions at sea were so perilous that if the spice ships returned at all, they normally dropped anchor with significantly fewer crewmembers than when they had left.

But this is relatively recent history: before humans could leave historical records, they were seasoning their food with aromatic plants. Later, the ancient Egyptians used spices to flavor the lives of the living and to preserve the bodies of the dead. The Chinese were importing cloves from the Moluccas over two millennia ago, and spices were traded in Europe before Rome was founded. It was not unknown for Arab merchants to guard the identity of their sources and hide spice routes by inventing bizarre and horrifying tales to discourage other entrepreneurs. In Roman times wealthier households made a conspicuous display of using spices in their daily cuisine and thereby increased their social standing. Later, Crusaders returning from the Holy Land brought with them spices and inspired fortune seekers, merchants, and adventurers to ply the seas for spices, Christian converts, and new continents. Spices became ingrained in everyday life, and their uses far exceeded enhancing the taste of unpalatable or insalubrious fare: in many towns one could pay taxes, tolls, and rent as well as bribe judges with just the right amount of pepper. Spices were ground into medical compounds; curative wines were enhanced with saffron; and sick rooms were liberally fumigated with spice-bearing smoke. The economic and political fortunes of vying global powers, notably Venice, Genoa, Spain, Portugal, England, and the Netherlands, were directly linked to their ability to control trade routes and their hegemony over the Spice Islands. The colonization of the New World ultimately created a new and highly motivated merchant class that was able to successfully undercut its competitors. The markets of the world became flooded with less expensive spices, and with the increased availability of sugar, coffee, tea, and cocoa, the sun began to set on the sovereignty of the peppercorn and its kin.

The value of a man's life was once equivalent to a bag of pepper; in light of this, it seems frivolous if not obscene to consider the current price of spices. In the spice *souks* it seems equally disrespectful to be able to simply walk by such historical wealth with modern indifference. Nonetheless, as I do, the breeze from my passing causes a slight tremor, and a few grains of allspice hover in the air like dust motes. I freeze—how much money have I inadvertently wasted? An annoying mechanical noise jars me from my spice-guilt, and I turn to watch a man in the Khan Al-Khalili operating what looks like a wood chipper, grinding curled cinnamon bark into its more common powdered form. Connecting with my imaginary cinnamon stick persona, I wince in sympathy for my fallen comrades.

In the Nubian markets of Aswan—the southernmost point of pharaonic Egypt and the most "African" in temperament and temperature—I buy henna to color my hair. The ancient Egyptians likewise dyed their hair and tattooed their bodies with these dried plant leaves. After spending an afternoon sitting on the balcony of my hotel with malodorous goop on my head, I fear that my hair more closely resembles the garish locks of the Egyptian Museum's dehydrated mummies. In the *souks* of Khartoum, I buy kilograms of frankincense from Somaliland. I have no clue what I will actually do with it—my experience with frankincense is limited to the Three Magi and interminable high masses from my childhood—but know that I must have it. In a world where Catholic parishes are increasingly offering incense-free masses—O *tempora! O mores!*—I can indulge my obsession for a fragrant hit of this freakishly sinus-purging but soothing sweetness behind closed doors. In a charred brass pot from India, I set charcoal briquettes alight and sparingly add a few grains of the amber-like resin—sparingly because the smoke is so prolific that I must disconnect my smoke alarm beforehand lest I invite the entire fire department into my home.

In Fès, considered by many the largest living medieval city in the world, I visit a *khan* or *caravanserai* (from the Persian for "merchant's inn") still guarded by colossal wooden doors able to admit laden camels and still kept secure by massive iron locks so large that I cannot cover them with my two hands. These hostels served the caravans that traversed the East and North Africa and were ingeniously designed around an open concept to cater to its entire clientele, both man and beast. Spices and goods were stored under lock and key; camels were kept safe in stalls on the ground floor courtyards; and merchants were lodged in the overlooking upper galleries. Looking about this now-derelict building, I am momentarily transported to a bygone era of travel—I am certain that I hear the tinkle of camel bells. Peering out the great doorway, I see instead a white mule pass by loaded with plastic crates of clanking Coca-Cola bottles. Caravans of cantankerous camels no longer wind their way through the twisting alleyways of Fès's *souks*, but deliveries haven't changed much in the past nine hundred years.

Not long ago, I presented my mother with an unlikely souvenir from Africa: nutmegs from Marrakech. When I was a girl, my mother baked cookies flavored with nutmeg. Unlike my friends' mothers, she grated her own spice and stored the scraped brindled nut in the receptacle of her nutmeg grater—an aged tin coffin that was affixed to the kitchen wall. It was no wonder to me that her molasses cookies were the world's best. On a rainy afternoon in Marrakech, I sought refuge in the *souk*, where I forewent indigo leather slippers and Berber carpets for a clutch of nutmegs the size of robins' eggs. These formidable nutmegs made their grocery store counterparts pale in comparison; indeed, they were so large my mother's grater could not hold them. Her home on the south shore of Nova Scotia completed these nutmegs' journey, which possibly had begun in Madagascar. Thus the cycle continues. The trade route lives even if a knapsack has replaced a Portuguese sailing vessel. This ancient gift of spice still feels like a serious and somber business, and it should—execution awaited thieves who stole nutmeg trees from the Dutch.

I play with my coffee cup and watch the foam and cinnamon sprinkles swirl about the sides of the cup, leaving Rorschach patterns for my contemplation. I think about Herodotus and his giant birds. I wonder if he was the victim of a dodgy merchant hoping to protect a source or if perhaps, just maybe, cinnamon sticks once had such fabulous origins. I finish my cappuccino, now grown cold, with a quick gulp and wistfully hope that they did. ◉

Winter 2007, volume 7, number 1

fred chappell |

Include Me Out

THERE ARE PEOPLE WHO EAT cold pasta salad. They enjoy despoiling their greenery with gummy, tasteless squiggles of tough, damp bread dough that are usually made palatable only when heavily disguised with hot tomato sauce and a stiff mask of Parmesan cheese. This salad does have the virtue of economy. Wednesday leftovers can be marketed to Thursday customers of perverse taste.

It is probably perversity also that accounts for the prevalence of ice tea in our American South. It was Edgar Allan Poe who first diagnosed this immitigable contrariness of human nature in his short story "The Imp of the Perverse," and he undoubtedly saw it as a normal trait of Dixie character. But please include me out. I am one southerner who detests that dirty water the color of oak-leaf tannin and its insipid banality. When I am offered ice tea by one of our charming sourthern hostesses I know I'm in for a long afternoon of hearing about Cousin Mary Alice's new baby and its genius antics in the playpen.

Hot tea makes sense. It can relax as well as stimulate and in fact may be sipped as a soporific. It can offer a bouquet pungent or delicate and causes us to understand why the Chinese designated certain strains of flowers as "tea roses." It can be a topic of conversation too, as southerners revive the traditional English debate as to whether the boiling water should be brought to the pot or the pot fetched to the water. Such palaver reassures us that all traces of civilization have not disappeared under the onslaughts of video games and e-mail.

But if you ice the stuff down it cannot matter in the least whether the water or the pot has journeyed. Any trace of the tea's bouquet is slaughtered and only additives can give this tarnished liquid any aroma at all. There is, of course, plenty of discussion about these added condiments. Even the mildest of southern ladies may bristle and lapse into demotic speech when they consider that a glass of ice tea has been improperly prepared.

Notice that we say "ice tea." Anyone who pronounces the successive dentals of "iced tea" is regarded as pretentious. And if you say "Coca-Cola" you will be seen as putting on airs, just as obviously as if you employed "you" as a collective pronoun. Down here we say "you-all," "CoCola," and "ice tea" and collect monetary fines from strangers who misspeak. Ignorance before the law is no excuse.

In recent years some enterprising women have seen the futility of the pot/water controversy and have begun making "sun tea," a beverage that is never acquainted with either stove or teapot. They simply fill a gallon jug with water, drop in a flock of tea bags, and set the collocation out on the back porch to brew in the broiling August sunshine. If this method does not make the kitchen more cheerful, it does at least lessen the hypocritical

chatter about proper procedure. Ice cannot harm sun tea; it is created beyond the reach of harm or help.

Now as to the recipe for ice tea:

Lemons are essential and should be of the big thick-skinned variety, cut into sixths. They are never—repeat: *never*—squeezed but only plumped into the pitcher, four or five slices. Extra slices are offered on a cut-glass plate six inches in diameter. Mint may be added, but it is always submerged in the pitcher and never put into a glass, where it would glue to the interior side like a Harley Davidson decal.

And sweetening is the soul of this potation. The sugar bowl passes from hand to hand at a pace so dizzying it is like watching the rotating label on an old 78-rpm record. Southerners demand sweetness. The truly thoughtful hostess shall have already sweetened the tea for her guests with a simple sugar syrup that excludes the possibility of unpleasant graininess from bowl sugar. Sugar syrup for ice tea is concocted by adding one pound of Dixie Crystal sugar to a tablespoon of water.

In the South sweetened ice tea is taken for granted, like the idea that stock car racing is our national pastime and that the Southern Baptist church is a legitimate arm of the Republican Party. If you order ice tea in a restaurant it will arrive pre-sweetened. If you want it unsweetened you must ask for it. Actually, you must demand it with pistol drawn and cocked. And you

Above: Fred Chappell and his hairstylist, Falstaff. PHOTOGRAPH © ALLEN JOSEPH

will have to repeat your demand several times because tea unsweetened is as abstruse a proposition to most servers as a theorem of Boolean algebra. Even then you can't be sure. My wife, Susan, once ordered unsweetened but it arrived as sweet as honey. The waitress pleaded for understanding. "We couldn't figure how to get the sugar *out*," she said.

Why southerners are so sugar-fixated may be a mystery, but it is an indisputable fact. We are a breed who makes marmalades of zucchini, tomatoes, onions, and even watermelon rinds. Our famous pecan pie ("puh KAWN pah") is a stiff but sticky paste of boiled Karo corn syrup studded with nuts. Since this is not sweet enough, it will likely be served with a gob of bourbon whipped cream dusted with cocoa powder and decorated with vegetable-peeler curls of milk chocolate.

"Do you want ice tea with that?"

"Oh yes. Sweetened, please."

Well, I'll confess that, though born in North Carolina, I make a poor example of a southerner. I don't even capitalize the name of the region. I'm a Democrat, a non-Baptist, and don't care what kind of car I drive. To me, adding broiled marshmallows to yams is like putting raspberry jam on porterhouse. I once spotted a recipe in the magazine *Southern Living* for CoCola cake and had to fight down a surge of nausea. I flee as if pursued from fatback, spoon bread, barbecue, grits, and—ice tea.

Susan tells me I need sweetening. ☻

Fall 2001, volume 1, number 4

merry white |

Evacuation Day,
or A Foodie Is Bummed Out

THERE ARE MANY REASONS not to eat, but none so humiliating as a day of preparation for that ultimate insult to the flesh, the camera up the ass. Like other boomers, especially those of us who hide sheer gluttony behind our "connoisseurship" in food, I have undergone a colonoscopy. Here, then, is my tale of learned humility, with new realizations about the true breadth of the field of food studies.

Before Evacuation Day, everything I had ever learned (and taught) about food studies concerned foodways—not the lower end of the digestive process. Thus, in the colonoscopic experience, all my efforts to develop palatal sensitivity were for naught, or for very new uses. Getting my gut ready for this procedure, I had to reverse a lifetime's notions of food and taste and satisfaction in eating. If you don't mind my getting graphic about it, this necessary insult to our systems is food connoisseurship turned upside down. And yet, there it is, demanding attention, that last stage of the bodily food chain. What new rank of scholars in cultural enterology will rise to the occasion and accord this field a name worthy of its significance? Post-digestism, perhaps? Or post-intestinal colonialism?

For those of you who are pre-colonoscopic (mostly under fifty), a colonoscopy scans your upper and lower bowels for polyps, benign or malign, by means of a tiny camera inserted on a probe. This procedure may remind you of an old science-fiction movie in which miniaturized scientists and their instruments travel through a human patient's arteries, but in this case the camera is, I believe, unmanned.

The patient's role in a colonoscopy is an active one, for the day before the procedure you must eat nothing but clear substances and, toward the end of the day, induce in yourself a dramatic purge of everything that might be in your digestive tract. Beyond that, we get a chance to think about what we're doing. Most food academics are not professionally interested in the end of the line—you might say, we don't give a shit. But it is time to fill that gap, and I have my own case study to offer as grist for the new field's analysts. No matter what methodology you choose—from anthropology's "thick description" to enology to the study of taste and culture—you have the tools. And, of course, the opportunity for participant-observation awaits you.

Fasting as personal purge and cultural ritual is a staple of our field. I have read works with titles like "You Are What You Don't Eat" that discuss the purification of the soul through denying the flesh; articles on subversion of the dominant (male) code through denying food to the self and others; and scholarly treatises on fasting and body image in advertising: waste your waist to get a man. During the week before my "field work," the questions of how a person who lives for her next superb meal manages the spartan regime sounded like an interesting exercise, and I began by dreaming up the limpid broths, perfect aspics, and fresh fruit gelatins I would make in preparation. I thought I could improve on the regulations from the doctors, which specify limiting your intake to "clear liquids (tea, coffee, and clear juices), broth or bouillon, and clear Jell-O (do not use red Jell-O)." As it turned out, though, the day before fast day was extremely busy. A raucous dinner party (this is when you decide to invite your first husband and his third wife for a reunion with your old professors) meant no time to prepare the *cuisine maigre* required for the next day. And there sat the delicious leftovers from the party…So I succumbed. For the fast day I made only yellow Jell-O and green Jell-O: "lemon" and "lime" do not describe their taste.

Fasting in itself had some appeal: maybe I would appreciate subtle tastes better, maybe I would learn a lesson of restraint for the future, maybe I would lose weight. It is not just the fact of a day or more of not eating. (Tip for the uninitiated: be sure to schedule your event for early morning—at least then you don't have all those additional hours of emptiness.) It is also what must happen at the end of that day: the hours on the toilet, with time off to sip more of the potion that will keep you there. For me, fear of pain (or, more remotely, the outcome of the test) was matched only by fear of the taste of the laxative. I had been prepared by horror stories—*the most appalling taste! disgusting! choke it down if you can!* With the bottle before me I read: "Sip slowly 1.5 oz at four P.M. and another 1.5 oz at seven P.M." My heart sank, reminding me of a child who said to his mother when he heard how he and his baby brother were made, "You mean, you had to do that TWICE???" Except that the child's mistake doesn't apply: in the case of sipping this potion, the act really is distasteful! As the picture of myself in an hour's time clutching my belly and crampily whining loomed, I feared failure of nerve. Would I give up? I would fail.

It is not the colon being tested; it is one's palatal tolerance.

Desperate for a strategy to sustain my courage, I determined to write my way through it. I placed a notebook and pen on the small table next to the toilet. Herewith are my confessional field notes from a participant-observer trip to the bottom of the bowel. Shocking but true.

Tasting Notes

What is your taste "wall" and how do you know when you've hit it? I ask my students in my culinary anthropology class this question, and they come up with things like squid or licorice. Those wanting to impress me cite that Japanese fermented soybean dish, *natto* (which I, against all the established notions about foreigners in Japan, happen to like), or witchetty grubs, or if they think I'm an anti-junk foodie, Hostess Twinkies or Marshmallow Fluff. As for me, I really can eat just about anything: culinary anthropologists are not supposed to have any ingrained dislikes, and I inwardly object to dinner guests who say "I don't eat this." I do have foods I can let alone. But now I have found my wall: it is Fleet Phospho-Soda.

Fleet Phospho-Soda is off any taste map. I try to use the relative language of wine tasting to describe the stuff, but it belies any allusion to food or drink. It is not a foodstuff. Nor is it a gussied-up medicament (I will never like cherry flavoring after Robitussin, or grape jelly after enduring my mother's method of grinding aspirin into it for me as a child). It is a substance designed to clear your bowels, an oral enema, a super-laxative.

I have bitten the bullet, and it is metallic; the taste almost clangs against my palate and tongue. But pursuing the taste despite a strong feeling of "Why am I doing this?" (as I once did at a salt-tasting event held by my local Slow Food Convivium), I persist and try to break the flavor down before it breaks me. The dominant taste is salty. The label says "lemon ginger," but for the life of me I can't find where these flavors are lurking. There is an undertaste of sweetness, but it is that flat, dead-end effect of artificial sweeteners. Not "leather" or "pencil lead" or "dark and sultry" or "effervescent, summery, and *petillant*," words I read in my wine books to describe liquids you might actually sip with pleasure. The mouth-feel is an attack of salt on the palate and tongue: It is a physical slap rather than a "taste"—we are not talking of flowers and fruits and spring breezes—and the slap makes you cringe and pull back. Remember *Rosemary's Baby* and the "chalky undertaste"? Not far away are the fluorescent green glow and the devilish cackles—and the exorcist.

I await the cramps, which do not come, and the purge, which does. The second round is no better than it should have been, and I am losing the battle to observe and record. I just want to sleep and forget. Instead, I read *New Yorkers* and cheerfully tell people who call that they are interrupting a porcelain séance and would they please wait until my gut is empty? A great way to get a telemarketer off the phone, by the way!

I drink coffee, tea, and loads of water. The yellow and green Jell-Os begin to taste good.

The High Priest

Early in the morning, I wait my turn for the probe in elegant ritual attire, the robes that victims don before human sacrifice. I scarcely have the mental energy to wonder why the doctors are called "endoscopists"; is it because they scope out our ends? And it is a very humble me, suffering a caffeine-withdrawal headache (no coffee, or anything else, before the test, please!), waiting passively to be poked. Too exhausted to feel the shame of cowardice, I tell the nurse to max up the drugs.

I am told to watch the monitor if I want to see my gut displayed in real time, and I imagine a twisted mass of garden hose, the kind I struggle with annually, or a videogame in which you hurtle down a tunnel with horrible challenges (and evil polyps) at every turn. Nothing I want to see. I turn my head to the priest instead, and he seems to want to talk about Japan. The last thing I remember hearing the white-coated doctor say is, "I remember so well walking around Kyoto…"

Good Drugs and Graham Crackers

"But nothing happened! Did they make a mistake and not do me?" I ask the nurse who nudges me awake. She insists that they've done the deed and hands me a graham cracker. Tastes real good on the high I have (an amnesia-inducing drug; they swear I was awake the whole time).

So for all you age-mates waiting in fear, procrastinating, or leaving town with no forwarding address, I thought I'd just give you a foodie's roadmap of a process we seldom address in our studies of the sensual delights of food, to remind you of the vast amount of research and fieldwork yet to be done. As for me, I'm pleased to say that I won't have a return engagement for a decade: plenty of time to prepare the veal aspic, the freshly squeezed lime and kiwi gelatin, and the herbal infusions with ginger and rose petals.

As for the outcome, let's just say it all came out right in the end. ☉

Summer 2003, volume 3 number 3

louise glück |

Ripe Peach

1.
There was a time
only certainty gave me
any joy. Imagine—
certainty, a dead thing.

2.
And then the world,
the experiment.
The obscene mouth
famished with love—
it is like love:
the abrupt, hard
certainty of the end—

3.
In the center of the mind,
the hard pit,
the conclusion. As though
the fruit itself
never existed, only
the end, the point
midway between
anticipation and nostalgia—

4.
So much fear.
So much terror of the physical world.
The mind frantic
guarding the body from the passing,
the temporary,
the body straining against it—

5.
A peach on the kitchen table.
A replica. It is the earth,
the same
disappearing sweetness
surrounding the stone end,
and like the earth,
available—

6.
An opportunity
for happiness: earth
we cannot possess
only experience, and now
sensation: the mind
silenced by fruit—

7.
They are not
reconciled. The body
here, the mind
separate, not
merely a warden:
it has separate joys.
It is the night sky,
the fiercest stars are its
immaculate distinctions—

8.
Can it survive? Is there
light that survives the end
in which the mind's enterprise
continues to live: thought
darting about the room,
above the bowl of fruit—

9.
Fifty years. The night sky
filled with shooting stars.
Light, music
from far away—I must be
nearly gone. I must be
stone, since the earth
surrounds me—

10.
There was
a peach in a wicker basket.
There was a bowl of fruit.
Fifty years. Such a long walk
from the door to the table.

Winter 2001, volume 1, number 1

how others eat

My McDonald's | *Constantin Boym* **198**

Great Apes as Food | *Dale Peterson* **202**

The Bengali *Bonti* | *Chitrita Banerji* **212**

The Best "Chink" Food: Dog Eating and the Dilemma of Diversity | *Frank H. Wu* **218**

constantin boym |

My McDonald's

MY FIRST ENCOUNTER with McDonald's was like a sitcom episode. A young and energetic émigré from Moscow, I arrived in Boston in 1981. By a stroke of good fortune I managed to get a job at an architectural firm, even though I could barely speak—let alone understand— basic English. My greatest desire was to blend in with my new colleagues, to be as normal and socially acceptable as possible. I noticed that the architects would sometimes return from lunch and tell everyone about a new place they'd found for a good sandwich, and that this information would usually generate a lively conversation. One day at lunchtime, I wandered a little farther than usual from my office. Suddenly I came upon a strange new restaurant. It was all red and yellow, and very brightly lit. The prices were just right for my wallet. I ordered at random and tasted something I had never tried before: a hamburger, French fries, ketchup… Back at the office, I made an announcement: "Well, today I found a really great place to have lunch. You guys should try it, too." "Really? What is it?" several voices asked. "It's called McDonald's," I said proudly. Nobody laughed or said anything sarcastic, but I could see from their faces that something was wrong…

I remembered this story many years later, when the Iron Curtain started to sag, and the first incredulous visitors from the Soviet Union trickled into the West. I was taking one of these overwhelmed guests, an old school friend, on a long walk through Manhattan. We eventually settled into a small, comfortably dark restaurant in the Village, at the choice window table. Even before the menu arrived, I noticed that my friend was uncomfortable. He was turning in his chair, peeking out the window, looking distracted and anxious. On the other side of the street, in plain view, was a brightly lit McDonald's in all of its red and yellow glory. I made an immediate decision. "Do you want to go there instead?" I asked. My friend eagerly leaped from his seat.

What is it about McDonald's that attracts children and immigrants alike? As a rule, immigrants, like children, are very sensitive creatures. In their desire to blend in, they are conscious of making the wrong gesture, looking funny or different, standing out in any conspicuous way. The simple experience of entering a restaurant, asking for a table, and talking to a waiter can be intimidating. In this respect, McDonald's is the ultimate populist place. No one can be excluded; you can come and go as you please. It's okay to bring your children and to make a mess. Toys are given away along with nutritional information: there is something for everyone.

The most important populist aspect of McDonald's is, of course, the food. Even though the American hamburger has been around since the late nineteenth century, it did not seize the public imagination until the 1940s. At that time, America was obsessed

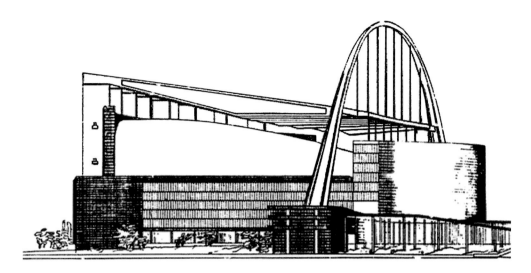

with self-service. The wartime workforce was scarce and expensive, while mechanization had made a giant leap. The drive to cut labor as much as possible resulted in a rapid proliferation of self-service gas stations, department stores, cafeterias, and fast-food restaurants. It is not by chance that the hamburger became a staple of these new eating establishments. American food has always been characterized by meals composed of distinct elements. Instead of one-pot meals, so common in old Europe, the American dinner has historically had a tripartite structure: meat, potato, and vegetable. According to historian James Deetz, this difference points to a world view that places a greater emphasis on the individual and free choice.

Fast-food restaurants proposed a quite different trinity: hamburger, french fries, and soda. Importantly, however, the entire fast-food meal is composed of separate, modular, interchangeable elements. The inner structure of the burger itself can easily be separated into further components, all open for inspection. The assembly of each hamburger has a clearly mechanical nature. Even the look of the different parts alludes to various technological processes, rather than having the conventional appearance of cooked food. Thus the beef patty is produced by molding to a great degree of precision, just like plastic parts (the diameter of a McDonald's burger is exactly 3.875 inches). Like aluminum extrusions, fries are shaped in precise square sections that have nothing to do with the shape of a potato. American cheese, itself a perfectly square yellow tile, is molded around the burger in a process that approximates thermo-forming. Only the bun still maintains some resemblance to conventional bread, but even there, the precise slicing creates two matching parts similar to the male and female parts of a mold. Individually added servings of ketchup play the role of oil and grease necessary for the working of any mechanical assembly.

Much has been written about McDonald's development of special technologies that allowed the company to truly mechanize the fast-food business. Less often commented upon, however, is the fun component of all this necessary and unnecessary mechanization.

Above: Detail from Le Corbusier, Palace of the Soviets (elevation drawing). © 2000 ARTISTS RIGHTS SOCIETY (ARS), NEW YORK/ADAGP, PARIS/FLC

Here, in my opinion, lies the real secret of McDonald's popularity, because Americans love to play with things industrial, mechanical, and technological. From children to adults, we enjoy having more video games, cars, telephones, and now, computers, than any other nation in the world. American roadside restaurants contributed to this obsession by bringing technology and play into the realm of basic food consumption.

At the outset of the twenty-first century, in an age of theme restaurants, the idea of having fun while eating seems obvious. It was not so when the McDonald brothers started their enterprise. The image of a typical roadside restaurant at the time was either faux-historical or cozily domestic. The spirit of the meal generally expressed simplicity and efficiency. As such, it was a far cry from the romance of, say, a contemporary American car. The famous golden arches of McDonald's introduced a brave attempt to tie together architecture, food, and technology into a single unified, entertaining experience. The arches were the intuitive invention of Richard McDonald, who insisted on their incorporation into his new restaurant building. Legend has it that several architects turned him down, not willing to deal with such a "tasteless" client. Eventually, one Stanley C. Meston, a local California architect, reluctantly accepted the commission. By the end of his work on the project, the arches had assumed their characteristic parabolic shape. As often noted, the curve most likely derived from Eero Saarinen's prize-winning St. Louis Arch, not yet built but widely published at the time. The interesting thing is that Saarinen's arch itself was probably influenced by a famous 1931 project, also unbuilt, by the great Le Corbusier. Yes, the first "golden arch" was proposed for Moscow, USSR, as the main compositional element for the giant Palace of Soviets. The rest is history. Indeed, history is full of such improbable, ironic coincidences. Not only would the symbol of populist America derive from a high-Modernist architectural icon, but the ultimate capitalist machine of McDonald's would be related to a palace for Communist Party congresses!

This connection became quite literal in the late 1980s, when newly liberalized Russia opened its doors to Western corporations. McDonald's was one of the first, and certainly the most noticeable, of the foreign companies who seized the opportunity. The site of the first Russian McDonald's was carefully chosen in the spiritual center of Moscow, across the street from the monument to Russia's national poet, Pushkin. Even though it was reported to be the largest McDonald's in the world, the lines to get in stretched around the block at all hours and in every kind of weather. Anecdotes circulated about business travelers who, after waiting in line for hours, would take the burger and fries (only one dinner was allowed per person) to their children deep in the provinces. After a long train journey, they would arrive days later to have the exotic food reheated and tasted by the whole family. Images of the local crowds, policemen in uniform, and the statue of Pushkin with the triumphant big M in the background became an obligatory part of any Western reportage about Russia in transition.

I visited the Moscow McDonald's a few years later, when the queues were long gone. It was evening, and the brightly lit place stood out even in its sumptuous Pushkin Square surroundings. The restaurant building was strangely attached to a conventional Soviet-style hi-rise, as if to permanently emphasize the existential collision of cultures. Driven by idle curiosity, I walked in and looked around. Surprisingly, the inside did not seem to differ from the familiar atmosphere of an American McDonald's. Families with children, groups of teenagers, people of all ages and financial means seemed busy and at ease. A young uniformed girl at the register addressed me in Russian not with the local "Next!" but with "Can I help you?", a hard-to-translate idiom that she was proud to say again and again. Suddenly, I felt at home. Because you can take McDonald's out of America, but you can't take America out of McDonald's. ⊕

Winter 2001, volume 1, number 1

dale peterson |

Great Apes as Food

GORILLA MEAT, so Joseph Melloh, a former commercial meat hunter from Cameroon, once told me, is "sweet, very sweet." Some people have a strong preference for it. "If you love somebody," Joseph explained, "you love somebody. If you don't, no matter how it's viewed, you know, how beautiful the woman is: no way. Same for those who eat gorilla meat as their precious meat. Just because they love it."

Chimpanzee, on the other hand, tastes "definitely different from gorilla. For one thing, chimpanzee meat stinks a little bit."[1]

That the three African apes—chimpanzees, bonobos, and gorillas—have traditionally been a food source for many people living in Central Africa's Congo Basin (a largely forested region claimed by the nations of Cameroon, Central African Republic, Congo, Democratic Republic of Congo, Equatorial Guinea, and Gabon) should surprise no one. Around the globe, people living in or on the edges of the world's great forests have always taken the protein offered by wild animals: true in Asia, Europe, and the Americas, as well as in Africa. But the African tropical forests are particularly rich in variety and have provided Central Africans a very diverse wealth of game species—collectively known as *bushmeat*. Gabonese, one informant tells me, eat every kind of bushmeat except owls, frogs, small lizards, and giant land snails.[2] Southern Congolese, a member of one southern ethnic group once declared, will eat almost every animal, gorillas included—but for various reasons still eschew the meat of chimpanzees.[3]

It is important to remember, however, that traditional eating habits in Central Africa depend not upon one's membership in the modern nation states, which are, after all, a recent invention, but rather upon one's allegiance to a tribe or ethnic group; and the tribal or ethnic food preferences and taboos in this part of the world remain subtle and complex as a result of subtle and complex historical traditions.[4]

Some religious prohibitions (notably, the Muslim prohibition against eating primate meat) and a number of village or tribal traditions have kept apes off the menu in a scattered patchwork across the continent. The local traditions are often rationalized according to familiar myths, and in the case of apes these ancient tales ordinarily evoke the theme of kinship. The Oroko of southwestern Cameroon consider that, since people are occasionally turned into chimps, any hunter discovering and sparing a wild chimp will find the grateful ape has deliberately chased other animals his way; conversely, killing the chimp can cast misfortune onto the hunter's family. (Nevertheless, a dead chimp is still edible food for the Oroko.)[5] The Kouyou of northern Congo traditionally forbade the hunting of at least four species—gorillas, chimpanzees, leopards, and bongo antelopes—and in the case of the two apes, that prohibition was based upon their closeness to humans. Likewise, the Mongandu people of north central Democratic Republic of Congo (former Zaire) have always, since anyone can remember, eaten everything in their forests except for leopards, tree hyraxes, and bonobos. While their neighbors to the south of the Luo River, the Mongo people, will happily hunt and eat bonobos, the Mongandu say that bonobos are simply too much like people to eat. They look human, and when actual humans are not watching, these animals will even stand upright on their hind legs.[6] (Chimpanzees and gorillas also sometimes walk upright, but bonobos, in fact, are the ape most distinguished by this surprising tendency. They will even walk considerable distances on two legs, often when their hands are full, so the Mongandu prohibition is based upon good observation and a sensible interpretation.)[7]

And yet the human resemblance that places apes on the prohibited list for some traditions actually lands them on the preferred list in others. Apes look like humans but possess a superhuman strength.[8] This combination may help explain why apes are, in some places, culturally valued as a food for ambitious men who would like to acquire the strength, and perhaps also the supposed virility, of an ape. For this reason, possibly, ape meat is strictly a man's meat for the Zime of Cameroon, so one tribe member told me.[9] Baka villagers in the southeast of that nation once told me the same thing.[10] For the Ewondo of Cameroon, according to one informant, women can eat gorilla meat at any time except during pregnancy, out of concern about the effects such potent fare might have on the unborn child.[11] This important "masculine" meat also turns out to be a special treat sometimes offered to visiting dignitaries and other powerful men. The recently elected governor of Cameroon's Eastern Province was regularly served up gorilla as he toured his new constituency. Likewise, the Bishop of Bertoua, according to one report, is offered gorilla hands and feet (considered the best parts) when he goes visiting.[12]

These food preferences, based partly upon symbolic value, blend into the preferential logic expressed by symbolic medicine. Symbolic (or "fetish") medicine is a thriving business in the big cities of Central Africa;[13] my own experience suggests that a person can rather easily locate ape parts in the city fetish markets. In Brazzaville, Congo's capital, I once looked over gorilla heads and hands. The hands, so the fetish dealer explained, are used especially by athletes who would like to be stronger. They boil pieces of the flesh until the water is all gone. Then they grind the remnants at the bottom of the pot down to a powder and press the powder into a cut in the skin, thus magically absorbing great strength from the great ape.[14] Likewise, according to Mbongo George, an active commercial meat hunter in southeastern Cameroon, rubbing pulverized gorilla flesh into your back will cure a backache, and chimp bones tied to the hips of a pregnant young girl will ease the process of labor when her own hips are narrow.[15]

ASIDE FROM BONES AND HAIR, virtually every part of an ape is edible, with some rare exceptions. In parts of Cameroon, at least, a male gorilla's testicles and scrotum will be rejected for reasons, so I am told, of taste.[16] But the ape's intestines and soft organs make the

central ingredients of a soup or stew. A gorilla's head is so big it might be cooked in its own pot. Likewise, gorilla hands and feet, especially desirable parts, may be cooked separately.

Ape meat, both smoked and fresh, is singed over a fire to remove any hair, then washed thoroughly, and cooked by boiling—a couple of hours for gorilla. Out in a hunters' camp the final meal may be quite simple: boiled meat with salt, oils, a few wild spices, perhaps a vegetable or two. In villages and towns and cities, though, a wide variety of oils and spices, starches and vegetables are available, and the cooking of ape or any other kind of bushmeat is likely to produce a rich and tasty soup or stew.[17]

YES, THERE ARE ALTERNATIVES to bushmeat in Central Africa. The city markets offer domestic meats, both imported and home grown—and, indeed, at least some of the bushmeats sold in the city markets are more expensive than some domestic meats. I am persuaded this is true for chimpanzee and elephant meat, compared to beef and pork, at least, because I once asked an ordinary citizen in Cameroon's capital city of Yaoundé to buy—bargaining as he would in ordinary circumstances—equivalent-by-weight amounts of chimpanzee, elephant, beef, and pork. In that way, I acquired a strange collection of flesh in my hotel room (severed hand of chimp, slice of elephant trunk, cube of cow, etc.), which I weighed and otherwise compared, and concluded that city people were paying approximately twice

Above: Gorilla hand with beer. PHOTOGRAPH BY KARL AMMANN © 2003

as much for chimpanzee and elephant as for beef and pork. Why would anyone pay more for chimp and elephant? Taste is clearly an important consideration in people's food preferences, though not the only one. Many Central Africans still prefer the taste of bushmeat, in all its prolific variety, but millions of recent urbanities also value bushmeat as a reminder of their cultural identity and roots in traditional villages.

In the rural areas where people are in many cases still living in a style close to traditional village life, the market cost hierarchy is reversed, with domestic meats more and bushmeat less expensive. For many rural Africans, then, bushmeat is also attractive simply because it's cheaper.

The standard dynamics of supply and demand mean that this pattern of consumption is about to hit a wall. While Africa is by far the most impoverished continent on the planet, it is also (and not coincidentally) the fastest growing. A natural rate of increase of 3.1 percent per year for Middle Africa indicates that human numbers are doubling every twenty-three years in this part of the world.[18] If food consumption habits continue, in short, demand for bushmeat as a source of dietary protein will double in little more than two decades.[19]

While the demand increases so rapidly, the supply is simply collapsing as a result of at least three factors. First, traditional hunting technologies are being replaced by ever more efficient modern ones, including wire snares, shotguns, and military hardware, and, as a direct consequence, animals across the Basin are being very efficiently *mined*, rather than *harvested*, out of the forests. Wire snares are particularly devastating because they kill indiscriminately; and, since snare lines are only periodically checked, they allow for considerable waste from rot.[20] Wire snares tend to maim rather than kill bigger animals like the apes, but modern shotguns loaded with large-ball *chevrotine* cartridges enable many of today's hunters to target such larger and more dangerous species with impunity.[21] Apes, who would have been unapproachably dangerous quarry for many (though certainly not all) hunters even a few years ago, are now attractive targets offering a very good deal in hunting economics: ratio of meat to cartridge.

Second, a one-billion-dollar-per-year commercial logging industry, run primarily by European and Asian firms to supply ten million cubic meters per year of construction, marine, and finish hardwoods primarily for the pleasure and benefit of European and Asian consumers, has during the last two decades cast a vast network of roads and tracks and trails into profoundly ancient and previously remote forests across the Congo Basin.[22] Loggers degrade these forests, haul in large numbers of workers and families, and often hire hunters to supply the bushmeat to feed the workers and their dependents. Most seriously, though, the loggers' roads and tracks and trails allow hunters in and meat out for the first time in history (and the ecological history of these great forests takes us back to the era of the dinosaurs). Vast areas of forest that even a decade ago were protected by their remoteness are today no longer protected at all.

Third, as a result of the new hunting technologies and the new opportunity offered by all those roads and tracks and trails cut by the European and Asian loggers, a small army of African enterpreneurs has found new economic opportunity in the bushmeat trade, which has quite suddenly become efficient and utterly commercialized. Bushmeat is now big business. Bushmeat is now no longer merely feeding the people in small rural villages and other subsistence communities but instead reaching very deeply into the forests and then stretching very broadly out to the towns and big cities throughout Central Africa. In Gabon alone, the trade currently amounts to a fifty-million-dollar-per-year exchange.[23] Altogether, this commerce today draws out of Central Africa's Congo Basin forests an estimated and astonishing five million metric tons of animal meat per year.[24] That amount is absolutely unsustainable. The depletion of the supply of wild animals and their meat, in short, is not even remotely balanced by the replenishment offered via natural reproduction in a stable ecosystem.[25]

A GENERALLY ACCEPTED ESTIMATE holds that around 1 percent of the total bushmeat trade involves the meat of the great apes—chimpanzees, bonobos, and gorillas. A blind and drunk optimist might imagine that 1 percent even of five million metric tons is a somewhat tolerable amount. It is not, of course. And even in the best of circumstances, where apes happen to inhabit legally protected forests (that is, national parks and reserves), a recent survey based on responses from professional field workers tells us that chimpanzees are hunted in 50 percent of their protected areas, bonobos in 88 percent, and gorillas in 56 percent.[26]

The impact of the current explosion in market hunting across the Congo Basin is threatening the existence of several wild animal species—but it disproportionately devastates the great apes. Biologists theoretically examining the sustainability of hunting consider, among other things, the ability of a species to replenish itself. A species with a quick rate of replenishment can likely, other factors being equal, withstand a high rate of depletion from hunting. Thinking about the impact hunting has on the survival of any particular species, in other words, requires us to examine that species' reproduction rates, and the great apes are unfortunately very slow reproducers. Perhaps because they are intelligent animals requiring extended periods of immature dependency while the young learn from their elders, apes wean late, reach independence and puberty late, and produce surprisingly few offspring. Altogether, the apes show about one quarter the reproduction rate of most other mammals.[27]

Given such a slow reproduction rate, biologists calculate that chimpanzees and bonobos can theoretically withstand a loss of only about 2 percent of their numbers per year and still maintain a steady population. Gorillas may be able to tolerate losses of 4 percent per year. Monkeys have about the same low tolerance for loss, ranging from 1 to 4 percent, depending on the species. Ungulates, depending on the species, should be able to withstand yearly losses ranging most typically around 25 percent; and rodents can do just fine with losses from 13 percent to 80 percent per year, again depending on the species. In an ideal world, hunters would be equipped with pocket calculators to keep track of how sustainable their hunting is. In the real world, commercial hunters usually shoot whatever happens to wander in front of their guns. As a result, active hunting in a forest tends to deplete the fauna in a predictable progression. Apes and monkeys go first. Ungulates next. Rodents last. Indeed, it ought to be possible to measure the faunal disintegration of a forest by comparing the ratio of monkeys to rats sold in local markets.[28]

The best, most recent estimates tell us that approximately 150,000 to 250,000 chimpanzees survive in the wild, at the most some 50,000 bonobos remain, and roughly 120,000 wild gorillas are still there.[29] Based on the "informed consensus of experts," though, the commercial hunting of apes for meat is "out of control and unsustainable," and it continues "to spread and accelerate."[30] With the current levels and patterns of demand for apes as food, how long can they last?

One measure of how fast commercial hunting can reduce an ape population has been provided by the history of eastern Democratic Republic of Congo's Kahuzi-Biega National Park, supposedly protected as a UNESCO World Heritage Site but not protected well enough to keep out the professional hunters. In only three years during the 1990s, hunters in Kahuzi-Biega earned a living by transforming into meat ("if our worst fears prove founded," so one investigator writes cautiously) some 80 to 90 percent of the 17,000 individuals who until then constituted the subspecies *Gorilla gorilla graueri*.[31]

In sum, conserving biodiversity—saving the apes from extinction—amounts to one argument against using apes as a human food. A second argument has to do with public health. Perhaps all meats amount to a fair bridge for animal-to-human infection. Domestic meats, for example, offer *E. coli* 0157, salmonella, and the hypothetical "prion" that causes mad cow disease among cattle and the deadly Creutzfeldt-Jakob syndrome among humans who eat cattle. But most domestic meats are regularly inspected and controlled to protect the carnivorous public, while bushmeat is not. Ape meat is particularly suspect if only because it is illegal, often sold covertly, and therefore particularly difficult to monitor or control.

Chimpanzees and gorillas, in any event, appear to be about as vulnerable to the extremely infectious and frequently lethal Ebola virus as people are, and recent events in Central and West Africa have demonstrated that apes can also, like humans, readily transmit that virus not only to each other but also to any humans nearby—hunters handling meat, for instance.[32] Virologists have also recently identified an SIV virus endemic to chimpanzees as the culprit, the historical source of HIV 1 (subtypes M, N, and O) in humans, which accounts for the infection of around 99 percent of today's globally distributed AIDS victims.[33] The remaining 1 percent have been infected with HIV 2, a closely related virus that we now know comes from an SIV endemic to the West African monkey popularly known as Sooty Mangabey. A reasonable presumption is that the three historical moments of viral transmission from chimpanzees to humans (producing today's three viable HIV 1 subtypes)—three separate episodes when a chimpanzee SIV successfully leapt into a human host—occurred not during the eating of ape meat, since cooking kills viruses, but during the butchering phase.[34] In any case, since that event has already happened, a person might imagine that the danger has passed: deed already done. In fact, apes are susceptible to a large variety of diseases that will also infect humans, including bacterial meningitis, chicken pox, diptheria, Epstein-Barr virus, hepatitis A and B, influenza, measles, mumps, pneumonia, rubella, smallpox, whooping cough, and so on.[35] Far more serious, however, is the possible scenario of a person already infected with HIV 1 or HIV 2 coming into intimate contact (through butchering, for instance) with one of a number of related viruses—the SIVs endemic among several monkey species—thereby producing a successful cross, a recombinant virus that could become HIV 3. The government of Cameroon recently sponsored an extended study on primate viruses where researchers tested the blood of 788 monkeys kept as pets or sold as meat and discovered that around one fifth of those samples were infected with numerous varieties of SIV, including five previously unknown types. So the potential for new epidemics based on recombinants should be taken very seriously.[36]

The final argument against apes as food is perhaps the one many people think of first but often have trouble describing fully or convincingly, and that is the moral argument. The great apes—the three species commonly known as chimpanzees, bonobos, gorillas in Africa, and orangutans in Southeast Asia—are special animals because they are so close to human.

This idea is one long held in several, though not all, African traditions, as I have already suggested, and now, increasingly, in the European tradition. One of the earliest European reports on the existence of the great apes in Africa, English sailor Andrew Battell's tale (told to a collector of explorers' narratives probably in 1607) of two types of humanoid "monsters" in Africa may have provided the seminal inspiration for Shakespeare's evocatively humanoid "howling monster" Caliban, in *The Tempest* (1611).[37] A few live apes created some more generalized interest, as they began arriving in Europe by the middle of the seventeenth century; and in 1698, British physician Edward Tyson dissected the recently deceased body of the first live chimpanzee ever to appear in England and announced before the Royal Society the existence of *Homo sylvestrius*, an animal with a profound anatomical similarity to humans.[38] That sort of rather casual enthusiasm was, during the nineteenth century, replaced by less casual studies in comparative anatomy. Charles Darwin himself was inspired to speculate that the African great apes would most likely turn out to be our own closest living relatives, though he lacked the data to prove it.[39]

Around the turn of the century, George Nuttall, an American expert on ticks lecturing in bacteriology at Cambridge University, pressed the comparative science beyond observable anatomy by examining the molecular structure of blood from different species, via antibody reactivity, and demonstrated the surprising fact that the blood of apes resembles human blood far more than it resembles monkey blood.[40] By midcentury, behavioral studies in the field began adding to the picture—perhaps most dramatically through Jane Goodall's first observations in 1960 that the chimpanzees of Gombe Stream Reserve in East Africa were making and using simple tools to capture termites.[41] Subsequent behavioral research shows that wild chimpanzees fashion and exploit an impressive variety of tools according to locally different cultural traditions and that they live in provocatively humanlike social systems, complete with a Machiavellian style of male power-politics and lethal, male-driven territorial wars between adjacent chimp communities.[42] Around the same time, laboratory projects in the United States and Japan were starting to demonstrate the astonishing reality that apes—all four species—are capable of learning and using sign language for communication purposes.[43] A few of those early studies still continue at full strength, as I write, and they have successfully responded to the earliest cries of disbelief from astonished skeptics.[44]

By the end of the twentieth century, techniques and technologies for genetic analysis had become sophisticated enough that it was possible not only to demonstrate to the satisfaction of every scientifically informed observer the undeniable reality of this closeness between humans and the great apes, but also to quantify it. The numbers go like this: Humans and orangutans share 96.4 percent of their genetic code. Humans and gorillas are genetically 97.7 percent identical. And, finally, humans share with both chimpanzees and bonobos an amazing 98.7 percent of their DNA. Genetically, you and I are 98.7 percent identical to both those ape species.[45]

A somewhat careless reader required to examine two books in which 98.7 percent of the words, sentences, and paragraphs are identical and placed in the identical order might complain at the serious injustice of having been forced to read the same book twice. A moderately careful reader, perhaps noticing that the two books have different titles—*Homo sapiens* for one and *Pan troglodytes* for the other—might express outrage at the unimaginative effrontery of this plagiarism.

No wonder, then, that the apes we see in zoos and on stage, in laboratories or in the wild, provoke that strange shock of recognition, serve as that often unexamined source of fascination and sometimes revulsion, of jokes and insults, of hidden concerns and even considered ethical assessments. The four non-human apes, our closest relatives, mirror our faces and bodies, our hands and fingers, our fingernails and fingerprints. They seem to share our perceptual world. They appear to express something very much like the human repertoire of emotions. They look into a mirror and act as if they recognize themselves as individuals,[46] laugh in amusing circumstances,[47] are manifestly capable of learning symbolic language, share with us several recognizable expressions and gestures....[48] Chimpanzees, the hunters sometimes say, will beg for their lives when cornered, with that desperately hunched posture, pleading expression, and pathetically outstretched hand—oh, quite in the style of real beggars you see in the city. ◉

NOTES

1. Joseph Melloh, interviewed in Lomié, Cameroon, by the author, August 2000. Taste is surely one reason why people prefer some foods over others. Since I have never myself eaten ape meat, I cannot form a reasonable opinion about the taste. Interestingly enough, though, a mystery meat experiment (not including ape meat) conducted with thirty European and thirty Nigerian tasters reached the conclusion that both groups harbored a distinct preference for the taste of wild animal meat, while both also ranked domestic beef near the bottom. The Europeans gave their highest scores to the taste of cane rat, while Nigerians preferred bushbuck and giant snail most of all. G.H.G. Martin, "Carcass Composition and Palatability in Some Wild Animals," *World Animal Review* 53 (1985): 40–44.

2. David Edderai, interviewed in Libreville, Gabon, by the author, August 2000.

3. Dale Peterson and Jane Goodall, *Visions of Caliban: On Chimpanzees and People* (Boston: Houghton Mifflin, 1993), 66.

4. Cameroon, for instance, is a single modern nation, but the 15.5 million people living within Cameroon's borders worship according to three major religious systems (Christian, Muslim, and indigenous African), speak twenty-four major African languages and two European languages (English and French), and retain their own cultural identity as members of more than two hundred different tribes. Thus, describing "Cameroonean food traditions" is likely to be incorrect in the particular even while it may be correct in the general.

5. Benis Egoh, letter to author, February 2002.

6. Takayoshi Kano, letter to author, 1996; see also Takayoshi Kano, *The Last Ape: Pygmy Chimpanzee Behavior and Ecology* (Stanford, CA: Stanford University Press, 1992).

7. Personal observation; also Kano, *The Last Ape*, 125.

8. One early experiment in the United States demonstrated that even caged, bored, and out-of-condition chimpanzees can be, pound for pound, three-and-a-half to four-and-a-half times stronger than uncaged, eager, and fully in shape college football players. John Bauman, "Observations on the Strength of the Chimpanzee and Its Implications," *Journal of Mammalogy* 1 (1926): 1–9.

9. Mbongo George, interviewed in Djodibe (hunting camp), Cameroon, by the author, August 2000.

10. Several villagers interviewed in Casablanca, Cameroon by the author, August, 2000.

11. Pierre Efe interviewed in Yaoundé, Cameroon, by the author, August 2000.

12. Karl Ammann, letter to author, September 2000.

13. Personal observation; see also Moses A. Adeola, "Importance of Wild Animals and Their Parts in the Culture, Religious Festivals and Traditional Medicine of Nigeria," *Environmental Conservation* 19 (1992): 125–134.

14. Peterson and Goodall, *Visions of Caliban*, 66.

15. Mbongo George, interviewed in Djodibe (hunting camp), Cameroon, by the author, August 2000.

16. Ammann, letter to author, March 2002.

17. Mbongo George, interviewed in Djodibe (hunting camp), Cameroon, by the author, August 2000; François Kameni, interviewed in Yaoundé, Cameroon, by the author, August 2000; Marcellin Agnagna, letter to author, March 2001; Benis Egoh, letter to author, February 2002; Christina Ellis, letter to author, March 2002; Joseph Nnomo Abah, *L'Art Culinaire Dans le Sud Forestier du Cameroun* (Silver Spring, MD: The Jane Goodall Institute, 2001).

18. *The World Population Data Sheet* (Washington, D.C.: Population Reference Bureau, 1998).

19. Standard consumption rates include a Congo Basin average of forty-seven kilograms per person per year of meat, reasonably comparable to the thirty kilograms per person per year in the "northern industrial countries." David S. Wilkie, "Bushmeat Trade in the Congo Basin," in *Great Apes and Humans: The Ethics of Coexistence*, edited by Benjamin B. Beck, et al. (Washington, D.C.: Smithsonian Institution Press, 2001), 89.

20. Andrew J. Noss, "Cable Snare," *Conservation Biology* 12 (1998): 390–398.

21. Raymond B. Hames compares the efficiency of traditional and modern weapons and reaches the conclusion that shotguns are 231 percent more efficient (meat per hunting time) than bow and arrow. One problem is that time saved using a shotgun may be lost in economic activities required to buy shotgun cartridges. See Raymond B. Hames, "A Comparison of the Efficiencies of the Shotgun and the Bow in Neotropical Forest Hunting," *Human Ecology* 7 (1979): 219–252.

22. *Sold Down the River: The Need to Control Transnational Forestry Corporations, a European Case Study* (Cambridge: Forests Monitor, 2001).

23. Elisabeth A. Steel, *A Study of the Value and Volume of Bushmeat Commerce in Gabon* (Libreville, Gabon: WWF and Gabon Ministère des Eaux et Forêts et d'Environnement, 1994).

24. According to a recent study by John Fa, reported in Fred Pearce, "Death in the Jungle," *New Scientist*, 9 March 2002, 14; a survey of earlier studies on bushmeat consumption rates can be found in David S. Wilkie and Julia F. Carpenter, "The Impact of Bushmeat Hunting on Forest Fauna and Local Economies in the Congo Basin: A Review of the Literature" (unpublished draft manuscript, 2001).

25. See, for instance, David S. Wilkie and Julia F. Carpenter, "Bushmeat Hunting in the Congo Basin: An Assessment of Impacts and Options for Mitigation," *Biodiversity and Conservation* 8 (1999): 927–955; or "U.N. Warns of 'Bushmeat' Crisis," Reuters News Service, 12 March 2001.

26. Andrew J. Marshall, James Holland Jones, and Richard W. Wrangham, *The Plight of the Apes: A Global Survey of Great Ape Populations* (Cambridge, MA: Briefing for United States Representatives Miller and Saxon, 2002), 10.

27. Ibid.

28. Sustainable offtakes for apes, ibid.; for general concept and all other species, John G. Robinson, "Appendix: Calculating Maximum Sustainable Harvests and Percentage Offtakes," in *Hunting for Sustainability in Tropical Forests*, edited by John G. Robinson and Elizabeth L. Bennett (New York: Columbia University Press, 2000), 499–519.

29. Tom Butynski, "Africa's Great Apes," in *Great Apes: The Ethics of Coexistence*, 3–56.

30. Ibid.

31. Ian Redmond, *Coltan Boom, Gorilla Bust: The Impact of Coltan Mining on Gorillas and Other Wildlife in Eastern D. R. Congo* (private report sponsored by the Dian Fossey Gorilla Fund and the Born Free Foundation, 2001), 3.

32. Joel G. Breman, et al., "A Search for Ebola Virus in Animals in the Democratic Republic of the Congo and Cameroon: Ecologic, Virologic, and Serologic Surveys, 1979–1980," *Journal of Infectious Diseases* 179 (Suppl 1, 1999): s139–147; Pierre

Formenty et al., "Ebola Virus Outbreak Among Wild Chimpanzees Living in a Rain Forest of Côte d'Ivoire," *Journal of Infectious Diseases* 179 (Suppl 1, 1999): s120–126; Pierre Formenty et al., "Human Infection Due to Ebola Virus, Subtype Côte d'Ivoire: Clinical and Biologic Presentation," *Journal of Infectious Diseases* 179 (Suppl 1, 1999): s48–53; Alain-Jean Georges, "Ebola Hemorrhagic Fever Outbreaks in Gabon, 1994–1997: Epidemiologic and Health Control Issues," *Journal of Infectious Diseases* 179 (Suppl 1, 1999): s65–75; C.J. Peters and J.W. LeDuc, "An Introduction to Ebola: The Virus and the Disease," *Journal of Infectious Diseases* 179 (Suppl 1, 1999): ix–xvi.

33. Beatrice Hahn et al., "AIDS as a Zoonosis: Scientific and Public Health Implications," *Science* 287 (2000): 607–614; Feng Gao et al., "Origin of HIV-1 in the Chimpanzee *Pan troglodytes troglodytes*," *Nature* 397 (1999): 436–441.

34. Hahn et al., "AIDS as a Zoonosis."

35. Tom Butynski, "Africa's Endangered Great Apes," *Africa Environment and Wildlife* 8 (2000), 30.

36. Martine Peeters et al., "Risk to Human Health from a Plethora of Simian Immunodeficiency Viruses in Primate Bushmeat," *Emerging Infectious Diseases* 8 (2002).

37. See Samuel Purchas, *Hakluytus Posthumus, or Purchas His Pilgrimes, Contayning a History of the World in Sea Voyages and Lande Travels by Englishmen and Others* (Glasgow: James MacLehose and Sons, 1625, rpt. 1905). The full argument supporting the theory of Battell's influence on the creation of Shakespeare's Caliban is elaborated in Peterson and Goodall, *Visions of Caliban.*

38. Geoffrey Bourne, *Primate Odyssey* (New York: G.P. Putnam's Sons, 1974), 281, 282.

39. Nineteenth-century anatomical comparisons include those reported in Thomas H. Huxley, *Man's Place in Nature* (New York: D. Appleton, 1863; 1894).

40. George H.F. Nuttall, *Blood Immunity and Blood Relationship: A Demonstration of Certain Blood-Relationships Amongst Animals by Means of the Precipitin Test for Blood* (Cambridge: Cambridge University Press, 1904); see also Richard Wrangham and Dale Peterson, *Demonic Males: Apes and the Origins of Human Violence* (Boston: Houghton Mifflin, 1996), 35–37.

41. See, for example, Jane Goodall, *The Chimpanzees of Gombe: Patterns of Behavior* (Cambridge, MA: The Belknap Press of Harvard University, 1986), 248–251.

42. Ibid., 530–534.

43. See, for example, Roger Fouts, *Next of Kin: What Chimpanzees Have Taught Me About Who We Are* (New York: William Morrow, 1997); R. Allen Gardner and Beatrix T. Gardner, eds., *Teaching Sign Language to Chimpanzees* (Albany, NY: SUNY Press, 1989); H. Lyn White Miles, "Language and the Orang-utan: The Old 'Person of the Forest,'" in *The Great Ape Project: Equality Beyond Humanity*, eds. Paola Cavalieri and Peter Singer (New York: St. Martin's Press, 1993); Francine Patterson and Eugene Linden, *The Education of Koko* (New York: Holt, Rinehart and Winston, 1981); and Sue Savage-Rumbaugh and Roger Lewin, *Kanzi: The Ape at the Brink of the Human Mind* (New York: John Wiley and Sons, 1994).

44. The most vocal skeptic: Herbert S. Terrace. See his "In the Beginning Was the 'Name,'" *American Psychologist* (September 1985): 1011–1028; and *Nim* (New York: Columbia University Press, 1979; 1987). To find the best and most thorough response to the criticism, see Savage-Rumbaugh and Lewin, *Kanzi*; also Fouts, *Next of Kin.*

45. Charles C. Sibley and Jon E. Ahlquist, "The Phylogeny of the Hominoid Primates, As Indicated by DNA-DNA Hybridization," *Journal of Molecular Evolution* 20 (1984): 2–15; also Feng-Chin Chen and Wen-Hsiung Li, "Genomic Divergences Between Human and Other Hominoids and the Effective Population Size of the Common Ancestor of Humans and Chimpanzees," *American Journal of Human Genetics* 68 (2001): 444–456.

46. George G. Gallup, Jr., "Chimpanzees: Self-Recognition," *Science* 167 (1970): 86, 87; George G. Gallup, Jr., "Self-Recognition in Primates," *American Psychologist* 32 (1977): 329–338.

47. Peterson and Goodall, *Visions of Caliban*, 180, 181.

48. Adriaan Kortlandt, "Handgebrauch bei Freilebenden Schimpansen," in *Handgebrauch und Verständigung bei Affen und Frümenschen*, ed. B. Rensch (Bern: Huber, 1968): 59–102.

chitrita banerji |

The Bengali *Bonti*

How big is the difference between sitting and standing? A cultural universe, when you examine posture in the context of food preparation. In the kitchens of the West, the cook stands at a table or counter and uses a knife. But mention a kitchen to a Bengali, or evoke a favorite dish, and more often than not an image will surface of a woman seated on the floor, cutting, chopping, or cooking. In the Indian subcontinent, especially in its eastern region of Bengal, this is the typical posture. For centuries, the Bengali cook and her assistant have remained firmly grounded on the kitchen floor, a tradition reflecting the paucity of furniture inside the house. A bed for both sleeping and sitting was usually the most important piece of furniture, but outside the bedroom people sat or rested on mats spread out on the floor, or on squares of carpet called *asans*. In the kitchen they often sat on small rectangular or square wooden platforms called *pinris* or *jalchoukis*, which raised them an inch or so above the floor.

From this closeness to the earth evolved the practice of sitting down both to prepare and to cook food. Enter the *bonti*, a protean cutting instrument on which generations of Bengali women have learned to peel, chop, dice, and shred. Despite the recent incursion of knives, peelers, graters, and other modern, Western-style kitchen utensils, the *bonti* is still alive and well in the rural and urban kitchens of Bengal.

A Bengali lexicon compiled by Jnanendramohan Das reveals that although the term *bonti* has been in the Bengali language for many years, it actually derives from the language of the ancient tribal inhabitants of the eastern regions of the subcontinent. Das traces the word *bonti* back to ancient Bengali narrative poems, such as Ghanaram Chakrabarti's poem "Dharmamangal," composed during the reign of Dharma Pala (A.D. 775 to 810), the second ruler of Bengal's Pala dynasty. In his definitive history of Bengal, *Bangalir Itihash*, the historian Nihar Ranjan Ray presents compelling evidence of the proto-Australoid peoples who settled Bengal long before the Aryans came to India and whose language, customs, and ritualistic beliefs still permeate the cultural life of Bengal. Ray also notes that Buddhist terracotta sculptures from the days of the Pala dynasty depict people using the *bonti* to cut and portion fish.

Basically, the *bonti* is nothing more than a curved blade rising out of a narrow, flat, wooden base. Sometimes the blade is mounted on a small iron tripod to increase its height. Its versatility comes from the many different types and sizes of both blade and base, as well as from the various uses to which it is put. The *bonti*'s uniqueness comes from the posture required to use it: one must either squat on one's haunches or sit on the floor with one knee raised while the corresponding foot presses down on the base. As in other "floor-oriented"

cultures, such as Japan, the people of Bengal were accustomed to squatting or sitting on the floor for indefinite periods of time. An 1832 volume by Mrs. S.C. Belnos, *Twenty-four Plates Illustrative of Hindoo and European Manners in Bengal*, depicts a Bengali kitchen complete with utensils and a woman seated in front of a low stove, cooking. The author comments: "Their furniture consists of low beds, small stools, a chest or two, perhaps an old-fashioned chair on which the master sits with his legs crossed under him, a Hookah of cocanut [*sic*] shell on a brass stand." Even today, in rural Bengal where many cottages are sparsely furnished, people—especially men—squat comfortably on porches or under large shade trees as they smoke and chat. Only after the European presence was well established later in the nineteenth century did the living room or dining room equipped with couches, chairs, and tables become part of the ordinary Bengali home.

The *bonti* also appears in Kalighat paintings, a body of indigenous works produced in the vicinity of the Kalighat Temple, built in 1829 on the banks of the river Hooghly (a branch of the Ganges) in Calcutta. As Calcutta grew under British rule, and its Bengali residents developed a semi-decadent "babu" culture, the Kalighat painters focused their attention on urban, rather than the canonic rural, life.

To use a knife of any size or shape, the cook must bear down with one hand on the item being cut, at the same time holding the food with the other hand to prevent it from slipping.

Above: Nineteenth-century Kalighat painting of a woman cutting a whole fish, possibly a carp, on a *bonti*. COURTESY OF BISWARANJAN SARKAR, CALCUTTA

Intérieur d'une hutte de natifs.   *Interior of a native Hut.*

But unlike the more familiar knife, the *bonti* uses horizontal, rather than vertical, force. The cook positions herself in front of the tool, one foot pressed firmly against the wooden base. She then uses both hands to slide the vegetable, fruit, fish, or meat against the curving blade that faces her. To those used to working with a knife, the delicacy with which the rigidly positioned blade cuts seems miraculous: it peels the tiniest potato, trims the tendrils from string beans, splits the fleshy stems of plants, chops greens into minute particles for stir-frying, and even scales the largest fish. At the great fish markets, as in Calcutta, fishmongers sit tightly packed as they dismember giant carp and *hilsa* (a type of shad) on huge, gleaming *bonti*s, all the while engaging in jocular repartee about who has the better fish.

Like knives, *bonti*s come in many different sizes, with blades varying in height, width, and shape. Women using the instrument at home generally have two medium-sized *bonti*s, one for cutting vegetables, the other for fish and meat (the animal products collectively known as *amish*). This separation of vegetarian and non-vegetarian food was rigidly practiced in all traditional Hindu homes until fairly recently and led to the term *ansh-bonti* for the tools used to cut fish or meat (*ansh* means "fish scale"). Professional cooks dealing with large volumes of food use considerably heftier *bonti*s than the housewives. Their *ansh-bonti*s must be strong enough to cut a twenty- or thirty-pound carp, and the blades are proportionately wider and higher. The *bonti* blade is generally made of iron rather than stainless steel, and it tends to rust if not immediately dried. Repeated use blunts the blade, so itinerant experts roam the cities with special gear for sharpening *bonti*s and knives.

An interesting blade is found on the *kuruni*, a *bonti* used for the specific purpose of grating coconuts. In this type of *bonti*, the blade curves out of the wooden base in the usual way, but its tip is crowned with a round, serrated piece of metal. The cook sits in front of the *kuruni* with the front end of its base on a woven mat or tray, or even on a piece of newspaper. Holding one half of a fresh coconut in both hands, she scrapes it with circular motions against the metal disk as the coconut flesh rains down in a stream of white.

Such are the day-to-day uses of the *bonti* in the Bengali kitchen. But as with any implement with a long history, this tool is endowed with a wealth of associations reaching far beyond the mundane. Although professional male chefs use the *bonti*, it is inextricably associated with Bengali women, and the image of a woman seated at her *bonti*, surrounded by baskets of vegetables, is a cultural icon. Holding the vegetable or fish or meat in both hands and running it into the blade makes the act of cutting a relatively softer, gentler motion than the more masculine gesture of bringing a knife down with force on a hard surface: the food is embraced even as it is dismembered.

In the days when most Bengalis lived in extended, multi-generational families, women had to make large meals every day. Usually the elderly grandmother or widowed aunt was responsible for cutting the vegetables, while the younger women took on the more arduous task of cooking over the hot stove. This ritual of cutting, called *kutno kota*, was almost

Left: "Interior of a Native Hut," from S.C. Belnos, *Twenty-four Plates Illustrative of Hindoo and European Manners in Bengal*, 1832. BY PERMISSION OF THE HOUGHTON LIBRARY, HARVARD UNIVERSITY

as important as the daily rituals carried out for the household gods. Some of my fondest childhood memories involve sitting near my grandmother on the floor of the large central space in her Calcutta house as she peeled and sliced the vegetables for the day's main afternoon meal. A grand array of shapes and colors surrounded her: purple and greenish-white eggplants; green-and-white striped *patols* (a favorite gourd-like vegetable); leafy greens of the *noteshaak* with their fleshy, rhubarb-like stems; yellow crescents of pumpkin; pale-skinned potatoes. During holidays and school vacations I always sat and watched my grandmother at the *bonti*…

She takes a long, purple eggplant and dexterously halves it against the blade, then starts cutting one of the halves into smaller pieces. I pick up the remaining half and inspect the white, seed-studded flesh. Something is moving. A worm, secretly embedded in the flesh, is now forced into the open. What kind of insect is it, I ask my grandmother, what kind of insect lives hidden inside the eggplant and what does it eat? She smiles at me, takes the eggplant from my hands and cuts off the infested portion. Then she embarks on a story from an ancient Hindu text about a king who lived inside a glass palace without any openings, to protect himself from the wrath of the snake king who had become his sworn enemy. But one day, when the king bit into a mango, a tiny worm came out from inside the flesh and within seconds was transformed into a huge serpent that stung him to death. I look at the still-crawling worm in the discarded bit of eggplant with new respect…

The woman at the *bonti*, however, is not always an elderly narrator. The young, nubile daughter of the family and the newly married bride sitting at the *bonti* are also part of Bengali iconography. As she joyfully manipulates food against the versatile blade, the young woman epitomizes feminine abilities. When marriages were arranged in rural Bengal, the bridegroom's family would come to look over the prospective bride, asking to see her kitchen skills and noting how well she could chop with the *bonti*. In the southern district of Barisal in Bangladesh, it was not enough for a prospective bride to chop just any vegetable. Her future in-laws often demanded that she sit at the *bonti* and cut a bunch of *koloishaak*, the leafy greens of the legume *khesari daal*, whose fibrous leaves and stem have to be chopped very fine before stir-frying. The ideal bride had to be able to reduce the resistant bunch into minute particles of green. Yet handling the *bonti* well had another advantage in Barisal. The local women used their *bonti*s to defend themselves and their homes against gangs of armed robbers who attacked prosperous homesteads when the men were away.

Bengali literature contains many references to another, less domestic aspect of the woman at the *bonti*. Recurring images portray her as young and demure, sitting with her head bent, concentrating on her hands as she moves the vegetable or fish toward the lethal blade. Often a married woman is pictured, her head modestly covered with the shoulder end of her sari, whose colorful border frames her face and hair. But the discreet posture and modest covering are a foil for a flirtatious element in extended family life, which offers virtually no privacy. Men—whether a husband or a romantic interest—can expect many eloquent, sidelong glances cast with surreptitious turns of the head as the woman goes about her domestic tasks with the *bonti*.

An extension of this mild titillation is found in *Shobha*, a fascinating album of photographs by Gurudas Chattopadhyay published around 1930. His photographs portray some of Calcutta's best-known prostitutes and are obviously intended for erotic stimulation. But this is no collection of *Playboy*-like nudes. Instead, each woman has been photographed fully clothed and seated before a *bonti*! Here is a study in body language: the straight back, the bifurcated legs (one crossed, the other raised), the coy eyes peeking out from under the sari covering the head. To the Bengali viewer/voyeur of the time, the *bonti*, by enforcing this posture, created a uniquely erotic vision of the female figure, rich in implication and suggestiveness.

Despite its long history, it is probably inevitable that in the new global century the *bonti* will eventually vanish. The kitchens of Bengal are rapidly changing. Knives rather than *bontis* are becoming the cutting implements of choice. Tables and countertops are triumphing over the floor; chairs, tables, and couches are becoming as integral to the home as its doors and windows. Women no longer live in extended families, nor do their mornings consist of the leisurely ritual of *kutno kota*, when several women worked together, forming a sisterhood of the *bonti*. Now women are likely to work outside the home, which leaves little time for that kind of domestic fellowship. But for those of us who remember, the *bonti* will continue to be a potent symbol of multi-faceted femininity. ◉

Spring 2001, volume 1, number 2

frank h. wu |

The Best "Chink" Food

Dog Eating and the Dilemma of Diversity

"People live too easy, that's the trouble with the world," he said. He wiped the bloody knife again and again on his apron. "They watch the stupid TV, they read the stupid Reader's Digest and the stupid best sellers, they eat trucker tomatoes that got no taste and no color, no value in the world except they're easy to ship, they go to work, go home again, just like cows to the milking—" He picked out another knife, a long one with a blade eight inches wide, raised it, and brought it down once very hard, WHUMP!—and the dog's head fell off, blood splashing…. The dog's head looked up at me with the tongue hanging out through the big, still teeth, an expression of absolute disbelief…. The horror was too solidly there to look away from.

—John Gardner, "The Art of Living"

Buster and Ding Ding

I love dogs. I live with two of them in a canine-centered household.

Buster is a ninety-five-pound mutt I adopted after he, as an unwanted Christmas gift, had been abandoned at a local pet shelter. He is named after the dog my wife's cousin raised when he was director of the Peace Corps mission in Tonga years ago. The original Buster eventually vanished, allegedly eaten by the neighbors after he killed their pig. Our Buster has needed extra training to overcome his many anxieties. A deep-chested shepherd mix with gold fur and white paws, a white tip on his tail, and a scar on his nose from breaking through a second-story window, he is powerful but timid. He spends his days chewing on tennis balls and lounging on top of his crate. But at the first murmurings of thunder, he runs to the basement to hide.

Ding Ding is a twenty-five-pound stray I rescued when she was a puppy. She is named after the beach resort in Taiwan where I found her, wandering alone and scavenging for insects. At six months of age she was issued a doggie passport verifying that she had had all the requisite vaccinations, and I was able to tuck her into a basket under the airplane seat. Resembling an elegant cross between a basenji and sight hound, with a black-and-tan coat, long legs, and a doe-like face, Ding Ding is spoiled and fussy. She barks at strangers and likes to sleep in guests' laps.

I subscribe to the school of thought summarized by the quip "The more I know of man, the better I like my dogs." I am appalled by the idea that anybody would eat dogs. The question

Right: Dog meat for sale at the weekly market in Yangzhou, China, December 2006. PHOTOGRAPH © CHARLIE GROSSO

of whether Asians, in particular, eat dogs also appalls me. How we as a society address the taboo on dog eating presents an excellent case study for contemplating the meanings and limits of diversity in all of its forms. Dog eating is neither as easy to accept as chopsticks instead of silverware, nor as easy to forbid as violence against women when justified as a venerable custom.

Dilemmas of Diversity

It may be that the question "Do Asians eat dogs?" can best be answered by another question: "What do you think?" Why an individual asks the first question and how we as a society structure the discussion are important, but dialogue itself is only a process without an end— always tentative, never definitive. The dialogue must be self-reflective, and if successfully critical, it can serve as a model for approaching the dilemmas of diversity. These dilemmas are greater for the open-minded, who embrace all experience, than for the closed-minded, who eat only familiar foods without nausea. Cosmopolitan principles conflict with paro-chial practices, and as we discover that tolerance has its limits, we often take recourse in what intellectual rigor most loathes: ambivalence and ambiguity.

We only sample diversity. Our festivals of diversity tend toward the superficial, as if America were a stomach-turning combination plate of grits, tacos, sushi, and hummus. But we also know intuitively that "food permits a person to partake each day of the national past," as philosopher Roland Barthes wrote, with the French expressly in mind.[1] For most Americans, dog eating is not even conceivable as a gustatory pleasure representative of the national past.

The most popular feature of the ethnic carnivals organized in city parks every sum-mer is the long line of food booths giving off the intermingled aromas of their individual fare. Each of the family-owned restaurants renting a space competes energetically to sell a comestible introduction to the national culture its owners represent, giving the misleading impression that to eat is to understand. Nowadays, Asian flavors are foremost on the menus. Passersby can satisfy their appetites with Americanized versions—at once bland, cheap, and greasy—of *pho* soup, chicken satay, *bi bim bop*, samosas with chutney, shrimp and veg-etable tempura, or fried dumplings with soy sauce. They can refresh themselves with iced coffee sweetened by condensed milk, or a mango *lassi* yogurt drink. They may even be able to find *sac sac* grape juice, green tea ice cream, or red beans on shaved ice.

It is unlikely, however, that any of the Asian entrepreneurs would dare to offer up a bite of dog stew, even though it would be authentic—it once could be found throughout China, Korea, Vietnam, the Philippines, and elsewhere in the Pacific Rim. Dog meat has been the subject of lurid stories from epicurean tourists ever since Captain Cook and his crew landed on what they referred to as the Sandwich Islands (which we now know as Hawaii). At the Bishop Museum in Honolulu, a multitude of necklaces consisting of innumerable pale yellow dog teeth strung together are still exhibited in glass cases along-side other artifacts of the former island glories. Yet even the editor of a volume called *The*

Anthropologists' Cookbook acknowledges that "there are limits, nevertheless, in matters of taste," and "some readers may object" to the instructions for preparing roast dog in an earth oven.[2] On his global tour of the culinary world for cable television in 2001, host Anthony Bourdain refused to try dog meat, despite ingesting live cobra heart and boiled iguana.[3] At a luau, the slow-moving and reputedly dim-witted *poi* dogs, named after the taro root (*poi*) on which they were fattened until ready to be baked at two years of age, have long since ceased to be the main dish. In St. Louis, which once had an area named Dog Town due to sensationalized legends about Filipino visitors to the 1904 World's Fair, it is improbable that dogs would be grilled for guests today.

Asian cookbooks in English abound, but dog eating is not on the menu anywhere. There is no literary champion savoring *asosena* ("dog meat" in the Filipino dialect of Tagalog) as the specialty of a Manila street vendor, as M. F. K. Fisher would have savored a rustic repast of pâté, cheese, and a proper digestif at a Provençal inn, sharing her talent for giving readers a vicarious taste.[4]

An exception is the late novelist John Gardner, whose short story "The Art of Living" provides the epigraph to this chapter. In the title piece of his 1981 *Art of Living* collection, which exemplifies his moral fiction, Gardner portrays dog eating as a reverential ritual. A motorcycle gang steals a dog so a chef can prepare a banquet centered on Imperial Dog. The chef is paying homage to his son, who had written to him about eating dog before being killed in the Vietnam War. The story, illustrated with woodblock prints, ends with everyone beholding a vision "in the darkness beyond where the candles reached." The lost son is surrounded by "a thousand thousand Asians bowed from the waist."[5]

A more typical reference to dog eating is the warning given by a dying man to his dog, Mr. Bones, in novelist Paul Auster's *Timbuktu*: "You get yourself a new gig, or your days are numbered," man's best friend is told, because "there's a Chinese restaurant on every block, and if you think mouths don't water when you come strolling by, then you don't know squat about Oriental cuisine."[6]

Dog eating is an international urban legend with some truth to it. Everybody knows that Asians eat dogs. Transcendentalist Ralph Waldo Emerson joked about it in his journals: "The Englishman in China, seeing a doubtful dish set before him, inquired, 'quack-quack?' The Chinese replied, 'bow-wow.'"[7] The sheep's head hanging in the window of the Chinese shop is supposed to be a signal that the shopkeeper will sell dog meat to those privy to the secret. In *Strange Foods: Bush Meat, Bats, and Butterflies: An Epicurean Adventure Around the World*, explorer Jerry Hopkins states that the Chinese Kuomintang political party began their meetings by eating dog. Hopkins tried dog as a staple and treat as he wandered across Asia, finding in Thailand "a kind of Oriental dog tartare, where raw dog meat is chopped almost to a mince, mixed with a few spices and finely chopped vegetables, and served with the dog's blood and bile" and dog "deep-fried into a sort of jerky that was very hard to chew." (In the same adventuresome spirit, he ate the placenta after the birth of his son.)[8]

Even in Asia, dog eating has become simultaneously a source of shame and pride. When the Olympic games were hosted by Seoul, Korea, in 1988, the government, in order to enhance its image in the West, attempted vigorously to ban dog eating. Since then, during major sporting contests high officials have continued to make a show of opposition to the culinary custom. Boosted by vocal support from many of the visiting athletes, their efforts have met with no more than modest success. Prior to the 2002 soccer World Cup, the Korean government tried the compromise of formally legalizing dog eating while simultaneously regulating it. Recent studies have found that over one-third of adults in the country eat dog stew in a given year. Press reports on the controversy usually include quotes from Koreans who are indignant about the denigration of their way of life. They are not about to be lectured by foreigners with an air of superiority.

In the United States, the response to dog eating is more likely to be revulsion. In 1989, in Long Beach, California, Cambodian refugees bludgeoned to death a German shepherd puppy before slashing its throat and skinning it. The judge dismissed the misdemeanor indictment against them. He found that they had not inflicted unreasonable pain. Animal rights groups were outraged by the ruling. As one of their spokespersons stated, "I think that what these defendants did offends the sensibilities of the community."[9] To ensure that the next prosecution was successful, the California legislature passed a statute making it a misdemeanor to eat dog or cat. They later amended the statute to encompass any animal ordinarily kept as a pet or companion. The only recently reported case in which a defendant was convicted of eating a dog concerned a man, apparently not Asian, who barbecued the ribs of his neighbor's dog to avenge a perceived insult. In that 1992 California case, the unrepentant defendant received a sentence of three years.[10]

Performance artist Joey Skaggs, who stages elaborate pranks, fooled activists and the media alike with a 1994 stunt in which he mailed letters to animal shelters nationwide, offering to buy dogs for export as food at ten cents per pound. Masquerading as a Korean businessman, he sent letters from a non-existent company whose name, Kea So Joo, translates as Dog Meat Soup. "Dog is good food. Dog is good medicine," his letter read. "Dog no suffer. We have quick death for dog." Callers to his answering machine, which played a bilingual greeting with dogs yapping in the background, left thousands of messages denouncing the scheme before it was revealed as a hoax. Skaggs received messages calling him a "filthy yellow devil" and suggesting that Asians be deported or killed. He stated mischievously that he wanted to demonstrate the vagaries of cultural chauvinism.[11]

"Do Asians Eat Dogs?"

Let us consider the range of potential reactions to the clichéd allegation that Asians eat dogs. When comedian Joan Rivers, hosting a television program before the 2000 Academy Awards, quipped before a commercial break that viewers could take their dogs for a walk, or if they were Filipino, eat them, protests by Filipino organizations goaded Rivers into subsequently delivering a halfhearted apology. (The following year Rivers remarked, "It's wonderful to see so many Asians here. It just gives [the program] a whole international flavor.") The joke that makes the rounds nowadays substitutes the Hmong for the other Asian ethnicities that used to be the butt: "What's the name of the Hmong cookbook? *101 Ways to Wok Your Dog.*"[12] The Asian-American child who is taunted that the fastest animal on the street is her pet Rover, who must run awfully fast to avoid ending up in the dinner pot, probably does not realize either the complex implications of what is being said or the various options open to her in formulating a response.

How Filipino-American organizations, how the child, how each Asian-American responds to the stereotype ends up affecting all of us. To the mocking inquiry "Do Asians eat dogs?" no riposte, however sharp, can effectively convey that "I speak for myself alone." The question is common enough to list with the others that define the sensation of being a perpetual foreigner, so familiar to Asian-Americans, however well they can pass themselves off on the phone as White, and even if they are startled to see in the mirror that they are not: "Where are you *really* from?" and "How do you like it in our country?" and "When are you going home?" Inevitably, even if these questions lead to the compliment "You speak English so well," they also contain the subtext "If you don't like it here, you can go back to where you came from." And somehow, even if that racial dictate were obeyed, the cultural supremacy cannot be evaded: Even if we were to "go back," we are no better off, for we are not to eat dogs there, either.

"Do Asians eat dogs?" must—but cannot—be countered.

The initial assimilationist answer to the charge is face-saving defiance: "*Asians don't eat dogs.*" But ironically, a denial serves as an admission. Indeed, the angrier the answer, the more assimilated the answerer. To refute the claim that Asians eat dogs is to admit that it would be wicked to do so. To protest also allows people to speak of Asians as a whole, so that the protester is actually acquiescing to the general practice of stereotyping.

Novelist May-Lee Chai, a resident of Laramie, Wyoming, invoked this kind of protective stereotyping in a letter to the editor of the *New York Times* in 1994. She wrote to complain about a news item telling of dog eating in mainland China, calling it "false information" and recounting a tradition of keeping dogs as pets and honoring them in artwork as symbols of fidelity. She closed her letter with an anecdote that reversed the roles: "In my two years of working and traveling in China, the only people I saw eating dog there were a group of American students. The Americans, newly arrived in Nanjing, went about the city in search of a restaurant that served dog. They found none. Finally they persuaded a private entrepreneur to procure a dog (for a sizable fee) and found someone willing to cook it in a stew. When the time came for the 'feast,' a crowd of amazed Chinese gathered and snapped pictures as the Americans ate a German shepherd."[13]

The subtler assimilationist answer may be more truthful, if no more satisfying: "*Other Asians might eat dogs, but I don't; I don't even condone it.*" Like the earlier disclaimer, this retort reflects the majority norm that devouring dogs is deviant behavior, but it draws a line between the group and the individual. In this manner, the respondent repudiates both the reputation and the culture. The hint that Asians are not all alike comes at the cost of disavowing other Asians, even the community of which the respondent is a part. She may be sacrificing her family to cultivate a relationship with the majority, saying, in effect, "Bad Asians eat dogs; I am not like them."

This is a plausible interpretation of the Korean government policy. The title of Jessica Hagedorn's first novel, *Dogeaters*, which was nominated for a National Book Award in 1990 and adapted for Broadway a decade later, refers to the name the rich call the poor.[14] High culture distances itself from low culture. The dog-eating recidivist is the superstitious peasant, not the urbane sophisticate.

Asked "Do Asians eat dogs?" the multi-culturalist accepts the description but rejects the prescription: "*Asians eat dogs, and who are you to criticize them?*" This aggressive argument applies to a limited extent, but it falters at an emotional level. The subject is literally too visceral. The censure is a gut feeling.

Many Asians dine on delicacies that would disgust most Anglos, but as a consequence their supper becomes a spectacle. Raw fish has become enough of an upscale fashion that sushi aficionados can order the delectable belly tuna (*toro*) as easily as they can the plain tuna (*maguro*), just as the appetizer of seaweed salad is "in." Tofu, ranging in texture from firm to silky, is a vegan staple, stocked at every supermarket in multiple brands. Bee pollen, ginseng, *kava*, and all sorts of herbs and medicinals have become domestic harvests lining the shelves at health-food stores. Edamame, boiled and salted fresh soybeans that are eaten with drinks, are beginning to rival beer nuts. Shrimp chips can be found alongside pork rinds. Calpis (say it aloud) and Pocari Sweat sport drinks are being imported, embarrassing names and all. On the other hand, eyes plucked out of a steamed fish head, stinky tofu, slimy sea cucumbers, bear paw, warm snake bile, congealed blood, wrinkled chicken feet, slimy giant water bugs, savory baked cocoons, bitter cow dung, and fried duck embryos have attracted no broader following than non-Asian ethnic dishes such as pigs' feet. Because most of us were not exposed to these foods by our parents, they do not appear likely to follow the bagel into the gastronomic mainstream as comfort food.

It is too facile, though, to note that most dietary restrictions, even religious proscriptions, are socially constructed and historically contingent. Although their origins lie in sensible precautions to stave off food poisoning and infection in times before refrigeration and the germ theory, they have since developed into an elaborate set of customs that help shape identity. Eschewing beef or pork may once have been a sanitary concern, but it has become as much an ethical apprehension. Hindus who think of the cow as sacred or Jews who deem the pig filthy should be protected as minorities. But in a society where strictly observant Hindus or Jews are the majority, it would be imprudent to advocate for an increased intake of steaks or pork chops.

Nowadays, few Americans keep chickens in the backyard and wring their necks for dinner, and a diminishing number still shoot game for their family's sustenance. Whether we shop for bulk discounts at the supermarket warehouse or graze on the latest organic concoction at the health-food chain store, we are largely phony gourmands without any conception of how our food reaches the table. The staunch individualist Henry David

Thoreau fantasized about eating a woodchuck raw while he lived in his cabin by Walden Pond. There was a brief moment—after the advent of the civil rights movement and before "White flight" cleared out the city's core—when African-Americans, Asian-Americans, and White ethnics would shop together on weekends at downtown warehouses where "fresh" meant alive, and catfish swam in tanks next to display cases of organs and blood sausage, below a row of hooks from which hung almost every type of carcass fit for human consumption. But no more.

Another multi-culturalist answer proposes a philosophical attitude: *"I don't eat dog, but if I did, what would be wrong with that?"* There is no great incentive for pressing this intellectual viewpoint. The individual who in fact does not eat dogs but who protects the right of others to do so must in turn persuade others to permit and respect practices they neither engage in nor approve of. But dogs are too much members of our household, especially as we Americans lavish our largesse on them, paying for cosmetic surgery to enhance their competitiveness in the show ring, hiring professional walkers to take them, ten at a time, for a stroll in the park, equipping them with designer trench coats and high-tech booties to protect their paws from snow and rain, buying them miniature sofas and cedar-chip-stuffed beds for their relaxation, giving them the same anti-depressants we swallow for self-help for their personality development, and feeding them super-premium kibble for their health. We are no more tempted to put them in the broiler than we would our own children. Most Americans are indisposed to permit dog eating in spite of the Latin maxim *de gustibus non est disputandum* ("There's no arguing about taste")—no matter that the great physician of antiquity, Hippocrates, reported that puppies could be eaten as a curative, and dog recipes were published in Paris as recently as 1870.

Even if we are convinced, as most are, that freedom of expression is laudable, few of us espouse an unconditional moral relativism. While we might acquiesce to the eating of dogs, that does not mean we would like to broaden our open-mindedness to human cannibalism. For that matter, we are unlikely to sanction the gobbling up of powdered horns and preserved penises from species on the verge of extinction, especially if the justification is based on unfounded claims about aphrodisiac properties. Nor would we necessarily accept chewing up live octopus in the macho rite of *ikezukuri* before its death struggle chokes the intrepid diner; or cutting open the skull of a live monkey to scoop out its brains even though it shares most of its genes with us.

"Do Asians eat dogs?" The worst reply diminishes the possibility of a civic discourse to which everyone can equally contribute. *"Whether or not I eat dogs, you don't have to worry because I promise I won't eat your dog."* This response is flippant and does not deal with the real question, which is whether eating one's own dog is wrong. There is no need to declare that it is inappropriate to eat the dogs of others. Even if that person's dog is reduced to chattel—mere property—eating it violates their property rights, if nothing else. The Honolulu newspapers reported a dispute in 1950 that foreshadows later anxieties about dog eaters. A man said by Margaret Acosta to have eaten her missing dog, Floppy, successfully defended himself by admitting that he had eaten a dog on the night at issue.

He said, however, that his meal had been a black dog, not a white one. He was acquitted, because Floppy was white.[15]

But because the reassurance about not eating other people's dogs forecloses discussion, it is the worst reply. It isolates each of us within a culture and makes us outsiders to all others. Each of us can watch these others and study them, but none of us can comment or interact. The animal rights groups that censured the Cambodians in Long Beach were not mollified that the perpetrators were eating only their own dog, which was certainly not a pet. In bringing into play "the sensibilities of the community," they denied that immigrants might contribute to those sensibilities or be part of that community.

We forget that people can eat Asian foods but still have contempt for Asians. They can tune in to the Japanese television show *Iron Chef*—where a challenger and a master compete to produce a meal from the theme ingredient in Japanese, French, Chinese, or Italian cuisine—but still make fun of the antics of Asians, as if a game show epitomized a culture and the host, who parodies Western showmen of the past, represented an entire people. They can be patronizing toward the obsequious maitre d' and the subservient waiter, confusing the deferential manner of service professions with the behavior of racial groups. They can talk about the best "Chink" food or the best "Jap" food, even as they attempt clumsily to use their chopsticks to stab that morsel they have dropped on the table. Eating at a Chinese restaurant is not the same as "breaking bread" with Chinese people. A patron at a Japanese restaurant can racially ridicule the *teppenyaki* chef, who he has erroneously assumed cannot comprehend his rank prejudice. More than one Asian-American customer has cringed at the spectacle of the next table, where an Asian immigrant is humiliated by the Whites he is serving, the Asian smiling nervously in a gesture that is misconstrued by Whites as assent to the abuse. The spectator may be more keenly aware of the humiliation than the subject, but be similarly powerless because there is no means of saving face.

"What Do You Think?"

There is a better answer to the question "Do Asians eat dogs?" It answers the question with another question: "What is the point of asking whether I eat dogs?" The accuser herself is cross-examined.

This rebuttal ensures that the question is not rhetorical, a set-up rather than an invitation to talk. Joan Rivers cannot be taken seriously, but she cannot be left alone. Detractors of dog eaters, such as those infuriated by Joey Skaggs, must be dispatched because they proceed in earnest. They believe that Asian-Americans are dog eaters and do not hesitate to reprimand them on that basis. In San Francisco in 1989, as officials sought to respond to rumors that Vietnamese immigrants were hunting dogs in Golden Gate Park, Vu-Duc Vuong, executive director of a refugee center, said, "There have been very few, if any, instances of pet eating… Far more numerous are anti-Asian prejudices and violence based on no more than false or racist stereotypes of Asian-Americans."[16]

Reducing the inhabitants of the Asian continent to dog eaters, i.e., defining them by a minor aspect of their multifaceted ways of life, is absurd. That characterization, however, often forms the basis for believing that Asians are inferior: the dogs are cute; the people are despicable. It is a circular trap. Only by assuming that American culture is superior can its vantage point be used to judge Asian culture in this regard. Insiders assume that their own culture is superior. They then find, based on their assumption, that it is so. In short, dog eating becomes an excuse to make Asians the butt of jokes and ultimately to disrespect complete cultures as primitive.

Instead, we need to inculcate within ourselves a sense of proportion. The behavior of Asian-Americans may be of interest to non-Asian-Americans for various reasons, but asking whether Asian-Americans are in the habit of eating dogs should not be used as a point of entry into exploring that behavior. Asian immigrants adjust their dietary routines as they adjust other aspects of their lives. Studies of Asian students who have moved to the United States show them gobbling up generous quantities of American-style junk foods, to their detriment.[17] Asian parents lament that their American children clamor for hamburgers and French fries, turning their noses up at even the celebratory dishes served on holidays. Pacific Islanders put together ingredients of their own with those from the United States, in a home-made fusion cuisine. They have invented, for example, the inimitable snack of Spam *masubi*. The Spam, a processed meat product identified with food stamps and cargo cults, is first fried, then wrapped in seaweed and placed on top of vinegared rice—a gristly variation of sushi, unlikely to be ordered up by yuppies sampling haute cuisine. Due to the islanders' genetic adaptation to food scarcity, the imported, fatty diet they now enjoy is causing an epidemic of morbid obesity.[18]

A few more rules are conducive to discussion. Whoever attacks a cultural practice must first understand it. Few of us have suffered as many Southeast Asians have—as civilians on the battlegrounds of war, with homes destroyed and stomachs empty—or as Koreans and Chinese have—enduring famine brought on by the authorities. Asian immigrant mothers may tell their children to finish the meat first because it has the highest nutritional value, but they probably do not tell their children to think of the starving children in Europe in order to cajole them into cleaning their plates.

If we critique a cultural practice, its origins and its context are relevant. Dogs compete with humans for resources. University of Pennsylvania professor James Serpell reports in his book *In the Company of Animals: A Study of Human-Animal Relationships* that in Chinese culture, "whereas the ruling elite took their affection for dogs or cats to bizarre and outrageous extremes, the mere idea of being fond of a dog or indeed any other kind of domestic animal was a concept alien to the mentality of the majority peasant population."[19] Eating dogs appears to be a compensatory adaptation to material deprivation and the lack of reliable sources of other meats.

So if you can criticize my cultural practices, I should be able to criticize your cultural practices. The criticism must be reciprocal and between equals. If either of us calls on standards that are not generated within the culture we are criticizing, we must do our utmost to make such standards as neutral as possible rather than just the enlargement of our preferences. It may be impossible to produce principles in a vacuum without the influence of our own backgrounds so as to bracket and set aside everything that is culturally specific, but at least we can become conscious of the constraints of either an Eastern or a Western worldview and conduct our discussion accordingly. Lest you be a hypocrite, you should be able to live up to the standards you would set.

And if, as a nation, we settle on stopping the practice of dog eating here and elsewhere, we are likely to be more effective if the means we use blend internal calls for reform with external demands for conformity. Otherwise, Asian-Americans who may not crave dogs may become justifiably resentful about regulations imposed on us without our input. Asian-Americans who refuse to submit to any interrogation about dog eating, frivolous or humorless, should be viewed sympathetically. No more than individuals do groups take kindly to being told what to do by the self-righteous.

These prerequisites to conversation should pertain to all communications across cultures. Without such indications of good faith, the responses—ranging from hostility to indifference toward what appears to be an unfair game—become much more appealing to Asian-Americans and anyone else who has minority status. The question "Do Asians eat dogs?" should not make Asian-Americans feel vulnerable.

It may be too difficult to satisfy all the conditions. We may need to proceed imperfectly, but each proviso that is not satisfied compromises the argument. For instance, former starlet Brigitte Bardot's campaigns against dog eating are a luxury for her, disguising her involvement with French right-wing groups that aim to curtail immigration for racial reasons. She connects mistreatment of animals with an influx into France of non-Western peoples. Her high-profile antagonism toward dog eating is a confirmation of her privileged position and part of an extreme political agenda. It does not seem to be the result of study. Dealings with her and with those who argue similarly do not occur on fair terms.

The power to control the exchange distorts it. In Michael Moore's 1989 documentary satire *Roger & Me*, the pundit interviews an impoverished woman who is selling rabbits by the roadside. She asks him if he wants one for a pet or for food. While those in the audience laugh out of squeamishness, they may be touched by her naive honesty. She recognizes poignantly both her own predicament of poverty and the fate of her furry animals.

The case against eating dogs that ought to command respect, possibly the only case that merits real attention, is the ascetic case for a vegetarian lifestyle. The prohibition against eating dogs becomes only a particular example in that line of reasoning. Many animal rights groups recognize as much. Peter Singer's influential argument for animal liberation is based on the premise that some animals are sentient enough to share with us the traits that we believe give us moral autonomy and that prohibit us from treating individuals as a means to an end.[20] There could be no harsher reduction of any organism we recognize as having person-hood to the status of an object than to consume it literally and unnecessarily. It matters not that we may do so because we are satiated in the act. From such a perspective, the more enjoyment we derive, the worse our sin.

Although the animal-rights movement has long been derided as sentimental, if not hysterical, it has profited greatly from scientific advances. It is opposition to animal rights that now often seems motivated by ideology rather than empirical research, as in the indignant claim that God gave Adam dominion over the beasts, even as the latest studies substantiate both the notion that animals are like us and the suspicion that we are driven by material desires. Still, the biblical directive issued in Eden at the beginning to name the fish and the fowl—so unlike the injunction not to eat from the tree of knowledge—reminds us of the importance in Western culture of the divine Word and of the resonance, in any culture, of words in general.

It is only through our shared language that we can come to terms with ourselves and others. Higher primates have been taught enough American Sign Language to host a tea party and show a sense of humor. The best-trained hunting dogs, the retrievers in the field, can learn a vocabulary of as many as two hundred words. Both are restrained by the language we use: it is the language we expect to be obeyed, instantly and without quarrel. The dogs are limited further by our lack of fluency in their body language, growls, howls, and yelps: as Yi-Fu Tuan, a Chinese émigré essayist working deftly with European high culture has argued, we dominate our pets.[21] Conventionally, the roles are fixed and we are paternalistic. We would be as alarmed at the sight of dogs walking upright as in a Franz Kafka tale as we would be aghast at the sight of them being basted over the holidays or prodded with a meat thermometer.

This meta-discourse about dog eating—talking about how we can talk— turns out to be imperative. Setting the terms for the discussion becomes the discussion itself. The terms of discussion are transformed. And it is at this point, though not before, that the concession can be made that killing dogs to eat them is not a commendable activity. The dogs who are eaten are beaten to death to tenderize their flesh. They are intelligent enough to know about their impending execution; they are trusting enough to consent to it; and, most of all, they are sensitive enough to feel pain.

Pursuant to the revised argument, the objection to eating dogs must be expanded to include other animals—for example, pigs. It should be extended to similar cases to prevent being suspect as a selective sensitivity. Pigs also can be housebroken, though they will revert to feral status in just two generations if returned to the wild. Vietnamese pot-bellied pigs even acquired momentary status as chic pets. More than dogs, pigs resemble human beings, which is why pigs are widely used in medical research on human disease, and xenotransplants of porcine hearts are a realistic possibility. The modern processing plants for pigs are hardly more humane for the efficiency of their mass slaughter. Upton Sinclair's muckraking 1906 novel, *The Jungle*, was an accurate report of the grisly methods of meat packing.[22] If any stage of the process were photographed, the pictures of "Babe" from the movies meeting his demise would be as disturbing as that of any dog hanging by a homemade noose. Were we all still to visit the local butcher before cooking supper, or if we had to raise and slaughter our own fowl for guests, rather than ingesting packaged and prepared products, we might more easily embrace the eating of dogs or swear off eating all meat.

After all, the guests at a down-home pig pick'n line up to help themselves to moist pork plucked by hand from the remains of a pink and smooth-skinned suckling who sports a baseball cap that has scrawled on it the name he was given the day before in homage to the guest of honor who is being feted. The swine has a tomato stuffed in his open mouth and cherries where his eyes once sat; his ears are still pricked up as if to hear the comments about his delicious haunches. The replacement of a word identifying the dead mammal that has been tended diligently all day as it turned on the barbecue spit or that is hidden under the lid of a fancy serving tray in the buffet line is enough to turn our impatient craving into the urge to vomit. How puzzling it is. ◉

NOTES

1. Roland Barthes, "Toward a Psychosociology of Contemporary Food Consumption," in Carole Counihan and Penny Van Esterik, eds., *Food and Culture: A Reader* (New York: Routledge, 1997), 24.

2. Jessica Kuper, ed., *The Anthropologists' Cookbook*, revised edition (London: Kegan Paul International, 1997), xii. For general information on food taboos and dog eating, I recommend Frederick J. Simoons, *Eat Not This Flesh: Food Avoidances from Prehistory to the Present*, 2nd ed. (Madison: University of Wisconsin Press, 1994). I also have consulted Alan Davidson, *The Oxford Companion to Food* (New York: Oxford University Press, 1999); and Stanley J. Olson, "Dogs," in Kenneth F. Kiple and Kriemhild Coneè Ornelas, eds., *The Cambridge World History of Food* (Cambridge: Cambridge University Press, 2000), 508. To understand the role of food in culture, I have consulted Donna R. Gabaccia, *We Are What We Eat: Ethnic Food and the Making of Americans* (Cambridge, MA: Harvard University Press, 1998); Carolyn Korsmeyer, *Making Sense of Taste: Food and Philosophy* (Ithaca, NY: Cornell University Press, 1998); Marvin Harris, *Good to Eat: Riddles of Food and Culture* (New York: Simon & Schuster, 1985); Richard Pillsbury, *No Foreign Food: The American Diet in Time and Place* (Boulder, CO: Westview, 1998); and Waverley Root and Richard de Rochemont, *Eating in America: A History* (New York: The Ecco Press, 1981).

3. Barbara E. Martinez, "Names & Faces," *Washington Post*, Jan. 1, 2002, C3.

4. Among her many books, however, M.F.K. Fisher did write *How to Cook a Wolf* (New York: North Point, 1988), which exhibits her usual open-mindedness and great talent.

5. John Gardner, "The Art of Living," in John Gardner, *The Art of Living and Other Stories* (New York: Knopf, 1981). The epigraph is taken from pages 302–303.

6. Paul Auster, *Timbuktu* (New York: Henry Holt, 1999), 5.

7. Linda Allardt, ed., *The Journals and Miscellaneous Notebooks of Ralph Waldo Emerson*, vol. 12 (Cambridge, MA: Harvard University Press, 1976), 237.

8. Jerry Hopkins, *Strange Foods: Bush Meat, Bats, and Butterflies: An Epicurean Adventure Around the World* (Hong Kong: Periplus Editions, 1999), 4–9, 62–63.

9. David Haldane, "Judge Clears Cambodians Who Killed Dog for Food," *L.A. Times*, March 15, 1989, B1.

10. "Man Bites Dog," *Jet*, Jan. 20, 1992, 19.

11. John Tierney, "The Big City: Falling for It," *The New York Times*, July 17, 1994, F16.

12. Anne Fadiman, *The Spirit Catches You and You Fall Down: A Hmong Child, Her American Doctors, and the Collision of Two Cultures* (New York: Farrar, Straus and Giroux, 1997), 190.

13. May-Lee Chai, "When the Old Order in China at Last Changes; Dog's Place in History," *The New York Times*, August 26, 1994, A28.

14. Jessica Hagedorn, *Dogeaters* (London: Pandora, 1991).

15. George Engebretson, *Poi Dogs and Popoki: Animals and Pets in Hawaii* (Hong Kong: Hawaiian Humane Society, 1997), 97.

16. Katherine Bishop, "California Journal: U.S.A.'s Culinary Rule: Hot Dogs Yes, Dogs No," *The New York Times*, Oct. 5, 1989, A22.

17. Yi-Ling Pan, "Asian Students Change Their Eating Patterns After Living in the United States," *Journal of the American Dietetic Association* 99, no. 1 (Jan. 1999): 54–58.

18. Ellen Ruppel Shell, "New World Syndrome," *Atlantic Monthly*, June 2001, 50–53.

19. James Serpell, *In the Company of Animals: A Study of Human-Animal Relationships* (Cambridge: Cambridge University Press, 1996), 45. I also have relied on James Serpell, *The Domestic Dog* (Cambridge: Cambridge University Press, 1995).

20. Peter Singer, *Animal Liberation*, 2nd ed. (New York: New York Review of Books, 1990).

21. Yi-Fu Tuan, *Dominance and Affection: The Making of Pets* (New Haven: Yale University Press, 1984).

22. Upton Beall Sinclair, *The Jungle* (New York: Penguin, 1989).

Spring 2002, volume 2, number 2

Charlie Grosso's photo essay "Meat and Market" appeared in Summer 2008, volume 8, number 3

close to the earth

Organic in Mexico: A Conversation with Diana Kennedy | *L. Peat O'Neil* **234**

Mr. Clarence Jones, Carolina Rice Farmer | *Jennie Ashlock* **247**

"GM or Death": Food and Choice in Zambia | *Christopher M. Annear* **255**

Wine, Place, and Identity in a Changing Climate | *Robert Pincus* **267**

Episode with a Potato | *Eric Ormsby* **277**

I. peat o'neil

Organic in Mexico
A Conversation with Diana Kennedy

DIANA KENNEDY IS RUMMAGING in a kitchen cupboard. "I don't like using foil. I use parchment," she says. "It's here someplace." Reaching high up to a shelf on the wall of her rustic kitchen, Kennedy eventually extracts a carefully folded packet of used foil. I watch as she tucks the creased foil over a ceramic tray of stuffed *pasilla* chilies from Oaxaca.

Diana Kennedy, the culinary historian and cookbook author who explains regional Mexican cuisines to a global audience, has invited me for lunch to talk about agriculture in Mexico. Her Mexican home, designed as an ecologically efficient building by local architect Armando Cuevas, is hidden by a thicket of vines and trees on a hillside above San Francisco Coatepec de Morelos, a hamlet in Michoacan near Zitacuaro, about three hours west of Mexico City on twisting rural roads.

"Come into my laboratory," she says, shaking my hand at the gate. I follow her up a stretch of jungle-shaded driveway into a traditional tiled Mexican kitchen with tortilla grills set into the counters and baskets hanging from the ceiling chock full of dried chilies. We met minutes ago, yet she's so easygoing that we're soon busying ourselves with food preparation like familiar friends.

She pours some sour pomegranate *agua fresca*—fruit pulp mixed with water. Strained and faintly sweetened, the fruit juice is a counterpoint to our multicourse lunch. "These sour pomegranates might be the original biblical variety," Kennedy speculates. "I make them into a marmalade used in Middle Eastern cooking. Sour pomegranates jell much better than other pomegranates."

The meal begins with *crema de flor de calabaza*, squash flower soup. Kennedy uses small flowers from the *calabacita* that she grows in the garden below her house and also buys large squash flowers from the market. "Sauté the onion and garlic in a bit of oil until translucent, then add flowers and cook for about 10 minutes. The thickening agent is the flower," she explains. "Add a light chicken broth to dilute." She keeps small quantities of the soup frozen for personal meals. "At the moment you serve it, add a touch of crème fraîche."

Our meal continues with the chilies, now hot from the oven. They're stuffed with a filling of shredded pork and beef, plus raisins and pine nuts. Kennedy makes the filling in half-kilo batches and keeps it frozen, ready for stuffing chilies. The plump chilies are topped with *queso fresco*, which melts under the creased recycled foil. "Here, have a taste of this cheese. Isn't it divine?" she asks. It is indeed. The slightly tangy flavor of the whole milk cheese summons mental pictures of green pastures dotted with clumps of wild chives.

Kennedy, a tad coyly, never reveals the name of the creamery, saying only that it is a small organic creamery in Hidalgo state, too small for commercial production. She's not about to reveal her sources.

The tomatoes she has roasted and reduced for the sauce are also from her garden. "The best harvest is usually in February," says Kennedy. "First you char them just until they're…," she stops and makes a slow gesture of squeezing her hand, as if the tomatoes were in a loose jelly stage, "with the skins still intact. Then freeze them whole. Later, puree with garlic and cook," she concludes the oral recipe. The result is a dense tomato flavor. Diana Kennedy is one fine cook.

Kennedy hustles back to the kitchen, leaving me at the table outdoors, but curiosity overwhelms me and I join her, hoping to learn some obscure culinary lore. Kennedy suggests that we toast the violet tortillas in residual heat from the oven instead of on the tortilla grill built into the tiled counter. She spoons white rice flavored with a fresh herb into a rustic ceramic bowl. I learn the next day that this herb is *oreganon*.

As we eat, our discussion turns to climate change. The fruit trees on Kennedy's property were a gift from the village mayor years ago, a gift she then shared with her neighbors. In the past she harvested wild cherries, but that tree no longer bears fruit. "The unexpected heat in January and February forces fruit trees to blossom, but subsequent cold nights bruise or kill the buds and production fails," she explains.

However, the grapefruit, curiously, fruited abundantly after fifteen years of bearing no fruit at all. Usually, raspberries fruit in March, Kennedy tells me, but in 2003 on Christmas

Above: Diana Kennedy and her back-roads truck. PHOTOGRAPH BY M. CALDERWOOD

Day, she collected a small handful. These and other examples of climate change affect smallholder farmers who don't have access to orchard management systems such as spraying trees with water that freezes and creates a protective ice shell around the blossoms.

Quinta Diana

The helpers who tend Kennedy's property—her *finca*—are themselves local landholders—or their children are—who know the rhythms of the climate. "It's all very nice to talk about *terroir*, but the quality of the soil is hit and miss here," Kennedy notes. She grows some maize for *masa* (corn dough). Seed from the corn crop is set aside each year for planting the next. She also has coffee bushes and shares the processed coffee with friends.

Kennedy gestures to the lime trees and other citrus trees that clearly are flourishing. "It was bare earth when I started." Her *finca* is a hideaway, yes, but it is marked by daily life, a working life. Kennedy picks clumps of herbs as we stroll around the gardens close to the house. "You see what people can do if they set their minds to organize a garden. We use compost and cow manure. Some guano is brought in. If it looks like fertile soil, it's because it's been enriched over a twenty-year period. I either get a lot of produce or not—it varies by the season."

A dog barks in the distance, and the boy who led me from the village to *Quinta* Diana reappears, ready to wash dishes. "The youngsters who work here understand sustainable living; they grew up with it," Kennedy explains. She takes village life seriously; but the locals are reticent. "I've been here twenty-five years, and I've only just been told some things about the problems the families here experience. I didn't understand how difficult their lives were."

After another trip to the kitchen, she shows me a handful of precious morels, very late for the season. "Found them last night," she confides. "There are several types in this area. I saw *campesinos* with a bucket of mushrooms and asked what they had. The indigenous people come down from the hills. They forage for mushrooms, wild berries, and wild fruit, but they won't tell me where they find things; don't want to let on where they go."

Pots of chives and basil, mint, oregano, and *oreganon* cluster on the patio. Orange and lime trees shade the expanse. In taller trees vines weave between the branches and air succulents—orchids—form a green screen surrounding the patio and sheltering the house from the penetrating sun. River rocks surround the trunks of the trees. Two capacious ovens where Kennedy smokes hams and bacon and bakes bread dominate one side of this outdoor "room," along with two outdoor grills. Behind them, hidden behind vines, stands a cement water tank, one of several water reserves on the property.

I peek inside the house; Kennedy has promised me a tour later, but I can't resist asking about the huge boulder in the middle of the house. "We built walls around the rock," says Kennedy. That decision fits with her pantheist and organic foundation, I think, as I nose around the kitchen while she takes a phone call. Chilies piled in baskets with labels detailing names and origin hang from the rafters. She catches me fingering crisp dried chilies in one of the baskets.

"Chilies normally last a long time, but there's been a problem with mold during the rainy season. I've had to replace the stock. The kitchen is like a laboratory. I keep buying new things. Experimenting." Wooden shelves and a massive counter are crammed with pans, tools, and jars of utensils, *molcajete* and *tejolote* (volcanic rock mortar and pestle), and a nightmare collection of cleavers. Near the window Kennedy keeps binoculars and a bird book. Her helpers are learning about birds by keeping a record of their sightings.

Later, around teatime, Kennedy probes recesses in the refrigerator, looking for preserves to make Mother's Fruit Slice from her cookbook *Nothing Fancy*.[1] The stuffed fridge reminds Kennedy of her dear friend Peter Kump, founder of the Manhattan cooking school now called the Institute of Culinary Education. Kump attended Kennedy's Mexican cooking classes when they both lived in New York City. They nursed a running joke between them, discussing legacies. "Peter told me, 'Diana, just leave me the contents of your refrigerator.' But then, sadly, he died before me." She brandishes a jar of homemade preserves and starts rolling pastry dough before sentimental memories overtake the moment.

While the fruit slice bakes, we tour the house. Beneath the stairs a cool larder stores Kennedy's wine, preserves, and bottled vinegars, which she offers for a taste. The main floor focuses on a stone fireplace and the boulder. A greenhouse towers above the living room. On the upper levels are a guest bath and bedroom and her private space, spread above the kitchen.

As the afternoon fades to twilight, we perch in Kennedy's office and talk about writing. "As far as I can see," says Kennedy, "I write oral history that is disappearing with climate change, agribusiness, and loss of cultivated lands. In the past people had a sense of taste and a sense of where they came from. They were conscious of what they were eating and what they consumed and about not wasting.

"*The Cuisines of Mexico* was an eye-opener for a lot of people. Mexicans are very generous," she adds, acknowledging the cooks who share recipes with her. "I always give credit to the person who tells me the original recipe. I can't say that other food writers give me that," she sniffs, a whiff of bitterness coloring her words. Kennedy points out that she was cooking in Mexico years before some of the current crop of chefs and food writers were born. "There's so much pretension among food experts," she grouses. She is particularly peeved at Mexican-born culinary commentators who don't live in Mexico but use nationality as a basis to question her authority on Mexican food.

Agricultural Frontiers

Kennedy is using her position as an expert in Mexican cuisine to focus attention on the plight of small farmers in the post-NAFTA (North American Free Trade Agreement) years. While organic coffee growers in Mexico's southern states have organized production and distribution networks, other small-scale farmers are struggling to obtain organic certification and access to markets.

Kennedy notes that progress in sustainable agriculture is slow here, if it comes at all, especially in terms of government transparency and corruption. "Things start here, but if the politician loses the election, or loses interest…." Her voice trails off in disappointment. "There are few controls on chemical fertilizers. Often, they're spraying every fifteen days, without masks."

Kennedy is pessimistic about the future. "I don't know what will happen to corn. I know of many chili varieties you can't find now. *Plagues* [plant diseases] have wiped them out."

The future of corn cultivation is central to the Mexican small farmer's perception of the impact of NAFTA. The Mexican government has embraced the agreements implemented over the past eleven years.[2] Yet, groups of *campesinos* have complained that they were shut out of the negotiating process.

The Mexican *campesino* groups and advocates like Diana Kennedy worry that genetically engineered seed will pollute the seed stock of their culinary patrimony—corn, beans, and chilies.[3] Unregulated genetically modified corn was found in Capulalpam, Oaxaca, in 2001, most likely imported with the six million tons of corn that enter Mexico each year from the United States, 30 percent of which is genetically modified. Mexico is debating a biosecurity law, anticipating the 2008 deadline when the remaining corn import quotas are lifted, as stipulated in NAFTA.[4]

In response to the NAFTA phaseout of agricultural tariffs and farm subsidies in 2003, grassroots groups with picturesque names such as "El Campo No Aguanta Mas" (The Countryside Can't Stand It Anymore) trumpeted their cause to the government. The gist of their message: small farmers need financial protection from imports to survive the changes brought by NAFTA.[5]

The groups marched and demonstrated in the capital, calling for changes to the agricultural section of NAFTA. The Mexican government agreed to sponsor reform talks with the agricultural groups early in 2003. By May 2003, a few agricultural groups and the government had signed the Countryside Agreement, promising federal assistance to the farmers.

Though she's not marching with the *campesinos* from the Independence Monument to the *Zocalo* in Mexico City, Diana Kennedy is just as forceful in articulating ideas to improve the lot of small farmers in Mexico. "First, we've got to have a strong government. A government that will look at the farms and farmers' situation. The government's mindset is 'what can you get out of it?' There's no continuity of planning. Take their idea of conservation of the *campo*—fields that used to be planted in corn are now converted to sorghum and fed to the cows. That's so wasteful."

It's not that Mexico doesn't have land for farming. As the world's twelfth-largest country in landmass, with about fifty-seven million acres of arable land, Mexico is a leading agricultural producer. But nearly two-thirds of Mexico's land is arid or semiarid. One in five Mexicans works in farming, and agriculture affects the nation's economic and political processes. Despite the endless stretches of industrial farmland, most Mexican farmers—more than half—work farms of ten acres or less, often in remote rural areas far from distribution centers, markets, and financial services.[6]

"Not enough people or governments recognize the potential this country has," complains Kennedy. "People who are living in marginal conditions could be growing and marketing their produce. Mexico has biodiversity that is astonishing. The question is how many people are willing to invest in it. Alternative technologies haven't been pursued because the steps toward development are difficult, and there's a bombardment from the north."

The "bombardment" she's talking about is the massive volume of food imported from the United States. The produce section of any grocery store in Mexico City is stuffed with lettuce, apples, plums, spinach, celery, carrots, and more, all branded with small stickers proclaiming "Product of USA."

"I can't help but be pessimistic," Kennedy says. "The land is Mexico's heritage, but the soil is filthy and the rivers polluted. The rules are being relaxed here by the government of Mexico to accommodate incoming manufacturers," she said. "Parts of rivers are completely dead, but who takes note?"

She launches into a friendly rant on the Mexican Green Party (Partido Verde Ecologista de México, or PVEM). "The Green Party needs to learn how to communicate issues. They need to learn how to speak in public and on television." She points out that Mexico's Green Party is forward thinking. On its Web site the PVEM promotes sustainable agriculture "in harmony with the types of earth."[7] And perhaps with a nod to its urban roots in Mexico City, the Mexican Green Party promotes balance between urban and rural areas. Their stated objectives include stopping the growth of the great large cities, reversing the flow of farmers to the great cities, and forming smaller, self-sufficient communities.

The Green Party's lofty goals may be inspiring, but Mexico's entrenched rural politics are dominated by the PRI, the party that held the nation's reins for seven decades until Vicente Fox won the presidency in 2000. Diana Kennedy maintains cordial relations with the local progressive political party, much like British country gentry keep an ear to the ground during local elections. Still, she knows it is unlikely that the PRI will lose its political base of *campesinos* grateful for preelection cash handouts; nor is the entrenched party likely to initiate programs that would advance their vote-by-rote supporters to political awareness.

Research Roots

Diana Kennedy nurtures deep connections to Oaxaca, where the sustainable agriculture effort and product branding as "Fair Trade organic" first turned up in the coffee business.[8] She spends part of every year there, researching recipes, foraging for new ingredients, tracking down plant genealogies. Kennedy's current project is focused on Oaxaca's regional recipes, which she gathers during research trips in remote areas of the state.

"I go out on the back roads," she explains, palming the gearshift of her white Nissan extended-bed pickup. She taps the dashboard. "That's why I have this truck." She has asked me to tag along during a quick errand, so we are tooling through the village to the market town of Zitacuaro, about twenty minutes from her house. I marvel at her upper body strength as she maneuvers the truck, which lacks power steering, along the twisty unpaved tracks and through the narrow walled *calles* of Zitacuaro. People on foot greet her, and as we inch past oncoming vehicles squeezing in the narrow lanes, she trades with the other drivers the joking pleasantries that ease Mexican daily life.

"For me it's all about how the people live, how people manage to get by in their lives. This is a starting point for mutual understanding. When I'm gathering recipes, I ask, watch, and listen. Mostly listen. You'll know the proportions are wrong and something is always missing." Usually, Kennedy finances her own book research in Oaxaca. She consults with ethnobotanical experts who help her identify edible wild plants.

For dinner we'll be tasting tamales—recipes from the new book, she announces. The first is a bean yucca tamale from the Chinantla area where it meets Vera Cruz state. "The yucca is cassava pulverized, then the starch is squeezed out. Avocado leaves are toasted and mixed in with the frijoles," Kennedy recites. The second *tamale de yucca* is cooked with *hoja santa* (holy leaves, *Piper sanctum*) and pork filling. The third tamale is from the Isthmus of Tehuantepec. "Eat it without sauce," Kennedy instructs. "Inside, there's

Above: Callito grinding tamale *masa.* PHOTOGRAPH BY DIANA KENNEDY

dried shrimp and *molito* of pumpkin seeds [ground-up pumpkin seeds]. The corn *masa* is heavier in these tamales."

The next morning I return to see Kennedy's greenhouse and gardens. After subduing the guard dogs, Kennedy leads me through the greenhouse. Her rapid-fire botanical lesson is tough to keep up with as I scribble plant names in Spanish, English, and Latin. Later, I fill in the blanks with facts culled from Kennedy's many cookbooks.

"This is from the Tabasco area—lowland tropical *perejil* [parsley]. It grows wild. This is *tequelite*, from Vera Cruz." Kennedy plucks a leaf and gives it to me. It smells like cilantro. "This one is called *oreganon*, originally from Africa, but the leaf is too fleshy to dry." One whiff and I realize that *oreganon* is the herb she had mixed with rice the day before. Kennedy points out that this herb is not the same as the oregano grown in the Mediterranean region. She steers me toward the main garden to continue the tour, then charges ahead, past fruit trees, past the chicken yard, down a hill to the garden.

"Limes have been prolific this year," she exults, poking at fallen fruit with her walking stick as we pass. "This yellow lemon took a while to flourish. Someone gave me a seed, and I planted it, a Eureka lemon, which is used for pickled lemons in Moroccan cooking." As we stroll through the vegetable garden, she notices chilies ready to harvest. She plucks a few and heaps them on the ground for one of the assistants to collect later, and to remind him to pick the rest of the ripe chilies.

Kennedy points to dense growth on one side of the path. "I keep a wild piece for the birds. I have a family of owls. Saw them sitting on a bough."

I ask about the neighboring farms. "'Farm' isn't a word you can use here," she replies. "The few acres belonging to a smallholder—perhaps two to six hectares [about five to twenty-two acres]—are called *una pequeña propriadade*. *Comunidades* are the big tracts of farmland held in common. There's nothing that could be called typical," she says.

Practicing what she preaches about preventing the influx of engineered corn varieties, Kennedy manages a small plot of corn to produce seed for her future needs. "We plant corn, but we don't mix varieties. And usually we're planting our own seed from the previous harvest." I also learn that farmers isolate corn varieties by cutting the tassels from the corn stalks in rows of adjacent varieties.[9]

"Recently, there's interest in heirloom fruit," she says. "Locals don't get fair prices because of low-priced fruit that comes in from Chile and Argentina. As far as new crops here in Michoacán, you'll see more sorghum than wheat. More sophisticated people buy the organic produce. Still, it's a very small group of people," acknowledges Kennedy. "More and more of the upper-echelon restaurants use organic produce. I wish they'd be bolder in announcing that they are using organic produce and support the farmers."

NAFTA Rules

Diana Kennedy sends me to talk to a neighboring small-scale farmer. "Pablo and I don't see eye-to-eye sometimes," she warns. "But I want you to hear what he has to say."

Pablo Span owns a country inn and tends thirteen acres cultivated with coffee, citrus trees, papaya, and mango, as well as guava, boysenberry, and blackberry. The thirty-three beehives on his property take care of pollination and add to the income stream.

"NAFTA is the best thing that's happened to Mexico," says Span. "There are two faces to NAFTA. On a scale of pluses and minuses, the pluses are much more, yet the negatives have the loudest voices." Originally from Yugoslavia, Span and his French-born wife, Lisette, settled in San Cayetano, Michoacán, thirty-four years ago.

"There have always been agriculture problems, but now people blame NAFTA. The solution is for small plotholders to stop planting maize. They've done it for centuries so that it has become a way of life. They should concentrate on tropical fruits. This is the ideal climate for passion fruit, for example. And there's no competition in the United States and Canada, which offer huge markets for tropical fruit. They should start growing *maracuya* (passion fruit) and then market it."

Span describes a successful example of tropical fruit production and marketing. "Guava used to be falling on the ground and rotting. For ten years no guava was harvested, but now Michoacán is the number-one producer of guava in the nation, with exports to Japan, Canada, and the US," he says.

"We dry coffee, roast it, and grind it for our clients." Span also sells honey, preserves, and *ates*, a local version of fruit paste, made by his daughter. "She sells the preserves in delicatessens and gourmet stores," he says proudly. "We try to make added value. Cooperatives don't function here; they don't trust each other. They know politicians will run things with or without the co-op." Span obtains information from the agriculture office in Zitacuaro, advice on topics like black fly disease. "The experts are trusted, and their service is free. They know more than the farmers," Span explains. Some producers in Michoacán are banding together to establish agricultural sales channels. And regional initiatives such as the *Asociación de Bioproductores del Estado de Michoacán* are in process, or at least on the drawing board.[10]

Culinary Queen

Even if she does criticize some of the high-profile chefs, Diana Kennedy retains her throne as culinary queen in Mexico. *DF Magazine*, a glossy lifestyle periodical, featured Kennedy in the April 2004 issue. The editors escorted her to fancy restaurants in Mexico City and asked for her comments.[11] Kennedy later confided to me, "Sol y Aguila wasn't that great.... Fleur de Lis, the tamales are not what they used to be....Izote, not a memorable meal."

In January 2005, during a book signing in Mexico City at the restaurant El Cardenal in the Hotel Sheraton Centro Historico, Kennedy fielded questions from a standing-room-only audience that seemed bent on extracting a global ranking for Mexican cuisine. "Is it second after French cuisine?" asked one woman. "Would you put Mexican cuisine ahead of Chinese and Indian?" Rather than parsing culinary technique, Kennedy steered the conversation to the unique ingredients that Mexico offers. "Should we push for UNESCO world heritage status for Mexican cuisine?" lobbed a questioner from a corner of the room. Kennedy deftly hedged the politically sensitive issues. "Mexico's ingredients are unique, but every culture treasures a traditional cuisine," she said. She ended the prickly discussion by recommending that chefs focus on the unique properties of Mexican flavors and learn French culinary technique.

"The young chefs all want to create, and some of them are quite inventive. They mix things up and put new flavors together. But many of today's chefs lack knowledge on how to bring out flavor. They're using ingredients in creative ways but missing flavor. If you know how to cook and manage ingredients, this shouldn't be a problem." She said that some chefs combine ingredients for menu shock value, to impress clients. The results are innovative, though sometimes inedible. "I don't want to see chili ice cream," she joked to an appreciative audience.

Farm Aid

Recently, when I read about the Autonomous Indigenous University of Mexico, I remembered Diana Kennedy's statement that educational programs for rural farmers fizzle out for lack of funding or logistical planning. Mexico made a stab at offering no-cost higher education to the indigenous rural farmers by opening the university in 2003. However, the school was located in Mochicahui, a colonial town eight hundred miles northwest of Mexico City, nearly a two-day journey by bus for students who hail from the far southern states of Chiapas and Oaxaca, where indigenous farmers have toiled for generations without access to education. Students who need to return home to help with farm chores or who wish to sustain the deep family ties that Mexicans enjoy might well decide that such a distant school is too difficult for the family. Underfunded and lacking teachers, the college struggles to accomplish its mission.[12]

But not all is bleak.

In November 2003 Slow Food, the international consumers movement, awarded Mexico's Jose N. Iturriaga de la Fuente an award "For the Defense of Biodiversity," one of ten honorees around the globe. Iturriaga de la Fuente, a historian whose team of researchers has published fifty-four books on Mexico's indigenous and imported culinary heritage, collected information on celebrations, plants, recipes, and cooking methods. The award acknowledges his work to protect Mexico's food heritage, which is in danger of being lost in the migration of *campesinos* from country to city.[13]

International nongovernmental organizations (NGOs) are assisting small farmers in Mexico with using organic cultivation methods and with moving their produce to the marketplace. In May 2004 Rainforest Alliance and USAID established a three-year project to promote sustainably produced and certified timber, bananas, and coffee exports from Central America and Mexico.[14] But it's slow going.

In a recent e-mail Salvador V. Garibay, a consultant with the Research Institute of Organic Agriculture (FIBL) based in Frick, Switzerland, who works on organic agricultural projects in Mexico and Central America,[15] noted that Mexican government agencies offering support to small farmers include the agricultural ministries of some individual states, the Mexican Coffee Council, the Mexican government's office of regional programs (SEMARNAP), a government agency dedicated to helping the poor form businesses (FONAES), and some state governments, such as those in Tabasco, Chihuahua, and the state of Mexico.

"Government aid is recent and has not recognized the potential of organic agriculture," he wrote. "Support by government has little coordination among institutions. Current constraints on the development of organic agriculture in Mexico are the lack of financial support and credit, deficient standards, and the lack of planning at national level." Diana Kennedy said much the same thing during our talks.

"Most important for the small producers is that they are organized to develop market initiatives [collective sales] for their organic products," Garibay continued. "To be successful, producers need to form networks at the local, regional, and national level for export. They need suitable communication strategies to position their products. Producers need to adapt prices and receive appropriate financing. Finally, they need access and knowledge of market conditions [market intelligence]. The consumers recognize the benefits of organic products, but the farmers need to have suitable promotional campaigns."

Garibay cited one association for organic farmers in Mexico—the Unión Nacional de Productores Orgánicos A.C. (UNAPRO)—which is just getting off the ground with a few organic producers.[16] Another group, ECOMEX, is made up of coffee producers, beekeepers, and producers of organic hibiscus, the flowers used in *agua de jamaica*, a popular *refresco* made by soaking the dried calyxes of hibiscus blossoms in water and adding honey, sugar, or another sweetener to taste.

In 2004, thirteen representatives of the Comité Nacional de Producción Orgánica in Oaxaca agreed to plan an organization that would integrate all the elements of the Mexican organic movement. Currently, the Guatemalan organization Mayacert offers organic certification for Latin American growers, including some in Mexico.[17]

Despite the presence of organizations and government agencies charged with assisting small farmers, there is little promotion of organic agriculture. For a country the size of Mexico, this amounts to abandoning organic agriculture. Garibay envisions a project for the promotion of Mexican organic produce that would build consumer awareness through publicity campaigns, launch a guaranteed "organic" mark or label to create the desired consumer demand, provide market information for the participating farmers, create a business directory, encourage participation in fairs such as a regional Bio-Expo, and facilitate direct contact and promotion to agricultural traders who would launch organic marketing initiatives. To achieve successful development of the organic agriculture movement in Mexico, he recommends organizing and developing "organic pilot projects" in different regions of Mexico.

To Market, to Market

From Diana Kennedy to chefs to vegetable growers to health food store managers, people involved with growing, selling, cooking, and promoting organic food in Mexico agree that the biggest problem for Mexican small farmers is getting produce to a market that offers the highest revenue. Less than 5 percent of Mexico's organic products are sold in natural food stores and restaurants.[18] While there are successful organic producers such as the Del Rancho dairy, whose products with their trademark black and white spotted cows on the labels are found in most supermarkets, it is difficult to find *Hecho en Mexico* on certified organic products.

It's hard enough for a poor farmer to get the produce to the next town, let alone to better-paying urban markets. Shipping produce to the marketplace means lugging hoppers of vegetables on the community pickup truck that serves as a rural bus or loading the family burro. Mexican farmers may soon lack even burros: donkey breeding has waned as workers in the United States send money back to their families in Mexico to buy tractors and pickup trucks. Yet, in hilly regions burros have better traction than vehicles.[19]

In remote areas the small landowner might well be farming with centuries-old organic methods, but farmers aren't branding the produce as organic. For rural farm families, distribution and delivery usually mean that the womenfolk haul bundles of onions, fruit, foraged herbs, and mushrooms or watercress to the nearest town on market day. Unfortunately for the poor rural farmer, the clientele that pays handsomely for fresh organic produce lives in urban centers.

Planting for the Future

As we review the state of organic agriculture in Mexico, we sip Chilean wine, easier to find in the Mexico City supermarkets than Mexican wine. Diana Kennedy and I also discuss how to implement sustainable living. "People need to think about every aspect of their lives. They may eat organic and pay the high prices but still won't separate their garbage," she says as I watch her refold the washed aluminum foil for another use. "Sustainable living isn't incompatible with quality. No one needs to live on a handful of beans. Variety is necessary for quality of life. If people paid more for foodstuffs, they wouldn't waste as much. And along with that goes reasonably sized—not gigantic—portions in restaurants."

Which leads Kennedy to ride a favorite hobbyhorse: packaging for take-out food and "doggie bags" for the huge portions in restaurants in the United States. "Why aren't governments and the public not insisting on biodegradable packaging? Europe is requiring biodegradable plastic for shopping bags; the materials exist. There's a lack of civic interest in trying to preserve the planet for future generations. We are only caretakers of the earth."

As we study the dimming sky, I hear a chorus of frogs and peepers. Conversation turns to Diana Kennedy's latest passion, early twentieth-century English composers—Tavener, Britten, and Elgar. "I cook to opera and jazz," she says. "As you get older, you have to push out. Move into fresh areas." Outside, sundown birds swoop past. A second later I realize that the black shapes whizzing by the terrace are bats.

"We must do more for the future. We're leaving behind a planet strewn with garbage on the Himalayas and the South Pole. We must work for the future. Somewhere down the line, people will realize. I plant trees for the future." ☉

NOTES

1. Diana Kennedy, *Nothing Fancy: Recipes and Recollections of Soul-Satisfying Food* (San Francisco, CA: North Point Press, 1989), 145.

2. Steven Zahniser, ed., NAFTA *at 11: The Growing Integration of North American Agriculture*, Electronic Outlook Report from the Economic Research Service/US Dept. of Agriculture, WRS-05-02, February 2005, www.ers.usda.gov.

3. Reed Lindsay, "Campesinos Demand End to GM Imports," *Mexico News*, 17 October 2001, database: Business Source Premier, Worldsources, Inc.

4. *The Economist*, 25 September 2004, 50; Will Weissert, "US, Mexico Disagree on Corn Importation," *Washington Post*, 10 November 2004.

5. www.unorca.org.mx/ingles/movementactivities.htm.

6. www.ers.usda.gov/Briefing/Mexico/.

7. www.pvem.org.mx/c-accion.htm.

8. Margot Roosevelt, "The Coffee Clash," *Time.com*, 8 March 2004, www.time.com/time/insidebiz/article/0,9171,1101040308-596156-1,00.html.

9. Tim King, "Indigenous Agriculture in Mexico, Traditional Farm-Based Communities," *Acres USA*, November 2004, 19.

10. www.bioplaneta.com.

11. David Lida, "¿Quién le teme a Diana Kennedy?" *DF, la revista de la Ciudad de Mexico*, 28 April–11 May 2004, 12–20.

12. Marion Lloyd, "Educating Mexico's Indians," *Chronicle of Higher Education*, 24 January 2003, 49: 20, A-38.

13. www.slowfood.com/eng/sf_premio/sf_premio_vincitori.lasso.

14. www.rainforest-alliance.org/news/2004/news92.html.

15. www.fibl.org/english/index.php.

16. www.new-ventures.org/opportunities.investors.airesdecampo.html.

17. www.mayacert.com.

18. Lisa J. Adams, "Mexico Spreading Organic Eating at Home," *Washington Post*, 30 September 2004.

19. Mary Jordan, "Mexico Up Against a Burro Deficit," *Washington Post*, 7 November 2004.

Winter 2006, volume 6, number 1

jennie ashlock |

Mr. Clarence Jones, Carolina Rice Farmer

THE CAPE FEAR REGION, a peninsula on the southeastern coast of North Carolina, is surrounded by estuaries, tidal creeks, and marshlands. The soil along the Cape Fear River is dark and rich, and the river itself provides enough tidal energy to flood the area where rice fields once cut through the marshes bordering the river's edge.

Rice came to Cape Fear in the 1730s. Searching for new economic opportunities, wealthy planters from Charleston, South Carolina, migrated to the area, bringing well-developed systems of slavery and rice production. Rice became a major enterprise on plantations along the Cape Fear River, second only to the naval store industry (the production of tar, pitch, and turpentine from pine resin). Rice from the Lower Cape Fear was particularly prized as seed on South Carolina plantations where the ground was nutrient-poor from years of heavy production.

The earliest variety known to have been grown along the southeast coast was Carolina Gold. While there were probably many introductions of the grain into North America, the most commonly accepted account states that Carolina Gold arrived by ship from Madagascar in the late seventeenth century. The ship's captain gave the rice to a Charleston planter, and the rest is history.[1] Planters as far south as Jacksonville, Florida, planted the grain; the Cape Fear River was its northernmost growing area.

I had the opportunity to see some Carolina Gold growing on a former rice plantation outside Savannah, Georgia. True to their name, the ripe Carolina Gold rice plants had a warm, golden hue. When properly cooked, however, each grain is pristine white.

After nearly two hundred years, the rice industry ended on the southeast coast and moved west. Three main factors contributed to its demise, the most obvious being the loss of the slave labor force at the end of the Civil War. After the war, former slaves continued working the fields as sharecroppers. The work was long, hot, and tedious. An article from a Wilmington newspaper dated August 23, 1899, suggests one way planters explored rebuilding their workforce: "Mr. Kidder said that in his opinion the convict system was the best means of operating these [rice] farms."[2]

Mother Nature also played her role. A series of devastating hurricanes hit the southeast coast in the late nineteenth century, greatly reducing crop returns. Carolina Gold is not only a tender grain, it is a tender plant. Growing over five feet tall, it tends to bend and break in high winds. It cannot withstand a hurricane.

With the development of new machinery and harvest techniques, the rice industry changed drastically. Unfortunately, southeastern rice fields were very soft and moist and could not support the weight of the heavy equipment. For two hundred years, mule, plow, and human hands had been the primary agricultural equipment in southern rice fields. Southeastern rice planters could not compete with large harvests coming from the new rice-growing regions of Louisiana, Texas, and Arkansas, where the new machinery was successfully used.

The southeastern rice industry is now coming back, but on a much smaller scale. Most sites grow not Carolina Gold, but hardier hybrids that are easier to grow. Today, however, there is an urgent environmental reason to revitalize the former rice fields, as these wetlands are a haven for a wide variety of wildlife. Construction and river pollution threaten the delicate balance in our natural coastal environment. In the Cape Fear area, the Coastal Land Trust, a nonprofit organization, is saving former rice fields through land easements in order to create much-needed green space. According to Bruce Watkins, a riparian specialist at the Land Trust, the goal is to protect the wetlands from being built upon or modified in any way.[3]

Scientists are also exploring modifications to the rice in order to increase yields. Dr. Merle Shepard, Professor of Entomology and resident director of Clemson University's Coastal Research and Education Center in Charleston, South Carolina, is collaborating with the International Rice Research Institute (IRRI) in the Philippines to develop a new variety of Carolina Gold. He is working with Dr. Gurdev Khush, senior rice breeder with the IRRI, to cross Carolina Gold with a shorter Japonica-type, high-yielding, aromatic variety. Basically, they hope to keep the grain and shorten the stalk.

At the time of this writing (April 2001), Dr. Shepard was waiting for the seeds to pass through the USDA/APHIS Plant Quarantine Service. Once he receives the seeds, he will grow them for one season at the Research and Education Center to ensure that they are not harboring any pathogens. If successful, he will find local farmers willing to grow the new varieties.[4]

THE STORY OF THE RICE INDUSTRY made me eager to interview Mr. Clarence Jones, who once worked on the Cape Fear rice plantations. At ninety-two, he lives in a comfortable home on the land his grandmother farmed in Brunswick County, North Carolina, across the Cape Fear River from Wilmington.

Like so many of his relatives, Mr. Jones started out sharecropping in the rice fields at several plantations along the Cape Fear River. When the rice industry collapsed in the 1930s, he became the head gardener at Orton Plantation, a once-thriving rice plantation originally owned by one of the first South Carolina planters to settle the area in the eighteenth century. Magnificent azaleas and camellias replaced rice as the plantation's economic mainstay. Today, the plantation grounds are open to the public, and Mr. Jones is often found in the gardens he tended for seventy years.

Right: Mr. Clarence Jones at home. PHOTOGRAPH BY JENNIE ASHLOCK © 2001

I asked Mr. Jones if Whites ever worked in the rice fields. No, he replied, it was a segregated industry. And, importantly, the arduous method of growing rice with human labor did not change much between the 1700s and 1930s. Mr. Jones said that his experiences are much the same as those of his ancestors, who years before him worked in the same fields.

This interview took place on September 9, 1999.

On Growing Rice

Jennie Ashlock: *Do you remember growing rice at Orton Plantation?*

Clarence Jones: Well, I do, really do, some. You know, the last crop of rice was raised down there in 1931…. That was the year I got married. I got married that year in 1931. And we were workin' in the rice field, my wife and me were both workin' down there in the rice field. Quite a job at that time.

JA: *Tell me about it.*

CJ: First you had to get the soil ready for plantin' the seeds. Well, you take the harrow. You know what a harrow is? And we didn't have a tractor, you know, we had mules. They'd get this land ready. Dry the field off. You know, it's gate controlled with the water. And you dry it off good and dry. And you put the harrow in there and plow it up. Get it all disked, then you get that all level. Then you take a marker, they call it, a marker. You know what a marker is, but I'll tell you what it is. You take an 8 × 8 timber, on the bottom of it you bore holes. Well, say you're going to put your rice that far apart. Then you bore a hole in there and put a peg in there, you see? And then you move on down as far as you want and make rows. You understand me now? Yes, see, that's in order you can run your rows straight. So if you want five rows you have five pegs or six. And you put that together. And you put shares on it and put that on the mule and then he pull it, he pull it up and down. Go down one way and come down another and he'd mark it. Then, after he'd get it marked then the girls would come along with the sowin'. Sowin' gourds. Well, they were trained, oh well trained, they could take that thing and sow rice any kind of way you wanted it. If you want it thick they could sow it thick. Or if you want it thin they could sow it thin. Any kind of way. And they was really good at it because they could sow a field with 'em a couple of 'em in a day.

JA: *And how big was a field?*

CJ: Oh, about ten acres. So then you sowed the rice. And after you sowed it then you put a soakin' throw on it…the first flooding, but you don't flood it over. You just soak it. That is, the water get probably that deep. Well, just get the ground soppy. And then it germinate, the rice. And then after you get it to germinate, come up, immediately when it get up off the ground about an inch or so tall, then you flood it again with the water. You put the water on it again. Then you put a flood on it again. And you let that flood stay on it a while. Stay so many days. Then when your rice get a certain size, then you go in there, you know the grass is growin' real fast. Dry it off. Dry. Dry the fields dry. As dry as you can, you know. Then you take a hoe. And you go in there, up and down each row. You weed the grass out of it. Get the grass out of that. Well, you gotta know grass from rice, you know, you have to do that. Then you go down one row. You take two rows at a time, choppin', you know. Until you get it all chopped out. And then after you get it chopped out, then you flow it again. Put the water on it again. Your rice is this high then.

JA: *A couple of feet by this time.*

CJ: And you flow it again and then you leave that water on there for a while, and see that's the roundin' up flow. Then you're formin' the head. Getting the heads ready for to come out, you see. But they have to have that water to push 'em, push 'em out. Well, you let it stay at 'em till they round on up and it's up. Cut all flows off. No more flow. Then your rice stay there until they get ripe. And that takes a while for that to happen. And then after it get ripe, you go down with...well, we didn't have no harvesters then to cut it, you know, for to cut it. So they had reef hooks. You know what a reef hook is? Well you take that reef hook and then you go in there and cut it and lay it on the [ground], you have to know how to lay it. Cut it, cut it and lay till you cut a field. How much you want to cut. Then you come back the next day, after it dry, and bundle it up. Take up so many pieces in a bundle, say a bundle that big and then you tie it, sew it together. And you do that until you get it all cut and tied. Then you come back, after you get it all cut and tied, and you come back and shock it up in the field.

JA: *And what is "shock it up"?*

CJ: You seen these little "wigwams" they call 'em in the field, you know, some little tent? You put two sticks of timbers like that on the ground, keep it from bein' on the ground and you start laying layers around and round and round and round until you get it high as you want 'em. And it stays there a good while like that in the field. Then in the fall of the year, you bring it into the barn. And they had a big barn. And they would bring that rice out to the hill and then load it on the wagons and take it to the threshers. And they had a crew there to thresh the rice and bag it up. And then they'd take it back to the river, put it on the boat, ship it up to Wilmington. They had a place over there that they would husk the rice. Take the husk off it and get it ready for sale, see? Rice at that time, you didn't ever have to buy rice because we had plenty of rice free.

JA: *Did you get a portion of what was grown in the field?*

CJ: The rice? Oh yeah, all the rice you want. Go to the barn and get it, you know. Plenty of rice left. And then we had something called a maul and pestle.

Yeah, well, you know how that works. So that's how you clean your rice up Friday for Saturday, Sunday, and you get the rice ready and it was good rice, too.

JA: *What kind of rice was it?*

CJ: I don't know the name of it. I go to the barn and get a bag, a pail of rice and that was one of my jobs I hated [*laughing*]. I had to beat it out, you know, and get it clean. My mother would come and look at it and say "Noo, beat it some more." You'd better be careful not to beat it up so you break the grains. You had to know how to do it. And then you'd go down to the barn where the corn was, in the barn, you know, and you'd shuck three or four ears of corn. Then you'd take those shucks when you get the brown husk off the rice then you had to *whiten* it.

JA: *So you didn't eat the brown rice?*

CJ: Oh no, you had to whiten it. Then you'd take these shucks and put it in the maul, stir it up. Then you'd beat that pestle in there until that white rice come white as that. You see, the shucks would whiten the rice somehow or other…. Then you get the husk off it, then you pick it up out of the maul and hold it like that [*blows twice*] and whistle. When you whistle the wind would blow, see [*laughing*]. Sounds funny, but that did it. Just whistle and the wind would blow and the husk would go. And the rice would go back in the maul; clear, clean and everything.

And one more problem we had. Birds. They'd eat you out, they'd [eat] the rice in an hour if you didn't keep them out of there. We had the shotgun. You know what a shotgun is. They'd take the shots out of the shell and just have the waddin' and the powder in there, and that "boom" they would fly away and they wouldn't stay long. They'd come right back. And you had to do that all day long, and there wasn't no sense in knockin' off because them birds would stay there until dark. And then be there in the mornin' at four o'clock. Your birds would be in the field. Well, you don't never eaten a bird taste as good as one of those rice birds [bobolink]. Best bird you ever eat in your life. Quail, doves and all those other birds didn't have no taste to them like a rice bird and a coot.

JA: *What was it like to work in the rice fields?*

CJ: What was it like? Well, first it was a job. And if you wanted money then you did most anything in a job that you could do to get it. But workin' in the rice field was not a good job. It wasn't a nice job, I'll tell you that. Because it was hard, hard work. And hot. You see you had no shade. Nothin'. You just workin' in full sun. Yeah, and you didn't work by the hour. You work at something they called a task. You do so much for your task. When you finish that you go home or you want to do another one or whatsoever. So that's the way they operate in the rice field. They did it by task.

JA: *What was your task?*

CJ: My task? We'd chop about two pieces. And that was two 70 × 70 squares, and you did that and that was your task. But we did it and made a living. Yeah. Made a living. Sometime we made 4 dollar a week, sometime $3.50, sometime 2 dollar. Well, if you made 3 dollar, you's rich. Had plenty of money. Oh, Lord [*laughing*]. Oh, you'd work hard, child. You'd work haaard. And you work long enough and hard enough to make $3 or $4 that week, boy you was tired when Friday come.…I worked other plantations too. Well, it just like anything else. You finish over here and we move on over. And we'd move other places. I ducked the rice fields as much as I could. No, it wasn't my favorite work.

On Eating Frog Legs

CJ: When you put the frogs, skin 'em, take 'em home and you dress 'em. Get 'em all washed up clean. Then you put 'em in the bag, you know, with salt and pepper. And you sprinkle flour on 'em and get 'em all ready. Get your grease good and hot. Then you have to have a lid, you know, to lower over the frying pan. 'Cause when you put the frog legs in there they jump out. They'll jump out and run! So you put them in there and put the lid on quick and they'll be there when the grease hit them.

On Hunting and Eating Alligator with His Friend Duncan McKoy

CJ: So we'd take the little ones and skin 'em, and he'd take the tail and sell him to different people, you know, that wanted it. And his wife was one of the best cooks you ever see in your life. She know'd how to cook anything. Didn't matter what it was. So she'd take this 'gator. It was, oh you'd take a 'gator that long and have about that much tail. That little part you wouldn't bother with it. But you'd it cut down and around into round pieces, you know round, until you get as many steaks out of it as you could. Then you'd take it and put it in the pan and salt it. Pour just a couple of teaspoons full of vinegar in that water. Then stir it up and put your 'gator in there and sit it on the shelf. Now they didn't have refrigerators long then, you know. You had to sit it on the shelf and pray to the Lord it won't spoil. So you'd set it up and nothin' happened to it! And next mornin' you'd get up and check that tail and check the pan and wash it off good. Take it out of that water and wash it off good. Clean. And get you some flour. Sprinkle a little black pepper in that flour and mix that up. Then you lay it in that flour and then turn it over and lay it in there like that. You know, and turn it over. Just keep turnin' it 'til you get it good and floured. Have your fryin' pan ready, see. Grease just a poppin'. And you fry that and it kind of puffles. It will puff up a little bit with the flour. Gets crispy. And he'd turn it over carefully and he'd [turn] it over a time or two. Take it out and lay it on a platter. Well, I tell you, when you holler supper or breakfast they'd so never did come runnin'. 'Cause the 'gator tail was right. So they'd eat it. Don't get me wrong. I'd eat it too, cause it was good. No question about it. Good eatin'.

On Killing Hogs

CJ: See, well, he [my grandfather] died and then she [my grandmother, Fanny Brown] come into possession. Everybody in the neighborhood would come down and "Fanny how 'bout a hog. We need a hog!" "Go on out there and get you a hog. Go yon and get you one." Just give it to them 'cause she had plenty. During that time there was something they called a No Fence law. I don't know if you heard of it or not. But no fence. You didn't have to fence your garden in, or you didn't have to fence your nothing. You could let your hogs and cattle run out. If you had a garden, you would have to fence it in yourself to keep these things out of it. 'Cause there wasn't no law that say "well, if your cow went in my garden you'd have to pay me for it." No, that wasn't true. And 'til the No Fence law was abolished, if you had a stock of cattle or hogs, they just growed and growed and growed. And they took care of themselves in the woods. You didn't have to feed 'em. The only thing you'd have to do is in November you'd go out and get about ten or twelve hogs and bring 'em home. And you'd put 'em in the pen. Fatten 'em up. Get ready for the hog killin' for Christmas. You see Grandma, she would kill eight and ten hogs every Christmas.

When they kill a hog, the first thing they did is to take the liver out and give it to the cook. And then they'd have liver and cornbread and sweet potatoes and all that and turnip greens and all that good stuff ready. So when we kill a hog, in about an hour or so, start for dinner and had a big table spread out everywhere, you know, and then they'd eat hardy. They didn't have time to cook no cakes or nothin' like that. Didn't really go into that part of it. Only time you got cake or pie was on Sunday.

When I thanked Mr. Jones for his time, he responded:

CJ: Yeah, well, thank you, thank you so much. I hope you got something out of it.

JA: *Well, look at what we learned. We learned about rice, frog giggin', and eating alligator.*

CJ: That's old time livin', missy. Yeah, that's old time stuff. ☺

For more information on the history of rice in the Southeast, contact:

The Rice Museum
Intersection of Front and Seventh Streets
P.O. Box 902
Georgetown, SC 29442–0902
843-546-7423

NOTES

1. David Doar, *Rice and Rice Planting in the South Carolina Low Country,* and Daniel Littlefield, *Rice and Slaves: Ethnicity and the Slave Trade in Colonial South Carolina,* as cited in Karen Hess, *Carolina Rice Kitchen* (Columbia, South Carolina: University of South Carolina Press, 1992), 17–18.

2. "Concluded Its Work," *The Morning Star,* Wilmington, North Carolina (23 August 1899), front page.

3. Bruce Watkins, telephone conversation with the author, 26 April 2001, Wilmington, NC.

4. Dr. Merle Shepard, e-mail correspondence with the author, 13 April 2001.

Fall 2001, volume 1, number 4

christopher m. annear |

"GM or Death"
Food and Choice in Zambia

FOOD IS COMPLICATED NOURISHMENT that feeds more than the belly. As recent events in Zambia have shown, it has the capacity to make (or break) relationships before even a morsel is raised to lips. In 2002 Zambian president Levy Patrick Mwanawasa sparked international controversy when he banned genetically modified (GM) foods from entering Zambia, including in the form of famine aid. Since then, contentious debate has ensued that transcends questions regarding the relative virtue of GM foods, in terms of both nutritional safety and geoeconomic prudence. The potency of President Mwanawasa's words and the strong international, almost exclusively Western, repudiations of his declaration reveal a tenuous relationship between African and Western donor countries over the topics of food aid and food values. What he has shown, in effect, is that food can constitute political poison even when it is gastronomically edible.

Mwanawasa's GM food remarks drew—perhaps even courted—criticism from beyond the borders of his midsized south-central African country for his purported insensitivity to the food needs of his own people. Due to the effects of El Niño on the preceding two growing seasons (2001, 2002), southern Africa has been reported to be a virtual famine zone. Therefore, the posited relationship between food and affected African countries is often discussed as if it were linear and axiomatic: the hungry continent requires food, any food. In this article I discuss the paradox that, on the one hand, debate is encouraged concerning the possible health risks of certain foods for people who can buy them; yet, on the other, donor governments deny the right of choice to those people in other countries who receive them at no immediate economic cost. I examine two ideas central to this controversy: one, that the privilege of food choice is present only in prosperous, industrialized countries; and two, that food is conceptualized symbolically, culturally, and ethically in a variety of ways. In sub-Saharan Africa this is no less the case than in Western countries, yet when Africans attempt to exercise choice concerning GM foods they are told: "Beggars can't be choosers."[1] Such sentiments suggest that Africans are denied the right of free food choice because Western nations, many of which are also aid donors, have already tacitly determined food pathways to and for Africa.

The news reports and opinion pieces published in response to President Mwanawasa's decision have been less refutations of his argument against GM foods than comments on his perceived arrogance and ignorance in denying food to "his own starving people." While this Western response to African hunger has been seen before, Mwanawasa's initial declaration, and perhaps even more his stubborn adherence to an anti-GM stance, is rather less orthodox. In order to better analyze Mwanawasa's political position this article will do what many others have not: it will reserve judgment long enough to examine the social, political, and gastronomic environment in Zambia that helped to generate the president's antagonistic posture, articulated in one editorial as the choice of either "GM or death."[2]

"Africa Becomes Battleground for Genetically Altered Food"[3]

No controversy—nuclear power, global warming, or even the eerie possibility of cloning human beings—occupies a larger space in that disturbing arena where science, social values, and commerce collide [than GM foods].[4]

The controversy over genetically modified foods is one of those rare topics that draw together cultural, economic, and religious values. Although typically presented as a scientific issue, genetic modification of foods also tends to inspire emotional reactions that speak to global issues of economic and cultural power. Before July 2002, the Western debate on GM foods focused on juxtapositions pitting international producers against local consumers[5] and occasionally agribusiness against individual farmers,[6] but rarely did it concern itself with ameliorating hunger. These parameters were tested when international media began running a seemingly paradoxical story: "We Would Rather Starve Than Get Genetically Modified Foods, Says President,"[7] which reported that Mwanawasa was considering refusing any food aid that included genetically modified elements. Articles written in response to the Zambian president's political stance articulated a range of opinions, from aloof dismissal of what was regarded as "yet another case" of an African leader posturing with dictatorial bravado to expressions of disbelief and anger. Advocates, and even some opponents of GM foods being allowed into European markets, voiced their indignation at a president who would refuse food aid to his own starving people, regardless of its value or content.[8]

I suspect that the reason for ignoring the issue of food *quantity* in a debate that until Mwanawasa's statement had been primarily about food *quality* is that it reshuffled the political arguments. One of the main sticking points with GM foods has been the long-term health effects of bioengineering on the land on which they are grown and on consumers. However, the capacity of such seeds to enduringly fulfill promises of improved yields is rarely questioned. Moreover, agribusiness firms have often promoted genetically modified organisms as the next hunger-ending "Green Revolution."[9] Based on the generally accepted notion that GM crops will bring enhanced productivity, Africa and GM foods seemed to be an ideal match: the continent "ravaged by hunger" is given high-yielding crops. But a problem arose when Africans themselves began to challenge this relationship.

Defining Food in Contemporary Zambia: Rural Perspectives

In an industrial society getting a meal is an interval or a conclusion to the day's work; in a [pre-industrial] society, getting a meal is the day's work.[10]

The debate over whether to accept or refuse GM foods in Zambia is inextricably connected to the symbolism of food. The late New Zealand anthropologist Raymond Firth's observation above offers a useful point of departure. Firth is correct—food production and procurement are essentially different activities in industrial and agrarian societies. Therefore, the meanings associated with food in these societies are likely to be dissimilar as well. However, modern Zambia, along with most other countries of the world, must also account for both urban and rural modes of labor and production, which coexist and interact through both meanings and markets within its national borders.

At least 60 percent of Zambians live in nonurban areas.[11] Many rural people rely on urban wage-remittances, severance payments, and other forms of imported income, and they, along with the vast majority of Zambians, subsist on locally cultivated staples such as maize, cassava, and finger millet. Rural residents typically produce the daily meals they consume through carefully planned year-round agricultural labor, and thus are intimately involved in the precarious process of food cultivation and harvest. Not surprisingly, therefore, among the attributes of highly valued foods is the ability to generate consistent and reliable results. Foods laden with the richest symbolic meanings are most likely to be "traditional"[12] ones that are known and trusted locally.

Defining food in rural, agrarian areas at first appears deceptively simple: food is what fills a person's stomach, food is what fuels strength for work. Symbolic subtleties, however, emerge upon consideration of which foods fulfill these requirements. Moreover, it is not just the type of food, but also the processes by which it is prepared, for whom, and at which times, that shape value. In the Luapula region, and throughout northern Zambia, the most significant food is *nshima*,[13] a thick porridge made from maize, cassava, and sometimes finger millet, which is eaten at almost every meal. Consuming several hearty portions of *nshima* means that a person will be "satisfied," which in turn results in them having strength for work. The concept of being satisfied (*ukwikuta* in Chibemba, the most widely spoken language of northern Zambia) implies more than merely filling emptiness with food. To eat an adequate amount of locally valued food "delivers one from hunger" or "chases the hunger away" (*ukutûka nsala*). N*shima* is considered so significant to the Zambian diet that a common complaint following the consumption of several ears of roasted maize or a hearty plate of peeled and boiled sweet potatoes without the basic staple dish is "Alas, we are dying of hunger. We have not had a bite to eat all day."[14]

Nshima in Zambia is often discussed in terms of the energy and gastronomic satisfaction that it confers upon individuals, yet it provides something more significant still: a sense of social coherence. Eating is a social activity, with *nshima* the anchor of every meal. Raymond Firth underscores this notion of food as socially cohesive. He discusses food production and meanings among Tikopian islanders of the South Pacific as a collaboration between the pragmatic and symbolic:

> The relationship of people to food in Tikopia is strongly pragmatic, empirical. They want to
> eat it, they are anxious about the supply of it, they organize a great deal of their activity around

getting it and making it ready for eating. They also are very interested in the idea of food, intellectually and emotionally. They talk a lot about food; they enjoy their own foods cooked in their own way; they are very hospitable in pressing food upon visitors; and very pleased when visitors enjoy it too. With all this the Tikopia have quite an elaborate set of symbolic concepts in which food figures—either being symbolized by other things or itself symbolizing activities and relationships.... Strictly speaking there are no symbolic objects—there are only symbolic relationships.[15]

Similarly, the symbolic relationships invested in and reflected by important foods are key to understanding the emotional responses of people in places like Zambia to genetically modified foods.

Symbolic Consumption: Relationships, Values, and Choices Encoded in Food

There are objects or substances which are not edible by their physical nature, because they cannot be masticated or cannot be digested or their flavour is antipathetic: earth, wood, grubs, some marine fauna, etc. Then there are others which are inedible because of their social nature.[16]

Now, to return to a question suggested earlier: what makes food bad to eat even when it is gastronomically edible? Among the variables that affect the morality of consumption are time, place, and social standing. Certain foods may not be appropriate, or might even be considered temporarily unpalatable during episodes of mourning, in rites of initiation, or due to one's age. Groups, rank, and gender are further delineated and variously amalgamated through the idiom of food. It is often through eating that social relationships are realized and symbolically represented.

Matrilineal clan aggregates in northern Zambia are often united under the banners of foods and animals. *Ubowa* (mushroom), *ubwali* (*nshima*), and *isabi* (fish) are commonly found group titles. While in some circumstances the consumption of the clan emblem is prohibited to members, clan names can also foster cooperation and familiarity among groups. Certain clans maintain special joking relationships that involve mutual obligation and the social leeway to act especially rudely toward each other without incurring the same ire as one would in typical interactions. These relationships are founded on the complementary nature of the clan names. For example, members of the mushroom and rain clans are "joking cousins" because mushrooms cannot grow without rain; likewise, the fish and crocodile clans are paired because crocodiles subsist on fish.[17]

Food is also used as an idiom to represent and transform interethnic relations in Zambia. Comparable to many other practices throughout the world, people are sometimes grouped by the foods they are purported to eat. An example is found in the Bemba proverb "*abalya mbulu, balapalamana,*" which translates loosely as "those who eat water monitors (a large species of lizard) gravitate together." In a similar manner, ethnic Bembas and Ngonis have in part transformed their previously hostile rivalry into a peaceful joking relationship through gastronomic teasing. Members of each group playfully mock the other for their respective "repulsive" culinary habits. Bembas are criticized by Ngonis for their atrocious willingness to eat monkeys, while Ngonis are mercilessly harassed for their "disgusting" habit of regularly consuming a certain type of rat. This manner of mischievous banter is so pervasive that Bembas and Ngonis are iconographically represented in house paintings and public murals as monkeys and rats throughout Zambia. As shown by interethnic and clan joking relationships, "fighting" via ethnic foodways can diffuse tension and invite sociability. As elsewhere, food in Zambia bestows richer sustenance than merely the sum of its constituent nutrients. Nourishment is endowed upon the social consumer through the symbolic relationships that are both represented and conferred via food. Such messages and meanings are, of course, as various as the foods that are eaten. Concepts appear especially diverse when comparing areas where food is bought and where it is harvested. However, I argue that the *processes* that pervade the social content appropriated through food are very much the same in urban and rural regions. These include communicating through symbolic representation, fighting for political leverage, and demanding the right to accept (and reject) foods.

Ndlovu's Thinking:[18] Urban Values and Involvement

Although rural people are usually more physically vulnerable than urbanites to calamities that might be set in motion by GM crops, the debate in Zambia has nonetheless been almost exclusively an urban one. With few exceptions, urban values and definitions of food are the ones that drive public discourse.[19] This is generally the case wherever GM foods are debated—in North America, the European Union (EU), and Africa. One of the most significant elements of delineation between urban and rural areas is access to mass media. While much has to do with the capability to receive incoming news and ideas, perhaps even more consequential are the outward channels for sending messages. However, there is a difference between sending and communicating. Compared to those in rural areas, city residents have much greater access to information from foreign sources, yet few ideas coming from Africa seem to be heard in international discourse. In Zambia, the GM foods debate has presented a temporary solution, which has served to open communication with the outside.

In this way the GM foods debate presents an opportunity to economically marginal so-called Third World nations—the "privilege" of international voice. Urban Zambian opinions seem to be greatly influenced not only by the content of perspectives expressed in the West, but also by a desire simply to be involved. The GM foods debate appears to be viewed in Zambia as a modern and cosmopolitan issue that connects the country to outside nations socially and, Zambians hope, economically.

Most Zambian news articles and opinion pieces discuss food issues by focusing on Zambia's relationship with the EU. Unlike in rural areas, food is not considered to be meaningful for its local productive significance in cities such as Lusaka and Kitwe. Instead, it is recognized for its value as a trade commodity that opens social and economic links with western Europe. Furthermore, due to the current anti-GM mood in most EU member countries, fears that GM-contaminated food products could be refused in Europe have increased the stakes for hopeful exporters such as Zambia.[20] Interestingly, these anxieties are at present wholly academic, since Zambia does not to any significant extent export edible crops to Europe.

Therefore, the urban Zambian debate ostensibly concerning GM foods can be viewed as a pseudoscientific discourse about international power and modern Zambia's role in the world. The newspaper article entitled "Ndlovu's Thinking" is a good example of such discussion. It is an editorial written as a rebuttal to Zambian member of parliament Alfred Ndlovu, whose original written piece expressed general confidence in the willingness of the United States to provide healthful foods as aid to drought-stricken regions of Zambia.

The editorialist disagrees with Ndlovu, calling him naïve for trusting a capitalist country to have moral rather than economic motives propelling decisions concerning GM food products. He expresses pragmatic disillusionment with Zambia's relationship to Western countries and reminds readers of how international aid donors, especially the United States, have previously sent understudied medical products such as the antidiarrheal Immodium to Africa, only to later ban it after many Africans died. Although cautionary, the writer is not entirely dismissive of Western countries. He wants Zambians to be cognizant of the nature of capitalistic, profit-minded decision making; nonetheless, he counsels his readers not to sever international relations. Ultimately, the editorialist is hopeful that greater international parity can be achieved among countries through careful and constructive engagement.

This rebuttal to Ndlovu expresses sentiments that echo the majority of Zambian commentaries. Common themes declare that GM foods might be poisonous and that crossbreeding between GM and indigenous varieties could permanently contaminate national food supplies,[21] resulting in a decrease of endemic biological diversity.[22] Despite the scientific rhetoric that consistently peppers these pieces, this mainly urban debate actually concerns power and international relations. Zambians often lament their lack of political power; inclusion in GM debates perhaps allows for a measure of engagement. For many Zambians, simply being recognized by Western countries as a participant in such a debate is a victory unto itself.

"Dignity in Hunger"[23]

It is all about economics. If you have economic power you can choose what you eat and eat what you want from where ever it is produced. On the other [hand,] you eat what is thrown at you, and [are] forced to give what you want, unless you have dignity. "Uwakwensha ubushiku bamutasha lilya bwacha!" [One who drives at night is only thanked in the morning].[24]

In Zambia, involvement in the GM foods debate generates international interaction that is otherwise nearly nonexistent. Whereas North American and European news sources tend to dismiss African skepticism of the healthfulness of GM foods as arrogant and irresponsible,[25] Zambians assert their opinions with self-confidence and the expectation that they are—or should be—equal partners in the discussion. However, the de facto reality of international news coverage is that political and scientific issues tend to be reported as if they exclusively concern Western countries. Individual non-Western voices are thus very rarely included in news accounts of debates that do not explicitly refer to their country or region of origin. It appears that international news outlets covering Zambia's response to being "force-fed" GM foods have been dismissive because of the tacit belief that Zambia is overstepping its role as a donor-dependent nation.

The sentiments in the quote above underscore the opinions of many residents of the cities and towns of Zambia. However, what about the perspectives of the rural Zambians who are reported to be starving? The few articles that depict the plights of Zambian villagers have been published almost exclusively in Western newspapers,[26] and tend to express an overwhelming willingness on the part of rural people to eat whatever food is given to them. Moreover, while Western media report starving African masses, Zambian newspapers tend to contradict these reports, often agreeing with President Mwanawasa's stance that "There has been a false picture being painted to the outside world that people in Zambia are dying of hunger."[27]

In reality, the current state of hunger in Zambia is neither wholly desperate nor satisfactory—nor, of course, is it a singular circumstance nationwide. Shortages appear to be most acute in the south and southwest of the country, where diminished rainfall has hampered the cultivation of maize for the past two seasons.[28] During those same two growing seasons, in Luapula Province a combination of more acceptable rainfall and the general reliance on the hardy cassava plant, which matures over the course of two to three years, has produced a relative bumper crop. Nevertheless, anecdotal evidence suggests that localized food shortages are still occurring in some areas, due less to poor harvests than to overselling by individuals attracted to exceptionally high prices for staple foods. Even in areas where food is scarce, poor Zambians may be suffering more from governmental inability (or unwillingness) to distribute Zambian-grown foods than from environmental capriciousness. At the very least, the current problem has certainly been exacerbated by a dysfunctional political system that has failed to distribute available food resources.

Conclusion: Relief-Induced Agonism— Starving for International Attention

This article has considered the Zambian role in international debate over genetically modified foods. President Mwanawasa's initial skepticism and later ban prohibiting GM foods from entering the country (including in the form of aid) have elicited a wide range of international and national responses. Despite spirited debate on many sides of this provocative issue, none of the news or editorial pieces I have come across presents compelling analysis that helps to explain why Zambians, and above all their president, have

expressed the opinions discussed throughout this article. In an effort to replace rhetoric with comprehension, I suggest that Zambian urban and rural perspectives on GM foods, as well as Western media reaction to the Zambian government's controversial stance, can be viewed as an extension of Robert Dirks's notion of "relief-induced agonism."[29]

Dirks describes relief-induced agonism as a condition of predictable and patterned aggression that follows after acutely underfed populations first receive enough nourishment to regain some strength. Perhaps counterintuitively, the reciprocal act of aid recipients is not merely to be unappreciative of the efforts by relief workers, but to act out aggressively, at times even physically abusing the people who fed them. The very people, therefore, who assisted the early recuperation of starving populations become the targets of their aggression.

Some populations in Zambia may currently be in dire physical condition; however, what has so amazed Western donor nations is the unexpected *analytical* belligerency exhibited by Zambia's government and citizenry. Zambian urbanites are angry at perceived international inequality and the apparent Western unwillingness to treat African countries as anything more than "dumping grounds" for their unwanted and/or unused resources. The writer of "Ndlovu's Thinking" articulates his anger as follows:

> What I am saying is that neither the world, the UN nor anyone will protect your citizens. It is
> for the government to ensure [that] its people and nation…[are] protected. This is fraught with

Above: Mr. Nason L. Chibwe displaying non-GM cassava root grown on his farm in Kansele on the Luapula Plateau during his independently organized agricultural show and farmer workshop, October 1999. PHOTOGRAPH BY CHRISTOPHER M. ANNEAR © 2004

hardships and danger when you are a small nation without economic muscle and without a strong infrastructure, because you will always be held to ransom on aid, loans and others unless you accede to certain programmes etc....Africa in the world pecking order comes bottom of the pile, fact not sentiment.[30]

What Zambia may be expressing is a relief-induced agonism of the analytical rather than physiological sort—a reaction to perceived political starvation. I am not suggesting that Zambian rejection of genetically modified food aid is necessarily an automatic reflex reaction of a starving people, but that it is instead a calculated response by a geopolitically hungry people. Debate of GM foods has been recognized in Zambia as a conduit for varied urban and rural responses that reach outside the African region. There are, of course, sincere anxieties in Zambia about the future health effects of genetically modified foods. However, what has been considered here is how the GM foods debate has become a forum for expressing urban frustration over both the scarcity and the tenor of social, political, and economic engagement with the world outside of Africa.

Conversely, the presence of such rapacious urban voices serves to magnify the rarity of national media engagement with rural areas, even though these are where most hypothetical GM contamination would occur. If Zambia and other politically and economically marginal countries are to succeed at building the internal strength and stature that they so desire, then all people must be given voices both inside and outside of national borders. Foods, Firth reminds us, mark symbolic relationships. Meanings are therefore neither fixed nor unidirectional. Just as urbanites seek to be recognized as participants in worldwide discussions concerning GM foods, rural perspectives must also be heard in order to reach meaningful accord.

The Zambian rejection of genetically modified foods is significant and noteworthy, even if heavily skewed toward urban channels of communication. For the attentive observer, it is more than just President Mwanawasa's defiant anti-GM declaration that can be heard emanating from Zambia. His act was one of calculated political opportunism; however, by making his pronouncement he inadvertently initiated a debate over economic power and choice that included a country which was hitherto a silent recipient of aid. While international response to his position has been largely critical, it has also focused a temporary spotlight on a hungry country, a small but considerable consolation for the many Zambians who see few options other than to express their relief-induced agonism. As a nation that is generally politically stable but slowly deflating economically, Zambia, like many other countries in similar straits, might be too weak to rise up, yet it is still strong enough to take a nip at the hand that feeds it. ☉

NOTES

The author acknowledges Parker Shipton, Diana Wylie, James A. Pritchett, James C. McCann, and Ruth H. Kerkham as well as two anonymous reviewers for insightful editorial comments. Additionally, appreciation is extended to Dr. Kenneth D. Kaunda, the first president of Zambia, and his assistants, Mr. Godwin Mfula and Mr. Gabriel Banda, for offering illuminating perspectives during his yearlong residency with the Boston University Balfour African President in Residence program, 2002–2003. This article is dedicated with great fondness and respect to the late Mr. Nason L. Chibwe, *bashikulwifwe*.

1. Zambia has been told by the United States to either use fifty million dollars to buy America's GM maize through the World Food Programme or face starvation. When the United States had earlier tried to force GM food aid on India, an unnamed USAID spokesman told the media: "Beggars can't be choosers." See Robert Vint, "Force-Feeding the World: America's 'GM or Death' Ultimatum to African Reveals the Depravity of Its GM Marketing Policy," AgBioIndia Mailing List, http://www.connectotel.com/gmfood/ag020902.txt, 2002.

2. Ibid.

3. Emily Gersema, "Africa Becomes Battleground for Genetically Altered Food," *Associated Press*, 9 September 2002.

4. Michael Spector, "The Pharmageddon Riddle: Did Monsanto Just Want More Profits, or Did It Want to Save the World?" *New Yorker*, 10 April 2000.

5. See, for example, Mark L. Winston, *Travels in the Genetically Modified Zone* (Cambridge, MA: Harvard University Press, 2002); Kathleen Hart, *Eating in the Dark: America's Experiment with Genetically Engineered Food* (New York: Pantheon Books, 2002); and Bill Lambrecht, *Dinner at the New Gene Café: How Genetic Engineering Is Changing What We Eat, How We Live, and the Global Politics of Food* (New York: Thomas Dunne Books, 2001).

6. Winston, *Travels in the Genetically Modified Zone.*

7. This headline is an excerpt from comments made by the president to the British news outlet Sky News. Sky News must have considered this story very important because Mwansabombwe, where the ceremony is held, is quite remote, one thousand kilometers from the national capital, Lusaka. "We Would Rather Starve Than Get Genetically Modified Foods, Says President," *Zambian Post*, 30 July 2002.

8. See, for example, Elizabeth Neuffer, "Unpalatable to the Starving: Food for Thought," *Boston Globe*, 1 September 2002; Henri E. Cauvin, "Between Famine and Politics, Zambians Starve," *New York Times*, 30 August 2002.

9. See, for example, "Bring on a Gene Revolution," *Financial Mail* (South Africa), 6 September 2002; Isabel Vincent, "Zambia Refuses Food Despite UN Assurances: Officials Fear Genetically Modified Grain Will Destroy Their Crops," *National Post* (Canada), 27 August 2002.

10. Raymond Firth, *Symbols: Public and Private* (London: Routledge and Kegan Paul, 1973), 244 (emphasis in original).

11. Central Statistics Office of the Republic of Zambia, *Preliminary 1990–2000 Census Data* (Lusaka: Central Statistics Office, 2002). The precise figure for rural populations is 61 percent, up from 60 percent in 1990.

12. I put the qualifier "traditional" in quotes to highlight the relatively rapid integration of nonendemic crops such as cassava and maize into the small group of trusted and reliable staples in Zambia. Cassava likely reached the northern region of Zambia in the early eighteenth century via Portuguese and African traders and slavers. Although maize originally reached Zambia by similar means, what is now widely grown is a hybrid form of the crop called SR-52, one of the first agricultural hybrids developed in southern Africa. Linda C. Jackson and Robert T. Jackson, "The Role of Cassava in African Famine Prevention," in Rebecca Huss-Ashmore and Solomon H. Katz, *African Food Systems in Crisis: Part Two: Contending with Change* (New York: Gordon and Breach Science Publishers, 1990), 207–225. See also Johan Pottier, *Migrants No More: Settlement and Survival in Mambwe Villages, Zambia* (Bloomington: Indiana University Press, 1988), 20–21.

13. The term *nshima* is used generically throughout Zambia to refer to this staple food. *Ubwali* is the specific term used in Luapula and much of northern Zambia, where the language Chibemba is primarily spoken.

14. Audrey I. Richards, *Land, Labour and Diet in Northern Rhodesia: An Economic Study of the Bemba Tribe* (London: Oxford University Press, 1939), 47. Despite the date of Richards's work, this sensibility continues to be voiced in Zambia today.

15. Firth, *Symbols*, 245.

16. Ibid., 248.

17. Audrey I. Richards, "Reciprocal Clan Relationships among the Bemba of N. E. Rhodesia," *Man* 37 (1937): 188–193.

18. "Comment: Ndlovu's Thinking," *Zambian Post*, 9 September 2002.

19. Winston, *Travels in the Genetically Modified Zone.*

20. See, for example, "Better Dead Than GM-Fed? Europe's Green Are Helping to Keep Africans Hungry," *Economist*, 21 September 2002; Rachel Wynberg, "High Risks and Dubious Benefits: The Case against the Introduction of GMOs," *African Wildlife* 5 (2001): 9–11.

21. "Comment: Ndlovu's Thinking," *Zambian Post.*

22. Wynberg, "High Risks and Dubious Benefits."

23. "Comment: Dignity in Hunger," *Zambian Post.*

24. Ibid.

25. "Feeding Hungry Gets More Challenging," *Seattle Post-Intelligencer*, 1 October 2002; Cauvin, "Between Famine and Politics, Zambians Starve."

26. Devon Walsh, "Earth Summit," *Independent*, 30 August 2002; Davan Maharaj and Anthony Mukwita, "Zambia Rejects Gene-Altered U.S. Corn," *Los Angeles Times*, 28 August 2002.

27. "Aid Workers Deny Food Crisis Exaggerated," *United Nations Integrated Regional Information Networks* (IRIN), 20 September 2002.

28. But apparently not the 2003 growing season. This most recent harvest has been a dramatic improvement over the 2001 and 2002 seasons, respectively. See "Kaoma District Expects 21,000 Tonnes of Maize," *Times of Zambia*, 1 August 2003.

29. Robert Dirks, "Famine, Hunger Seasons and Relief-Induced Agonism," in Rebecca Huss-Ashmore and Solomon H. Katz, *African Food Systems in Crisis: Part One: Microperspectives* (New York: Gordon and Breach Science Publishers, 1989), 295–302.

30. "Comment: Ndlovu's Thinking," *Zambian Post*.

Spring 2004, volume 4, number 2

robert pincus |

Wine, Place, and Identity in a Changing Climate

THE LINKS AMONG WINE, place, and identity are both cultural and agricultural. Local tradition often informs the many decisions made during the growing of grapes (viticulture) and the making of wine (viniculture), but wine also reflects the physical environment in which the grapes are grown—a combination of geology, aspect, and weather that the French call *terroir*. Thus wine production techniques are (in principle, at least) adapted to local conditions, resulting in wines that can be strongly connected to their particular place in the world.

Products made on a small, individualized scale are not very practical in the twenty-first century, and commercial pressures are pushing wine production toward more uniformity and less site-specificity. But there is a greater long-term threat to the traditional connection between wine and place. Climate change, the fruit of the Industrial Revolution and continued population growth, is beginning to make decades of winemaking expertise irrelevant. In an increasingly warm world, the particular associations between wine and place will be difficult or impossible to maintain.

This article explores ways in which the changing climate will affect wine production, and how winemakers must adapt in order to continue making wines that reflect their particular region and site. I use simulations of future climate to represent the ways in which weather and climate are likely to change in the coming decades in several wine growing regions; I also describe the reactions of several vintners to the simulations, focusing on the range of responses they are considering.

How Climate Change Breaks the Traditional Links Between Wine and Place

Some wines are so strongly identified with a particular place that they are emblematic, like California Zinfandel or Pinot Noir grown in Burgundy. The link arises because grapes grown in favored sites can express themselves and that place with extraordinary clarity, while the same grapes grown somewhere else may have something else entirely to say, or may be mute. The connection between site and flavor is strongest in Europe, where centuries of experimentation have led to precise ideas about which grape varieties and growing techniques make the most desirable wine in each region. In many locations this knowledge has evolved from tradition into legislation, formalized by authorities called controlled appellation boards. At a minimum, these organizations define the geographic extent of the wine growing area and specify the varieties that may be grown within its borders. The mandates may go further, specifying ripeness levels for harvest or particular viticultural practices. The boards essentially define the regional wine, then tell growers and vintners how to produce bottles as close to this ideal as possible.

Appellation regulations are intended to make it easier to fashion wine that suits the physical characteristics of the region, most importantly the local climate and geology. Soil and landscape are virtually immutable on a human time scale (absent some catastrophic event), and the typical year-to-year changes of weather patterns are part of vintners' collective experience. But the rate of climate change is now faster than it has ever been, and the changes are only expected to become more dramatic. If the local weather changes significantly, the grape varieties and viticultural techniques that have been so carefully refined over time will begin to fail, because weather exerts such a strong influence on the taste of wine.

Though decisions in the winery and cellar have some influence, much of a wine's flavor is determined by the way the grapes taste at harvest. Flavor is determined in part by the geology of the site and by the grape variety, then shaped by the trajectory of ripening, the distribution of sunlight, and the amount of heat and rainfall to which the fruit is exposed over the course of the growing season.[1] Ripening begins with *veraison*, typically forty to sixty days after the fruit sets, when grapes begin to soften, sweeten, and take on color. Over time, sugars accumulate in each berry, the tannins in the seeds and skins mature, acidity levels drop, and secondary flavors develop. Growers ideally harvest when the grapes have reached the peak of physiological ripeness, when sugars and acids are balanced and the other flavoring elements are mature. Ripening is driven by ongoing photosynthesis, which requires warm weather and sunshine. By and large, sugar levels increase as warmth and light accumulate, while the tannins and other flavors require many weeks on the vine to develop.

The requirements for ripeness depend on the variety, and different growers may try to obtain different qualities in their grapes. As a general rule, white wine varieties ripen earlier than do grapes used to make red wine, which is why warm viticultural regions like central California and southern Australia are known for rich, alcoholic red wines, and cool climates like Champagne are associated with white wines. Vines also "remember" the weather from one year to the next, since the shoots on which berries form begin to grow the year before the flowers bloom. If the fall weather is poor or if an early frost arrives before the shoots mature, the next season's growth will begin in a weaker state. Grape development depends not on what happens on any particular day, but rather on the accumulation of weather over the course of the growing season, such as overall amounts of precipitation and sunshine.

Weather, Climate, and Climate Change

To say that a particular variety ripens well in a given location means that in most years the berries eventually mature enough to have good flavor but don't get so much sun and warmth that their sugar levels become excessive or their acidity falls too much. In any given year, though, the ripeness on a specific day is almost entirely unpredictable. This dichotomy illustrates the difference between weather and climate: climate is weather in all of its variety. Climate includes the likelihood of extreme events like hailstorms or cold snaps, the likely distribution of temperatures, and the complete range of possibilities for every element of the atmosphere that might matter. Weather predictions are accurate in their specifics for a week or ten days at most. Climate prediction, on the other hand, is an exercise in probability rather than certainty. The long-term forecast (measured in decades) is at once vague and robust: the world will almost surely be warmer than today, though it is hard to say by how much, when, and where.

Predictions of overall warming can be made with confidence because the fundamental principles causing the change are very well understood. Temperature is a manifestation of energy, and human-induced changes to the atmosphere are affecting the way the earth exchanges energy with the rest of the universe. This transfer of energy is accomplished by light, also called radiant energy or radiation. The planet is bathed in sunlight, some of which is reflected back to space by bright clouds and ice, but most of which is absorbed by the oceans, land, and atmosphere. Energy moves around the earth by warming the land, evaporating water from the ocean, or making the wind blow. Eventually, the energy is transformed into infrared radiation. This invisible light is emitted back toward space, exactly balancing the absorbed sunshine.

The atmosphere is transparent to sunlight but doesn't easily allow infrared radiation to pass through. By slowing the energy's escape, the atmosphere makes the planet warmer. This has been happening since the earth was formed, and it is, in part, the reason that life is possible here: without the atmosphere's warming effect, the planet would be an icy ball with a temperature near -20°C (0°F).

Only some of the gases that make up the atmosphere absorb infrared radiation; two of the most common are carbon dioxide and water vapor. If the amount of these absorbing ("greenhouse") gases increases, the atmosphere will become more opaque to infrared radiation, and the planet's temperature will tend to rise. And of course many human activities, but most of all the burning of fossil fuels, increase the amount of carbon dioxide and other greenhouse gases in the atmosphere.

Our actions are changing the composition of the atmosphere in a way that makes the atmosphere trap more energy and pushes the planet toward a warmer state. This much is undeniable. But the internal workings of the climate are so enormously tangled that exact predictions of future climate are uncertain. Climate and weather are influenced by nearly every physical, chemical, and biological system on the planet, and each of these systems varies from place to place. The amount of rainfall in a given location helps determine the kind of vegetation that thrives there, for example, which in turn influences how much sunlight is absorbed. The interactions that are already known are enormously complicated, and it's certain that others exist that haven't yet been identified.

Like weather prediction, climate simulations are made with huge computer programs that divide the world into boxes, then keep track of the energy (temperature), water, and momentum (air motion) in each box. This view of the world is blurry, however, since the current limitations of computer power mean that the individual boxes into which the world is divided are fairly large (tens of kilometers across for weather prediction programs, and hundreds for climate models). It's also crude, because the complicated processes and interactions have to be cartoonishly simplified. Weather services make predictions every day for the coming week or two, a span of time during which many things vary little, if at all (what plants are growing where, how warm the ocean is); climate predictions, in contrast, need to account for changes in almost every one of the earth's many components. This complexity means that while predictions about global changes are probably broadly accurate, the predictions that matter to individuals—those that describe the changes in specific locations at specific times in the future—are at best a rough guide.

Adapting to Change

Viticulture is in some ways more vulnerable to climate change than other aspects of agriculture, because decisions can take years to play out. Should a winegrower decide to replant a vineyard with a more heat-loving variety, for example, the vines will take three or four years to bear fruit, and at least a decade or more to produce the highest quality grapes. This delay between action and result puts pressure on winegrowers, who must understand the ways in which climate may change in years ahead so that they can think about adaptive strategies.

Some winemakers believe that the climate has already changed in the last few decades, and statistics do show a trend toward earlier flowering and harvesting. (In fact, because grapes have been cultivated for so long and so much attention has been paid to them, viticultural records have been used inversely to help reconstruct the climate over the last few hundred years.[2]) Some contend that warming may have contributed to better wine,[3] though this is hard to disentangle from the evolution of vinicultural techniques. The climate of the last decade has almost certainly had an effect on style, making richer, lusher (or at least more alcoholic) wines possible nearly everywhere in the world.

What might wines be like in twenty-five years if the climate continues to warm? At that time, many of the people currently running wineries will still be working. These men and women, with their firsthand experience of the traditional wine styles of their regions, will preside over the transition from the older styles that have held sway for tens or hundreds of years to the wines of the twenty-first century.

With this thought in mind, I used simulations[4] from a global climate model[5] to get rough estimates of how climate may change in several wine producing areas by the year 2025 and then asked winegrowers from each region what changes they might expect in vini- and viticultural practices and in the wines they produced. I assessed climate changes by comparing two twenty-year time periods (1980–1999 and 2015–2034). For each year I computed the meteorological quantities most closely tied to wine quality[6]: total rainfall, surface sunshine, frost dates, and warmth as measured in degree-days[7] for each season based on daily values at the model grid point closest to the region. This approach gives a sense of how year-to-year variations may themselves change in the future, as well as of how the average climate might change. Two global predictions are relevant to winemakers: the day-to-night temperature difference is predicted to decrease slightly with time; and there is likely to be a somewhat higher risk of thunderstorms, with the attendant risk of damaging hail.

In these discussions, the growing season is inexactly considered to be the spring, summer, and fall of every year. Each season of the year lasts three months; spring begins on March 1. As a general rule, the average changes between the climate projected for 2025 and the current climate are no larger than the range of current year-to-year variations.

The following accounts are only the beginning of the story. The geography of wine regions is intensely interesting to both vintners and aficionados because the exact location, slope, and exposure of a particular parcel can dramatically affect the way grapes grow and ripen. Given the coarse resolution of the climate simulations (about 280 km, or 175 miles), the available predictions are only a rough guide to the changes that may actually occur. Furthermore, neighboring winegrowers can hold diametrically opposing views on how to grow their grapes, not to mention how to adapt to climate change.

France's Alsace

The vineyards of Alsace nestle up against the eastern slope of the Vosges Mountains, running parallel to the Rhine River in the northeast corner of France.[8] The mountains create a rain shadow, and the resulting sunny days and mild temperatures allow grapes to ripen at this extreme latitude (of the French wine producing regions, only Champagne is slightly farther north). The current climate is just warm enough for wine to be produced in most years, and chapitalization (the addition of extra sugar to increase alcohol levels) is not uncommon. The varieties permitted in the *appellation contrôlée* are those that favor cool weather, many of which are grown across the river in Germany but not elsewhere in France—Riesling, Gewürztraminer, Muscat, and a little Pinot Noir, the only permissible red variety.

The climate projections for Alsace are as follows:

- Rain and snowfall may decrease slightly, though they will be more uniform from year to year. Springtime will tend to be drier. Summers will vary more dramatically from year to year than they do today, and falls will generally be more consistent.

- Sunshine over the growing season will increase by about 1.5 percent, with most of this change occurring in the summer months. The variations from year to year will be larger, and some years will be much sunnier than they currently are. Fall sunshine will be more variable but spring sunshine more consistent.

- Frosts in late spring may become more common, with the last frost occurring one to three weeks later than it now does. The first frost of fall, however, will be delayed by about a month.

- There will be about three hundred more degree-days during the growing season than there are today. This is a very small percentage increase, corresponding to an average daily temperature change of about 1.1°C. Most of the change will occur in summer and fall.

Jean Hugel of Hugel & Fils in Riquewihr has worked fifty-five vintages and remembers seventy-seven. He takes the long view. "Normally we have blossoming around the 10th of June, in early years at the end of May. In 1307 the blossoms emerged at the end of April, and the crop came in at the end of July," he says, quoting historical records.[9] Then again, the vines froze on May 22, 1146.[10] Vintners have always contended with the vagaries of weather and climate, and in Hugel's view the current climatic changes are not extraordinary. "If grapes ripened early in more years, I'd be delighted, but not convinced."

Alsatian wines are remarkable for their delicacy, floral aromas, and relatively low alcohol levels. Hugel feels that even in the presence of overall warming these traits can be maintained by making careful changes in vineyard and cellar practices. He foresees earlier harvests to limit sugar concentrations and, to a limited extent, changes in crop levels. "We pick Pinot Gris at 13.5 degrees potential alcohol," he asserts. "At 14.5 degrees it won't finish fermentation." He does worry a little about the impact of earlier harvests: "In my experience, a longer ripening period leads to better microchemistry and a better nose." He can imagine, perhaps, greater planting of relatively late-harvested varieties, like Riesling, at the expense of more reliable but less unusual selections like Pinot Blanc or Pinot Gris. But, he adds, "I am opposed to the planting of more Pinot Noir. We are a white wine region."

Germany's Mosel

It's hard to believe that anyone would seriously try to cultivate anything along the banks of the Mosel. The river's course through western Germany is so tortuous that one might start facing east, walk following the flow for a kilometer or two, and wind up facing west. The banks are vertiginous slopes of loose sheets of rock, climbing several hundred meters to wooded hilltops at angles of forty-five degrees or more, terrain so convoluted that it gives rise to entire taxonomies of microclimates. But in the warm oxbows, where the slopes face the low sun and the light and warmth are reflected from the river onto the dark slate, some of the finest Riesling in the world is grown. Grapes in the Mosel typically spend long, mild falls on the vine before harvest and so retain enough acidity to balance the apple and citrus fruit flavors and to age magnificently. In exceptional years, some growers may also take the risk of leaving grapes hanging in the vineyards to develop the fungus *Botrytis cineria*, the "noble rot" that dehydrates the grape, concentrating the juice inside the berries and adding a haunting flavor of honey. *Botrytis*-affected grapes become the sweet *Beerenauslese* and rare *Trockenbeerenauslese* wines. A few vintners make the further gamble of leaving fruit on the vines until December or later, when the hard frosts arrive and the water in the berries begins to freeze, concentrating the sugars within the grape. The fruit (sometimes picked at night) is pressed frozen to become intensely sweet *Eiswein* (ice wine).

The climate changes projected for the Mosel are:

• Precipitation will decrease by about 5 percent on average. Drier falls will become more common, although the wettest winters will be much wetter than today's.

- Sunshine over the growing season will increase by about 1.5 percent, though this will be more variable from year to year than it is now. Summers, in particular, are likely to be sunnier than today. Extremely sunny or cloudy years will become somewhat more frequent, though still rare.

- There will be about three hundred more degree-days during the growing season. Spring and summer will be uniformly warmer, and fall somewhat warmer but more variable than today.

- Frosts of –7°c (hard enough to make *Eiswein*) will arrive about a week later than they do now, and they will arrive in about 25 percent fewer years.

To Johannes Selbach of Selbach-Oster and J.H. Selbach in Zeltingen these predictions sound as much like history as a possible future. "It was the rule that in a decade you would have a couple of bad vintages [when grapes didn't ripen sufficiently] and a couple of great ones. Since 1988 every year has been good to outstanding," he explains.[11] Warmer weather in the past has been a boon for the Mosel, which is "on the brink of viticulture," and further warming in coming decades will allow Selbach to produce richer, riper wines. German law mandates ripeness levels for various designations of wine; warmer weather would allow Selbach to "put more meat on the bones of every category," as he has begun to do in recent years.

The greatest threat from the changing climate has nothing to do with grapes. "If the Mosel floods," Selbach points out, "we sit in the water." The valley is so narrow that villages lie right next to the river, and the mountains come down steeply to the shore. Like many of his colleagues', Selbach's cellar is in the basement of his home. "If all your money sits under water, it's a bad feeling." Flooding has become more frequent in recent years, a trend that is likely to continue as the winters become wetter. Selbach and others of his generation think it inevitable that they'll have to move from their homes, some of which are hundreds of years old, to higher ground.

Selbach also worries that there will be a vinicultural downside to climate warming in the Mosel. "Hot summers and early ripening would be detrimental to the cause of Mosel Riesling," he asserts, since grapes will lose the acidity that sets Mosel wines apart and lets them age so well. The climate projections don't indicate much danger of this in the next few decades, but they don't bode well for *Eiswein*. Even in the current climate, leaving perfectly good grapes on the vine in the hope of a hard frost is a big risk, because if the freeze does not arrive by January, the grapes will have been damaged by wind, sleet, and hail, and may be wasted. If the frequency of hard frosts in early winter diminishes, growers may become much more reluctant to make the wager. "Not to be able to make *Eiswein*, and not to be able to drink it, would be a real loss," says Selbach. "It's an exciting wine. I'll still try to make it, but I'll make a smaller gamble."

Austria's Kamptal

To read an Austrian wine label is to get a crash course in a whole new vocabulary of varieties grown nowhere else in the world—Blaufränkisch, Zweigelt, Sankt-Laurent. Wine is produced throughout eastern Austria, near the borders with Slovenia, Hungary, Slovakia, and the Czech Republic. Some of the loveliest Austrian wine is produced in the regions along the Danube—the Wachau, Kamptal, and Kremstal. In Austria, which is substantially farther south than Alsace or Germany, it is much easier to ripen grapes fully, so the wines tend to be richer and fuller than their northern counterparts. Austria's vinous heart is Grüner Veltliner, a white variety with structure, mineral content, and complexity, which pairs almost flawlessly with food, especially legumes and vegetables. Grüner Veltliner is a picky grape, requiring fastidious geology and just the right combination of warm days to mature and cool nights to stay fresh, and it thrives in Austria as in no other place on earth.

The climate projections for Austria are that

- Rain and snowfall may increase by about 10 percent on average, with most of this precipitation occurring in spring. Summer rainfall may tend to cluster, so that a given summer will be either rainy or dry, but not enormously different from today's summers in regard to precipitation.

- Sunshine over the growing season will increase by about 2 percent, though this will vary from year to year. Summers, in particular, are likely to be sunnier than they are today. Extremely sunny or cloudy years will become somewhat more frequent, though they will still be rare.

- Growing season degree-days will increase by about two hundred and fifty (i.e., the average daily temperature will increase by about 1°C). Fall, in particular, will be warmer, as will summer, though to a lesser extent. Summers will also be more variable: years are more likely to be either cool (and cloudy) or hot (and sunny) but not as moderate as today.

Like Johannes Selbach, Willi Bründlmayer of Weingut Bründlmayer in Langenlois is not surprised by the predictions. "We appreciate by now that a climatic change has already taken place. Our wines are getting more body and less acidity [and growers are] beginning to plant red wines."[12] But because grapes in the Kamptal already receive enough sun and warmth to ripen, Bründlmayer is concerned that more insolation and higher temperatures will push some of the vines too far. "We will drop out of optimum position for Grüner Veltliner," he says bluntly. And although Chardonnay is a more adaptable variety than Grüner Veltliner and is already grown with great success in Austria, Bründlmayer wants to keep producing something more distinctive. "The advantage of Zweigelt or Sankt-Laurent is that they're something new in the world," he explains. These are, in other words, the varieties that distinguish Austrian wine from all others, and Bründlmayer is devoted to the special qualities of what he grows. "If this forecast were 99 percent sure," he says, "I would pursue with vigor new sites for planting Grüner Veltliner. I would find new vineyards for the new situation." But the decision is not his alone to make. European Union regulations don't permit a net increase in any country's vineyard area, so new, exploratory plantings would have to come at the expense of existing sites. Adjustments at this scale would involve the whole Kamptal, or perhaps all of Austria.

For Bründlmayer, climate change "puts the complete system of *appellation contrôlée* into question." Ten years ago, in an action steeped in tradition, he helped found a small group[13] devoted to finding the best matches among soil, rootstock, and varieties in the Kamptal and neighboring Kremstal appellations. More recently, though, he has begun to believe that "if the future climate [proves] to be fluctuating and uncertain, a long-term fixed relation of vineyard site, rootstock, and variety may not be sensible, [and] a more dynamic approach might be reasonable." The group had already begun discussing these ideas when Europe was unexpectedly drenched by torrential rains in the summer of 2002, which caused one-hundred-year floods along the Danube and inundated several winery cellars in the Kamptal and nearby Wachau. They were forced to turn in a moment from patient investigation to the very short-term, pragmatic question of how to help the growers devastated by the waters. Although the summer's dramatic weather can't definitively be attributed to human activities or climate change, extreme events (like droughts and floods) that were previously rare have become more frequent almost everywhere on the planet.

Wine and Identity in a Changing World

One could say that we experience weather, as we feel the heat of the day or find that the winter has been especially wet. But we do not experience climate, which occurs on a time scale longer than we can really perceive. Yet climate inexorably affects the way that we live. It's almost certain that the climate will change over the next several decades, and wine producers, like everyone else, will have to adapt. Some will try to use their skill and experience to continue making wines in the traditional style of their region. In colder regions, where ripe grapes and great vintages have historically been rare, their jobs may become a little less stressful. Some adaptations will involve choices made by individuals, such as changes in vineyard management or the replacement of one grape variety with another; others will require more far-reaching changes, including cooperation with governing bodies and appellation boards. But where the culture of wine production is tightly coupled to the current climate, something will have to give.

What are certain to change as a result of adaptation are the links between particular wines and their traditional home. Ice wine, though rare even in Germany, is one of the purest expressions of that chilly climate, a vinicultural turning of lemons into lemonade. Grüner Veltliner is Austria's beloved treasure. Yet both of these wines will likely be much more difficult to produce in the coming decades than they currently are. Even where the impact of climatic change is less dramatic, decades, even centuries, of vinicultural experience will be rendered irrelevant. ⊕

NOTES

I appreciate helpful conversations with wine producers Willi Bründlmayer (Weingut Bründlmayer, Langenlois, Austria); Randall Grahm (Bonny Doon, Santa Cruz, US); Jean Hugel (Hugel & Fils, Riquewihr, France); Michael Moosbugger (Schloss Gobelsburg, Langenlois, Austria); Johannes Selbach (Selbach-Oster, Zeltingen, Germany).

1. See, for example, D. Jackson and D. Schuster, *The Production of Grapes and Wine in Cool Climates* (Aotearoa, New Zealand: Lincoln University Press, 1997).

2. See, for example, C. Pfister, "Monthly Temperature and Precipitation in Central Europe 1525–1979: Quantifying Documentary Evidence on Weather and Its Effects," in *Climate since A.D. 1500*, edited by Raymond S. Bradley and Philip D. Jones (New York: Routledge, 1992), 118–142.

3. R.R. Nemani, M.A. White, D.R. Cayan, G.V. Jones, S.W. Running, and J.C. Coughlan, "Asymmetric climatic warming over coastal California and its impact on the premium wine industry," *Climate Res.* 19 (2001): 25–34.

4. The simulations were made by the National Center for Atmospheric Research (NCAR) as a contribution to the Intergovernmental Panel on Climate Change's Third Assessment. In this study I've used the calculations for Scenario A, "Business as usual," in which greenhouse gases increase with time. The atmosphere, ocean, and land surface all interact with one another. The scenarios are described in *Climate Change 2001: The Scientific Basis* (Cambridge: Cambridge University Press, 2001).

5. The NCAR climate model is described in M. Blackmon and twenty-five coauthors, "The Community Climate System Model," *Bull. Amer. Meteor. Soc.* 82 (2001): 2357–2376.

6. A more complete treatment of this idea applied to a single region can be found in G.V. Jones and R.E. Davis, "Using a Synoptic Climatological Approach to Understand Climate-Viticulture Relationships," *Int. J. Climatol.* 20 (2000): 813–837.

7. Because vines begin to grow at temperatures above about 10°C, each day warmer than this base temperature contributes the temperature excess to the total degree-days (i.e., five days of 15°C temperatures contribute twenty-five degree-days to the total).

8. A useful source on the geography of viticultural regions worldwide is *Oz Clarke's Wine Atlas* (London: Websters International Publishers, 1995).

9. Telephone interviews with Jean Hugel on 21 November and 27 November 2001.

10. M. Boesch, *800 ans de viticulture en Haute-Alsace* (Guebiller: Privately published, printed at L'imprimerie Art'real, 1983).

11. Telephone interview with Johannes Selbach on 22 November 2001 and ongoing correspondence.

12. Telephone interview with Willi Bründlmayer on 26 November 2001 and ongoing correspondence.

13. The group Traditionsweingüter maintains a Web site (in German) at www.traditionsweingueter.at.

Spring 2003, volume 3, number 2

eric ormsby |

Episode with a Potato

I was skinning a potato when it said:
Please do not gouge my one remaining eye!
My parer hesitated. The knob of the spud
comforted my hand-hold with its sly
ovoid, firm yet brittle as a fontanelle,
and I much enjoyed the way its cool lump
—all pulpy planes and facettings, with a starch
sheen that mildly slimed my fingers
(not to mention that tuberous smell
that lingers
like the shoulder of a clump
of creosote bushes or the violet mildew of an arch
no triumph still remembers)
—yes, I liked the way it occupied my pinch.

I understood at its tiny squeak
the power of pashas over the members
of their entourages. For a week,
whenever I passed, the potato would flinch.
Its one eye never slept.
I thought of the kingdoms it had crept
through under the ground, spud-
smug, amid the dust of the bones of shahs
and eunuchs, those generations of the Flood,
the Colossi and the Accursed,
the Great Hunger and the hegiras,
telemons and ostraca and worst,
immense anti-archives of dirt.

It hurt
me to do it but I scooped out its eye
and ate it and felt utterly triumphant: I
ingested all that a potato could personify.

Summer 2002, volume 2, number 3

technologies

A Plea for Culinary Modernism: Why We Should Love New,
Fast, Processed Food | *Rachel Laudan* **280**

The Patented Peanut Butter and Jelly Sandwich:
Food as Intellectual Property | *Anna M. Shih* **293**

The Clockwork Roasting Jack, or How Technology Entered the Kitchen | *Jeanne Schinto* **302**

Grinding Away the Rust: The Legacy of Iceland's Herring Oil
and Meal Factories | *Chris Bogan* **314**

rachel laudan |

A Plea for Culinary Modernism

Why We Should Love New, Fast, Processed Food

MODERN, FAST, PROCESSED FOOD is a disaster. That, at least, is the message conveyed by newspapers and magazines, on television cooking programs, and in prizewinning cookbooks. It is a mark of sophistication to bemoan the steel roller mill and supermarket bread while yearning for stone-ground flour and brick ovens; to seek out heirloom apples and pumpkins while despising modern tomatoes and hybrid corn; to be hostile to agronomists who develop high-yielding modern crops and to home economists who invent new recipes for General Mills. We hover between ridicule and shame when we remember how our mothers and grandmothers enthusiastically embraced canned and frozen foods. We nod in agreement when the waiter proclaims that the restaurant showcases the freshest local produce. We shun Wonder Bread and Coca-Cola. Above all, we loathe the great culminating symbol of Culinary Modernism, McDonald's—modern, fast, homogenous, and international.

Like so many of my generation, my culinary style was created by those who scorned industrialized food; Culinary Luddites, we may call them, after the English hand workers of the nineteenth century who abhorred the machines that were destroying their traditional way of life. I learned to cook from the books of Elizabeth David, who urged us to sweep our store cupboards "clean for ever of the cluttering debris of commercial sauce bottles and all synthetic flavorings." I progressed to the Time-Life *Good Cook* series and to *Simple French Food*, in which Richard Olney hoped against hope that "the reins of stubborn habit are strong enough to frustrate the famous industrial revolution for some time to come."[1] I turned to Paula Wolfert to learn more about Mediterranean cooking and was assured that I wouldn't "find a dishonest dish in this book....The food here is real food...the real food of real people." Today I rush to the newsstand to pick up *Saveur* with its promise to teach me to "Savor a world of authentic cuisine."

Culinary Luddism involves more than just taste. Since the days of the counterculture, it has also presented itself as a moral and political crusade. Now in Boston, the Oldways Preservation and Exchange Trust works to provide "a scientific basis for the preservation and revitalization of traditional diets."[2] Meanwhile, Slow Food, founded in 1989 to protest the opening of a McDonald's in Rome, is a self-described Greenpeace for Food; its manifesto begins, "We are enslaved by speed and have all succumbed to the same insidious virus: Fast Life, which disrupts our habits, pervades the privacy of our homes and forces us to eat Fast Foods....Slow Food is now the only truly progressive answer."[3] As one of its spokesmen was reported as saying in the *New York Times*, "Our real enemy is the obtuse consumer."[4]

At this point I begin to back off. I want to cry, "Enough!" But why? Why would I, who learned to cook from Culinary Luddites, who grew up in a family that, in Elizabeth David's words, produced their "own home-cured bacon, ham and sausages…churned their own butter, fed their chickens and geese, cherished their fruit trees, skinned and cleaned their own hares" (well, to be honest, not the geese and sausages), not rejoice at the growth of Culinary Luddism?[5] Why would I (or anyone else) want to be thought "an obtuse consumer"? Or admit to preferring unreal food for unreal people? Or to savoring inauthentic cuisine?

The answer is not far to seek: because I am a historian. As a historian I cannot accept the account of the past implied by Culinary Luddism, a past sharply divided between good and bad, between the sunny rural days of yore and the grey industrial present. My enthusiasm for the Luddites' kitchen wisdom does not carry over to their history, any more than my response to a stirring political speech inclines me to accept the orator as scholar. The Luddites' fable of disaster, of a fall from grace, smacks more of wishful thinking than of digging through archives. It gains credence not from scholarship but from evocative dichotomies: fresh and natural versus processed and preserved; local versus global; slow versus fast; artisanal and traditional versus urban and industrial; healthful versus contaminated and fatty. History shows, I believe, that the Luddites have things back to front.

That food should be fresh and natural has become an article of faith. It comes as something of a shock to realize that this is a latter-day creed. For our ancestors, natural was something quite nasty. Natural often tasted bad. Fresh meat was rank and tough, fresh milk warm and unmistakably a bodily excretion; fresh fruits (dates and grapes being rare exceptions outside the tropics) were inedibly sour, fresh vegetables bitter. Even today, natural can be a shock when we actually encounter it. When Jacques Pepin offered free-range chickens to friends, they found "the flesh tough and the flavor too strong," prompting him to wonder whether they would really like things the way they naturally used to be.[6]

Natural was unreliable. Fresh fish began to stink, fresh milk soured, eggs went rotten. Everywhere seasons of plenty were followed by seasons of hunger when the days were short, the weather turned cold, or the rain did not fall. Hens stopped laying eggs, cows went dry, fruits and vegetables were not to be found, fish could not be caught in the stormy seas. Natural was usually indigestible. Grains, which supplied from fifty to ninety percent of the calories in most societies, have to be threshed, ground, and cooked to make them edible. Other plants, including the roots and tubers that were the life support of the societies that did not eat grains, are often downright poisonous. Without careful processing, green potatoes, stinging taro, and cassava bitter with prussic acid are not just indigestible, but toxic.

Nor did our ancestors' physiological theories dispose them to the natural. Until about two hundred years ago, from China to Europe, and in Mesoamerica, too, everyone believed that the fires in the belly cooked foodstuffs and turned them into nutrients.[7] That was what digesting was. Cooking foods in effect pre-digested them and made them easier to assimilate. Given a choice, no one would burden the stomach with raw, unprocessed foods.

So to make food tasty, safe, digestible and healthy, our forebears bred, ground, soaked, leached, curdled, fermented, and cooked naturally occurring plants and animals until they were literally beaten into submission. To lower toxin levels, they cooked plants, treated them with clay (the Kaopectate effect), and leached them with water, acid fruits and vinegars, and alkaline lye.[8] They intensively bred maize to the point that it could not reproduce without human help. They created sweet oranges and juicy apples and non-bitter legumes, happily abandoning their more natural but less tasty ancestors. They built granaries for their grain, dried their meat and their fruit, salted and smoked their fish, curdled and fermented their dairy products, and cheerfully used whatever additives and preservatives they could—sugar, salt, oil, vinegar, lye—to make edible foodstuffs. In the twelfth century, the Chinese sage Wu Tzu-mu listed the six foodstuffs essential to life: rice, salt, vinegar, soy sauce, oil, and tea.[9] Four had been unrecognizably transformed from their naturally occurring state. Who could have imagined vinegar as rice that had been fermented to ale and then soured? Or soy sauce as cooked and fermented beans? Or oil as the extract of crushed cabbage seeds? Or bricks of tea as leaves that had been killed by heat, powdered, and compressed? Only salt and rice had any claim to fresh or natural, and even then the latter had been stored for months or years, threshed, and husked.

Processed and preserved foods kept well, were easier to digest, and were delicious: raised white bread instead of chewy wheat porridge; thick, nutritious, heady beer instead of prickly grains of barley; unctuous olive oil instead of a tiny, bitter fruit; soy milk, sauce, and tofu instead of dreary, flatulent soy beans; flexible, fragrant tortillas instead of dry, tough maize; not to mention red wine, blue cheese, sauerkraut, hundred-year-old eggs, Smithfield hams, smoked salmon, yogurt, sugar, chocolate, and fish sauce.

Eating fresh, natural food was regarded with suspicion verging on horror, something to which only the uncivilized, the poor, and the starving resorted.[10] When the compiler of the Confucian classic *Book of Rites* (ca. 200 B.C.) distinguished the first humans—people who had no alternative to wild, uncooked foods—from civilized peoples who took "advantage of the benefits of fire…[who] toasted, grilled, boiled, and roasted," he was only repeating a commonplace.[11] When the ancient Greeks took it as a sign of bad times if people were driven to eat greens and root vegetables, they too were rehearsing common wisdom.[12] Happiness was not a verdant Garden of Eden abounding in fresh fruits, but a securely locked storehouse jammed with preserved, processed foods.

Local food was greeted with about as much enthusiasm as fresh and natural. Local foods were the lot of the poor who could neither escape the tyranny of local climate and biology nor the monotonous, often precarious, diet it afforded. Meanwhile, the rich, in search of a more varied diet, bought, stole, wheedled, robbed, taxed, and ran off with appealing plants and animals, foodstuffs, and culinary techniques from wherever they could find them.

By the fifth century B.C., Celtic princes in the region of France now known as Burgundy were enjoying a glass or two of Greek wine, drunk from silver copies of Greek drinking vessels.[13] The Greeks themselves looked to the Persians, acclimatizing their peaches and apricots and citrons and emulating their rich sauces, while the Romans in turn hired Greek cooks. From around the time of the birth of Christ, the wealthy in China, India, and the Roman Empire paid vast sums for spices brought from the distant and mysterious

Spice Islands. From the seventh century A.D., Islamic caliphs and sultans transplanted sugar, rice, citrus, and a host of other Indian and Southeast Asian plants to Persia and the Mediterranean, transforming the diets of West Asia and the shores of the Mediterranean. In the thirteenth century, the Japanese had naturalized the tea plant of China and were importing sugar from Southeast Asia. In the seventeenth century, the European rich drank sweetened coffee, tea, and cocoa in Chinese porcelain, imported or imitation, proffered by servants in Turkish or other foreign dress. To ensure their own supply, the French, Dutch, and English embarked on imperial ventures and moved millions of Africans and Asians around the globe. The Swedes, who had no empire, had a hard time getting these exotic foodstuffs, so the eighteenth-century botanist Linnaeus set afoot plans to naturalize the tea plant in Sweden.

We may laugh at the climatic hopelessness of his proposal. Yet it was no more ridiculous than other, more successful, proposals to naturalize Southeast Asian sugarcane throughout the tropics, apples in Australia, grapes in Chile, Hereford cattle in Colorado and Argentina, and Caucasian wheat on the Canadian prairie.[14] Without our aggressively global ancestors, we would all still be subject to the tyranny of the local.

As for slow food, it is easy to wax nostalgic about a time when families and friends met to relax over delicious food, and to forget that, far from being an invention of the late twentieth century, fast food has been a mainstay of every society. Hunters tracking their prey, fishermen at sea, shepherds tending their flocks, soldiers on campaign, and farmers rushing to get in the harvest all needed food that could be eaten quickly and away from home. The Greeks roasted barley and ground it into a meal to eat straight or mixed with water, milk, or butter (as the Tibetans still do), while the Aztecs ground roasted maize and mixed it with water to make an instant beverage (as the Mexicans still do).[15]

City dwellers, above all, relied on fast food. When fuel cost as much as the food itself, when huddled dwellings lacked cooking facilities, and when cooking fires might easily conflagrate entire neighborhoods, it made sense to purchase your bread or noodles, and a little meat or fish to liven them up. Before the birth of Christ, Romans were picking up honey cakes and sausages in the Forum.[16] In twelfth-century Hangchow, the Chinese downed noodles, stuffed buns, bowls of soup, and deep-fried confections. In Baghdad of the same period, the townspeople bought ready-cooked meats, salt fish, bread, and a broth of dried chick peas. In the sixteenth century, when the Spanish arrived in Mexico, Mexicans had been enjoying tacos from the market for generations. In the eighteenth century, the French purchased cocoa, apple turnovers, and wine in the boulevards of Paris, while the Japanese savored tea, noodles, and stewed fish.

Deep-fried foods, expensive and dangerous to prepare at home, have always had their place on the street: doughnuts in Europe, *churros* in Mexico, *andagi* in Okinawa, and *sev* in India. Bread, also expensive to bake at home, is one of the oldest convenience foods. For many people in West Asia and Europe, a loaf fresh from the baker was the only warm food of the day. To these venerable traditions of fast food, Americans have simply added the electric deep fryer, the heavy iron griddle of the Low Countries, and the franchise.[17]

The McDonald's in Rome was, in fact, just one more in a long tradition of fast food joints reaching back to the days of the Caesars.

What about the idea that the best food was country food, handmade by artisans?[18] That food came from the country goes without saying. The presumed corollary—that country people ate better than city dwellers—does not. Few who worked the land were independent peasants baking their own bread, brewing their own wine or beer, and salting down their own pig. Most were burdened with heavy taxes and rents paid in kind (that is, food); or worse, they were indentured, serfs, or slaves. Barely part of the cash economy, they subsisted on what was left over. "The city dwellers," remarked the great Roman doctor Galen in the second century A.D., "collected and stored enough grain for all the coming year immediately after the harvest. They carried off all the wheat, the barley, the beans and the lentils and left what remained to the countryfolk."[19]

What remained was pitiful. All too often, those who worked the land got by on thin gruels and gritty flatbreads. North of the Alps, French peasants prayed that chestnuts would be sufficient to sustain them from the time when their grain ran out to the harvest still three months away.[20] South of the Alps, Italian peasants suffered skin eruptions, went mad, and in the worst cases died of pellagra brought on by a diet of maize polenta and water. The dishes we call ethnic and assume to be of peasant origin were invented for the urban, or at least urbane, aristocrats who collected the surplus. This is as true of the lasagne of northern Italy as it is of the chicken *korma* of Mughal Delhi, the moo shu pork of imperial China, the pilafs, stuffed vegetables, and baklava of the great Ottoman palace in Istanbul, and the *mee krob* of nineteenth-century Bangkok.[21] Cities have always enjoyed the best food and have invariably been the focal points of culinary innovation.

Nor are most "traditional foods" very old. For every prized dish that goes back two thousand years, a dozen have been invented in the last two hundred.[22] The French baguette? A twentieth-century phenomenon, adopted nationwide only after World War II. English fish and chips? Dates from the late nineteenth century, when the working class took up the fried fish of Sephardic Jewish immigrants in East London. Fish and chips, though, will soon be a thing of the past. It's a Balti and lager now, Balti being a kind of stir-fried curry dreamed up by Pakistanis living in Birmingham. Greek moussaka? Created in the early twentieth century in an attempt to Frenchify Greek food. The bubbling Russian samovar? Late eighteenth century. The Indonesian *rijsttafel?* Dutch colonial food. Indonesian *padang* food? Invented for the tourist market in the past fifty years. Tequila? Promoted as the national drink of Mexico during the 1930s by the Mexican film industry. Indian tandoori chicken? The brainchild of Hindu Punjabis who survived by selling chicken cooked in a Muslim-style tandoor oven when they fled Pakistan for Delhi during the Partition of India. The soy sauce, steamed white rice, sushi, and tempura of Japan? Commonly eaten only after the middle of the nineteenth century. The *lomilomi* salmon, salted salmon rubbed with chopped tomatoes and spring onions that is a fixture in every Hawaiian luau? Not a salmon is to be found within two thousand miles of the islands, and onions and tomatoes were unknown in Hawaii until the nineteenth century.

These are indisputable facts of history, though if you point them out you will be met with stares of disbelief.

Not only were many "traditional" foods created after industrialization and urbanization, a lot of them were dependent on it. The Swedish smorgasbord came into its own at the beginning of the twentieth century when canned out-of-season fish, roe, and liver paste made it possible to set out a lavish table. Hungarian goulash was unknown before the nineteenth century, and not widely accepted until after the invention of a paprika-grinding mill in 1859.[23]

When lands were conquered, peoples migrated, populations converted to different religions or accepted new dietary theories, and dishes—even whole cuisines—were forgotten and new ones invented. Where now is the cuisine of Renaissance Spain and Italy, or of the Indian Raj, or of Tsarist Russia, or of medieval Japan? Instead we have Nonya food in Singapore, Cape Malay food in South Africa, Creole food in the Mississippi Delta, and Local Food in Hawaii. How long does it take to create a cuisine? Not long: less than fifty years, judging by past experience.

Were old foods more healthful than ours? Inherent in this vague notion are several different claims, among them that foods were less dangerous, that diets were better balanced. Yet while we fret about pesticides on apples, mercury in tuna, and mad cow disease, we should remember that ingesting food is, and always has been, inherently dangerous. Many plants contain both toxins and carcinogens, often at levels much higher than in any pesticide residues.[24] Grilling and frying add more. Some historians argue that bread made from moldy, verminous flour, or adulterated with mash, leaves, or bark to make it go further, or contaminated with hemp or poppy seeds to drown out sorrows, meant that for five hundred years Europe's poor staggered around in a drugged haze subject to hallucinations.[25] Certainly, many of our forebears were drunk much of the time, given that beer and wine were preferred to water, and with good reason. In the cities, polluted water supplies brought intestinal diseases in their wake. In France, for example, no piped water was available until the 1860s. Bread was likely to be stretched with chalk, pepper adulterated with the sweepings of warehouse floors, and sausage stuffed with all the horrors famously exposed by Upton Sinclair in *The Jungle*. Even the most reputable cookbooks recommended using concentrated sulphuric acid to intensify the color of jams.[26] Milk, suspected of spreading scarlet fever, typhoid, and diphtheria as well as tuberculosis, was sensibly avoided well into the twentieth century, when the United States and many parts of Europe introduced stringent regulations. My mother sifted weevils from the flour bin; my aunt reckoned that if the maggots could eat her home-cured ham and survive, so could the family.

As to dietary balance, once again we have to distinguish between rich and poor. The rich, whose bountiful tables and ample girths were visible evidence of their station in life, suffered many of the diseases of excess. In the seventeenth century, the Mughal Emperor, Jahangir, died of overindulgence in food, opium, and alcohol.[27] In Georgian England, George Cheyne, the leading doctor, had to be wedged in and out of his carriage by his servants when he soared to four hundred pounds, while a little later Erasmus Darwin, grandfather of Charles and another important physician, had a semicircle cut out of his dining table to accommodate his paunch. In the nineteenth century, the fourteenth shogun of Japan died at age twenty-one, probably of beriberi induced by eating the white rice available only to the privileged. In the Islamic countries, India, and Europe, the well-to-do took sugar as a medicine; in India they used butter; and in much of the world people avoided fresh vegetables, all on medical advice.

Whether the peasants really starved, and if so how often, particularly outside of Europe, is the subject of ongoing research.[28] What is clear is that the food supply was always precarious: if the weather was bad or war broke out, there might not be enough to go around. The end of winter or the dry season saw everyone suffering from the lack of fresh fruits and vegetables, scurvy occurring on land as well as at sea. By our standards, the diet was scanty for people who were engaged in heavy physical toil. Estimates suggest that in France on the eve of the Revolution one in three adult men got by on no more than 1,800 calories a day, while a century later in Japan daily intake was perhaps 1,850 calories. Historians believe that in times of scarcity peasants essentially hibernated during the winter.[29] It is not surprising, therefore, that in France the proudest of boasts was "there is always bread in the house," while the Japanese adage advised that "all that matters is a full stomach."[30]

By the standard measures of health and nutrition—life expectancy and height—our ancestors were far worse off than we are.[31] Much of the blame was due to the diet, exacerbated by living conditions and infections which affect the body's ability to use the food that is ingested.[32] No amount of nostalgia for the pastoral foods of the distant past can wish away the fact that our ancestors lived mean, short lives, constantly afflicted with diseases, many of which can be directly attributed to what they did and did not eat.

Historical myths, though, can mislead as much by what they don't say as by what they do. Culinary Luddites typically gloss over the moral problems intrinsic to the labor of producing and preparing food. In 1800, ninety-five percent of the Russian population and eighty percent of the French lived in the country; in other words, they spent their days getting food on the table for themselves and other people. A century later, eighty-eight percent of Russians, eighty-five percent of Greeks, and over fifty percent of the French were still on the land.[33] Traditional societies were aristocratic, made up of the many who toiled to produce, process, preserve, and prepare food, and the few who, supported by the limited surplus, could do other things.

In the great kitchens of the few—royalty, aristocracy, and rich merchants—cooks created elaborate cuisines. The cuisines drove home the power of the mighty few with a symbol that everyone understood: ostentatious shows of more food than the powerful could possibly consume. Feasts were public occasions for the display of power, not private occasions for celebration, for enjoying food for food's sake. The poor were invited to watch, groveling as the rich gorged themselves.[34] Louis XIV was exploiting a tradition going back to the Roman Empire when he encouraged spectators at his feasts. Sometimes, to hammer home the point while amusing the court, the spectators were let loose on the leftovers. "The destruction of so handsome an arrangement served to give another agreeable entertainment to the court," observed a commentator, "by the alacrity and disorder of those who demolished these castles of marzipan, and these mountains of preserved fruit."[35]

Meanwhile, most men were born to a life of labor in the fields, most women to a life of grinding, chopping, and cooking. "Servitude," said my mother as she prepared home-cooked breakfast, dinner, and tea for eight to ten people three hundred and sixty-five days a year. She was right. Churning butter and skinning and cleaning hares, without the option of picking up the phone for a pizza if something goes wrong, is unremitting, unforgiving toil. Perhaps, though, my mother did not realize how much worse her lot might have been. She could at least buy our bread from the bakery. In Mexico, at the same time, women without servants could expect to spend five hours a day—one third of their waking hours—kneeling at the grindstone preparing the dough for the family's tortillas. Not until the 1950s did the invention of the tortilla machine release them from the drudgery.[36]

In the eighteenth and early nineteenth centuries, it looked as if the distinction between gorgers and grovelers would worsen. Between 1575 and 1825 world population had doubled from 500 million to a billion, and it was to double again by 1925. Malthus sounded his dire predictions. The poor, driven by necessity or government mandate, resorted to basic foods that produced bountifully even if they were disliked: maize and sweet potatoes in China and Japan, maize in Italy, Spain, and Romania, potatoes in northern Europe.[37] They eked out an existence on porridges or polentas of oats or maize, on coarse breads of rye or barley bulked out with chaff or even clay and ground bark, and on boiled potatoes; they saw meat only on rare occasions.[38] The privation continued. In Europe, 1840 was a year of hunger, best remembered now as the time of the devastating potato famine of Ireland. Meanwhile, the rich continued to indulge, feasting on white bread, meats, rich fatty sauces, sweet desserts, exotic hothouse-grown pineapples, wine, and tea, coffee, and chocolate drunk from fine china. In 1845, shortly after revolutions had rocked Europe, the British prime minister Benjamin Disraeli described "two nations, between whom there is no intercourse and no sympathy… who are formed by a different breeding, are fed by a different food, are ordered by different manners, and are not governed by the same laws…THE RICH AND THE POOR."[39]

In the nick of time, in the 1880s, the industrialization of food got under way long after the production of other common items of consumption, such as textiles and clothing, had been mechanized. Farmers brought new land into production, utilized reapers and later tractors and combines, spread more fertilizer, and by the 1930s began growing hybrid maize. Steamships and trains brought fresh and canned meats, fruits, vegetables, and milk to the growing towns. Instead of starving, the poor of the industrialized world survived and thrived. In Britain the retail price of food in a typical workman's budget fell by a third between 1877 and 1887 (though he would still spend seventy-one percent of his income on food and drink). In 1898 in the United States a dollar bought forty-two percent more milk, fifty-one percent more coffee, a third more beef, twice as much sugar, and twice as much flour as in 1872.[40] By the beginning of the twentieth century, the British working class were drinking sugary tea from china teacups and eating white bread spread with jam and margarine, canned meats, canned pineapple, and an orange from the Christmas stocking.

To us, the cheap jam, the margarine, and the starchy diet look pathetic. Yet white bread did not cause the "weakness, indigestion, or nausea" that coarse whole wheat bread did when it supplied most of the calories (not a problem for us since we never consume it in such quantities).[41] Besides, it was easier to detect stretchers such as sawdust in white bread. Margarine and jam made the bread more attractive and easier to swallow. Sugar tasted good, and hot tea in an unheated house in mid-winter provided good cheer. For those for whom fruit had been available, if at all, only from June to October, canned pineapple and a Christmas orange were treats to be relished. For the diners, therefore, the meals were a dream come true, a first step away from a coarse, monotonous diet and the constant threat of hunger, even starvation.

Nor should we think it was only the British, not famed for their cuisine, who were delighted with industrialized foods. Everyone was, whether American, Asian, African, or European. In the first half of the twentieth century, Italians embraced factory-made pasta and canned tomatoes.[42] In the second half of the century, Japanese women welcomed factory-made bread because they could sleep in a little longer instead of having to get up to make rice.[43] Similarly, Mexicans seized on bread as a good food to have on hand when there was no time to prepare tortillas. Working women in India are happy to serve commercially made bread during the week, saving the time-consuming business of making chapatis for the weekend. As supermarkets appeared in Eastern Europe and Russia, housewives rejoiced at the choice and convenience of ready-made goods. For all, Culinary Modernism had provided what was wanted: food that was processed, preservable, industrial, novel, and fast, the food of the elite at a price everyone could afford. Where modern food became available, populations grew taller and stronger, had fewer diseases, and lived longer. Men had choices other than hard agricultural labor, women other than kneeling at the *metate* five hours a day.

So the sunlit past of the Culinary Luddites never existed. So their ethos is based not on history but on a fairy tale. So what? Perhaps we now need this culinary philosophy. Certainly no one would deny that an industrialized food supply has its own problems, problems we hear about every day. Perhaps we *should* eat more fresh, natural, local, artisanal, slow food. Why not create a historical myth to further that end? The past is over and gone. Does it matter if the history is not quite right?

It matters quite a bit, I believe. If we do not understand that most people had no choice but to devote their lives to growing and cooking food, we are incapable of comprehending that the foods of Culinary Modernism—egalitarian, available more or less equally to all, without demanding the disproportionate amount of the resources of time or money that traditional foodstuffs did—allow us unparalleled choices not just of diet but of what to do with our lives. If we urge the Mexican to stay at her *metate*, the farmer to stay at his olive press, the housewife to stay at her stove instead of going to McDonald's, all so that we may eat handmade tortillas, traditionally pressed olive oil, and home-cooked meals, we are assuming the mantle of the aristocrats of old. We are reducing the options of others as we attempt to impose our elite culinary preferences on the rest of the population.

If we fail to understand how scant and monotonous most traditional diets were, we can misunderstand the "ethnic foods" we encounter in cookbooks, at restaurants, or on our travels. We let our eyes glide over the occasional references to servants, to travel and education abroad in so-called ethnic cookbooks, references that otherwise would clue us in to the fact that the recipes are those of monied Italians, Indians, or Chinese with maids to do the donkey work of preparing elaborate dishes. We may mistake the meals of today's European, Asian, or Mexican middle class (many of them benefitting from industrialization and contemporary tourism) for peasant food or for the daily fare of our ancestors. We can represent the peoples of the Mediterranean, Southeast Asia, India, or Mexico as pawns at the mercy of multinational corporations bent on selling trashy modern products—failing to appreciate that, like us, they enjoy a choice of goods in the market, foreign restaurants to eat at, and new recipes to try. A Mexican friend, suffering from one too many foreign visitors who chided her because she offered Italian, not Mexican, food, complained, "Why can't we eat spaghetti, too?"

If we unthinkingly assume that good food maps neatly onto old or slow or homemade food (even though we've all had lousy traditional cooking), we miss the fact that lots of industrial foodstuffs are better. Certainly no one with a grindstone will ever produce chocolate as suave as that produced by conching in a machine for seventy-two hours. Nor is the housewife likely to turn out fine soy sauce or miso. And let us not forget that the current popularity of Italian food owes much to the availability and long shelf life of two convenience foods that even purists love, high-quality factory pasta and canned tomatoes. Far from fleeing them, we should be clamoring for more high-quality industrial foods.

If we romanticize the past, we may miss the fact that it is the modern, global, industrial economy (not the local resources of the wintry country around New York, Boston, or Chicago) that allows us to savor traditional, peasant, fresh, and natural foods. Virgin olive oil, Thai fish sauce, and *udon* noodles come to us thanks to international marketing. Fresh and natural loom so large because we can take for granted the preserved and processed staples—salt, flour, sugar, chocolate, oils, coffee, tea—produced by agribusiness and food corporations. Asparagus and strawberries in winter come to us on trucks trundling up from Mexico and planes flying in from Chile. Visits to charming little restaurants and colorful markets in Morocco or Vietnam would be impossible without international tourism. The ethnic foods we seek out when we travel are being preserved, indeed often created, by a hotel and restaurant industry determined to cater to our dream of India or Indonesia, Turkey, Hawaii, or Mexico.[44] Culinary Luddism, far from escaping the modern global food economy, is parasitic upon it.

Culinary Luddites are right, though, about two important things. We need to know how to prepare good food, and we need a culinary ethos. As far as good food goes, they've done us all a service by teaching us to how to use the bounty delivered to us (ironically) by the global economy. Their culinary ethos, though, is another matter. Were we able to turn back the clock, as they urge, most of us would be toiling all day in the fields or the kitchen; many of us would be starving. Nostalgia is not what we need. What we need is an ethos that comes to terms with contemporary, industrialized food, not one that dismisses it, an ethos that opens choices for everyone, not one that closes them for many so that a few may enjoy their labor, and an ethos that does not prejudge, but decides case by case when natural is preferable to processed, fresh to preserved, old to new, slow to fast, artisanal to industrial. Such an ethos, and not a timorous Luddism, is what will impel us to create the matchless modern cuisines appropriate to our time. ◉

NOTES

1. Elizabeth David, *French Country Cooking* (London: Penguin, 1951; reprint 1963), 24–25. Richard Olney, *Simple French Food* (London: Penguin, 1974; reprint 1983), 3; Paula Wolfert, *The Cooking of the Eastern Mediterranean: 215 Healthy, Vibrant and Inspired Recipes* (New York: HarperCollins, 1994), 2. Even social historians join in the song: Georges Duby asserts that medieval food "responds to our fierce, gnawing urge to flee the anemic, the bland, fast food, ketchup, and to set sail for new shores." Foreword to Odile Redon, Françoise Sabban, and Silvano Serventi, *The Medieval Kitchen: Recipes from France and Italy*, trans. Edward Schneider (Chicago: University of Chicago Press, 1998), ix.

2. http://www.oldwayspt.org/html/meet.htm, 1999.

3. http://www.slow-food.com/principles/manifest.html, 1999.

4. http://www.slow-food.com/principles/press.html, 1999.

5. David, *French Country Cooking*, 10.

6. Julia Child and Jacques Pepin, *Julia and Jacques Cooking at Home* (New York: Alfred A. Knopf, 1999), 263.

7. Rachel Laudan, "Birth of the Modern Diet," *Scientific American*, August 2000; Laudan, "A Kind of Chemistry," *Petits Propos Culinaires* 62 (1999), 8–22.

8. For these toxins and how humans learned to deal with them, see Timothy Johns, *With Bitter Herbs They Shall Eat It: Chemical Ecology and the Origins of Human Diet and Medicine* (Tucson, Arizona: The University of Arizona Press, 1992).

9. Michael Freeman, "Sung," in K.C. Chang, *Food in Chinese Culture: Anthropological and Historical Perspectives* (New Haven: Yale University Press, 1977), 151.

10. For the survival of this view in eighteenth-century America, see Trudy Eden, "The Art of Preserving: How Cooks in Colonial Virginia Imitated Nature to Control It," in Beatrice Fink, ed., *The Cultural Topography of Food: A Special Issue of Eighteenth-Century Life* 23 (1999), 13–23.

11. E.N. Anderson, *The Food of China* (New Haven: Yale University Press, 1988), 41–42.

12. Andrew Dalby, *Siren Feasts: A History of Food and Gastronomy in Greece* (London and New York: Routledge), 24–25.

13. For Greek wines in Germany, see T.G.E. Powell, *The Celts* (London: Thames and Hudson, 1958; reprint 1986), 108–114; for Greek emulation of Persian dining habits and acclimatization of fruits, see Andrew Dalby, "Alexander's Culinary Legacy," in Harlan Walker, ed., *Cooks and Other People: Proceedings of the Oxford Symposium on Food and Cookery, 1995* (Totnes, Devon: Prospect Books, 1996), 81–85 and 89; for the spice trade, J. Innes Miller, *The Spice Trade of the Roman Empire* (Oxford: Clarendon Press, 1969); for the Islamic agricultural revolution, Andrew M. Watson, *Agricultural Innovation in the Early Islamic World* (Cambridge: Cambridge University Press, 1994); for stimulant drinks in Europe, James Walvin, *Fruits of Empire: Exotic Produce and British Taste, 1660–1800* (Cambridge: Cambridge University Press, 1997). For Linnaeus's efforts to naturalize tea and other plants, see Lisbet Koerner, "Nature and Nation in Linnean Travel," unpublished dissertation, Department of History, Harvard University, 1994.

14. For the history of sugar, see Philip Curtin, *The Rise and Fall of the Plantation Complex* (Cambridge: Cambridge University Press, 1990), and Sidney Mintz, *Sweetness and Power: The Place of Sugar in Modern History* (New York: Penguin, 1986); for apples in Australia, Michael Symons, *One Continuous Picnic: A History of Eating in Australia* (Adelaide: Duck Press, 1982), 96–97; for grapes in Chile and the Mediterranean, Tim Unwin, *Wine and the Vine: An Historical Geography of Viticulture and the Wine Trade* (London: Routledge, 1991; reprint 1996), ch. 9.

15. K.D. White, "Farming and Animal Husbandry," in Michael Grant and Rachel Kitzinger, eds., *Civilization of the Ancient Mediterranean: Greece and Rome*, vol. 1 (New York: Charles Scribner's, 1988), 236; Rinjing Dorje, *Food in Tibetan Life* (London: Prospect Books, 1985), 61–65; Inga Clendinnen, *Aztecs: An Interpretation* (Cambridge: Cambridge University Press, 1991), 119.

16. For fast food and take-out stands in ancient Rome, see Florence Dupont, *Daily Life in Ancient Rome* (Oxford: Blackwell, 1992), 181; for Hangchow, Chang, *Food in Chinese Culture*, 158–163; for Baghdad, M.A.J. Beg, "A Study of the Cost of Living and Economic Status of Artisans in Abbasid Iraq," *Islamic Quarterly* 16 (1972), 164, and G. Le Strange, *Baghdad during the Abbasid Caliphate from Contemporary Arabic and Persian Sources* (London: Oxford University Press, 1900; reprint 1924), 81–82; for Paris and Edo, Robert M. Isherwood, "The Festivity of the Parisian Boulevards," and James McClain, "Edobashi: Power, Space, and Popular Culture in Edo," both in James L. McLain, John M. Merrieman, and Ugawa Kaoru, eds., *Edo and Paris: Urban Life and the State in the Early Modern Era* (Ithaca: Cornell University Press, 1994), 114 and 293–95.

17. Richard Pillsbury, *No Foreign Food: The American Diet in Time and Place* (Boulder, Colorado: Westview, 1998), 175.

18. "Great cuisines have arisen from peasant societies." Michael Symons, *One Continuous Picnic*, 12. Symons is a restaurateur and historian of Australian food.

19. Quoted by Peter Brown, *The World of Late Antiquity* (London: Thames and Hudson, 1971), 12.

20. Daphne Roe, *A Plague of Corn: The Social History of Pellagra* (Ithaca, NY: Cornell University Press, 1973), ch. 5.

21. Lynne Rossetto Kasper, *The Spendid Table: Recipes from Emilia-Romagna, the Heartland of Northern Italian Food* (New York: Morrow, 1994), 165–69; K.T. Achaya, *Indian Food: A Historical Companion* (Delhi: Oxford University Press, 1994), 158–59; Semahat Arsel, project director, *Timeless Tastes: Turkish Culinary Culture* (Istanbul: Divan, 1996), 48–49.

22. For the baguette, see Philip and Mary Hyman, "France," in Alan Davidson, *The Oxford Companion to Food* (Oxford: Oxford University Press, 1999); for moussaka, Aglaia Kremezi, "Nikolas Tselementes," in Walker, ed., *Cooks and Other People*, 167; for fish and chips, John K. Walton, *Fish and Chips and the British Working Class, 1870–1940* (Leicester: Leicester University Press, 1992); for the samovar, Robert Smith, "Whence the Samovar?" *Petits Propos Culinaires* 4 (1980), 57–82; for *rijsttafel*, Sri Owen, *Indonesian Regional Cooking* (London: St. Martin's, 1994), 22; for *padang* restaurants, Lisa Klopfer, "Padang Restaurants: Creating 'Ethnic' Food in Indonesia," *Food and Foodways* 5 (1993); for tequila, José María Muría, "El Agave Histórico: Momentos del Tequila," *El Tequila: Arte Tradicional de México*, Artes de Mexico 27 (1995), 17–28; for tandoori chicken, Madhur Jaffrey, *An Invitation to Indian Cooking* ((New York: Knopf, 1973), 129–130; for soy sauce, sushi, and soba noodles, Susan B. Hanley, *Everyday Things in Premodern Japan: The Hidden Legacy of Material Culture* (Berkeley and Los Angeles: University of California Press), 161.

23. Dale Brown, *The Cooking of Scandinavia* (New York: Time-Life Books, 1968), 93; Louis Szathmary, "Goulash," in Davidson, *The Oxford Companion to Food*, and George Lang, *The Cuisine of Hungary* (New York: Bonanza, 1971, reprint 1990), 134–35.

24. For the natural carcinogens in plants, see Bruce N. Ames and Lois Swirsky Gold, "Environmental Pollution and Cancer: Some Misconceptions," in Kenneth R. Foster, David E. Bernstein, and Peter W. Huber, eds., *Phantom Risk: Scientific Interference and the Law* (Cambridge, Massachusetts: The MIT Press, 1993), 157–60. For toxins, Johns, *With Bitter Herbs*, chs. 3 and 4.

25. Piero Camporesi, *Bread of Dreams: Food and Fantasy in Early Modern Europe*, trans. David Gentilcore (Chicago: The University of Chicago Press, 1991), esp. chs. 12–15; Lynn Martin, *Alcohol, Sex and Gender in Later Medieval and Early Modern Europe* (New York: St. Martin's, 2000); Jean-Pierre Goubert, *The Conquest of Water*, trans. Andrew Wilson (Princeton: Princeton University Press, 1989), 58; J.G. Drummond and Anne Wilbraham, *The Englishman's Food: Five Centuries of English Diet* (London: Pimlico, 1939, reprint 1991), ch. 17; Richard Hooker, *A History of Food and Drink in America* (New York: Bobbs-Merrill, 1981), 298–301.

26. *Classic Russian Cooking: Elena Molokhovets's A Gift to Young Housewives*, trans. and ed. Joyce Toomre (Bloomington, Indiana: University of Indiana Press, 1992), 107; Daniel Block, "Purity, Economy, and Social Welfare in the Progressive Era Pure Milk Movement," *Journal for the Study of Food and Society* 3 (1999), 22.

27. Roy Porter, "Consumption: Disease of the Consumer Society," in John Brewer and Roy Porter, eds., *Consumption and the World of Goods* (London and New York: Routledge, 1993), 62; Anita Guerrini, *Obesity and Depression in the Enlightenment: The Life and Times of George Cheyne* (Norman, Oklahoma: University of Oklahoma Press, 2000); Hanley, *Everyday Things*, 159–60.

28. Peter Laslett, *The World We Have Lost*, 2nd ed. (New York: Charles Scribner's, 1965).

29. Emmanuel Le Roy Ladurie, *Histoire de la France rurale*, II (Paris, 1975), 438–440; Hanley, *Everyday Things*, 91; Peter Stearns, *European Society in Upheaval: Social History since 1750* (New York: Macmillan, 1967; reprint 1975), 18.

30. Olwen Hufton, "Social Conflict and the Grain Supply in Eighteenth-Century France," in Robert I. Rotberg and Theodore K. Rabb, *Hunger and History: The Impact of Changing Food Production and Consumption Patterns on Society* (Cambridge: Cambridge University Press, 1983), 105–33, 133; Hanley, *Everyday Things*, 160.

31. John Komlos, *Nutrition and Economic Development in the Eighteenth-Century Hapsburg Monarchy: An Anthropometric History* (Princeton: Princeton University Press, 1989), and Roderick Floud, Kenneth Wachter, and Annabel Gregory, *Height, Health and History: Nutritional Status in the United Kingdom, 1750–1980* (Cambridge: Cambridge University Press, 1990). For a critique of this method see James C. Riley, "Height, Nutrition, and Mortality Risk Reconsidered," *The Journal of Interdisciplinary History* 24 (1994), 465–71.

32. Thomas McKeown, in *The Modern Rise of Population* (New York: Academic Press, 1976), argued forcefully that nutritional level (not improvements in medicine) was the chief determinant of population growth in Europe. The nutritional thesis has been challenged by Massimo Livi-Bacci, *Population and Nutrition: An Essay on European Demographic History*, trans. Tania Croft-Murray (Cambridge: Cambridge University Press, 1991).

33. Stearns, *European History*, 15.

34. For spectators at feasts, see Per Bjurstrom, *Feast and Theatre in Queen Christina's Rome*, Nationalmusei skriftseries, no. 14 (Stockholm, 1966), 52–58; Peter Burke, *The Fabrication of Louis XIV* (New Haven: Yale University Press, 1992), 87; Barbara Wheaton, *Savoring the Past: The French Kitchen and Table from 1300–1789* (Philadelphia: University of Pennsylvania Press, 1983), 134–35.

35. André Félibien, *Les plaisirs de l'isle enchanté*, cited in Wheaton, *Savoring the Past*, 135.

36. Jeffrey M. Pilcher, *¡Que vivan los tamales!* (Albuquerque, New Mexico: University of New Mexico Press, 1998), 105.

37. Redcliffe Salaman, *The History and Social Influence of the Potato* (Cambridge: Cambridge University Press, 1949; reprint 1970), chs. 11–19; Arturo Warman, *La Historia de un Bastardo: Maíz y Capitalismo* (Mexico: Fondo de Cultura Económica, 1988), chs. 6, 7, 10, and 11; Sucheta Mazumdar, "The Impact of New World Crops on the Diet and Economy of India and China, 1600–1900," unpublished paper for the conference Food in Global History, University of Michigan, 1996.

38. For England, see John Burnett, *Plenty and Want: A Social History of Diet in England from 1815 to the Present Day*, part 2 (London: Methuen, 1966, reprint 1983); for France, Theodore Zeldin, *France 1848–1945*, vol. II (Oxford: Clarendon Press, 1974), 725–730; for Germany, Hans Teuteberg and Gunter Wiegelmann, *Der Wandel der Nahrungsgewohnheiten unter dem Einfluss der Industrialisierung* (Göttingen: Vandenhoeck & Ruprecht, 1972).

39. Benjamin Disraeli, *Sybil, or The Two Nations*, book II, ch. 5 (London: H. Colbourn, 1845).

40. John Burnett, *Plenty and Want*, 128 and 133; and Harvey Levenstein, *Revolution at the Table: The Transformation of the American Diet* (Oxford: Oxford University Press, 1988), 31–32.

41. Christian Petersen, *Bread and the British Economy, ca. 1770–1870*, ed. Andrew Jenkins (Aldershot, Hampshire: Scolar Press, 1995), chs. 2 and 4; Edward Thompson, "The Moral Economy of the English Crowd in the Eighteenth Century," *Past and Present* 50 (1971), 76–136, esp. 81.

42. Artusi, Pellegrino, *The Art of Eating Well*, trans. Kyle M. Phillips II (New York: Random House, 1996), 76–77.

43. Emiko Ohnuki-Tierney, *Rice as Self: Japanese Identities Through Time* (Princeton: Princeton University Press, 1993), 41; Camellia Panjabi, *50 Great Curries of India* (London: Kyle Cathie, 1994), 185.

44. Camellia Panjabi, "The Non-Emergence of the Regional Foods of India," in Harlan Walker, ed., *Disappearing Foods: Proceedings of the Oxford Symposium on Food and Cookery, 1994* (Totnes, Devon: Prospect Books, 1995), 146–49; Owen, *Indonesian Regional Cooking*, Introduction; Rachel Laudan, *The Food of Paradise: Exploring Hawaii's Culinary Heritage* (Honolulu, Hawaii: University of Hawaii Press, 1996), 7–8 and 209–210.

Winter 2001, volume 1, number 1

anna m. shih |

The Patented Peanut Butter and Jelly Sandwich

Food as Intellectual Property

THE WORDS "INVENTION" and "patent" often conjure images of mad inventors working frantically in their workshops, or of visionary technological developments such as the light bulb, the automobile, the airplane, the radio. A sandwich probably would not be among the objects that the general public would consider worth patenting.

Yet on December 21, 1999, the J.M. Smucker Company's Menusaver division obtained U.S. Patent Number 6,004,596 ("the '596 patent"), entitled "Sealed Crustless Sandwich." Several months later, Smucker's released the commercial embodiment of the patented sandwich. Marketed under the name "Uncrustables,"™ the sandwich is a round, crustless, frozen peanut butter and jelly sandwich sealed in an airtight foil wrapper. The frozen sandwich can be placed in a lunchbox in the morning so that by lunchtime, the thawed sandwich is ready to eat. The instructions on the Uncrustables™ box helpfully inform that the thawing process takes about half an hour, just in case the sandwich cravings are too urgent to ignore.

The '596 patent drew much criticism soon after it issued and even more criticism when Smucker's attempted to stop another company from making similar sandwiches. Various commentators, including a federal judge,[1] accused Smucker's of trying to patent a simple peanut butter and jelly sandwich with its crusts removed. The patent itself has been used as an example of "colossal idiocy" in patents[2] and a waste of taxpayer dollars.[3]

Much of the coverage in the popular media, however, misinterprets patent law, the patent itself, and the nature of Smucker's improvement over existing sandwich-making technologies. Patents are both technical and legal documents, and their interpretation is subject to many laws and legal decisions that challenge even experienced patent attorneys. As a result, the question remains: is the '596 patent as ridiculous as the media portrays it to be?

Anatomy of a Patent

One common misconception regarding patents is that inventions must involve large technological leaps to be worthy of patent protection. In reality, patents more commonly cover incremental improvements to known products and methods. Further, patents can be obtained in any technical field and are not limited to highly publicized areas such as electronics, biotechnology, chemicals, or mechanics.

Patenting food products and food-processing techniques is not new, or even uncommon. The U.S. Patent and Trademark Office (USPTO) has an entire category in its patent classification system devoted to food-related patents. Class 426, entitled "Food or Edible Material: Processes, Compositions, and Products," includes over five hundred sub-categories covering every aspect of food and food processing, such as flaked or puffed ready-to-eat breakfast cereal (subclass 621) and food-frying methods (subclass 438). Given the breadth of Class 426 and the value that many companies place on patents, nearly every food item in a supermarket or fast-food restaurant could conceivably incorporate at least one patented invention in its creation, and the patents could be directed to the food product itself, additives in the food product, the manner in which it is processed, or even the machinery used in the processing.

Patents may differ greatly in the technologies they cover, but the parts of a patent and the process patents undergo during examination in the U.S. Patent and Trademark Office are virtually identical, regardless of the technology they cover. Every patent starts its life as a patent application, which includes the proposed text and drawings to appear in the final patent itself if approved by the USPTO. Patents also include a brief abstract to help patent searchers understand the subject of the invention quickly, one or more drawings showing the invention, and a detailed description of the invention.

The patent may also include a background and summary of the invention to describe problems that previously known technologies encountered and the objectives fulfilled by the patented invention. For example, in the sandwich patent, the background of the invention states, "[S]ome individuals do not enjoy the outer crust associated with the conventional slices of bread and therefore take the time to tear away the outer crust from the desired soft inner portions of the bread." The invention then solves this perceived problem by creating a sandwich with the crusts already removed before reaching the consumer. The patent also explains that the invention "provides a sandwich primarily developed for the purposes of providing a convenient sandwich without an outer crust which can be stored for long periods of time without a central filling from [sic] leaking outwardly."

Once the patent identifies the problems to be solved by the invention, the detailed description and drawings describe the invention in more detail, providing sufficient information for a person in the same field to duplicate the invention. The drawings usually show several different views of the invention. The detailed description then identifies the components shown in each drawing, describes each component in greater detail, and explains the interrelationship between the components. The reason that the detailed description must be complete enough for someone to build the invention lies with the policy behind patent law: a patent acts as a bargain between the government and the inventor. In the bargain, the government grants a time-limited (around twenty-year) monopoly to the inventor, allowing the inventor to exclude others from making, using, selling, or importing the invention into the United States. In exchange, the inventor publishes the details of the invention so that other inventors can invent improvements, furthering technological progress.

The '596 patent is directed to a simple sealed, crustless sandwich, and therefore the detailed description is relatively brief. The patent includes drawings showing the sealed,

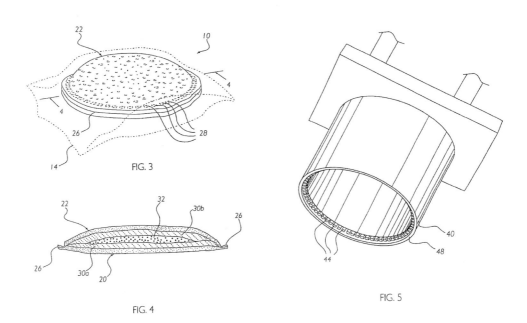

FIG. 3

FIG. 4

FIG. 5

crustless sandwich itself as well as the device used to create the sandwich (see figs. 3, 4, and 5). The patent also includes a series of drawings illustrating the sandwich-manufacturing process at different stages. Along with the drawings, the detailed description in the '596 patent enumerates possible materials that can be used for the sandwich filling, the various components of the sandwich-making device, and the way in which the device cuts and crimps the sandwich edges.

Although the detailed description can be lengthy, the numbered paragraphs following the detailed description form the actual heart of the patent. These numbered paragraphs, called "claims," form the legal definition of the subject matter the inventor actually owns. Grammatically, each claim is the direct object of the phrase "I claim" or "We claim" and may contain one or more items, or "elements," much like a component checklist for the invention. Claims are analogous to a land deed; just as the geographic description in a land deed describes the outer boundaries of a landowner's real property, claims in a patent define the outer boundaries of an inventor's intellectual property. The claims act as a fence around the inventive subject matter. And like a fence that encloses a person's land without encroaching onto another person's land, patent claims must define a boundary that does not encroach onto the boundaries of other people's inventions or information already known by the public. Because the claims dictate the scope of the inventor's protection,

Above, left: Fig. 3: Upper perspective view of the sealed crustless sandwich within airtight packaging. Fig. 4: Cross-sectional view from Fig. 3 disclosing the peanut butter sealing the jelly in between. Both from Kretchman et al., U.S. Patent application no. 6,004,596. Above, right: Fig. 5: Lower perspective view of the cutting cylinder. From Kretchman et al., U.S. Patent application no. 6,004,596.

the patent examination process in the USPTO and any disputes after the patent grant focus primarily on claim interpretation.

Claims can vary in scope from broad to narrow, covering different amounts of intellectual property. As the word "broad" implies, a broad claim lists fewer details and therefore potentially covers more product variations than a narrow claim. To catch a copyist under a given patent claim, the copied device must contain each and every element recited in the claim. For example, if a broad claim lists elements A and B and a narrow claim lists elements A, B, C, and D, an accused copyist having a device with elements A, B, and C would encroach on, or "infringe," the broad claim because the copied device has every element (A and B) in the broad claim. The copied device, however, would not infringe the narrow claim because it does not contain element D, which is explicitly required in the narrow claim.

Inventors applying for patents like to include multiple claims having different scopes for several reasons. The primary reason is that it is difficult to predict which claims will ultimately remain in the final patent after the patent application has been examined in the USPTO. The patenting process often involves negotiations between the inventor (or the inventor's attorney) and the patent examiner, with the claims being the central topic. It is not uncommon for the original claims in the patent application to be changed, revised, or even deleted during this process.

Multiple claims having varying scopes also help ensure that if the broader claims are invalidated during a lawsuit or a patent re-examination proceeding, the narrower claims will still remain intact for snaring infringers. A patent claim can be invalidated if a court or tribunal determines that the broader claims impermissibly cover products that were already known to the public, which may occur if the examination in the USPTO was not sufficiently thorough. To infringe a patent, the accused infringer need only infringe one of the claims. Patent drafters often include one narrow claim describing the invention that will be actually commercialized by the inventor, but as a general rule the claims describe the invention in a broader and more abstract way than the specific examples described in the rest of the patent.

Because claims play such an important role in defining an inventor's property rights, patent drafters choose each word in a claim carefully and draft each claim to describe the invention as precisely as possible (although some readers feel this focus on precision sacrifices clarity). To be patentable, the claims must meet standards of novelty, usefulness, and non-obviousness.[4] The novelty and usefulness requirements are relatively easy hurdles to overcome, because the invention merely needs to be new and usable to reach an attainable result. The non-obviousness requirement, however, is where most of the negotiations in the USPTO focus and where most patent disputes arise. Non-obviousness is a subjective standard and requires that the differences between the invention and publicly known information be non-obvious to an average person working in the same technological field as the invention at the time the invention was made.

How to Protect a PB&J Sandwich

The broadest claim in the '596 patent is claim 1, which reads as follows:

1. A sealed crustless sandwich, comprising:

    a first bread layer having a first perimeter surface coplanar to a contact surface;

    at least one filling of an edible food juxtaposed to said contact surface;

    a second bread layer juxtaposed to said at least one filling opposite of said first bread layer, wherein said second bread layer includes a second perimeter surface similar to said first perimeter surface;

    a crimped edge directly between said first perimeter surface and said second perimeter surface for sealing said at least one filling between said first bread layer and said second bread layer;

    wherein a crust portion of said first bread layer and said second bread layer has been removed.

In simpler terms, claim 1 covers any crustless sandwich that includes two layers of bread, a center filling that covers less than the entire bread layer to leave perimeter surfaces on both bread layers exposed, and a sealed, crimped edge around the sandwich's entire perimeter, formed from direct contact between the perimeter portions of the two bread layers.

The sealed, crimped edge, created from direct contact between the two bread layers, was considered by the inventors to be the critical difference between the inventive sandwich and conventional sandwiches. During patent examination, the patent examiner considered the inventive sandwich obvious in light of publicly available descriptions of similarly sealed sandwiches. The inventors, through their patent attorney, argued that known sandwich-manufacturing processes required applying a hydrolyzed starch layer between the bread layers to act as an adhesive in the seal, while the invention used direct contact between the bread layers to form the seal. They also argued that none of the sandwiches shown by the examiner have the claimed crimped edge.[5] By arguing that the claims require a crimped edge with direct contact between the bread layers, the inventors convinced the USPTO that their sandwich constituted a non-obvious improvement over known sandwich structures formed by other manufacturing processes. The patent subsequently issued.

Claim 9 recites a more specific sandwich structure:

9. A sealed crustless sandwich, comprising:

    a first bread layer having a first perimeter surface, a first crust portion and a first contact surface;

    a first filling juxtaposed to said first contact surface;

    a second bread layer having a second perimeter surface, a second crust portion and a second contact surface;

    a second filling juxtaposed to said contact surface;

    a third filling;

a crimped edge directly between said first and second perimeter surfaces for sealing said first, second and third fillings between said first and second bread layers;

wherein said first and second crust portions have been removed and said third filling is encapsulated by said first and second fillings.

While claim 1 covers any sealed, crustless sandwich, regardless of the filling inside, claim 9 requires three layers of fillings between the bread layers and also requires the second filling layer to be "encapsulated" between the first and third filling layers. Claim 9, in essence, describes the sandwich that Smucker's actually commercialized. As a result, a person who makes a sealed crustless peanut butter and jelly sandwich containing one jelly layer and one peanut butter layer would avoid infringing claim 9. Further, claim 9 would not catch an infringer that simply placed a jelly layer in between two peanut butter layers in the sandwich without sealing the peripheral edges of the peanut butter layers together around the jelly, because a simple three-layer filling structure would not enclose the jelly layer within the peanut butter layers; the open peanut butter layer edges would fail to form the requisite closed capsule encasing the jelly layer. This sandwich, however, would still fall under the broader description of claim 1, allowing the patent owner to catch the infringer with the broader claim.

While the sealed, crimped edge may seem like an insignificant change in the sandwich-manufacturing field, it does represent an improvement that provides Smucker's with a competitive advantage, particularly in markets requiring participants to adhere to strict specifications. School lunch programs are one significant market; in a request for bids, for example, the Oregon Department of Administrative Services required the bidders to provide price quotes for circular, crustless peanut butter and grape jelly sandwiches that were individually packaged and frozen.[6] Given that all competing bids must specify sandwiches meeting these minimum requirements, the sealed, crimped edge in the patented sandwich with its attendant leak resistance is an advantageous functional feature distinguishing the patented sandwich from competing sandwiches. Thus, even seemingly small changes to known products may be worth protecting, especially if the changes have commercial value.

Food Fights in the Courts and in the U.S. Patent and Trademark Office

The '596 patent alone provided sufficient ammunition for critics of the U.S. patent system, but when Smucker's decided to enforce its sandwich patent against Albie's Foods, a small Michigan-based business, commentators uniformly criticized Smucker's for attempting to prevent others from making its crustless peanut butter and jelly sandwiches. Albie's Foods received a letter from an attorney representing Smucker's Menusaver division, asking Albie's Foods to stop making its allegedly infringing sandwiches. From this letter, three separate proceedings emerged.

The first proceeding was a lawsuit initiated by Albie's Foods on January 11, 2001, in response to the cease-and-desist letter. Albie's Foods filed a complaint against Smucker's in a U.S. Federal District Court and selected the Eastern District of Michigan, its home jurisdiction, as the forum.[7] A proceeding filed by an accused patent infringer requesting patent invalidation is called a "declaratory judgment" action because the accused infringer is asking the court to declare the patent invalid.

Albie's Foods also filed a "request for re-examination" in the USPTO on March 9, 2001.[8] This type of proceeding is not a lawsuit because it does not involve suing another party. Instead, a re-examination is a confidential proceeding within the USPTO that involves reviewing and re-examining patent claims in view of additional information brought by the person requesting the proceeding. Usually, the requestor brings to the USPTO's attention a new patent or other publicly available reference that was not considered during the initial patent examination. The patent claims are then evaluated in view of the new reference to see whether the claims are still new, useful, and non-obvious, much in the same manner as for a regular patent examination.

Not to be outdone, Smucker's filed a patent infringement lawsuit against Albie's Foods in another U.S. Federal District Court, in its own home forum, the Northern District of Ohio, on May 17, 2001.[9] In this lawsuit, Smucker's formally accused Albie's Foods of infringing the claims of its '596 patent. In a patent infringement lawsuit, the elements of the patent claims are compared with the accused infringer's product. If the accused product contains each element of any one valid claim in the patent, the accused infringer must pay the patent owner damages and/or stop making the product.

Having three simultaneous proceedings over the same issue is not unusual, but the high costs and diverted business resources required to support even a single dispute force patent owners and accused infringers alike to avoid involvement in multiple disputes for all but the most commercially important patents and products. As of this writing, all three proceedings are in the early stages, and therefore little public information is available. What is available, however, is data indicating just how important the patented sandwich is to Smucker's business; in the year and a half after Smucker's obtained its patent, sales of the patented sandwich exceeded fifteen million dollars (over fifty million units), making the sandwich Smucker's fastest-growing product in many years. This figure does not include sales by other companies accused of copying Smucker's product and diverting sales from Smucker's.[10] Given these high stakes, quick resolution of any of the three proceedings appears improbable. Instead, Smucker's and Albie's will likely spend tens or even hundreds of thousands of dollars in legal fees as their patent attorneys parse each word in the claims and argue over each word's meaning in three different venues. Reaching trial at the district court level can take many months or even one or more years. Appellate proceedings can stretch the case for even more years, depending on the number of disputed issues.

Both sides can also expect to pay technical experts to testify on their behalf in all three proceedings, to help the judges understand the technology and the subtle differences between seemingly identical objects. In the USPTO proceeding, Smucker's has already filed a statement by one of its expert witnesses, an adjunct professor at Case Western Reserve University in the Mechanical and Aerospace Engineering department. The professor used his manufacturing-systems expertise to explain the differences between the patented sandwich and a sandwich generated by a spring-loaded device called the "Tartmaster" and sold by The Pampered Chef.[11]

With the attention surrounding Smucker's crustless sandwich patent, one would assume that such a sandwich must be special to eat. The glossy foil packaging encasing the precious patented sandwich, complete with the words "Patent No. 6,004,596" emblazoned on the back, invites at least some curiosity as to the sandwich's taste. Unfortunately, the crimping process formed the sandwich's edges into a stiff, chewy border with the texture of compressed Wonder Bread™. Air inside the foil packaging combined with freezing temperatures dried the outer surface of the thinly sliced bread to form its own unintentional crust, and a single bite into the sandwich mangled the first, second, and third filling layers into a gooey, homogenized, peanut butter and grape jelly mass between the bread layers. After I tossed the half-eaten sandwich into the trash, I decided to keep making my sandwiches the old-fashioned way, reminding myself not to remove the crusts or crimp the edges. ☻

NOTES

1. William W. Bedsworth, "Food Fight!" *The Recorder*, March 16, 2001.

2. Seth Schuman, "Owning the Future: PB&J Patent Punch Up," MIT *Technology Review*, May 2001.

3. This particular criticism is unfounded; the U.S. Patent and Trademark Office is funded completely through user fees and does not receive any money obtained from tax revenues. In fact, every year Congress diverts funds collected by the U.S. Patent and Trademark Office into the general treasury.

4. 35 United States Code, Sections 102 and 103.

5. Amendment filed July 12, 1999, *In re Kretchman et al.*, Appln. No. 08/986,581 (issued as U.S. Patent No. 6,004,596).

6. Oregon Department of Administrative Services, 2000 *Request for Bids*, Item D.3.1, Salem, OR.

7. Case No. 01-CV-10022 (Bay City, Michigan).

8. *In re Kretchman et al.*, Re-examination Proceeding Serial No. 90/005,949, filed March 9, 2001 (U.S. Patent and Trademark Office).

9. Case No. 01-CV-1182 (Cleveland, Ohio).

10. Declaration of Steven T. Oakland, *In re Kretchman et al.*, Re-examination Proceeding Serial No. 90/005,949, filed March 9, 2001 (U.S. Patent and Trademark Office).

11. Declaration of Malcolm Cooke, *In re Kretchman et al.*, Re-examination Proceeding Serial No. 90/005,949, filed March 9, 2001 (U.S. Patent and Trademark Office). In his statement, Professor Cooke noted, "The removal action of the sandwich [from the Tartmaster device] causes the edges of the sandwich to tear, thereby unsealing and damaging the edge of the sandwich which would allow the filling to escape."

Winter 2002, volume 2, number 1

The Patented PB&J Sandwich: An Update

Years later, the little round sandwiches known as "Uncrustables®" continue to provide revenue for Smucker's and work for Smucker's patent attorneys. Smucker's reported sales of $27.5 million in 2004, $12.5 million more than in 2001. To expand its patent portfolio, Smucker's filed more patent applications, twelve of which are publicly known. Out of those twelve applications, the USPTO has granted only one patent so far: U.S. Patent Number 6,874,409, which protects a mass-production machine for making sealed crustless sandwiches.

For the original peanut butter and jelly sandwich patent that started it all, the judges in both Michigan and Ohio dismissed their respective lawsuits, leaving the re-examination in the USPTO as the only ongoing dispute. During the re-examination, Smucker's canceled all of its existing patent claims and filed new claims protecting a sandwich having a specific configuration at its sealed edge. After the patent examiner rejected the application with the new claims, Smucker's appealed to the Board of Patent Appeals and Interferences and asked a panel to overturn the rejection. In its brief to the board, Smucker's attorney argued that existing sealed crustless sandwiches had smashed or pinched-off sealed edges that commingled the bread layers into an "amorphous homogenous mass of dough." Smucker's sandwich, by contrast, had a "surface-to-surface" seal where the surfaces of the bread slices were merely pressed together without full compression. The attorney noted that the two bread layers were separately visible at the sandwich's edge after they were sealed together, forming a distinct surface demarcation rather than "a single glob of dough." To bolster its patentability arguments, Smucker's submitted two expert witness reports that analyzed and compared the smashed sandwich edge formed by known sandwich crimper-cutters with the pressed edge recited in the patent application.

The attorney further argued that the inventive sandwich included a series of small, highly compressed depressions spaced inwardly from the outer edges of the sandwich to prevent the surface-to-surface seal from separating. Because the depressions were limited to isolated regions and were surrounded by areas of less compressed bread, the inventive sealed edge locked the bread layers together while keeping the layers distinct at the outer periphery of the sandwich. The attorney stated that this particular sealed edge configuration made the depressions relatively undetectable when the sandwich was eaten, preserving the "overall natural bread feel and taste."

Smucker's made similar arguments in a separate patent application directed to a method of making the crustless sandwiches. After the board rejected the application, Smucker's appealed the board's decision to a three-judge panel at the U.S. Court of Appeals for the Federal Circuit. Smucker's attorney argued that known crimping methods formed a smashed edge that created a homogenous mass at the sandwich's periphery, while Smucker's method formed a compressed surface-to-surface seal that kept the bread slices distinct. During the court hearing, one judge declared that compressing the edges of the bread according to Smucker's inventive method "smushed" the bread. Smucker's attorney corrected him, explaining that the bread was "sealed by compression, but it is not smushed." Another judge commented that his wife made sandwiches for their child by squeezing the edges of the bread together. "I'm afraid she might be infringing on your patent," the judge said. All three judges on the panel apparently agreed that Smucker's sandwich-making method was unpatentable; they affirmed the board's rejection two days after the hearing, reportedly one of the fastest decisions in the court's history. ◉

Winter 2006, volume 6, number 1

jeanne schinto |

The Clockwork Roasting Jack, or How Technology Entered the Kitchen

When you next set your watch, remember that Tompion was a farrier [blacksmith], and began his great knowledge in the Equation of Time by regulating the wheels of a common Jack, to roast meat.

—Matthew Prior, on the father of English clock-making, Thomas Tompion (1639–1713)

MY HUSBAND HAS BEEN COLLECTING antique clocks and other ingenious mechanical things for over twenty years. Two Aprils ago, he came home from the semi-annual science and technology sale at Skinner, Inc., held at its gallery in Bolton, Massachusetts, with two "clockwork jacks," as the auction catalogue had described them.

These events at Skinner every spring and fall are a gear-head's delight, featuring the likes of English pocket barometers and Italian diptych sundials; sphygmomanometers, galvanometers, and ship's wall clinometers; sextants, octants, and astrolabes; magic lanterns and combination kerosene-powered lamp-and-rotating-fans. I love the brass, mahogany, and real leather ingredients of these unnecessarily beautiful objects. But the guts of them I appreciate only from a distance. Machines are Bob's passion, not mine. So I was surprised to hear him say he had bought these clockwork jacks for me (in one lot for $350.00, plus 17.5 percent buyer's premium). For me? Yes, he said, putting them on the kitchen counter; they had something to do with cooking.

I grew more interested.

They were both from the nineteenth century, said the catalogue. One was English, the other French. The English one was brass and shaped like a bottle with a long neck. Its spring-driven mechanism was meant to be wound with a (missing) key. The manufacturer's name, "John Linwood," was pressed into a brass label on the front. The French one had no maker's name. It was made of black cast iron and resembled a miniature stove. It had a hand crank to wind its spring and an alarm bell. More elaborately designed than the

Right: The mechanics of a roasting jack. From Joseph Moxon, *Mechanick Exercises. Or the Doctrine of Handy-Works* (Printed for Dan. Midwinter and Tho. Leigh, at the Rose and Crown in St. Paul's-Church-Yard, 1703), p.38. COURTESY OF CHAPIN LIBRARY, WILLIAMS COLLEGE

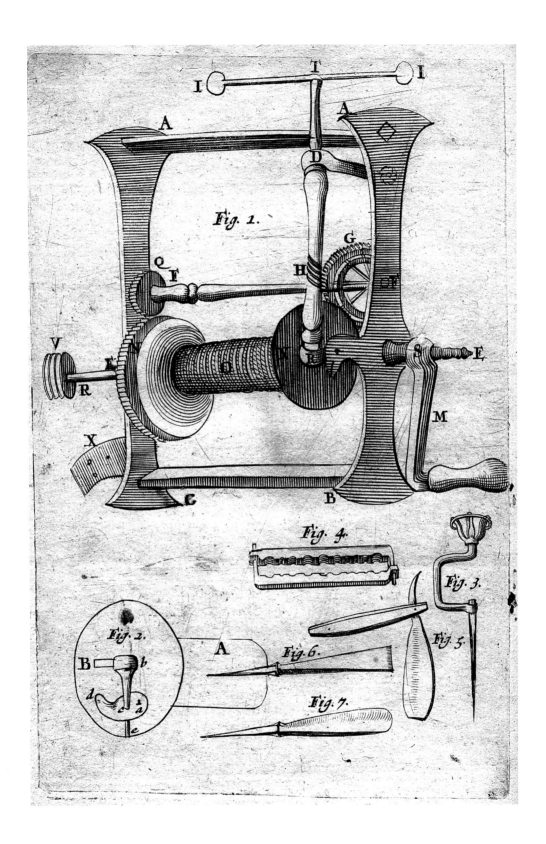

Fig. 1.

Fig. 4.

Fig. 3.

Fig. 2.

Fig. 6.

Fig. 5.

Fig. 7.

English one, it stood about fifteen inches tall on four little hoofed feet, and its top piece was decorated with a horn-playing cherub.

I began to look through books in Bob's horological library and found scattered references to "clockwork *roasting* jacks." These machines also went by other names, including "spit jacks," "spit engines"—and, what seems to be most common, the shortened "clock jacks." Their purpose: to turn spits of roasting meat before a fire without the need of anyone doing it by hand. Our English jack, I learned, would turn a vertical "dangle spit" in front of a fireplace or inside something called a "tin kitchen"; the French one turned a horizontal spit at hearth level, and when its bell rang, the cook would know it was time to rewind the spring. In either case, diners could anticipate that their meal would be "done to a turn."

Information in clock books was skimpy otherwise. Because clock jacks aren't actual time-pieces, horologists have not written in much depth or with much enthusiasm about them.[1] But food historians have. And so I was able to piece together the story of this chiefly British phenomenon,[2] which spanned the centuries roughly from 1550 to 1850. The clock jack, it is true, was not an earthshaking invention, like, for example, John Harrison's marine chronometer, or the cast-iron stove, but it has its place in annals. British food historian Rachael Feild, for one, cites the clock jack as the first successful mechanical device to enter the realm of the kitchen.[3]

The clock jack must also have been for many the locus of their first personal encounter with a self-powered machine of any kind, anywhere. For that reason alone, its significance goes well beyond the purely culinary.

Human-powered spit-roasting is, of course, a primeval cooking technique. A wrought-iron "fire dog," probably from the first century B.C., is pictured in C. Anne Wilson's *Food and Drink in Britain: From the Stone Age to the 19th Century.* Just as andirons are made to balance a log, fire dogs were made to balance the ends of a meat-laden spit. A person sat on the ground and, risking scorched palms, turned the spit by hand. In Feild's *Irons in the Fire: A History of Cooking Equipment* there is an illustration from the mid-fourteenth century of two men spit-roasting a piglet and two small fowl. Eons had passed since the Iron Age and, in terms of culinary technology, very little had changed—but it would soon. For as human groups grew larger, the task of food preparation naturally grew more complex. When knighthood was in flower, cooks were charged with feeding a castle's worth of people, and turning the spits by hand became a specialized task. Assigned to it were male scullions descriptively named "turnspits." Turnspits weren't known as refined characters; the horribly hot, tedious job inspired them to drink (and the word itself became a generalized slur). A drunken turnspit couldn't have been a reliable one, and in Tudor times, the human power of these menials was replaced by dog power.

A canine turnspit ran in a treadmill similar to a hamster's exercise wheel. A pulley system linked the dog's wheel to a smaller wheel attached to the end of the spit by a belt. As the dog ran, both wheels turned, along with the spitted meat. Thomas Rowlandson (1756–1827), the British caricaturist, drew a turnspit working such a wheel after a visit to Wales

in the late eighteenth century. The dog in the Rowlandson scene looks the way the breed has been described by many writers of the period: small, long-bodied, short-legged—and wretched. Mary Elizabeth Thurston, a contemporary commentator, illustrated her book *The Lost History of the Canine Race: Our 15,000-Year Love Affair with Dogs* with photos of the turnspit wheel at the Abergavenny Museum in Wales and of the museum's stuffed turnspit, "Whiskey," which looks like a cross between a dachshund and a rodent. Thurston is grateful to the inventors of clock jacks, believing that they allowed turnspit dogs to retire and mercifully grow extinct. But the histories of dog-powered and clockwork-powered jacks overlap considerably. Peter Brears, the British food historian who is a consultant to the National Trust, writes that clock jacks were already in use by 1587, "when the 'jacke which turneth the broche' is referred to in the will of William Hyde of Urmston in Lancashire."[4] One wonders why the term clock *jack* evolved, when the mechanism, too, might easily have been called a turnspit: the 1913 edition of Webster's says that the word "jack" meant a "mechanical contrivance" that took the place of an "attendant who was commonly called Jack"—the presumed equivalent of our own less than endearing "Bud" or "Mack."[5]

These earliest clock jacks were the weight-driven type. Their movements resemble the movements of the tall-case clocks that my husband temporarily removes from their cases and repairs for a living.[6] Clock jacks were traditionally attached high up on one side of the fireplace frame. They were made of iron by clever blacksmiths (as were early clocks). They were found not in small households but in taverns and in the kitchens of country estates,[7] where large quantities of food were prepared and fireplaces were tall enough to accommodate the long descent of the clock jack's weights.

The less-than-landed gentry, meanwhile, continued to roast their meat in more primitive ways. Usually, they drove a nail into their fireplace frame and hung a roast by a string.

Above: Thomas Rowlandson (1756–1827), *Kitchen at Newcastle Emlyn.* <small>COURTESY OF THE BRITISH MUSEUM</small>

Given a good twist, the string would rotate the roast for a few minutes in one direction, stop, then automatically rotate in reverse until all the energy was spent. (A child who twists himself or herself in a swing initiates a similar momentum.)

Hanging meat by a hook in the chimney was an alternative to the string method. It required no twisting, but to remove the meat at the end of the cooking time must have been a death-defying feat.

The chimney-hook method partly inspired another invention, the smoke jack, which rivaled the clockwork kind. Leonardo da Vinci (1452–1519) is often mentioned when the subject of smoke jacks comes up. Around 1500, he drew a sketch in one of his notebooks of a device meant to hang inside the chimney; it consisted of an arrangement of fan-like blades that turned by means of hot gases rising from the fire below it. A spit connected to that power source would turn a roast continually.

The Leonardo smoke jack was theoretical.[8] Real ones are mentioned in the diaries of Samuel Pepys[9] but they existed in Britain even earlier than Pepys's time—and they persisted. Brears lauds the smoke jack at Lowther Castle, built near Penrith between 1806 and 1811, as part of what was "probably the finest roasting range ever to have been made in this country."[10] It could power eight horizontal and four vertical spits at once, and a line drawing in Brears's book begs a comparison between it and machines in early factories: it dwarfs the man in the apron who operates it.[11]

However, smoke jacks, as compared to clock jacks, had at least one serious shortcoming: the fires under them had to be fed continually, requiring large amounts of fuel, or the smoke jack's blades wouldn't turn properly—and the roast would burn. Steam jacks, another clock jack rival, had a similar drawback. "In practice it may have proved to be a rather impractical machine," says a Smithsonian Institution appraisal of one in their collection, "inasmuch as uniform cooking requires constant rotation. Therefore interruptions for refilling the 'boiler' with water and the pause while it generates more steam would doubtless frustrate the housewife and scorch the supper in preparation."[12]

The Smithsonian's steam jack was sold in New York City by Browne and Pearsall in the mid-1790s. (It's uncertain if the firm also manufactured it.) That fact notwithstanding, jacks of any kind in early America were not a common sight. "The universal use of spit-engines in eighteenth-century England was not copied in Colonial America," Feild writes. "One new arrival wrote home complaining that her roasts were very poor for they had no spit-engine."[13]

Benjamin Franklin didn't improve the situation with what appears to have been an only half-serious idea for an electric roasting jack (foreshadower of the electric rotisserie, a fad of the 1950s that many of us will recall). In a letter to an English friend he wrote "somewhat humorously"[14] about his plans for an all-electric picnic on the banks of the Schuylkill River: "A turkey is to be killed for our dinner by the electrical shock, and roasted by the electrical jack, before a fire kindled by the electrified bottle: when the healths of all the famous electricians in England, Holland, France, and Germany are to be drank in electrified bumpers, under the discharge of guns from the electrical battery."[15] (Franklin actually did kill a turkey by electrocution, on Christmas Day 1750, and shocked himself in the process.)

Mary Beth Norton, the noted historian of early American life, reminds us that lacking mechanical means to turn roasts was the least of the colonists' hardships: "A majority of women in eighteenth-century America resided in poor or middling farm households." Women in the log cabins of the Midwest "had to cope with a far more rough-and-ready existence than did their counterparts to the east and south." One woman on the Ohio frontier who lacked a churn "was reduced to making butter by stirring cream with her hand in an ordinary pail"[16]—this, while various English lords and ladies, the Americans' colonizers, were up to their chins in spitted swans and peacocks.

Still, some high-style estates and busy taverns of the American colonial era did have jacks. Mount Vernon, for example, had both clock jacks and smoke jacks.[17] And the Golden Ball Tavern in Weston, Massachusetts, owned by a Tory merchant, Isaac Jones (1728–1813), had a clock jack and did a good business with it on the Boston Post Road, especially with all the traffic that passed by the tavern during the years of the Revolutionary War.

The Golden Ball's clock jack was sold to the Shelburne Museum in Shelburne, Vermont, in the 1940s, where it remains.[18] Another eighteenth-century inn, Longfellow's Wayside Inn in Sudbury, Massachusetts (originally Howe's Tavern when it was established in 1716), still owns a clock jack. It is bolted to a fireplace frame in one of its dining rooms, where it's been for decades, unused. No one knows if it's original to the inn or not. There are, as well, reproductions in working order at places like Colonial Williamsburg in Williamsburg, Virginia. However, to see a real one in operation in an authentic setting, you must go to another place in Massachusetts: the Salem Cross Inn in West Brookfield, near Old Sturbridge Village. The owners of the property—the brothers Henry and Bob Salem and their families—say theirs is the only restaurant in the country where an antique clock jack is regularly used to roast meat.

I visited the Salems' place last January to see this clock jack in the flesh—or, rather, while it was cooking flesh. Henry Salem, a congenial octogenarian, and his son, John, escorted me to the lower level of the inn, where a crowd of over a hundred was drinking mulled wine and cider in anticipation of spit-roasted prime rib, served as part of the inn's "Fireplace Feast."

The clock jack was busy working—slowly turning two horizontal wrought-iron spits, each attached to the clockwork above it by a leather belt. As I watched it, I understood for a moment why gear-heads feel the way they do about machines. The spits were formidable; they looked like weaponry—veritable spears laden with six pieces of beef, a total of 120 pounds. The world conspires against a would-be vegetarian; I began to salivate at the sight, and at the sound—the sizzle—and the smell.

Propped against the back wall of the fireplace were four upright logs that blazed fiery red. Even six feet back, the heat flushed my face. The size of the fireplace frame was mammoth—it looked like a threshold to a radiant room that only devils could enter. "We never have to clean the chimney," said Henry Salem. "It's self-cleaning because the heat is so intense." Still, I wanted to get closer. As I did, however, Henry and John called out warnings: if I didn't remove the reading glasses on top of my head, the plastic lenses would melt into my hair. I decided to keep my distance after all.

A slim, white-haired man named Jim Contacos was monitoring the clock jack. Contacos has worked for the inn "since the beginning"—the 1960s—so he was around when the inn first started cooking with the jack in the early 1970s, after another Salem brother-owner, Richard (1924–1996), picked it up "somewhere in Maine," said Henry.

"Uncle Dick, along with a retired machinist, figured out how to operate it," said John. "It took about three years. It was not self-evident. And it had not come with all its parts. One gear had two broken teeth, and they'd had to get those fixed."

"It's now known," said Henry, "exactly how many pounds of meat it will cook, how many you can feed with it, and so on."

"There's been a lot of interest recently," said John, "in other restaurants coming here to see how we do this. And they expect us to tell them. Excuse me!"

Henry and John would tell me at least this much for publication:

It's quite a trick to put the meat on properly. The pieces need to be balanced, or the spits will go around but the meat won't. That job is handled by the cooks in the kitchen.

It takes three-and-a-half to four hours to cook the meat once the fire gets up to temperature. The jack's weights are rewound every twenty or thirty minutes.

The inn has cooked other meat besides beef with the jack. On Thanksgiving, they usually cook two 50-pound turkeys. ("A local guy grows them for us," said Henry. "He keeps them going until they're about to explode.") Once, they roasted a pig. (Henry: "It weighed about 140 pounds when we put it on, and it kept shrinking and shrinking, because of the fat. Besides that, it took 16 hours. I was here for maybe 12 hours. It was a big disappointment.") They have also cooked fish in a basket spit, which looks something like a transparent watermelon, with stripes made of iron. That was good but not something easily cooked commercially.

When the Salems first got their jack, John went to the Essex Institute (now part of the Peabody Essex Museum) in Salem, Massachusetts, to do research on the subject. An architect with a strong interest in history (he has done quite a bit of architectural work on the inn buildings), John is fairly certain that the inn's clock jack is an import, English-made. "I don't think this was made in America. The colonists could be as artful as anyone else. But there wasn't much of a demand for clock jacks on this side of the Atlantic. We didn't have any castles. If you could afford one, you'd probably get it from London."

England was the source of a smoke jack that belongs to a friend of the Salems. But Henry didn't envy him the purchase. "They're a real maintenance problem," he said. A clock jack is far easier to clean and keep in good order than a smoke jack, which gets greasier and is much more difficult to access than its clockwork counterpart. The clock jack at the Salem Cross Inn is cleaned (as a clock is cleaned—taken apart, degreased, and reassembled) twice a year.

After the feast, which was served in a dining room upstairs (the meat was delectable, truly tender; I have tasted nothing else like it), John gave me copied pages from several books. Some of them were from J. Seymour Lindsay's *Iron and Brass Implements of the English and American House,*[19] including a line drawing of an eighteenth-century clock jack from the author's collection that looks nearly identical to the one at the inn, right down to the decorative front plate.

Other pages were from an eighteenth-century cookbook, *The British Housewife: Or, The Cook's, Housekeeper's, and Gardiner's Companion, Calculated for the Service both of London and the Country*, written by Mrs. Martha Bradley ("late of Bath"). The frontispiece shows a woman winding up the weights of a clock jack that is turning what appears to be a spitted lamb.

Mrs. Bradley knew about spit-roasting everything, from venison to quail, I discovered when I read the full text of *The British Housewife* at Radcliffe College's Schlesinger Library. ("Pick and draw the Quails, and have a very clear Fire; put round each a Slice of Bacon, and over that a Vine Leaf, then spit and lay them down; let them be done at a moderate distance from the Fire, for too near spoils them, and if they be kept too far off they never have their right Flavour."[20]) She knew, too, about the ailments of cattle and about how to scrub spits with a mixture of water and sand. Although she must also have known about jacks, unfortunately she didn't write about them here.

On that same January day at the Salem Cross Inn, John Salem took me into another room in the inn's lower level to see a tin kitchen. It was meant to be used with a bottle jack, like the kind I own. It looked like a small (three-foot-tall) tin barrel, halved and painted black. "This can't cook much—just a turkey or a goose," he said. "You're not going to cook for fifty or a hundred people with this."

That turkey or goose could be hung on a dangle spit and suspended from the tin kitchen's top, then rotated by the spring-driven bottle jack whose coiled power, unlike weight-driven power, required no drop. "This is probably late 1700s, early 1800s," John said, lifting it by its top hook to demonstrate that the whole thing was portable, so it could be stored away from the hearth when not in use. "After tin kitchens, bit by bit, comes the cook stove. But it's this kind of thing, capturing heat with metal, that becomes a twentieth-century oven."

The inn had never cooked anything with its tin kitchen. "We used to keep it in a dining room upstairs, one of the very refined front rooms. But it just didn't belong in there. It's definitely English-kitchen style." In fact, it was marked *Argyle Street, Glasgow*. "So it's just, right now"—John smiled—"an objet d'art."

That the bottle jack was meant for private households rather than inns or other institutions is noteworthy. By the mid-nineteenth century, Victorian kitchens would be positively festooned with mass-marketed kitchen gadgets, but these jacks were, for many, their first purchase—a veritable baptism by gear oil. Think of the weight-driven jack as analogous to a tower clock—communal; the bottle jack was the equivalent of a household clock—as personal as a personal computer.

It was with the bottle jack that Americans may have made their first contribution to technology—and technological progress in general.

Until 1783, when the Revolutionary War ended, the colonists were impeded as would-be manufacturers, not only by their lack of materials but also by their lack of skill. For example, anyone who called himself a clockmaker in the colonial era was probably primarily an importer who repaired clocks on the side. The age of Yankee ingenuity had not yet begun. However, whenever I mention the subject of clock jacks to any of Bob's clock-collector friends, the name of America's best known and most revered clockmaker, Simon Willard (1753–1848), is almost immediately uttered. Willard's clocks sell today for hundreds of thousands of dollars.[21] Even in the early nineteenth century, they weren't cheap. Willard's clientele were the people whose portraits were painted by the likes of John Singleton Copley. The keeper of Harvard's clocks for decades, Willard made timepieces for the United States Capitol and for Thomas Jefferson. In 1802, he patented the so-called Willard Improved Timepiece, known to us today as the American "banjo" clock. With its round face and modified-pyramid body that was about the height of a toddler, it was smaller, more compact, and more portable than a tall-case clock.[22]

But in the days directly after the war, as a young man getting himself established, Willard first turned to clock jack making. Does this, then, mean that Bob might well aspire to own a Willard clock jack someday, seeing that a Willard clock is, financially, out of the question? Not exactly. The trouble is, there is scant information about Willard's jacks. No one, not even Willard expert Robert C. Cheney, is sure what they looked like. The Willard House and Clock Museum in Grafton, Massachusetts, owns a bottle jack with a "Simon Willard, Grafton" nameplate affixed to it, but the curator, John Stephens, won't swear that it's authentic. It might well have been an import to which Willard (or some other, unscrupulous, person) affixed the label.[23]

Stephens showed me an original document hanging on the wall in the keeping room, where Willard was born. It gives directions for using Willard's "much esteemed patent weight-driven clock jack."[24] Stephens also showed me a copy of the patent issued by Massachusetts in 1784 (there was as yet no federal patent office). Another interesting document at the museum is an advertisement from a Massachusetts newspaper that describes what sounds like a Willard spring-driven bottle jack. The mystery only deepens.

Willard's jacks were apparently being sold in Boston by none other than "Colonel Paul Revere,"[25] according to correspondence at the Massachusetts Historical Society. I went there to read these tantalizing letters written by Willard to Revere, ca. 1784–1785. (The Revere end of the correspondence didn't survive.) The clockmaker seems to have struggled financially *and* mechanically. He wrote Revere with requests for money advances—and with apologies, because some of his clock jacks didn't work right initially. ("I understand some of the first that I made has got out of order intirely [*sic*] owing to their not being strung with proper strings. I will go around to them all & put in good order. I am your Humble Servt."[26])

Willard also wrote to Revere about his efforts to build a striking clock jack, as well as with another request for funds. ("Roxbury March 10, 1784 …Should you oblige me with the money I will not disappoint you [?], being very busy in fixing a Jack to strike."[27]) But whether it resembled my striking French clock jack, we'll probably never know. Willard went on to clock-making fame (if not fortune—he was a notoriously bad businessman) and left the clock jacks behind. What is more, cook stoves began to be produced,[28] sending clock jacks on their way to extinction.

The transition to cook stoves was slow, sometimes resisted by cooks who were skilled in hearth cooking. Why should they forsake their proven methods for a contraption that was, at least in its initial stages, unreliable and difficult to operate? Besides, cook-stove-cooked meat didn't taste as good as roasted meat did. Catherine E. Beecher and Harriet Beecher Stowe noticed the difference: "The introduction of cooking-stoves offers to careless domestics facilities for gradually drying-up meats, and despoiling them of all flavor and nutrient—facilities which appear to be very generally accepted," they wrote. "They have almost banished the genuine, old-fashioned roast-meat from our tables, and left in its stead dried meats with their most precious and nutritive juices evaporated."[29] The Beecher sisters recommended a giant step backwards, use of a variant of the tin kitchen. "Another useful appendage is a common tin oven, in which roasting can be done in front of the stove, the oven-doors being removed for the purpose. The roast will be done as perfectly as by an open fire,"[30] they promised. Ironically (and perhaps horrifyingly to the ghost of an old turnspit), the illustration shows that the tin oven had a hand crank!

By the time *Knight's American Mechanical Dictionary* was published in the 1870s, the definition of "roasting-jack" was "an *old-fashioned* device" (emphasis mine), even though *Knight's*, in describing it, harked back to the superior taste of a spit-roasted supper: "[All] the jacks have, unfortunately for the meat and the consumers, been superceded by the oven, which bakes but roasts not."[31]

I know someone who has spit-roasted a shoulder of ham, using a bottle jack. He's not a culinary friend of mine, but a clock-collector friend of Bob's. Les Tyrala, while living in England years ago, bought a bottle jack at the famous flea market in Bermondsey for fifteen or sixteen pounds. When he returned home to the United States, he got it working. "Yes, I actually took my roasting jack apart," Les told Bob and me. "I was just curious to see how it works. It was held together by simple set screws, like yours, so it was easy to open."

Les encouraged Bob to open up our model, which is pretty much identical to Les's, whose brand name is "Slater & Co." He hasn't yet. There's too much paying business in his workshop to be done. So the jacks remain inert, as much objets d'art as John Salem's tin kitchen, still waiting for a collaboration of Bob's talents at the clock bench and mine in the kitchen. ☉

NOTES

1. The principle of clockwork applies to clock jacks because both take a quantity of stored energy, in either a raised weight (as, for example, in most tall-case ["grandfather"] clocks) or a coiled spring (as in most old alarm clocks), and cause it to be released slowly over a period of time. However, the "heart" of a clock is its escapement, which provides accuracy through regular, regulated ticking; a clock jack does not have an escapement but merely a "transmission" to convert the power of the hanging weight or coiled spring into a slow rotation.

2. Eventually, as cooking in France grew to be a complicated "cuisine," it was the English "beefeaters" who perfected the art of roasting. But the French did have their share of clock jacks. There is a monumental one at the sixteenth-century castle Chenonceau on the River Cher in the Loire River Valley.

3. Rachael Feild, *Irons in the Fire: A History of Cooking Equipment* (Crowood House, Ramsbury, Marlborough, Wiltshire, England: The Crowood Press, 1984), 45.

4. *Lancashire and Cheshire Wills* (Chetham Society, 1860), 190. Cited in *The Country House Kitchen 1650–1900: Skills and Equipment for Food Provisioning*, Pamela A. Sambrook and Peter Brears, eds. (Thrupp Stroud, Gloucestershire: Sutton Publishing, in association with the National Trust, 1996), 95.

5. The horologists' explanation is more elaborate. They say that "jack" is short for *jaccomachiardus*, meaning "man in armour," or *jacquemart*, a compound word made from *jacques* plus *marteau* (i.e., hammer). These were names for the hammer-wielding

automatons that used to strike the hours in the earliest public clocks. The figures were modeled after the men who, dressed in protective armor, used to walk the streets counting off the hours with hammer and bell before their jobs were mechanized by the introduction of clocks. See *International Dictionary of Clocks*, Alan Smith, ed. (New York: Exeter Books, 1984), 63–64.

6. Similarly, early weight-driven clocks, ca. 1550–1625, weren't enclosed in cases, either, but were meant to be hung on the wall with movement, weights, and pendulum exposed.

7. Until the mid-sixteenth century, small households in Europe didn't have clocks, either. They relied on public clocks, which began to be built by the late thirteenth century and had become fairly common by the fifteenth century, although they did not have dials and hands, only bells that tolled the hours. It wasn't until the seventeenth century that the domestic-clock-making business began to flourish, particularly in England, which, by 1680, was the acknowledged horological center of the world, a preeminence it was to enjoy for about a century.

8. The reason Leonardo never actually made a smoke jack (or "chimney jack," as he called them), at least if vegetarians are to be believed, is that he didn't eat meat, roasted or otherwise, and had no use for one, but the truth about Leonardo's attitudes toward meat-eating is not verified. For the best compendium of primary sources on the subject, see David Hurwitz, "Leonardo da Vinci's Ethical Vegetarianism," www.ivu.org/history/davinci/hurwitz.html (on the Web site of the International Vegetarian Union).

It seems likely that the mind of Leonardo could also have theorized about clock jacks. His notebooks contain many descriptions of clocks and clockwork. He never made a clock, however, and he never sketched or made notes toward the building of a clock jack, either.

9. "So to White Hall, where I met Mr. Spong, and went home with him and played, and sang, and eat with him and his mother. After supper we looked over many books, and instruments of his, especially his wooden jack in his chimney, which goes with the smoke, which indeed is very pretty," 23 October 1660.

"The last night I should have mentioned how my wife and I were troubled all night with the sound of drums in our ears, which in the morning we found to be Mr. Davys's jack, but not knowing the cause of its going all night, I understand to-day that they have had a great feast," 12 November 1660.

10. Sambrook and Brears, *The Country House Kitchen*, 98.

11. Ibid.

12. See www.historywired.si.edu/detail.cfm?ID=188.

13. Feild, *Irons in the Fire*, 60.

14. Ronald W. Clarke, *Benjamin Franklin: A Biography* (New York: Random House, 1983), 75.

15. Letter of Benjamin Franklin to Peter Collinson, 29 April 1749. Cited in Clarke, *Benjamin Franklin*, 77–78.

16. Mary Beth Norton, *Liberty's Daughters: The Revolutionary Experience of American Women, 1750–1800* (Boston-Toronto: Little, Brown, 1980), 14.

17. "According to the 1799/1800 inventory, done shortly after George Washington's death, there was '1 Jack and chain,' valued at $10.00 in the first floor of the kitchen, and another jack, appraised at $5.00, in storage on the second floor. There is a smoke jack in the chimney of the kitchen at the current time. For many years, we had a clock jack on the wall to the left of the spit rack. It was removed several years ago, when the traffic pattern was changed in the kitchen, which made the clock jack vulnerable to touching by the public." E-mail to the author from Mount Vernon research specialist Mary Thompson, 3 February 2003.

18. *The Golden Ball Grapevine* 11, no. 1 (Autumn 1980): 3 (published by the Golden Ball Tavern Trust, Weston, MA).

19. First published in 1924 in London and Boston by the Medici Society; reprinted by Carl Jacobs, McKenzie Road, Bass River, MA, 1964.

20. Martha Bradley, *The British Housewife* (London: S. Crowder & H. Woodgate, 1770?), 226.

21. There were other clock-making Willards, three generations of them, including Simon's brothers and sons, but Simon's timepieces are the most sought after, and the most expensive. While the whole Willard family established Boston as the center of American clock-making, it was Simon who became known as the true horological genius.

22. One of the ingenious aspects of the Willard Improved Timepiece is its design for the drop of the weights: it requires only inches rather than feet for a week's worth of power. Why didn't he just use a spring? Having been apprenticed to an English clockmaker, John Morris, who had emigrated here, he was doubtless aware of spring-driven technology, and he also must have taken spring-driven imports into his shop for repair, but he didn't have ready access to springs here. It was an expensive technology at the time. Only specialized spring makers had the right kind of steel—and the practiced skill to make springs of sufficient strength not to break under the pressure.

23. For evidence that Willard may have imported some of his clock movements, see Robert C. Cheney, "Roxbury Eight-Day Movements and the English Connection 1785–1895," *Antiques Magazine*, April 2000: 606–614.

24. Original artifact at the Willard House and Clock Museum, Grafton, MA.

25. "This most useful machine was invented by Simon Willard, Clock Maker, Roxbury Street, near Boston, New England. It was recommended by the Academy of Arts; and the General Assembly, in order to encourage genius, have granted him a Patent, for the sole making and vending it for five years. It is valuable above the other roast-meat Jacks, as it is portable, and may be useful in any room. It requires less fire, and will roast meat in a shorter time.

"They are sold by him, at the above place, and by Paul Revere, directly opposite Liberty Pole, Boston." Advertisement in *Thomas's Massachusetts Spy, or Worcester Gazette*, 11 March 1784.

26. The Revere family papers, Massachusetts Historical Society, Boston, Massachusetts.

27. Ibid.

28. Thomas Robinson took out a patent for his kitchen range on October 21, 1780.

29. Catherine E. Beecher and Harriet Beecher Stowe, *American Woman's Home* (New York: J.B. Ford & Co., 1869), 181.

30. Ibid., 73.

31. *Knight's American Mechanical Dictionary* (New York: J.B. Ford, 1874).

Winter 2004, volume 4, number 1

chris bogan |

Grinding Away the Rust

The Legacy of Iceland's Herring Oil and Meal Factories

FOR THE PAST SEVEN YEARS, I have found thrill, adventure, and purpose while exploring the decaying industrial playgrounds of defunct fish oil and fish meal factories in Canada and Iceland. The first one I discovered had been idle for just over twenty years, and its slowly seizing machines still echoed the roar of the former factory. Others, silent for forty or fifty years, had crumbling concrete walls and rusted machinery exposed to pounding rains through open ceilings. The only evidence of some factories was their foundations, fighting for visibility among tall weeds and grasses, or occasional bricks and chunks of metal from derelict machines eroding along the rocky shoreline. I spent four years in Canada learning as much as possible about these factories. For the past three years I've been in Iceland, applying that knowledge to rebuild one such factory as a museum.

I saw my first herring oil and meal factory, also known as a reduction plant, in the spring of 1996. My infatuation was immediate. I was a new heritage interpreter at the Gulf of Georgia Cannery (GOG) in Steveston, British Columbia, an intact herring reduction plant that had operated from 1939 to 1979. That fall I became exhibit researcher, and over the next two years, I doted on the factory. I loved its beautiful collection of conveyors and cookers, presses and dryers, grinders and cyclones, separators and evaporators, boilers and tanks. I admired the seemingly endless network of piping that snaked along the floor, flew through the air, and criss-crossed everywhere in between. I compiled a personal encyclopedia of herring oil and meal production, my fascination growing until I became irreversibly hooked.

During my years of researching subjects for exhibits on the West Coast fishing industry, I began to appreciate the scope and significance of the herring reduction industry, not only in British Columbia, but also much farther afield. I realized that the production of herring oil and meal was a largely unknown chapter of industrial history, which needed to be told. To my surprise, in 1998 I discovered that Örlygur Kristfinnsson, director of the Herring Era Museum in Siglufjörður, Iceland, was as committed as I was to bringing the story of the herring oil and meal industry to the public.

Herring oil and meal production was Iceland's first heavy industry. Begun in 1911, the Icelandic herring reduction industry peaked in the late 1940s, was declining by 1960, and had expired by 1968 with the depletion of the nation's herring resources. During that nearly sixty-year period, many factories were built around the north and east coasts of Iceland, the majority in the town of Siglufjörður (Sigló), which became the heart of Iceland's herring reduction industry. Three generations of Icelanders made their livings from herring

processing, and towns like Sigló owed their existence to it. Decades later, a few remote ghost factories are the only evidence of this once-thriving industry.

A local effort led by Örlygur Kristfinnsson to develop a museum of the herring industry in Sigló in 1989 resulted in the Herring Era Museum, which opened to the public in 1996. Housed in a 1907 Norwegian-built fishing station, the exhibits focused primarily on the salting of herring in barrels for export and the lives of the factory workers. Aware that the story was incomplete, the museum embarked on an ambitious expansion between 1993 and 2003, which included collecting machinery from ghost factories at Ingólfsfjörður (Ingó) and Hjalteyri and constructing a new building to tell the whole herring reduction story.

Above: Looking across at Sigló from the ruins of the Evanger factory while collecting bricks by snowmobile, January 2002. (The smokestacks in the distance are at Sigló's modern fish oil and meal factory.) COURTESY OF CHRIS BOGAN

During the summer of 2000, I joined Kristfinnsson on this project, and it was a real treat for me. I had learned of the Herring Era Museum project from the museum's Web site in 1998, after having volunteered at the International Congress of Arctic and Sub-Arctic History held in Reykjavík that summer. Remarkably, while volunteering at the archives of the Icelandic Canadian Club of British Columbia in New Westminster, BC, I had occasion to meet an Icelander completing his Ph.D. at the University of British Columbia, whose wife was the sister of a close friend of Kristfinnsson; they made sure that I connected with Örlygur once I arrived in Iceland. We hit it off immediately, and the rest is history! Having recently completed an exhibit about herring reduction in British Columbia, I could think of nothing more exciting than diving headlong into a new reduction project. Three long, cold, dark winters later, the Grána Herring Oil and Meal Factory exhibit officially opened at the Herring Era Museum, the result of a ten-year effort. It was my great pleasure to help build that exhibit and serve as the caretaker of the machinery.

If my tenure in Steveston was a flirtation, my years in Sigló were far more intimate. Constraints had prevented me from satisfying my cravings for hands-on experiences with the reduction machinery at the GOG. But I found all of the manual work I wanted building the 1930s-to-1950s-era herring reduction factory in Sigló. I spent three long winters dismantling, cleaning, reassembling, rebuilding, and grinding away rust, and the machines had wonderful stories to tell. Most intriguing to me was that the restoration and rebuilding process drew a flood of stories out of the townspeople of Sigló. This industry was not as forgotten as I had originally believed.

The Industry Comes to Iceland

The production of herring oil for commercial purposes began in Norway around A.D. 800. The process was simple. The boiled fish were pressed between planks and stones, and the oil was collected. By the seventeenth and eighteenth centuries, the Norwegians were exporting herring oil to Great Britain, France, and Germany for use as lamp oil. By the early nineteenth century, production methods had changed little: herring were boiled in large iron cauldrons, and as the oil floated to the top, it was ladled off. The remaining oil was then squeezed from the cooked herring in hand-cranked presses. Layers of rough cloth were filled with the herring and placed between some twenty iron plates mounted onto a frame above a deep box. The force of three men cranking a long handle pressed the plates together and squeezed the herring in between. The oil ran out through the cloth, pooled in the bottom of the box, drained through a hole near the base, and was stored in large, oak shipping barrels. The cakes of pressed herring were sold as fertilizer.

The fish reduction industry developed at a similar pace in the mid-to-late nineteenth century in Norway, Sweden, England, and the United States. The application of steam and electricity to newly developed processing techniques in the industrial age gave rise to the first factories. Sweden's first herring reduction factory opened in 1856, and Norway's, using machinery from Sweden and the United States, opened in 1884. As the industry shifted from fertilizer making to the production of herring meal for animal feed, several factories, equipped with the latest American presses, were built in Norway between 1909 and 1911. A Norwegian named Thormod Bakkevig brought this technology to Sigló in 1911 and built a small herring oil and meal factory, the country's first.

The Industry Grows and Grows

Bakkevig was soon joined by the Evanger brothers, who built a much larger factory on an ill-fated site opposite the town on the east side of the fjord. Their factory was cast into the sea by an avalanche in the spring of 1919. Two additional factories operated that year, both on board ships, one owned by Norwegians, the other by Danes. In 1913, a Dane named Søren Goos built a factory in town. That same year, the first factory outside of Sigló was built at Krossanes in Eyafjörður. A new factory was built in Sigló in 1921 and another in 1929.

The industry's most significant growth occurred between 1934 and 1937, when factories were built throughout the north and east of Iceland at Norðurfjörður, Dagverðareyri, Djúpavík, Hjalteyri, Húsavík, and Seyðisfjörður, in addition to Sigló. Construction continued into the 1940s with factories at Ingó and again at Sigló. During this phenomenal period of growth, the amount of herring reduction increased from 680,000 hectoliters in 1934 to over 1,500,000 hectoliters four years later. By 1938, Iceland was exporting over 17,000,000 kilograms of herring oil and 21,000,000 kilograms of herring meal to major buyers in Denmark, Norway, Holland, Belgium, Germany, and the United States. Considering that Iceland had had but one small factory only a quarter century before, the growth was impressive.

The Wonderful Machinery of Herring Reduction

The grand scale of the factories and equipment reveals the incredible demand for these products in Europe and North America during the heyday of Iceland's reduction industry. It seems remarkable that a collection of specialized machinery was necessary to turn a small fish into two basic products. However, a fabulous array of giant machines moved, cooked, pressed, shook, spun, pumped, ground, dried, blew, and weighed the herring on its tumultuous journey through the factory.

When herring boats arrived at the docks, the fish were unloaded in one of three ways. In Sigló, barrels were lowered into the boat holds and filled with herring by men using special net-like shovels. The barrels were then hoisted to the dock and the contents were tipped into large wheeled carts, which were pushed along rails to storage bins. Other factories eliminated labor-intensive hand shoveling by employing automatic scoop-like shovels to unload the holds. At the factory in Djúpavík, massive motor-driven bucket-elevators and cranes unloaded the herring onto conveyor belts headed for the huge storage bins. Eventually elevators and cranes became the industry's standard unloading equipment.

Steam and electricity powered the factories of this period. The steam was generated either by coal-burning boilers, such as those at Ingó, or by oil-burning boilers, such as the

Babcock & Wilcox units used at Hjalteyri. As the herring arrived in bucket-conveyors, it was delivered into the funnel hoppers of cylindrical steam cookers, some over twelve meters long. A screw conveyor inside each cooker moved the herring along from the feed end to the discharge end. Once cooked into a mash by the machine's steam jets, the fish were carried by screw conveyors into the press hoppers. Inside the enormous presses, the fish mash was separated into liquids and solids, that is, into press liquor and press cake. (Press liquor and press cake, despite their sweet-sounding names, are not something anyone would enjoy tasting.) Presses of this period were typically five to seven meters long. American-made presses, such as those made by Renneburg and California Press, were used at Ingó and Sigló, respectively. The presses consisted of perforated tubes. A fast-turning screw drove the herring mash into a slow-turning tapered screw that forced the mash against increasingly smaller perforations until nearly all the liquid was separated from the solids.

The press liquor was pumped through vibrating screens to remove any residual solid particles. It was then fed through a series of centrifugal separators to remove the water. The oil was polished (a process that removes the last, minute percentage of impurities), then pumped into gigantic concrete storage tanks to await export. Almost all separators used in Iceland were made by De Laval, although Titan Roto-Jector separators started becoming popular in the mid-1940s because of their self-cleaning feature.

The press cake exited the press on a screw conveyor, passed through a fluffer that broke it up to facilitate drying, and fell into the huge, long, rotating drum of the dryer. Fish

Above: The massive concrete herring oil tanks at the Hjalteyri ghost factory. The metal tank held fuel oil for the boilers in the room on the left. Summer 2002. COURTESY OF CHRIS BOGAN

meal dryers of the period could be as large as fifteen meters long with a diameter of over two meters. The fluffed press cake was dried into meal by blasting heat generated in coal-burning fireboxes, such as the Riley-Stoker type used at Ingó, or in oil-burning fireboxes, such as the ones at the Rauðka factory in Sigló. Grinders or hammer-mills turned the meal into a powder, which was fed into weighing machines and bagged. The bags were sewn shut with industrial Singer sewing machines and dollied to a storage area for export.

Factory and Worker

The machinery in Icelandic factories typically occupied two to three stories and several rooms within or adjoining the main factory building. The rooms were designed to accommodate the specific purpose of each machine, such as the press house (*pressuhús*) for pressing or the dryer house (*þurrkarahús*) for drying.

Each factory employed over fifty men. There were the more menial jobs requiring many hands, such as unloading on the docks or bagging and storing in the meal house (*mjölhús*). In addition to several machinists and a carpenter or two, there were several other skilled positions, including steam and electrical engineers, oil-men in the oil house (*lýsishús*), press-men in the press house, and dryer-men in the dryer house. During the summer herring season when Iceland's reduction plants were in full swing, the machines ran around the clock, and the men worked in shifts. Summer after summer, hundreds of men made their living working in Iceland's herring factories.

The Products of the Industry Touched Everyone's Lives

The herring oil churned out day after day was exported to Europe and North America for use in an array of industrial and everyday products, and it returned to touch the workers' lives in surprising forms. Among other things, herring oil found its way into soap, cosmetics, paints, varnishes, lubricants, candles, insecticides, floor and furniture polishes, and foods such as margarine. It may also have been an ingredient in printing ink, linoleum, waterproofing materials, artificial leather, synthetic rubber, and plastics. The meal was exported to European and North American markets exclusively as high-protein animal fodder.

Rescuing Machines from Ghost Factories

In order to preserve this once-booming industry, it was necessary to have something to restore, such as an old factory. Unfortunately, the only surviving factories in Iceland, those at Ingó, Djúpavík, and Hjalteyri, were far too isolated and far too dilapidated to serve as public museums (although a local effort in Djúpavík has been making progress in offering guided tours through that city's derelict factory). Sigló, despite being the northernmost town in Iceland and some five hours from Reykjavík by car, was the perfect place for a factory museum. It was the undisputed center of the herring reduction industry, at one time boasting nine working factories. However, there were no ghost factories there. All of the elements necessary to build a factory exhibit would need to be removed from remote ghost factories and brought back to Sigló for conservation and display. Fortunately, the people of Sigló are not known for being daunted by obstacles like this.

The ten-year process of acquisition began in 1993 and involved several expeditions by boat, 4 × 4, and flatbed crane-truck to Ingó—a weekend trip because it is eight to nine hours from Sigló—and daytrips to nearby Hjalteyri. Each foray required the efforts of several volunteers, including former reduction workers and machinists. A typical task involved removing a massive seven-meter-long press weighing about fifteen tons that was cemented to the floor and connected by pipe and wire to the factory's long-dead water, steam, and electrical systems. Oxyacetylene cutting torches, blocks and pulleys, truck winches, ropes, chains, sledgehammers, prybars, crowbars, hammers, saws, tape measures, notebooks, pens, and cameras were the standard tools required. In addition, tents, camping gear, licorice, *harðfisk* (dried haddock), *kjötsúpa* (Icelandic meat soup), lambchops, potatoes, red wine, coffee, and cognac were equally important, as was warm clothing, since average summer temperatures at Ingó are only 2–8 degrees Celsius (36–46 degrees Fahrenheit.)

The majority of the heavy reduction machinery was hauled back to Sigló between 1993 and 2001. From Ingó came a large section of the original wood-framed herring intake elevator, the four-meter-high front face of a coal-burning boiler, a four-meter-long section of a cooker, three De Laval separators, a rare 1940s De Laval separator-bowl washing/scrubbing machine, a small press and variator, the front face of a Riley-Stoker dryer firebox, an oil pump, several gear wheels, machine motors, steam pumps, electrical circuit boxes, control switches and panels, original green enamel "China hat" factory lights, and an array of tools. From Hjalteyri came the front face of the five-meter-high oil-burning boiler, a massive steam control panel, a six-meter-long, fifteen-ton press with a steam engine, all kinds of steam and water piping, more "China hats," tools and spare parts, and the workbench from the machine shop. From both locations we collected everything we could to put the finishing touches on our factory, that is, objects that would lend human elements and in-operation realism to our exhibit. With this in mind we gathered coal, original light switches and wiring, oil and grease cans, empty soda, beer, and whisky bottles, coveralls and boots, faded calendars, and even tarnished nails for hanging the calendars.

Conservation and Installation of a "New" Old Factory

By the time I moved to Sigló in 2000, the bulk of this machinery was stored inside Grána, the recently completed herring reduction exhibit building. I knew I had found heaven when I saw it all for the first time, completely rusted, possibly seized, and covered in forty years' worth of dirt, bird droppings, and moss. I clearly remember my first tasks: polishing the "China hats" to prepare them for refitting with new electrical fixtures and tackling the noisome intake elevator. It was full of mold and moss and fish scales and dirt and a dead bird. But in the end, the gear wheels turned. Once I took apart the chain links and coated the wood with herring oil, it was good to go.

The cleaning and conserving were endless that first winter. We had no heat or light in the building, and I worked long days in my Icelandic thermal suit under the blinding glare of a large spotlight. For the most part, I spent my days grinding away rust. From the largest machine to the smallest tool, I had my Hitachi G 12SR2 disc grinder working overtime. I must have gone through at least fifty wire cup brushes that winter, not to mention two dozen or more large spray cans of WD-40. Afterwards, the bulk of the machinery was ready for rebuilding, installation, and display.

If conserving the machinery wasn't enough to bring me considerable joy, the long process of rebuilding and installation certainly was. I'll never forget the brickwork we did for the coal boiler from Ingó. It was an exceptionally cold January, and we decided that as a tribute to the Evanger brothers' factory, which was lost in the 1919 avalanche, we would collect the bricks from the factory walls that had been pushed far along the shore into the fjord. We traveled by snowmobile to the far side of the fjord and picked up over one hundred stray red bricks. We obtained our dryer in a similar fashion. After the collapse of Iceland's herring industry in the late 1960s, many dryers were cut into four-meter lengths and buried under local roads as drainage culverts. We exhumed one of them, sparing it this ignominious fate. It was work like this that made building the factory exhibit so consistently interesting and pleasurable. All of the cutting, welding, and concrete work was a bonus.

The Stories Machines Tell

When you spend day after day cleaning years' worth of grime and rust off machinery and tools, you begin to notice certain patterns of wear that tell an important story about the factory from which they came. For example, at Ingó I found many machine parts and tools with obvious signs of repair. Many critical moving parts had clear signs of having been welded back together more than once. That everything from the smallest wrenches to the largest parts had been fixed in order to keep the factory going—not simply discarded and replaced—spoke to the factory's isolated location. As the builders of the remote Djúpavík factory testified, everything down to the last box of nails had to be there right at the start. They could want for nothing because there was no communication except by boat. It was the same during the herring season. There were no spare parts on the way from Reykjavík or the United States. The men in the shop had to demonstrate considerable ingenuity in keeping things running. Part of that ingenuity is evident in the number of homemade tools we discovered. This was especially the case at Hjalteyri.

Stories Machines Bring Out of People

I was surprised at the ways in which working with the machinery brought stories out of the locals in Sigló. For example, when we decided to build a complete brick dryer firebox, a man named Njörður who had worked on building the fireboxes at the town's then-new factory, SR 46, in 1946, came to us. He told us everything we needed to know. He advised us on how to lay the bricks vertically and how to give the walls the necessary curve. This kind of input was essential to replicate a typical 1930s-to-1950s-era factory.

Recently, a fellow named Óskar came to us and, excited to see us preserving old herring equipment, told us about how he had worked at SR 46 for years. He told us that when machines were being scrapped he always collected the machine tags, and he donated his collection to the museum. Among others, it included tags from California Press, De Laval, Horton Tank, Nottingham, Renneburg, Verksmiðjan, and Enterprise, some dating as far back as 1918. His personal interest in the industry helped to create a valuable catalogue of specific machines used by the factory throughout the decades.

Most incredible was the Danish gentleman who came to us and said that he was the grandson of Søren Goos, who had built a factory in Sigló in 1913. It was his first trip to Iceland, and he wanted to see if there was any information about his grandfather at the museum. He was pleased enough with what he saw to donate two photo albums of pictures detailing the construction of the Goos factory in 1913. These examples demonstrate how the act of salvaging and conserving led to the preservation of something even more fragile: the human experience in the industry.

Future Factories

Should you come to Siglufjörður and visit our factory you will see two large boilers rusting out front. I hope you will think of them as I do: important objects beautiful in their decay, the kind of beauty that set me off on this path in the spring of 1996, the kind of beauty that John Steinbeck had in mind in *Cannery Row* when he described the faulty old boiler from the Hediondo Cannery in Monterey. The boiler was set up on blocks in the vacant lot between Lee Chong's and the Bear Flag Restaurant:

> The boiler looked like an old-fashioned locomotive without wheels. It had a big door in the center of its nose and a low fire door. Gradually it became red and soft with rust and gradually the mallow weeds grew up around it and the flaking rust fed the weeds. Flowering myrtle crept up its sides and the wild anise perfumed the air about it. Then someone threw out a datura root and the thick fleshy tree grew up and the great white bells hung down over the boiler door and at night the flowers smelled of love and excitement, an incredibly sweet and moving odor. (pp.28–29)

The image of this wonderful rusting boiler inspires me. Monterey is a famous cannery and fish meal factory town I have yet to explore. Now that the Grána Herring Oil and Meal Factory exhibit is complete, I can begin my search for another old reduction industry, perhaps in Alaska, Norway, Namibia, or in Chile and Peru. Many countries could do with a fish meal and oil museum or two. I am certain that there exist out there somewhere more ghost factories full of decaying machinery worth preserving; it's just a matter of finding them. As long as there are old factory towns and ghost factories to be discovered, or even just the odd rusting machine lurking in the weeds, I will be happy. ◉

SOURCES

Foredrag Ved Sildoljeindustriens Kursus I Bergen 22–27 November 1948. Bergen: A.S. J.W. Eides Boktrykkeri, 1949.

Hovland, Kari Shetelig. *Norske Islandsfiskere På Havet.* Bergen: Universitetsforlaget As., 1985.

Karlsson, Gunnar. *Iceland's 1100 Years: The History of a Marginal Society.* London: Hurst & Company, 2000.

Kristiansen, Svein, ed. *Sild: Havets sølv, bordets gull.* Tromsø: Grafisk Produksjon, 1983.

Kristinsson, Ástvaldur Eydal. *Síldveiðar og Síldariðnaður.* Reykjavík: Ísafoldarprentsmiðja H.F., 1941.

Kristinsson, Ástvaldur Eydal. *Silfur Hafsins.* Reykjavík: Helgafell, 1948.

Magnússon, Finnur. "Work and the Identity of the Poor: Work Load, Work Discipline, and Self-Respect," in *The Anthropology of Iceland,* ed. E. Paul Durrenberger and Gísli Pálsson. Iowa City: University of Iowa Press, 1989.

Pálsson, Gísli. *Coastal Economies, Cultural Accounts: Human Ecology and Icelandic Discourse.* Manchester: Manchester University Press, 1991.

"Saga síldarmannvirkja á Djúpavík og Hjalteyri," *Gangverk Fréttabréf* vst. Reykjavík, January 2000. [newsletter of the engineering firm vst]

Sigurðsson, Birgir. *Svartur sjór af síld: Síldarævintýrin miklu á sjó og landi.* Reykjavík: Forlagið, 1992.

Steinbeck, John. *Cannery Row.* Toronto: Bantam Books, Inc., 1970.

Western Fisheries. Vancouver, May 1948.

Þórðarson, Matth. *Síldarsaga Íslands.* Kaupmannahöfn: 2. Útgáfa. J. Jørgensen & Co., 1939.

Spring 2004, volume 4, number 2

pleasures
of the past

A la recherche de la tomate perdue: The First French Tomato Recipe? | *Barbara Santich* **326**

The Egg Cream Racket | *Andrew Coe* **332**

Frightening the Game | *Charles Perry* **345**

Alkermes: "A Liqueur of Prodigious Strength" | *Amy Butler Greenfield* **347**

Food for Thought | *Eamon Grennan* **356**

barbara santich |

A *la recherche* de la tomate *perdue*

The First French Tomato Recipe?

Text

Conserve de tomates

Il faut froter les tomatesse avec un linge s il y a de la terre, et ne point les mouiller les écraser avec la main et les metre dans un grand pot les faire bouillir pendant une journée entière apres les avoir assaisonnée en observant de ne point les laisser ruiner [?], le lendemain on les passe á un tamis fin, et apres y avoir ajouté un peu de Canelle et de girofle il faut les laisser bouillir jusquaceque quelle ressemble a une marmelade. Bien èpaisse et qu'on ny voiye plus d'eau Car C'est la le point éssentiel, C'est pour quoi il est Bon de ne pas le presser de la metre dans des pots parce quelles en rendant quelque fois encore Le lendemain allors il faut encore les faire Bouillir un peu et ne les fermer en fin que lorsqu'on est bien sur qu'elle est toutte consummee on La met en suite dans des petit pot audessu un peu dhuile ou graisse blanche fondüe et on couvres avec un papier il vaut mieux plusieurs petit pot qu'un grand parcequetant entamez ils peuvent se moisir une petite cuilliere á café bien delayée sufit pour un ragout.

—Pauline Barjavel de Carpentras, 1795

Tomato Conserve

You have to wipe the tomatoes with a cloth if they have dirt on them, but do not wet them; squeeze them with your hands and put them in a large pot and let them simmer for a whole day, but first season them, and watch that you don't let them spoil; the next day strain them through a fine sieve, and after adding a little cinnamon and cloves boil them until they are very thick, like a paste. It should be very thick and you should not be able to see any more liquid, for this is the most important point. This is why it is good not to press it to put it in pots because it sometimes gives out a little more liquid. The next day then you have to boil them again for a little and don't seal them until you are sure that all the liquid has gone; then put it in small jars and pour on top a layer of oil or melted fat and cover with paper; it is better to use several little jars rather than one large one because once opened they can go moldy; a small coffee-spoonful well mixed with liquid is enough for a ragout.

Commentary

Any dish described as *à la provençale* today evokes associations of tomatoes and garlic or, less typically, of aromatic herbs. In the eighteenth century, however, the phrase usually indicated that the dish was flavored with parsley, chives, garlic, mushrooms, and oil.[1] Tomatoes were not then the staple they have since become; in fact, it appears that they were rare in the kitchen and on the table before the last decades of the eighteenth century. There were no recipes for tomatoes in French cookbooks of the eighteenth century. *Les dons de Comus* (1742) includes a recipe entitled *Pommes d'amour* ("Apples of love"), but in reality these are little cakes, a *biscuit de Savoie* mixture baked in *"des moules à pommes d'amour,"* whose form and size I have not yet been able to ascertain.[2]

The serendipitous discovery of the mention of *recettes des tomates* in a catalogue of manuscripts belonging to the Archives Départementales de Vaucluse (a region in the south of France) promised exciting revelations—even if they were assumed by the cataloguers to be nineteenth-century documents.

Above: Raphaelle Peale, *Still Life with Fruit and Vegetables*, ca. 1795. Oil on wood. Note the ribbed, globular shape of the eighteenth-century tomato in the left foreground. THE WADSWORTH ATHENEUM MUSEUM OF ART, HARTFORD, CONNECTICUT, THE ELLA GALLUP SUMNER AND MARY CATLIN SUMNER COLLECTION FUND

Tomatoes in Southern France

According to Marcel Lachiver, there were tomatoes in the Languedoc around 1590.[3] Hyacinthe Chobaut, a former archivist in the Archives Départementales de Vaucluse, discovered a reference to *pommes d'amour* in gardens at Nîmes at the end of the sixteenth century. These were almost certainly decorative or rare plants rather than a useful, edible species, as indicated by the use of the term *jardin* (garden) rather than *potager* (vegetable plot).[4] At this time, however, there was still confusion between the tomato and the aubergine, so it is not certain that these *pommes d'amour* were indeed tomatoes, although the tomato was already being grown in Spain and Italy.[5]

By the late eighteenth century, it seems, tomatoes were quite widely grown, and grown commercially, in Mediterranean France. According to Rudolf Grewe, the catalogues of the seed company Andrieux-Vilmorin classified the tomato as an ornamental plant up to 1778, and from then on as a vegetable.[6] In *Les soirées provençales* (1786), Laurent-Pierre Berenger wrote rapturously of the displays of fruits and vegetables in the markets of Marseille and Toulon, probably in late summer or early autumn: "Here are piled thousands of watermelons and melons, heaps of pomegranates, aubergines and *pommes d'amour*; there, baskets of all shapes and sizes filled with huge grapes, white, black and pinkish in color, figs brown and golden; further on, baskets of golden yellow peaches, plums still covered with a fine bloom, succulent pears."[7] J. B. Guérin recorded both the *"grante tomate ou pomme d'amour"* and the *"petite tomate à fruit en poire"* in his 1795 inventory of vegetable gardens in the Vaucluse.[8]

By the early nineteenth century, tomatoes were available in Paris. Grimod de la Reynière mentioned them in the first year (1804) of his *Almanach des gourmands* (inexplicably, in his advice for the month of December).[9] Tomatoes are rarely available after St. Thomas's day (December 21), he noted; indeed, they are not really very good from the end of November. Nevertheless, this is the month Grimod chose to discuss tomatoes. According to his account, tomatoes had been introduced into Languedoc and Provence from Spain but were virtually unknown in Paris until around 1790, when they were popularized by the flood of southerners attracted to the capital by the Revolution. Initially they were very expensive, but by 1804 they had become quite common; indeed, in that year they were being sold in the markets from large baskets, whereas previously they had been so rare that they had been displayed on small wicker trays.

There is very little information, however, about how tomatoes were eaten, nor about who ate them. None of the household accounts from private households and religious communities in the Vaucluse of the mid- to late eighteenth century that I have consulted includes any mention of tomatoes, although such accounts typically exclude produce obtained from the household's gardens and orchards. According to Rudolf Grewe, the tomato had become a familiar culinary ingredient in Spain (Seville) by the mid-seventeenth century, and the first published European recipes for tomatoes date from the very end of the seventeenth century.[10] By the mid-eighteenth century, the *Nuevo arte de cocina* (1745) by Juan Altamiras included tomatoes in thirteen of its approximately two hundred recipes.[11] Italian cookbooks of the mid- to late eighteenth century, such as *Il cuoco galante* (1786) by Vincenzo Corrado, also included tomatoes in a significant number of recipes.[12] In 1804 Grimod de la Reynière gave advice on how tomatoes should be used, principally in a sauce for roast and boiled meats. He even included a recipe for tomatoes stuffed with a mixture of minced pork, breadcrumbs, garlic, and fresh herbs, which, he said, was a dish new to Parisians; possibly he became aware of this dish during his travels in southern France in the early 1790s.[13]

None of these recipes, however, bears any resemblance to the recipe from Pauline Barjavel of Carpentras.

The Recipe

Pauline's recipe was written on a single sheet of loose paper, of approximately standard European size (8 ¼″ × 11 ¾″). It was filed in a folder with other single manuscript sheets pertaining to medical treatments. Its punctuation is minimal, orthography inconsistent, accents sometimes confused, and words occasionally run together.

Several words have been struck out and rewritten. This could indicate either that the writer was copying from a written source (and therefore correcting words that had been mis-copied) or that the recipe was written from dictation, with the person dictating it watching the writing progress and pointing out mistakes. My inclination favors the latter explanation; the emphasis on "the essential point" and the hint to use several small jars rather than one large pot sound like someone speaking with the voice of experience.

Who Was Pauline?

At this stage I cannot determine whether Pauline was the "author" or "dictator" of the recipe, or simply the person who recorded it. It is known, however, that the Barjavel clan were wealthy landowners in and around Carpentras in the late eighteenth and early nineteenth century.[14] The most likely candidate to be associated with this recipe is Mme Catherine Pauline Barjavel, who was still alive in 1837 and therefore could have been in her twenties when the recipe was recorded. There must have been several branches of the Barjavel family, for Pauline's husband was Antoine Henri Barjavel, a surgeon, and she herself was the only child of François Xavier Barjavel. Her eldest son, François Henri Barjavel, was also a doctor.

Source of the Recipe

Pauline's recipe corroborates other evidence for the consumption of tomatoes in southern France before the end of the eighteenth century. Yet it appears in isolation. The highly concentrated preparation this recipe yields seems to be a precursor of today's ubiquitous tomato paste.

Of the Spanish recipes in *Nuevo arte de cocina*, several call for tomatoes as an acidify-ing alternative to lemon or orange juice ("*si no tuvieres tomates, echarás agrio de lima, o naranja*").[15] In other recipes, tomatoes appear as a more important ingredient, cooked with gourds to make a thickish sauce.[16] In the Italian *Il cuoco galante* of 1786, tomatoes are used to make a *colì*, or sauce, to be served with a diversity of dishes, including calves' heads, chicken, turtle doves, sturgeon, trout, and poached eggs. The section *Dei Pomidoro* has thirteen recipes in which tomatoes are the principal ingredient, often stuffed with a tasty filling.[17] Tomatoes had obviously found a favored place in Corrado's repertoire: "*I pomidori sono di piacere,*" he wrote. "Tomatoes are pleasurable."

As far as I am aware, the first French text to treat tomatoes similarly, as a familiar basic ingredient, was *Le cuisinier méridional d'après la méthode provençale et languedocienne*, first published (anonymously) in Avignon in 1835 and reissued in 1839.[18] This book gives a recipe for *Purée aux tomates*, a sort of tomato-flavored meat stock, and for *Sauce Tomate ou aux pommes d'amour*, a thick tomato puree that could accompany boiled mutton, crumbed cutlets of mutton, *Cotelettes d'agneau à la parmesane* (lamb cutlets, trimmed and coated with breadcrumbs and grated Parmesan), spit-roasted chicken and duck, fried marinated rabbit, and kidney omelette. Other recipes refer to this sauce as *marmelade de tomate*, used to thicken pan juices after roasting or braising, for example. "Marmelade" commonly referred to quince paste, so it can be assumed that this sauce was reasonably solid, or could be made so. This recipe would probably have resulted in a less concentrated preparation than Pauline's, but it appears to have had similar uses.

> *Sauce Tomate ou aux pommes d'amour.* Squeeze seeds and liquid from tomatoes, place on a slice of ham in bottom of pot, add some meat trimmings, onion, two carrots, clove, celery, season; cook over low heat, reduce, then moisten with good bouillon, when thick remove from heat, strain, press down on pulp, add nut of butter before serving.[19]

Curiously, however, the recipe that shows the most resemblance to Pauline Barjavel's recipe is American—the oldest American tomato recipe, according to Andrew Smith.[20] It belonged to the recipe collection of Harriott Pinckney Horry, later published as *A Colonial Plantation Cookbook: The Receipt Book of Harriott Pinckney Horry, 1770.*[21]

> Take ripe Tomatas, peel them, and cut them in four and put them into a stew pan, strew over them a great quantity of Pepper and Salt; cover it up close and let it stand an Hour, then put it on the fire and let it stew quick till the liquor is intirely boild away; then take them up and put it into pint Potts, and when cold pour melted butter over them about an inch thick. They commonly take a whole day to stew. Each pot will make two Soups. N.B. if you do them before the month of Oct they will not keep.

Smith adds that this was a common recipe, by the mid-1700s used throughout the Caribbean and Central America, and suggests that Horry's recipe came from Antigua, where her father was the British lieutenant-governor.[22] Considerable further research is needed to determine whether Pauline's recipe also has a Caribbean source, or whether its origin was much closer to home. However, Smith also points out that in 1758 a supplement to Hannah Glasse's *The Art of Cookery* appeared, which included a recipe using tomatoes (*To Dress Haddock after the Spanish Way*). Smith speculates that this recipe may have had a connection with Jamaica, which was under Spanish control from the early sixteenth century until captured by the British in 1655.[23]

Conclusion

While it is relatively easy to trace Pauline's recipe through later developments, it is frustratingly difficult to identify its precursors. The absence of such a recipe from contemporary Italian and Spanish cookbooks does not necessarily mean that in those countries the preparation was unknown; alternatively, it may have belonged to a category of home-style preserves that professional cooks regarded as outside their repertoire. Its intriguing similarity to a contemporaneous recipe from the Americas poses many questions. ☉

NOTES

The *conserve de tomates* recipe is from the Archives de Vaucluse. Archives de Carpentras, no. 2098, Recueil de médecine, fol. 236, Recette de tomates.

1. See, for example, the 1774 edition of Menon's *La cuisinière bourgeoise*, first published in 1746, as well as *Il cuoco piemontese*, first published in 1766.

2. *Les dons de Comus*, ed. Silvano Serventi, vol. 3 (Pau: Editions Manucius, 2001), 131 (first published 1742).

3. Marcel Lachiver, *Dictionnaire du monde rural: Les mots du passé* (Paris: Fayard, 1997), 1609–1610. Lachiver adds the possibly apocryphal story that the first tomatoes did not appear in Paris until 1792 when, on the day the Tuileries were taken, the troops from Marseille showed Parisians how to eat them, either raw or cooked with garlic.

4. Hyacinthe Chobaut, "Notes par Hyacinthe Chobaut, archiviste 1928–1950, sur les jardins et vergers. Note 49, 'Une ville au temps jadis, ou Nîmes en 1592,'" *Mémoires de l'Académie de Nîmes* (1883), 333–337.

5. Rudolf Grewe, " The Arrival of the Tomato in Spain and Italy: Early Recipes," *The Journal of Gastronomy* 3, no. 2 (1987): 66–82.

6. Ibid., 78.

7. Laurent-Pierre Berenger, *Les soirées provençales, ou Lettres sur la Provence*, II (Paris: Nyon, 1786), 322–327.

8. J. B. Guérin, *Jardins potagers de Vaucluse*, ms. 3111, fol. 48, an IV [1795], Archives Départementales de Vaucluse.

9. Grimod de la Reynière, *Ecrits gastronomiques*, compiled and edited by Jean-Claude Bonnet (Paris: Union Générale d'Editions, 1978), 217–220.

10. Grewe, "The Arrival of the Tomato," 74.

11. Ibid., 76.

12. Vincenzo Corrado, *Il cuoco galante*, 3rd ed. (Naples: Stamperia Raimondiana, 1786).

13. Grimod, *Ecrits gastronomiques*, 219.

14. Various mentions in archival documents, such as the Régistre d'Hypothèques de Carpentras, confirm that the Barjavel name was associated with a number of properties in and around Carpentras.

15. Juan Altamiras, *Nuevo arte de cocina* (Huesca: La Val de Onsera, 1994), recipe 73, *Perdices asadas con sardinas*.

16. Ibid., recipe 139, *Huevos en abreviatura*; recipe 163, *Calabaza rehogada*.

17. Corrado, *Il cuoco galante*.

18. *Le cuisinier méridional d'après la méthode provençale et languedocienne*, Avignon, 1839 (Avignon: Laffont, 1984).

19. Ibid., recipe 112.

20. Andrew Smith, *Souper Tomatoes: The Story of America's Favorite Food* (New Brunswick, NJ: Rutgers University Press, 2001).

21. Richard Hooker, ed., *A Colonial Plantation Cookbook: The Receipt Book of Harriott Pinckney Horry*, 1770 (Columbia: University of South Carolina Press, 1984).

22. Smith further speculates that refugees from France in the years immediately following the Revolution may have become familiar with the tomato recipe in Haiti or elsewhere in the Caribbean and introduced it to France on their return. (Personal communication.)

23. Smith, *The Tomato in America*, 20.

Spring 2002, volume 2, number 2

andrew coe |

The Egg Cream Racket

BEFORE WE TURN TO THE CRIMINAL CAREER of Harry Solomon Dolowich, let's pause for something cold and sweet. I know the perfect spot. A cheerful Brooklyn luncheonette called Tom's has been selling egg creams from its soda fountain since 1936. Let's observe the counterman's technique: He fills a glass about a third of the way up with milk and then whisks it under the soda spout and pulls back the lever. It takes only a few seconds for the bubbling blend of seltzer and milk to reach the rim. Next, he moves the glass under the pump a few inches to the right and precisely squirts one and a half shots of Fox's U-Bet Chocolate Syrup into the mixture. He briskly mixes it with a long-handled spoon and then finishes it with a floating halo of whipped cream. Since the pleasures of the egg cream are fleeting (the bubbles quickly disappear), you're supposed to consume the drink within three minutes of manufacture. On the first gulp the richness of chocolate fills your mouth. On the second the slightly sour/metallic taste of the seltzer comes to the fore. Then all that's left is the watery lees, a rime of chocolate syrup at the bottom, and a vague sense of disappointment. In truth, the egg cream tastes a little…thin.

Brooklynites have made egg creams the object of a local cult, with its own strict rules and rituals. (The whipped cream atop Tom's egg creams caused their entry's disqualification from the 2002 Brooklyn Egg Cream Extravaganza for "unnecessary decoration.") For the keepers of this cult, egg creams have become the symbol of a lost past, vaguely located in the "good old days" of post–World War II Brooklyn. One sip of chocolate, milk, and seltzer and the memories flood back unchecked: the old neighborhood, the sweet-stale smell of the corner candy store, the thwack of stickball bats on Spaldeens, the squeal of trolley wheels, the taunts of Dodgers fans at Ebbets Field. In fact, so powerful are those memories that they even infect the egg cream experience of those who didn't live through that supposedly simpler and more innocent era. The sweet, happy buzz you feel after imbibing one isn't just from the chocolate and sugar overload.

An air of uncertainty nevertheless lingers around the egg cream's milk-foam head. Take away the memories, strip the drink of everything but its basic ingredients, and questions arise with the seltzer bubbles. Why does it contain neither eggs nor cream? Why does it leave you strangely unsatisfied, neither refreshing like a lime rickey (a tart, fizzy drink made from limes, seltzer, and cherry syrup) nor satiating like an ice cream soda? Because the origins of the egg cream reach beyond the 1940s to an earlier and more desperate time.

Right: Ben and Dotty Abrams in Ben's Luncheonette, 2000 Holland Avenue, May 1951. This was one home of the authentic Bronx Egg Cream. THE BRONX COUNTY HISTORICAL SOCIETY LIBRARY COLLECTION

And we can detect that era's poverty, struggle, and even cruelty in the very particular mix of milk, seltzer, and chocolate syrup.

Egg creams were born on Manhattan's Lower East Side in the first decades of the twentieth century. The neighborhood was then the classic American slum, rife with poverty, disease, and crime, where Old World rabbis shared the sidewalks with hardened young gangsters like Meyer Lansky and Bugsy Siegel. Although its immigrant residents looked for the quickest way to move up and out, they also embraced what amusements they could afford: picture shows, music hall dancing, and soda fountain drinks.

A passion for cold, sweet, and fizzy soda-water concoctions then gripped the city. The drinks were dispensed from soda fountains that could be found everywhere from Times Square office buildings to country stores in the farthest reaches of the outer boroughs. In Manhattan's plusher districts customers at brass and marble fountains favored cream sodas (syrup, cream, seltzer) and ice cream sodas (syrup, ice cream, seltzer). The variation came from the flavored syrups, ranging from chocolate to any fruit under the sun to celery, pistachio, sarsaparilla, and on and on. For lunch many shunned solid food for something liquid and rich. A Twenty-third Street soda fountain served "creamed eggs" blended from raw egg, ice cream, syrup, and milk and the similar egg chocolate using egg, cream, chocolate syrup, seltzer, and ice. Depending on how many eggs and what the neighborhood could bear, these drinks cost fifteen, twenty, or even twenty-five cents.

Whereas the rich and middle class enjoyed their drinks in elegant comfort, down on the Lower East Side immigrants lined up at sidewalk soda-water stands where vendors squirted carbonated water into grimy, much-shared glasses. For a penny or two, anybody could afford a plain glass of seltzer. But who didn't want something more, like a real ice cream soda or the almost unimaginable luxury of an ice cream sundae? If a neighborhood soda fountain owner could whip up something similar, but costing a lot less, he could build a trade.

Debate has raged for years over who invented the egg cream: fountain owners Louis Auster or Hymie Weiss, a Parisian café proprietor, or some unknown soda jerk? Whoever it was, the actual innovation was nothing to write to the patent office about. They simply took the cream out of a cream soda and replaced it with milk. The real genius came in the marketing, in naming the drink an "egg cream." Somehow the lack of those two ingredients never bothered customers. Indeed, the name acknowledged their aspirations for something better, as if egg cream drinkers were saying, "We know it's a phony, but we'll take it until we can afford the real thing." And it only cost a nickel! Over the next decades the taste for egg creams grew into a craze in Jewish neighborhoods from Lower Manhattan to Harlem, Brooklyn, and the Bronx. Selling the drink brought a decent living not only to fountain owners but also to their suppliers, especially the manufacturers of seltzer water and soda fountain syrup. For some of them, however, that wasn't enough.

Harry Solomon Dolowich grew up amid the poverty and striving of the Lower East Side. Born in 1899 to Russian Jewish immigrants, he made his first home in a tenement on a gritty block of Willett Street. His family found modest but honest success, his mother, Tillie, as a dressmaker and his father, Abraham, selling insurance. Eventually, they moved to an apartment on the bustling business artery of Delancey Street. Up the building's air shaft rose sweet, chocolate- and fruit-scented fumes wafting from the first-floor factory of I. Lefkowitz & Son, manufacturer of soda fountain syrups. Health authorities twice cited Isaac Lefkowitz for adulterating his syrups with saccharin and other dangerous chemicals. Nevertheless, he paid his fines and remained in business, with trucks, employees, and hundreds of customers. He was someone to look up to, a role model for the young and hungry.

The Dolowich family, living the immigrant dream, moved steadily upward. Their eldest son, Irving, graduated from college and became a successful lawyer. Young Harry was next, receiving a BD in civil engineering from NYU in 1919. His yearbook photo depicts a slim, callow youth dressed in a crisp suit and tie. Under the picture the editors call him "Andsome Arry" and laud his skills at bullshitting: "He talks a wonderful game of basketball and…also speaks baseball, pool, and chess fluently. We predict success for this remarkable youth for, given sufficient time, he will convince anybody of anything." Despite their predictions, Harry clearly lacked direction in life. Engineering didn't work out, so he eventually entered Brooklyn Law School and in 1926 received his law degree in the "forenoon" class. He left no mark on the legal profession, however, apparently never practicing. Then in 1929 Harry married Isaac Lefkowitz's niece Charlotte and finally decided to get serious.

From Wall Street stocks to Brooklyn real estate, hungry young men could choose from scores of legitimate money-making opportunities in 1920s New York. For Harry Dolowich, however, the trick was not to work for it. Luckily for him, that wide-open era offered even more opportunities in the illicit occupations known as the rackets. He could choose from old standbys like bootlegging, gambling, or peddling worthless securities, or he could try one of the newfangled industrial rackets. In 1930 investigators counted over fifty city industries that had been taken over by racketeers, including kosher chickens, artichokes, neckwear, fish, laundries, restaurants, funeral parlors, construction, movie theaters, tailors, bakeries, furriers, grapes, and miniature golf courses. The racketeers' method was to take over an industry by threats and violence, then jack up prices and reap the spoils. Sure, they put a few people out of work just as the economy was plummeting downward, but those were the breaks.

Harry Dolowich's plans crystallized when Larry Fay hit the headlines in mid-1929. A rich, dapper ex-bootlegger, Fay ran a fleet of taxis and greeted celebrities at his chic El Fey Club on West Forty-fourth Street. On the side he presided over the New York Milk Chain Association, which prosecutors charged was a racket that controlled the city's milk sales. About one hundred independent milk dealers paid thousands apiece for membership in the Milk Chain; in return Fay guaranteed to keep the price of milk high. Those who couldn't afford the dues, or attempted to sell for less, found that wholesalers wouldn't supply them, health inspectors would harass them, and their customers would receive visits from the "dead wagons." These were association trucks that undersold recalcitrant dealers, causing retailers to drop their regular suppliers. After a few weeks of dead wagons, the holdouts usually had to shut their doors. Larry Fay's profit from his association was nine hundred dollars a day, enough to keep him in bespoke suits. For Harry Dolowich the news stories on Fay's arrest served not as a warning sign but as a road map for his own future.

In late 1929 fast-talking Harry Dolowich began to organize a racket in the soda-syrup business, a trade somehow overlooked by all the gangsters and tough guys who had recently embraced racketeering. Through his Lefkowitz connection he had contacts with all the major syrup makers, many of whom were now located in Brooklyn neighborhoods like Williamsburg, Brownsville, and East New York. Inside their doors the air was a thick, sweet fug of boiling syrup, fruit, and chocolate. Harry laid out his proposition to the owners: following Larry Fay's example, he wanted to form a syrup association that would allow members to raise prices, divide up new customers, and beat back the competition. Those who refused to join his racket, well, they would pay for it. His gift for gab finally paid off, as one by one the big syrup manufacturers fell in line, including Isaac Lefkowitz, Weller Syrup's Bernard Weller, and Herman Fox, the maker of Fox's U-Bet Chocolate Syrup.

Why did they trust Harry Dolowich? Because he told them he was a lawyer and had worked out a scheme to make it all look up-and-up: he would disguise their racket behind the trappings of a legitimate syrup company. His fronts were actually three corporations, Kings County Syrup, Standard Syrup, and Syrup Service, respectively covering Brooklyn, the Bronx, and Manhattan. Harry rented offices in one of the Lower East Side's fanciest buildings, hard by the El at the corner of Grand Street and the Bowery. His three companies shared a delivery truck, a secretary/bookkeeper, and even a big safe in which he kept the stock certificates bought by the shareholders. To drive the truck he hired two "salesmen" named Benny Troupp and Max Kaplan. The companies held regular meetings attended by the city's largest syrup men. There they supposedly discussed the manufacturing, buying, and selling of syrups, just as it said on the papers of incorporation.

But when Joseph Bershader, owner of Williamsburg Syrup, came to his first meeting, he quickly discovered that not all members were treated equally. There were insiders and outsiders, and Bershader was definitely an outsider. That evening about fifteen syrup men sat around the office. When the discussion turned to the division of new customers, Bershader said that he hoped they would be shared evenly. On hearing this Harry yelled at him: "Mind your own business! If you don't like it, get out of here!" Then Harry and a syrup maker named Yankowitz grabbed Bershader by the collar and threw him out the door. Bershader crept back into the office like a beaten dog despite the others' mocking laughter. This humiliation he could bear. What he really feared was that, if he quit the association, the others would steal his customers and destroy his business.

Harry Dolowich gave all the mom-and-pop syrup operations a choice: either join or be ruined. After her husband died Rebecca Kaplan took over his little East New York–based Yankee Syrup company. She cooked the syrups and drove the truck on deliveries, earning just enough to support herself and her children. One day while she was still in mourning, Harry Dolowich arrived on her doorstep. He advised her to join Kings County Syrup, or else. Mrs. Kaplan told him she couldn't afford the one-hundred-dollar initiation fee and the fifteen-dollar weekly dues.

"If you won't join," said Dolowich, "I feel sorry for you."

A day or two later a Health Department inspector visited and slapped her with a violation and a fine. Soon she lost 75 of her 125 customers, because Harry Dolowich's dead wagon had followed her delivery route. Driven by Max Kaplan and Benny Troupp, the dead wagon visited each of Mrs. Kaplan's customers and offered syrup for fifty cents a gallon, half of her wholesale price. (Bernard Weller had supplied the dead wagon's syrup at below cost, knowing he would be able to take over some of the widow's customers.) Her income cut by more than half, Mrs. Kaplan found herself nearly destitute, desperate from grief, and scrounging to feed her children.

Leon Rakowsky of Victory Syrup also received a call from Max Kaplan and Benny Troupp, who handed him a slip of paper saying, "Keep out of 132 Clinton Street." When Rakowsky persisted in selling to the Clinton Street soda fountain, somebody slashed his delivery truck's tires. Kaplan and Troupp spread rumors among soda fountain owners that some small syrup makers were selling a poisoned product. Rakowsky lost customers to their poison scares, as did Joseph Bershader, who overheard one of them telling a storeowner: "You bought that man's syrup? His wife cooks it in her wash basin."

The pair told another fountain owner that a boy had died after drinking a soda made with Isidore Trachtenberg's syrup. The cops had arrested the fountain owner, they said, and now were looking for Trachtenberg. Before this, Trachtenberg had actually joined the Kings County Syrup group, figuring they wouldn't target one of their own members. But then he ran afoul of one of the ruling clique, who coveted the "Pure Fruit" brand name Trachtenberg was using. When Trachtenberg refused to surrender it, the Health Department hit him with fines, the dead wagon followed his route, and Kaplan and Troupp began with the poison rumors.

Harry Dolowich's only real obstacles were the one or two big syrup men who refused to join his association. In late August of 1930, he called an accountant named Harry Merdinger and asked to meet him at the Williamsburg storefront of the syrup maker S. Snaider & Co. Merdinger assumed Harry wanted to talk about some kind of business deal with his client Samuel Snaider, who was out of town. He was wrong. As Merdinger sat there dumbstruck, Harry unfolded his plan to take over the syrup industry in New York City. He wanted Harry Merdinger to help destroy Snaider's business and then come to work for him—he needed a clever accountant to cook his books. Merdinger was told that he needn't worry about the consequences, because Harry would shoulder the responsibility if there was any trouble. "If anyone is going to take a rap," he said, "I will take it."

Merdinger refused, but Samuel Snaider finally caved in to the threats, paying a two-hundred-dollar initiation fee and six dollars per truck in weekly dues. The demands for money didn't stop there. In addition to his one-hundred- dollar weekly salary, Harry assessed members sixty dollars apiece toward buying him a new Studebaker and another time asked for one hundred dollars apiece. When Snaider asked what it was for, Harry snapped, "None of your business!" Snaider quit in disgust, only to rejoin four months later after Harry threatened to ruin him. He saw what had happened to other syrup dealers who tried to fight. First, however, Harry fined him two hundred dollars for quitting and another one hundred

dollars for the crime of soliciting a new customer. Harry then brought Snaider before a special meeting of the group's board of directors and told him that more punishment was on its way. Within two weeks the dead wagons driven by Max Kaplan and Benny Troupp had caused Snaider to lose almost four hundred of his five hundred customers.

By the spring of 1931, Harry Dolowich had remade himself. No longer the rudderless, unformed youth, he was a big shot, someone who mattered. Through his association he controlled well over half the syrup sold in New York. A large map of the city hung in his office, showing how he and his cronies divided the territory. Harry's efforts gave him not only his salary and the Studebaker but whatever he could skim out of the Grand Street safe. The slums of the Lower East Side were history; he and his wife now lived in a new elevator apartment building up in Washington Heights just steps from Riverside Drive. Best of all, his word was law, capable of inspiring respect and even fear. If anybody disobeyed him, he and his thugs would use threats, slashed tires, and the ability to ruin their businesses to bring them in line. His allies among the big syrup makers didn't complain, because each had gained hundreds of new customers. And that was just a start.

For the city's small syrup makers, however, Harry Dolowich's success was nearly fatal. This was one of the darkest years of the Great Depression, so they faced the bread

Above: Brooklyn, 1899. A soda water stand with Yiddish text is visible in the center of the photograph. THE BYRON COLLECTION OF THE MUSEUM OF THE CITY OF NEW YORK

line if forced to shut down. They decided to fight back. In June of 1931, a group of Harry Dolowich's victims asked for an interview at the offices of Manhattan district attorney Thomas C.T. Crain. Racketeering was big news during that era, and every politician right up to President Hoover promised swift and sure action to fight its evils. A distinguished-looking stalwart of the ruling Tammany Hall political machine, Crain was one of the loudest to beat this drum locally and had recently announced an all-out war on the rackets. An assistant district attorney took copious notes on the syrup makers' complaint and passed it up to the desk of Crain himself. They appeared to have clear evidence of an association racket. A day or two later the file came back with the notation in Crain's handwriting: "No cause for criminal action."

New Yorkers knew that under Tammany's corrupt reign most cops, prosecutors, and even judges were on the take, so maybe Crain was too. After all, Harry Dolowich himself had boasted about his political connections. (Months later a New York State investigation decided that Crain wasn't crooked, just incompetent and probably scared.) Realizing they would find no help from city authorities, the victimized syrup makers brought their case to the office of New York state's attorney general, long the scourge of urban corruption. Deputy Attorney General Joseph Flynn heard their story and immediately went before a judge, obtaining an order that empowered him to investigate the syrup racket. Fifty subpoenas were issued, and state investigators bearing warrants barged into the Grand Street office and seized all records of the phony syrup companies. Harry Dolowich was finally on the defensive.

For advice Harry turned to his brother Irving's law firm, which had previously filed the papers incorporating the three companies. (The association was something of a family business: Harry's sister-in-law Bella helped keep the books.) On August 3 Irving Dolowich convened a special meeting of the syrup association in his law offices at 148 Delancey Street, two doors down from their old building. In just three days Joseph Flynn would open public hearings into the syrup racket, with at least a dozen victims slated to testify. The meeting lasted late into the evening as the syrup makers worked out their strategy. To guard against any waverers who might consider ratting, Irving made all participants sign affidavits swearing that they had joined the companies voluntarily. He also advised them that with the attorney general on their tail, they had better think about dissolving the three corporations. However, that didn't mean that they would have to stop the activities of their lucrative little racket.

Harry Dolowich and his cronies were cocky as the hearings started. They sat smirking in the audience as one by one Samuel Snaider, Harry Merdinger, Rebecca Kaplan, Isidore Trachtenberg, Leon Rakowsky, and a troop of others recounted tales of threats and ruin at the hands of Harry Dolowich, Max Kaplan, Benny Troupp, and their syrup-maker allies. After Joseph Bershader told of how they had laughed after giving him the bum's rush from the meeting, he pointed to the men in the audience and shouted: "And they are laughing at me now!"

"Well, they won't be laughing long," Flynn assured him.

Three days into the hearings, Samuel Snaider returned to the witness stand to give the news that Herman Fox and Isaac Lefkowitz had repainted their trucks with the names of fictitious companies. Although the association truck had been impounded, their dead wagons would still roll through the streets of New York.

By the end of the week, however, the association's future looked a lot bleaker. Flynn had piled up evidence of both civil and criminal violations, including extortion, conspiracy, and running an illegal monopoly. He not only sent the hearing minutes to the city's district attorneys to pursue the criminal cases but also filed suit to dissolve the three companies and stop its officers from continuing any illegal practices. Harry Dolowich's syrup racket was effectively dead.

But this was still Tammany-run New York. Despite piles of evidence and the ample publicity the hearings received, prosecutors in Brooklyn and Manhattan refused to file charges. Even if the DAS weren't corrupt, they still sensed something about this case that made it too hot to handle.

Harry and his pals remained free, until the transcripts reached the desk of Charles B. McLaughlin, the district attorney of the Bronx and an enemy of Tammany Hall. A story told by Bronx syrup maker Philip Hertz, who had testified almost unnoticed in the hearings, became the basis of McLaughlin's criminal case against Harry Dolowich and Max Kaplan. The pair had visited Hertz at his Bronx syrup factory and told him he had better join their association or be put out of business. Hertz asked for a little time to think it over. Two days later he looked out the rearview mirror of his truck and saw Max Kaplan following him in the Studebaker. Hertz yanked the wheel of his truck toward the curb, cutting the car off. Here's what he later told the court about his confrontation with Kaplan:

"What's the reason you are following me?" yelled Hertz, in his Yiddish-inflected English.

"Don't get excited," said Max. "We only want you to join the association."

"Give me a little chance yet," Hertz responded, "and maybe I will."

A few weeks later Hertz wrote a check and went down to Grand Street for his first meeting of the association.

Harry and Max's lawyers staged a lengthy defense at the trial in February of 1932. The prosecution had first called Harry Merdinger and Samuel Snaider to testify about the operation of the syrup racket and then presented Philip Hertz as the star witness. For the defense eight of the principals in the syrup association took the stand, including Max Kaplan. Unfortunately, their testimony, mainly impugning Philip Hertz, was evasive, contradictory, and riddled with sudden memory losses. They failed to show that the syrup companies had any legitimate business, and most importantly, Max Kaplan failed to refute Hertz's testimony that he had followed Hertz's truck on its delivery route. The three judges hearing the case found Max and Harry guilty and sentenced them to a three-month to three-year term at the city's Welfare Island penitentiary.

Harry Dolowich did not enjoy prison. A few months earlier a gangster named Joey Rao had been sent to Welfare Island for running a Bronx seltzer-water racket. A murderer and narcotics dealer with a Mafia death warrant on his head, Rao preferred prison to the perils of the streets. He suborned the warden with bribes and threats and turned the penitentiary into his personal playground. Tended by valets and using the warden's office as his own, Rao lived like a king; to pass the time he ran gambling games and sold heroin that had been flown in by his flock of pigeons. He and his gang dined on steaks and chops, while ordinary prisoners, like Harry Dolowich, ate watery stew. To receive any sort of better treatment, they had to pay hefty bribes to Rao and his boys. Rao even sold the clothes the prisoners had worn into prison, so Harry reentered the world wearing some bum's ragged castoffs. Fittingly, he had learned what it was like to be on the receiving end of a racket.

Harry Dolowich didn't stick around to see the glory days of the egg cream. He moved to Philadelphia, a town where the drink came with eggs and cream, and never was heard from again. Back in New York, meanwhile, the sons and daughters of the Lower East Side moved to new neighborhoods in Brooklyn and the Bronx, carrying with them the egg cream habit. On streets with actual trees and playgrounds and good schools, the drink was transformed into something full of innocence and hope—the kind of treat a guy bought a girl on their first date. They drank them at soda fountains, which from the 1930s through the late 1950s enjoyed their last golden age. Freed from the baleful influence of Harry Dolowich, even the syrup manufacturers prospered and multiplied.

Limits remained, however, on the egg cream's acceptance. Its sales were largely confined to white lower- and middle-class neighborhoods in the boroughs, the kind dotted with candy stores, lunch counters, and soda fountains. In Manhattan the big cafeteria chains and fancy ice cream parlors kept nickel egg creams off their menus: they could make more money selling the more expensive ice cream sodas and sundaes. In order to gulp an egg cream, you had to belly up to down-market fountains in the Garment District or head down to raffish areas like Greenwich Village and the Lower East Side. And outside the New York City area the drink was unknown. No recipes for the drink exist in either the soda fountain formularies or *Soda Fountain* magazine or its successors. Even a 1944 *Soda Fountain* article on Krum's soda parlor in the Bronx, a center of egg cream consumption, makes no mention of the drink. A tinge of shame still seemed to follow this drink born in poverty.

After World War II a series of social and economic changes knocked the underpinnings from the New York City soda fountain business. Suburbia opened up, drawing the sons and daughters of Jewish, Italian, Irish, and German immigrants. In Brooklyn and the Bronx they were replaced by new arrivals who hadn't learned the soda fountain habit. At the same time supermarkets sprang up, selling bottled soft drinks that consumers could enjoy at home; New Yorkers didn't have to go down to the corner candy store anymore to enjoy a cold soda. Business dropped off, and soda fountains and candy stores began closing down at a rapid rate. The downturn rippled through all the related industries, from seltzer delivery to syrup manufacture. Dozens of suppliers shut their doors for good. By the 1960s the egg cream was disappearing fast, available at only a few dozen places scattered across the five boroughs.

Over the following decade, during which New York suffered one of its worst fiscal crises, young people began moving into some of the city's poorer neighborhoods looking for cheap places to live. These included neighborhoods like the East Village and the Lower East Side, which in places resembled bombed-out districts, pocked with abandoned buildings and piles of junk nobody wanted. In this rubble the new arrivals found, among other things, scrapped soda fountains and piles of old seltzer bottles. They also discovered a few vestiges of the district's long-gone Jewish population: little restaurants selling knishes and cheese blintzes and a newspaper stand called the Gem Spa offering something sweet and cold called the chocolate egg cream. This drink was cheap and different and "authentic"; it became a cult favorite of the artists, writers, and musicians who hung out in the East Village. Just when it was on its last legs, the egg cream had been reborn.

The egg cream revival was spurred by the resurgence of one of its principal ingredients: seltzer water. The counterculture grandchildren of the original immigrants bought up all those old seltzer bottles, located soda companies that could fill them, and began delivering seltzer to a new generation of consumers. Media savvy, they promoted seltzer water's many uses to local newspapers and television shows. The vast majority of the public were seltzer water novices, so reporters also gave instructions on how to use the fizzy water, including, for the first time, recipes for egg creams.

This campaign touched a chord in people of the older generation, those who had come of age during the egg cream's glory days. A whole stream of egg cream memories spilled into print, as people like Mimi Sheraton, Mel Brooks, and Avery Corman looked back on their childhoods in Brooklyn and the Bronx. (Interestingly, they remembered only Fox's U-Bet being squirted into their glasses, even though dozens of local companies sold chocolate syrup.) These stories inevitably led to arguments about the drink's invention and the proper way to mix an egg cream. The disputants agreed only that the days of their youth, replete with egg creams, were truly the "good old days," an idyllic period of safety and happiness. This spate of memories has overwhelmed all other meanings of the egg cream, including its origins in the crime and desperation of the slums.

For these purists, if the drink contains anything but milk, seltzer, and U-Bet chocolate syrup, it is not an egg cream. Nevertheless, the drink has resisted their efforts to lock it into a kind of culinary time capsule. While the Gem Spa still sells traditional egg creams, Ray's Candy Shop two blocks away offers the drink in sixteen flavors, including cherry, tamarind, papaya, and licorice. For the past decade a native Brooklynite named Jeff Glotzer has been selling bottled, premixed egg creams nationwide (blasphemy to anyone who believes the drink's joys are strictly evanescent). A West Village soda fountain called the Bespeckled Trout sells classic egg creams but also the drink mixed with a homemade syrup blended from high-end Venezuelan and Belgian chocolates—for the first time you can enjoy the oxymoronic luxury egg cream. And Artie's, a nostalgia-heavy Upper West Side delicatessen, sells its own invention, a "frozen egg cream." Made with syrup, seltzer, and ice cream, it is, in fact, exactly the same as an ice cream soda. Nearly a century after the egg cream's birth, the owners of Artie's have unconsciously returned the drink to its origins in the soda fountains of New York. ◉

SOURCES

Bonham, Wesley A. *Modern Guide for Soda Dispensers.* Chicago: A.O. Ellison, 1897.

The Bronx Cookbook. Bronx: The Society, 1997.

Gould, Jillian. "Candy Stores and Egg Creams." *Jews of Brooklyn,* Ilana Abramovitch and Seán Galvin, eds. Hanover: Brandeis University Press, 2002.

Kisseloff, Jeff. *You Must Remember This.* New York: Harcourt Brace Jovanovich, 1989.

Kreitzman, Sue. *Deli.* New York: Harmony Books, 1985.

Moynahan, Vin. "6,000 Fountain Services A Day." *Soda Fountain Service,* April 1944.

O'Neill, Molly. *New York Cook Book.* New York: Workman, 1992.

Saxe, D.W. *Saxe's New Guide.* Chicago: Saxe Guide Publishing, 1895.

"Seltzer: A Renaissance in Fizz." *New York Times,* 26 October 1979.

Sheraton, Mimi. "When Fun Was Your Very Own Ice Cream Soda." *New York Times,* 7 August 1982.

Stallworth, Lyn, and Rod Kennedy. *The Brooklyn Cookbook.* New York: Alfred A. Knopf, 1991.

Stern, Jane, and Michael Stern. *Real American Food.* New York: Alfred A. Knopf, 1986.

Summer 2004, volume 4, number 3

charles perry |

Frightening the Game

"BUT WITH THE MALE DOMESTIC FOWL, that has been fed on hemp seeds and oil of *?* (*ên?*), and on the butter of olive, [no fowl can stand the contest].—First, on the day it is killed one [must] chase and frighten it, and [then] must hang up [its] (foot), and then on the second day must hang it by the neck, and roast it on a spit."[1]

So it is said in a sixth-century Middle Persian manual of accepted gourmet opinions. It sounds peculiar to us, this idea of chasing and frightening a rooster—no matter how well fattened—before slaughtering. We know that if an animal is stressed by fear or violent exercise, its meat will become tough.

The reason is as follows: when the animal is killed without stress, the cells continue to use up their fuel, but since no fresh oxygen is available, its lactic acid byproduct can't be broken down. However, if the animal is killed after being stressed, more oxygen is available and some of the lactic acid does get broken down.

This makes the meat seem firmer and drier ("tougher"), since the proteins are better able to hang on to their water in this less acid environment and don't ooze as much. This also makes the meat spoil faster. (In the Middle East the latter consideration ordinarily doesn't have much weight, because slaughtered animals are not typically hung but slaughtered, butchered, and cooked the same day. The Persian book is unusual in saying to hang the bird overnight.)

"Another effect of stressing," the food science writer Harold McGee points out, "would be to speed the onset of rigor mortis, which comes when the muscle runs out of fuel and the contractile proteins lock into place, and then its passing as muscle enzymes begin to break the proteins down." This process happens faster at higher temperatures, McGee adds, so (depending on the climate and animal and timing) stressing might help speed the meat through rigor before cooking. He speculates that this might compensate somewhat for the lack of hanging.

Medieval Baghdad adopted Persian court customs wholesale, the idea of frightening your dinner included. The onager or wild ass had been a favorite game meat of the pre-Islamic kings of Iran, and in a tenth-century cookbook based on the personal recipe collections of the caliphs and their circle, the following medical information is included: "All that you eat of wild (ass) meat after exhaustion and pursuit [*al-kadd wal-tard*] is faster to digest and lighter in the stomach, and more beneficial, and more praised of consequence."[2]

Left: *Bahram Gur Hunting with Azada.* From the *Shahnama* (*Book of Kings*), 1352. THE METROPOLITAN MUSEUM OF ART, CORA TIMKEN BURNETT COLLECTION OF PERSIAN MINIATURES AND OTHER PERSIAN ART OBJECTS, BEQUEST OF CORA TIMKEN BURNETT, 1956 (57.51.32). PHOTOGRAPH ©1993 THE METROPOLITAN MUSEUM OF ART.

This does not necessarily refer to the hunt; the finest onager meat was held to come from animals that had been fattened in captivity.

What's going on here? M.M. Ahsan points out that the fear and exhaustion of the hunt were believed to make meat more "heating," and "heating" food digests more quickly.[3] But according to medieval medical doctrine, this would also make the meat positively dangerous to eat, and one would expect that passage to mention this. Meat was already a "heating" food, and stressed meat would unbalance the humors unless one was suffering from a "cold" illness or balanced it with "cooling" ingredients such as lettuce, sweetbreads, coriander, and camphor.

I happen to doubt that medieval people governed their diet by medical theory. Modern Americans are known for paying avid attention to dietary theories, but we still consume great quantities of meat, dairy products, and animal fats. Many of us call ourselves vegetarians, but a recent study showed that we tend to have idiosyncratic definitions of vegetarianism that permit us to eat meat whenever we feel like it. I suspect that medieval people were much the same: some followed their doctors' recommendations all the time, the rest got religion about it when they were sick, and formal dinners often made a great show of being "dietarily correct."

Some contexts make it clear that stressed meat was considered positively enjoyable. The same passage where the tenth-century Baghdad cookbook recommends eating exhausted onager quotes a poem in which the scribe Mahmud b. al-Hasan invites a friend to come enjoy a meal of fatted kid and a Persian dish of stewed sliced meat: "a *kushtâbiyya* of a gazelle meat that the hunting birds [*jawârih*] brought you after exhausting it."[4]

In hunting, that favorite diversion of aristocrats, animals are necessarily stressed before being killed, and it may be noteworthy that the above references to exhausting animals all come from sources in or near royal courts, whether of pre-Islamic Persia or the Baghdad of the caliphs. In the six later medieval Arab cookbooks, which were written by middle-class scribes, there is only one mention of stressing before slaughter. Perhaps the particular qualities of meat obtained in the hunt, like the "gaminess" of wild venison, were enjoyed simply because they were familiar in these circles. ◉

NOTES

1. *Husrav i kavâtân u rêtak ê* [the Pahlavi text *King Husrav and His Boy*], Jamshedji Maneckji Unvala, trans. (Paris: P. Geuthner, 1921), 19. I have amended the translation. Unvala says to hang the rooster's "trunk," but the Persian text has *pâdh*, "foot."

2. Ibn Sayyar al-Warraq, *Kitâb al-Tabîkh*, Kai Öhrnberg and Sahban Mroueh, eds. (Helsinki: Studia Orientalia, 1987), 127.

3. M.M. Ahsan, *Social Life under the Abbasids* (London and New York: Longman/Librairie du Liban, 1979), 207–229.

4. Ibn Sayyar al-Warraq, *Kitâb al-Tabîkh*, 127.

Fall 2005, volume 5, number 4

amy butler greenfield |

Alkermes

"A Liqueur of Prodigious Strength"

CAN STRONG DRINK SAVE A LIFE? If the scandalous memoirs of Lorenzo Da Ponte are any guide, the answer is yes. An Italian adventurer, Da Ponte was one of the great rogues of the eighteenth century, whose notoriously checkered career included a stint as a priest, numerous seductions, and a sentence of banishment from Venice. He redeemed himself, however, when it came to music, writing the librettos to some of Mozart's most exquisite operas.

Oddly enough, music also led to Da Ponte's encounter with one of Europe's rarest and most remarkable liqueurs. In the late 1790s, Da Ponte was scouring Italy for new singers, hoping to engage them for opera performances. On a bitter winter night, as he was nearing the end of his search, he met with a terrible accident on the snow-covered roads of Tuscany. As he recounted in his memoirs, he was dragged from the carriage wreck "more dead than alive." Injured and badly frostbitten, he was brought to a nearby inn, put to bed, and left to the care of the innkeeper's wife. She gave him some Chianti, then dosed him with "two or three glasses of kermes," described by Da Ponte as a "liqueur of prodigious strength." So miraculous was the effect of this kermes that Da Ponte claimed he was made a new man. "In less than three hours," he wrote, "I was in condition to proceed again."[1]

Da Ponte was given to embroidering the truth, but when it came to extolling the virtues of kermes liqueur, he had plenty of company. In Enlightenment Europe kermes liqueur and kermes syrups were widely praised for their purported medicinal powers. They were thought to be especially valuable for strengthening the heart, and they were credited with saving lives in dramatic circumstances.

What were the origins of this mysterious drink? How was it made? Da Ponte stints on details, though he believed that the liqueur he drank was produced "only in Florence."

In truth, however, the complex history of kermes liqueur began in a place and time far removed from eighteenth- century Tuscany. Still sought after by connoisseurs today, the liqueur has deep roots that stretch back over a thousand years to the golden age of ancient Baghdad — and kermes, the key ingredient of the liqueur, has an even more ancient culinary past.

Although it looks like a miniature berry, kermes is actually a parasitic insect, *Kermes vermilio*, that feeds on the Mediterranean oak. Humans have long treasured it for its vibrant red dye. As far back as the Neolithic age, the inhabitants of Provence consumed pâté made with kermes, barley, and meat. Later, the Sumerians, Phoenicians, and Greeks set great store by the dye. So, too, did the Romans, who demanded that Spain pay half its imperial tribute in kermes.[2]

As these civilizations were well aware, kermes was rare and expensive. *Kermes vermilio* flourished only in certain regions of the Mediterranean, and in those districts workers— mostly women—had to pluck the insects off the tree by hand, a costly and painstaking task. Killed with steam or vinegar, the insects were then dried and packed for the marketplace.

In the classical world kermes was valued primarily as a textile dye, famous for turning cloth a rich red. Despite the early example of Provence's Neolithic pâté makers, the dye failed to make much headway among cooks. Doctors, however, found a use for it. In the first century the Greek physician Dioscorides included the dye in his treatise *Materia medica*. He advised grinding the dye, mixing it with vinegar, and then applying it externally to wounds and other injuries to speed healing.[3]

After Rome fell, the advice of Dioscorides was largely lost to Europe. Among the scholars of the Arab world, however, interest in Greek science and medicine flourished. In the advanced medical schools of ancient Baghdad, students read Dioscorides and learned of the virtues of kermes. Eventually, Arab doctors created their own medicines using the dye, and by the early ninth century they had invented the precursor to kermes liqueurs: a potion called *confectio alchermes*. Unlike Dioscorides's prescription, this *confectio* was meant to be taken internally.

Who came up with the drink? Surviving sources credit the great Arab Christian physician Yūhannā Ibn Māsawaih. Born in 777, he was a pharmacist's son from Gundishapur, one of the great medical centers of the Persian empire. Later, he directed the medical school in Baghdad and served as personal physician to the caliph. His books contain hundreds of pharmaceutical recommendations, including the first known recipe for *confectio alchermes*.[4]

To modern eyes the recipe appears rather odd, not least because the first ingredient is a length of fabric—specifically, a pound of red silk "recently dyed with kermes." Ibn Māsawaih instructed his students to soak this silk overnight in apple juice and rosewater and then boil it till the liquid turned red. After the silk was squeezed and removed, a pound and a half of sugar was stirred in, until the contents reached "the consistency of honey." The sweet syrup was then spiced with a host of rare ingredients: ambergris, cinnamon, aloes, gold leaf, musk, and pulverized lapis lazuli and white pearls.[5]

An expensive and exotic concoction, *confectio alchermes* must have been intended for the caliph and his court and not for commoners. But for those who could afford it, the drink was said to have extraordinary effects that were not unlike those later attributed to Da Ponte's alkermes liqueur. According to Ibn Māsawaih, the medicine was a wonderful strengthener, curing palpitations of the heart, putting an end to fainting spells, and restoring minds disturbed by madness and depression.

The *confectio* later played an important part in the pharmacopoeia of other Arab physicians, and in time its fame spread beyond the bounds of the Arab world. It probably reached Europe courtesy of Judeo-Arab physicians from Spain and Sicily, but Latin translators of Arabic medical treatises also helped spread the word. By the thirteenth century the *confectio*

Right: A classic bottle of Alkermes from the Officina di Santa Maria Novella. PHOTOGRAPH BY DAVID GREENFIELD © 2006

had reached France, becoming a favored remedy at Montpellier, one of Europe's top schools of medicine. Among European physicians the *confectio* was esteemed chiefly as a cordial—the official term for a medicine that strengthened the heart—although, in imitation of Arab practice, it was also used against melancholy.[6]

As the Renaissance came into full flower, *confectio alchermes* met with increasing favor in Europe. Recipes for the drink appeared in numerous medical treatises and herbals, from the popular works of the English apothecary Nicholas Culpeper to the official pharmacopoeia handbooks of London and Amsterdam. In France, Queen Elizabeth's ambassador was treated with the remedy. The *confectio* traveled beyond Europe's borders, too. A handwritten cookbook from early colonial Virginia—later inherited by Martha Washington—contains a recipe calling for the *confectio*, and colonial physicians were familiar with the remedy.[7]

Yet even as the *confectio*'s fame increased, the recipe itself was undergoing a transformation. Some of the changes were subtle, involving the addition of one or two new ingredients. The alkermes given to Queen Elizabeth's ambassador, for instance, was said to

Above: An eighteenth-century engraving of cochineal production in Mexico. COURTESY OF AMY BUTLER GREENFIELD

have included an ingredient called "unicorn's horn" (possibly a ground-up narwhal tusk) in addition to the traditional gold, pearls, and musk.[8]

Other changes were more profound, including a move away from a key ingredient in Ibn Māsawaih's recipe: fresh kermes-dyed silk. According to the great Elizabethan herbalist John Gerard, boiling silk served no purpose since it did nothing at all "for the strengthening of the heart." Some apothecaries recommended replacing the silk with bristles dyed with kermes, but Gerard advised against this, too, noting that the bristles often contained poisons. Instead, Gerard urged apothecaries and physicians either to use kermes itself or to rely on a new red dye called *cochineal*.[9]

Recently arrived from the New World, cochineal was a luxury in Gerard's day. Nurtured by the ancient people of Mexico, it was derived from an American insect, *Dactylopius coccus*, a close cousin of kermes. When the cochineal reached Europe in the wake of the Spanish conquest, it caused a sensation. Everyone from dyers to duchesses fell in love with cochineal's luminous dye, which produced the most brilliant and intense red the world had ever seen—a color the English chemist Robert Boyle christened "a Perfect scarlet." Moreover, dyers soon discovered that ounce for ounce cochineal was far more potent than kermes. Within little more than a generation, cochineal drove kermes to the fringes of the European market.[10]

Dyers consumed the lion's share of cochineal, but Europeans were also eager to make use of the dried insects in the overlapping realms of cookery and medicine. In doing so, they were following in the footsteps of their counterparts in ancient Mexico. Long before the conquest Mexican cooks had been coloring tamales and other foods with the dye, a practice that may have had religious significance. Aztec physicians also made use of cochineal, mixing it with vinegar and applying it to wounds—a practice that uncannily parallels Dioscorides's use of kermes in ancient Greece. The Aztecs also prescribed cochineal poultices for heart, head, and stomach ailments. According to the sixteenth-century Spanish physician Francisco Hernández, the Aztecs praised cochineal as a dentifrice, too, noting that it "cleans the teeth extraordinarily well."[11]

Most Europeans knew nothing about the ways that cochineal had been used in ancient Mexico, but throughout the Renaissance and the Age of Reason, they were quite willing to experiment with the dye on their own terms. Since medieval times European cooks had used dyes like alkanet and sandalwood to create reddish food colorings, particularly when making confections and other sweet delicacies. When they discovered that cochineal produced clearer pinks and stronger reds, the Mexican dye became a desirable staple in kitchens that could afford it. The dye was also valued for its power to mask mistakes and faulty ingredients. Cooks in well-off households used it to make claret and currant jellies appear brighter and more appetizing, while professional bakers were accused of adding a pinch of cochineal "to make the apple and the gooseberry outblush the cherry and the plum."[12]

Cochineal also became extremely popular with European physicians, in part because the dye's similarity to kermes allowed it to slot neatly into established medical regimens. Yet rather than functioning as a mere substitute for kermes, cochineal came to be regarded as the superior substance, probably because it contained considerably more dye per ounce. At any rate, cochineal soon acquired medical renown beyond that of kermes.

By the seventeenth century cochineal was heralded as a substance that could cool fevers, produce sweats, and prevent infection. Perhaps it was for this reason that cochineal was given to England's Charles II—along with cinnamon, marshmallow leaves, violets, rock salt, and antimony—in an enema as he lay on his deathbed in 1680. Other physicians prescribed cochineal for jaundice. Sufferers were directed to mix the dyestuff with cream of tartar and Venetian soap and "take half a dram three times a day." (No doubt this was a foul-tasting potion, but it was preferable to some other jaundice treatments, which included swallowing "nine live lice every morning for a week, in a little ale.")[13]

Most often, however, physicians made use of cochineal as an ingredient in the *confectio alchermes*. In the seventeenth and eighteenth centuries, the *confectio* went from strength to strength. By 1721 it was said to be one of the "five great Compositions" of the apothecary shops in London, and it had become an essential remedy throughout Europe.[14]

As the *confectio* grew in popularity, its list of indications multiplied. Physicians still continued to prescribe it as a cordial and an antidepressant, but they also discussed other uses for it in medical journals and treatises. A number of doctors recommended the *confectio* as a treatment for the plague. Others believed it helped patients resist poison.[15]

By some accounts the *confectio* was also useful in affairs of the heart. No less an authority than Casanova confided in his memoirs that he had made a love potion containing the *confectio* among its many ingredients. (Thick enough to be made into sugary comfits, his concoction could more accurately be termed a "love paste.") Less-daring lovers could use the *confectio* to create "Aromaticum Lozenges" that made the breath smell sweet. When the time came to deliver the fruits of lovemaking, the *confectio* could be helpful, too. Jane Sharp, the author of a seventeenth-century treatise on midwifery, recommended that women in the midst of a hard labor be given "a dram of *Confectio Alkermes* at twice in two spoonfuls of Claret wine."[16]

Sharp's prescription indicates another way in which the use and administration of the *confectio* was changing during this period: increasingly, it was being combined with alcohol. Most Europeans accomplished this by adding the *confectio* to claret or wine, as Sharp did. In eighteenth-century Florence, however, the Dominican monks of Santa Maria Novella developed a considerably more sophisticated technique. Following in the footsteps of the Renaissance monasteries that had invented Benedictine and Chartreuse, the Dominicans created their own elixir in 1743: an alkermes liqueur that raised the *confectio* to new culinary heights.[17]

The exact composition of the Florentine liqueur was a well-kept secret, but it appears to have combined alcohol with the key ingredients of the confectio: sugar, rosewater, and red dye from kermes or cochineal. The more-exotic seasonings in Ibn Māsawaih's original formula—lapis lazuli, pearls, musk, and gold leaf—were apparently left out, but essences of cloves, nutmeg, and orange blossoms were added to improve the taste and health-giving properties of the liqueur.[18]

Known simply as *alkermes* or *kermes*, the drink could be purchased from the Dominicans' pharmacy in Florence, and it soon became one of the shop's top sellers. Like the *confectio*, it was thought to strengthen the heart and revitalize both body and mind. Taken regularly by some Italians as a restorative, it was also administered in desperate cases, which is no doubt why the innkeeper's wife offered alkermes to Da Ponte after his catastrophic accident.

Had Da Ponte been traveling through Italy a generation later, however, the innkeeper's wife might not have been so quick to offer him the drink. In the early nineteenth century people became more skeptical of the ability of spirits to effect miracle cures. Faith in the powers of the *confectio alchermes* also waned, to be replaced by trust in the new (and often exceedingly toxic) remedies offered by heroic medicine.[19]

Yet even as the *confectio* gradually faded from the pharmacopoeia, alkermes liqueur came increasingly into vogue, in a development that had more to do with the drink's sensuous aroma and taste than with its redoubtable medical background. Like many other monastery cordials, it became one of the pleasures of the table. Drunk at the end of a meal and used as an ingredient in fancy desserts, alkermes became quite fashionable in the nineteenth century. Imitators began manufacturing their own versions of the liqueur, and sales and exports of alkermes boomed.[20] The liqueur's success may even have inspired Gaspare Campari to use cochineal in his eponymous drink, first created in Turin in the 1840s.

In the end it was Campari—the more complex and astringent drink—that triumphed in the marketplace. By the late nineteenth century Campari's star was rising ever higher, and in the next century the brightly colored aperitif became a cocktail hour hit. Since then, Campari's fortunes have waxed and waned, but it has weathered the changes well. Its name remains in the public consciousness, and in banner years the drink seems to be everywhere.

Contrast that with the fate of alkermes, which virtually disappeared from the liqueur cabinet in the twentieth century. Cloying to many modern palates, its primary use now is in making Tuscan desserts like *zuccotto* and *zuppa inglese*, where it imparts a sweet flavor and rosy color to the dish.

No longer a popular liqueur even in its home country, alkermes is hard to obtain outside Italy. Even alkermes extract, a bright red alkermes-based liquid suited more to baking than drinking, is not easy to come by. But American fans of *zuppa inglese* can count themselves lucky: One supplier, Gasbarro's Wines of Providence, Rhode Island, will ship giant one-liter bottles of the extract anywhere in the United States. Another supplier, Polcari's Coffee in Boston's North End, ships half-ounce bottles, along with a recipe for using the extract to make alkermes liqueur.

For those in search of the classic liqueur, the best place to find it is at the Officina Profumo-Farmaceutica di Santa Maria Novella, the Dominicans' centuries-old pharmacy in Florence. Now in secular hands, the sweet-smelling shop remains open for business, and delicate glass bottles of ruby red alkermes liqueur are still sold over the counter. Recently, the shop has expanded its reach to America, and a Santa Maria Novella boutique in New York's East Village now carries the liqueur. To taste it is to savor the spirit of another age. A vibrant survivor, the spicy, sticky-sweet drink is the genuine article, the "liqueur of prodigious strength" that put new heart into Mozart's librettist on that snowy night in Tuscany so long ago.

Nicholas Culpeper's Recipe for *Confectio Alkermes* (1653)

Take of the juice of Apples, Damask Rose-water, of each a pound and an half, in which infuse for twenty-four hours, raw Silk four ounces, strain it strongly, and add Syrup of the berries of Cherms [kermes or cochineal] brought over to us, two pounds, Sugar one pound, boil it to the thickness of Honey; then removing it from the fire whilst it is warm, add Ambergris cut small, half an ounce, which being well mingled, put in these things following in powder, Cinnamon, Wood of Aloes, of each six drams, Pearls prepared, two drams, Leaf-Gold a dram, Musk a scruple, make it up according to art. ◉

SUPPLIERS OF ALKERMES LIQUEUR

Officina Profumo-Farmaceutica di Santa Maria Novella
Via della Scala 16.
Florence TOSCANA 50123
Italy
011-39-055-21-62-76
www.smnovella.it

SUPPLIERS OF ALKERMES EXTRACT

Gasbarro's Wines
361 Atwells Avenue
Providence, RI 02903
401-421-4170
www.gasbarros.com

Polcari's Coffee
105 Salem Street
Boston, MA 02113
617-227-0786
www.northendboston.com/polcaricoffee

NOTES

1. Lorenzo Da Ponte, *Memoirs*, Elisabeth Abbott, trans. (New York: New York Review of Books, 2000), 286.

2. R.A. Donkin, "The Insect Dyes of Western and West-Central Asia," *Anthropos* 72:861–862; Amy Butler Greenfield, *A Perfect Red* (New York: HarperCollins, 2005), 29–30.

3. Dioscorides, *The Greek Herbal of Dioscorides*, Robert T. Gunther, ed. (New York: Hafner, 1959), 440.

4. Donald Campbell, *Arabian Medicine and Its Influence on the Middle Ages* (London, 1926), 1:60–61; Donkin, "Insect Dyes," 862.

5. Yūhannā Ibn Māsawaih, *Opera de medicamentorum* (Venice, 1633), 89.

6. George Sarton, "Review: The Gate of Heaven," *Isis* 45: no. 1, 113–115; Donkin, "Insect Dyes," 862.

7. Nicholas Culpeper, *Physical Directory* (London, 1650), 117–118; Cecil Wall et. al., *History of the Worshipful Society of Apothecaries of London* (Oxford: Oxford University Press, 1963), 33; D.A. Wittop Koning, ed., *Amsterdam Pharmacoepia 1636* (Nieuwkoop, Netherlands: B. de Graaf, 1961), 53–54; Edward Eggleston, "Some Curious Colonial Remedies," *American Historical Review* 5 (1899): 201; Karen Hess, ed., *Martha Washington's Booke of Cookery* (New York: Columbia University Press, 1981), 407–408; Harold B. Gill, Jr., *The Apothecary in Colonial Virginia* (Colonial Williamsburg Foundation, 1972), 70–71.

8. Eggleston, "Colonial Remedies," 201.

9. John Gerard, *Herball* (London, 1633), 1343.

10. Greenfield, *Perfect Red*, 35–37, 75–78, 140–141.

11. Greenfield, *Perfect Red*, 40; Francisco Hernández, *Nova Plantarum* (Rome, 1651), 78.

12. Constance Hieatt et al., *Pleyn Delit* (Toronto: University of Toronto Press, 1995), recipe 114; Peter Brears, *The Compleat Housewife* (Wakefield, UK: Wakefield Historical Publications, 2000), 68; Hess, *Martha Washington's Booke of Cookery*, 360; Ralph Blegborough, *An Address to the Governors of the Surrey Dispensary* (London, 1810), 2.

13. Greenfield, *Perfect Red*, 83–84.

14. www.wlv.ac.uk/tradedictionary/dictionary_examples.htm.

15. John Christoph Gottwald et. al., "Abridgement of a Book Intitl'd, A Description of the Plague," *Philosophical Transactions of the Royal Society* 28 (1713): 139; Culpeper, *Physical Directory*, 118.

16. Jacques Casanova de Seingalt, *The Memoirs of Jacques Casanova de Seingalt*, www.gutenberg.org/catalog/world/file.php?file=files; *A Closet for Ladies and Gentlewomen* (London, 1608), 37; Elaine Hobby, "'Secrets of the Female Sex': Jane Sharp, the Reproductive Female Body, and Early Modern Midwifery Manuals," *Women's Writing* 8: no. 2, 201–212.

17. Jon Bresler (Manager of Santa Maria Novella USA), letter to the author, 11 May 2006.

18. Bresler, letter to the author, 11 May 2006.

19. Andrew Barr, *Drink: A Social History of America* (New York: Caroll & Graf, 1999), 203.

20. www.smnovella.com/english.html.

Winter 2007, volume 7, number 1

eamon grennan |

Food for Thought

Here is the space I'm sitting in: a garden
closed by fuchsia hedges, two sycamores,
a mountain ash, sally trees, some brambly
blackberry bushes. I note the grass is mostly
not grass at all but a tall-stemmed weed
with slim, down-covered, light green leaves.
I love the boulder with its pelt of moss,
and in one corner, low to the ground,
a patch of sheep's sorrel that I'll pick
and nibble for its cool and tart. Grass
too: I pull a blade or two and chew:
green butteriness fills my mouth. When a
poet mentions "a last dry fig," I remember
your hand holding a fresh almond in its
velvety green shell: you put the knife in
and out popped the heart you handed me:
cool crisp whiteness between my teeth.
What I like about poetry is porousness,
the way it will not fill its cracks but
seems linked in some set body-circuit
(ear, muscle, nerves, blood) with how
the brain is honeycombed, those spaces
between cell and cell where something
charged with light and riddled with affinities
is happening, where Hermes—keeper of
secret recipes—is bringing everything
to a steamy boil, is figuring things out.

Spring 2001, volume 1, number 2

richard wilbur has served as Poet Laureate of the United States. His many honors include the National Book Award and two Pulitzer Prizes. In addition to his poetry, Wilbur has written numerous essays and children's books, and he collaborated with Leonard Bernstein on the Broadway show *Candide*. His translations of Molière and Racine are often played, here and abroad, and he has lately rendered three works of Pierre Corneille. His most recent book of verse is *Collected Poems, 1943–2004*.

frank h. wu is the author of *Yellow: Race in America beyond Black and White* and coauthor of *Race, Rights and Reparation: Law and the Japanese American Internment*. From 2004 to 2008 he served as the dean of Wayne State University Law School. He has taught at Howard, George Washington, Maryland, Columbia, and Michigan, and he practiced law in San Francisco.

illustration credits

pp.a and b, Catherine Chalmers, four photographs from the series *Food Chain*. Courtesy of the artist.

p.ii, *Tomato Eater* © Gail Skoff.

p.viii, Luis Buñuel, *L'Age D'Or*. Collection Cinématique Suisse. Rights reserved.

p.8, Wayne Tiebaud, *Girl with Ice Cream Cone*. Hirschhorn Museum and Sculpture Garden, Smithsonian Institution, Joseph H. Hirschorn Bequest Fund, Smithsonian Institution, Joseph H. Hirschhorn Bequest Fund, Collections Acquisition Program and Museum Purchase, 1996. Photograph by Lee Stalsworth.

p.11, a trader from Western Nigeria. Photo courtesy Donald Vermeer.

p.14, edible clays at a market in Accra, Ghana. Photo courtesy Donald Vermeer.

p.52, Áslaug Snorradóttir, *Salmon Heads with Lemons*. Photo courtesy of the artist.

p.102, Andre von Morisse, *Pink Freud*, 2006. Oil on canvas, 60 × 42 in. Courtesy of the artist.

p.150, Andy Warhol, *Silver Coke Bottle*, 1967. Silver paint on glass Coke bottle with metal cap, 8 × 2⅜ in. © 2009 The Andy Warhol Foundation for the Visual Arts / ARS, NY.

p.180, Chema Madoz, *Sin Título*, 2000. © 2009 Artists Rights Society (ARS), New York/ VEGAP, Madrid.

p.196, David Sterenberg, *Breakfast*, 1916 (?). Oil on canvas, 88 × 72.5 in. © 2009 State Russian Museum, St. Petersburg.

p.232, Fausto Zonaro, *Girl with a Pumpkin*. Courtesy of Sakip Sabanci Museum, Sabanci University, Istanbul.

p.278, Jean Blackburn, detail of *Thick or Thin*, 1998. Wooden rolling pin and board 4 × 16 × 16 in. Courtesy of the Artist & Caren Golden Fine Art, NY. Photograph by Jeffrey Sturges.

p.324, Emily Eveleth, *Nigh*, 1998. Collection of Nancy and Robert Magoon, Aspen, CO. Courtesy of Danese Gallery, NY.

p.366, Catherine Chalmers, photograph from the series *Food Chain*. Courtesy of the artist.

The remaining illustration credits are provided with the captions.